TAKING SIDES

Clashing Views in

World History:
The Ancient World
to the Pre-Modern Era
Volume I

THIRD EDITION

Mc
Graw
Hill **Contemporary
Learning Series**

A Division of The McGraw-Hill Companies

TAKING SIDES

Clashing Views in

World History:
The Ancient World
to the Pre-Modern Era
Volume I

THIRD EDITION

Selected, Edited, and with Introductions by

Joseph R. Mitchell
Howard Community College

and

Helen Buss Mitchell
Howard Community College

Mc Graw Hill **Contemporary Learning Series**

A Division of The McGraw-Hill Companies

Photo Acknowledgment
Cover image: Emperor Justinian and retinue by
Meister von San Vitale in Ravenna—public domain

Cover Acknowledgment
Maggie Lytle

Manufactured in the United States of America

Third Edition

123456789DOCDOC09876

Library of Congress Cataloging-in-Publication Data
Main entry under title:
Taking sides: clashing views on controversial issues in world history, volume i/selected, edited,
and with introductions by Joseph R. Mitchell and Helen Buss Mitchell—3rd ed.
Includes bibliographical references and index.
1. World History 2. History, ancient. I. Mitchell, Joseph R., ed. II. Helen Buss, ed. III. Seris.
909
0-07-351499-3
978-0-07-351499-4
ISSN 1538-716X

Printed on Recycled Paper

Preface

In *Taking Sides: Clashing Views in World History: The Ancient World to the Pre-Modern Era,* we identify the issues that are typically covered in the teaching of world history, using scholarly and readable sources that argue these issues. We have taken care to choose issues that will make this volume multicultural, gender-based, and reflective of current historical scholarship. We frame its issues with preview and follow-up sections that are user-friendly for both teachers and students. Students who use this volume should come away with a greater understanding and appreciation of the value of studying history as well as enhanced skills in critical thinking.

Plan of the Book This book is made up of 18 issues that argue pertinent topics in the study of world history. Each issue has an issue **introduction**, which sets the stage for the debate as it is argued in the yes and no selections that follow. Each issue concludes with a **postscript** that makes some final observations and points the way to other questions related to the issue. In reading the issue and forming your own opinions, you should not feel confined to adopt one or the other of the positions presented. There are positions in between the given views or totally outside them, and the **suggestions for further reading** that appear in each issue postscript should help you find resources to continue your study of the subject. We have also provided Internet site addresses (URLs) in the **On the Internet** page that accompanies each part opener. At the back of the book is a listing of all the **contributors to this volume,** which will give you information on the historians and commentators whose views are debated here.

Using the Book Care has been taken to provide issues that are in various ways related. They could be used to: (a) compare/contrast those with like content; (b) show relationships between and among some topics across time, geographic, and cultural boundaries; (c) make connections between past historical events and their contemporary relevance. For example, Issues 1 and 3 cover the changing interpretations of Africa's role in human history, stretching back to the origins of humankind. Issues 6 and 8 analyze the reasons for the demise of two civilizations, one European, the other Mesoamerican. Issues 2, 5, and 11 explore the roles played by women in ancient Sumeria, early Christianity, and Renaissance Europe; Issue 16 explores their persecution as witches. Issues 4, 7, and 15 evaluate the influence of three historical figures: two men of arms—Alexander the Great and Justinian—and a man of God—Martin Luther. Issues 9 and 10 explore the historical relationship between the Islamic and Christian worlds. Issues 13, 14, and 18 deal with overseas exploration and expansion, from both Asian and European perspectives. Finally, Issues 12 and 17 show the power of ideas in shaping the history of two civilizations—one Japanese, the other Western.

A word to the instructor   An *Instructor's Manual With Test Questions* (multiple-choice and essay) is available through the publisher for the instructor using *Taking Sides* in the classroom. A general guidebook, *Using Taking Sides in the Classroom*, which discusses methods and techniques for integrating the pro-con approach into any classroom setting, is also available. An online version of *Using Taking Sides in the Classroom* and a corresponding service for *Taking Sides* adopters can be found at http://www.mhcls.com/usingts/.

　　Taking Sides: Clashing Views in World History is only one title in the Taking Sides series. If you are interested in seeing the table of contents for any of the other titles, please visit the Taking Sides Web site at http://www.mhcls.com/takingsides/.

Acknowledgments   We would like to thank Larry Madaras of Howard Community College—fellow teacher, good friend, coeditor of *Taking Sides: Clashing Views on Controversial Issues in American History*, and editor of *Taking Sides: Clashing Views on Controversial Issues in American History Since 1945*—for his past and present assistance in making our work possible. Special acknowledgment also goes to David Stebenne of Ohio State University—friend, scholar, teacher, and author of *Arthur J. Goldberg: New Deal Liberal* (Oxford University Press, 1996)—for his suggestions and advice. Thanks also go out to the library staffs of Howard County, Maryland; University of Maryland, College Park; University of Maryland, Baltimore County (UMBC); and Howard Community College, particularly Ela Ciborowska who secured interlibrary loans.

　　At McGraw-Hill Contemporary Learning Series, a debt of gratitude is owed to managing editor Larry Loeppke and developmental editor Susan Brusch, who guided us through the process of publishing this book, offering words of support and encouragement when they were most needed.

A final word   We would appreciate any questions or comments that you may have on our work, especially which issues work best in your classroom and which issues you never use. Please contact us at joemitch@bigjar.com. We will use this feedback in shaping future editions.

Contents In Brief

Contents

History professor Ivan Van Sertima argues that Mesoamerica's Olmec civilization was influenced by African sources that date back to both ancient and medieval civilization. Scholars Viera, Ortiz de Montellano, and Barbour counter that Mesoamerica's Olmec civilization developed on its own, with little, if any, influences from African sources.

Professor emeritus of Greek N. G. L. Hammond states that research has proven that Alexander the Great is deserving of his esteemed historical reputation. Professor Ian Worthington counters that Alexander's actions were self-serving and eventually weakened his Macedonian homeland; therefore, he does not merit the historical reputation he has been given.

Professor of New Testament Studies and the History of Ancient Christianity Karen L. King presents evidence from biblical and other recently discovered ancient texts to illuminate women's active participation in early Christianity—as disciples, apostles, prophets, preachers, and teachers. Art historian Lisa Bellan-Boyer uses mimetic theory to explain why women's richly diverse roles were severely circumscribed in the name of unity and in order to make the new religion of Christianity acceptable in the Greco-Roman world.

History professor Antonio Santosuosso states that the Roman Empire's inability to cope with demands involving the defense of the empire was responsible for its demise. Professor of history Peter Heather claims that the invasion of the Huns forced other barbarians to use tribal unity as a survival technique and to seek safety within the confines of the Roman Empire, thus permitting the invasion of the Huns to bring about the fall of the Roman Empire.

Professor of history and philosophy of education Mehdi Nakosteen traces the roots of the modern university to the golden age of Islamic culture (750–1150 C.E.) He maintains that Muslim scholars assimilated the best of classical scholarship and developed the experimental method and the university system, which they passed on to the West before declining. Emeritus professor of sociology Walter Rüegg calls the university "the European institution *par excellence*," citing its origin as a community of teachers and taught, accorded certain rights that included the granting of degrees, and as a creation of medieval Europe—the Europe of papal Christianity.

Historian Margaret L. King surveys Renaissance women in domestic, religious, and learned settings and finds reflected in their lives a new consciousness of themselves as women, as intelligent seekers of a new way of being in the world. Historian Joan Kelly-Gadol discovered in her work as a Renaissance scholar that well-born women seemed to have enjoyed greater advantages during the Middle Ages and experienced a relative loss of position and power during the Renaissance.

Religious scholar Winston L. King credits the monk Eisai with introducing Zen to the Hōjō samurai lords of Japan who recognized its affinity with the warrior's profession and character. Japanologist Catharina Blomberg emphasizes the diversity of influences on the samurai psyche—Confucianism, Shinto, and Zen—stressing the conflict between a warrior's duty and Buddhist ethical principles.

Journalist Nicholas D. Kristof states that China's worldview, shaped by centuries of philosophical and cultural conditioning, was responsible for its decision to cease its maritime ventures during the Ming dynasty. Naval historian Bruce Swanson acknowledges that China's worldview played a role in its decision to cease its maritime programs, but maintains that there were other, more practical considerations that were responsible for that decision.

Issue 14.   Did Christopher Columbus's Voyages Have a Positive Effect on World History?   242

YES: **Robert Royal**, from "Columbus and the Beginning of the New World," *First things: A Monthly Journal of Religion and Public Life* (May 1999)   *244*

NO: **Gabriel Garcia Marquez**, from "For a Country Within Reach of the Children," *Americas* (November/December 1997)   *253*

Robert Royal states although there were negatives that emanated from Columbus's New World discoveries, they continue to "remind us of the glorious and ultimately providential destiny on the ongoing global journey that began in the fifteenth century." Nobel laureate Gabriel Garcia Marquez argues that Columbus's voyages had a negative effect on the Americas, much of which is still felt today.

Issue 15.   Did Martin Luther's Reforms Improve the Lives of European Christians?   260

YES: **Robert Kolb**, from *Martin Luther as Prophet, Teacher, Hero: Images of the Reformer, 1520–1620* (Baker Books, 1999)   *262*

NO: **Hans Küng**, from *Great Christian Thinkers*, trans. John Bowden (Continuum, 1996)   *269*

Religion and history professor Robert Kolb contends that Martin Luther was seen as a prophetic teacher and hero whose life brought hope, divine blessing, and needed correctives to the Christian church. Theologian and professor emeritus of theology Hans Küng views Martin Luther as the inaugurator of a paradigm shift and as the unwitting creator of both bloody religious wars and an unhealthy subservience by ordinary Christians to local rulers in worldly matters.

Issue 16.   Were the Witch-Hunts in Premodern Europe Misogynistic?   277

YES: **Anne Llewellyn Barstow**, from "On Studying Witchcraft as Women's History: A Historiography of the European Witch Persecutions," *Journal of Feminist Studies in Religion* (Fall 1988)   *279*

NO: **Robin Briggs**, from "Women as Victims? Witches, Judges and the Community," *French History* (1991)   *288*

History professor Anne Llewellyn Barstow claims that the European witch-hunt movement made women its primary victims and was used as an attempt to control their lives and behavior. History professor Robin Briggs states that although women were the witch-hunt's main victims, gender was not the only determining factor in this sociocultural movement.

Distinguished professor emeritus of history and philosophy of science
Edward Grant argues that there was a revolution in science that took
place in the seventeenth century; however, it might have been delayed
by centuries if several key developments between 1175 and 1500 had
not paved the way for it. Professor of sociology and historian of science
Steven Shapin questions the idea of a Scientific Revolution, suggesting
greater continuity with the past and rejecting a single time/space event
we might call a Scientific Revolution.

Professor of history William H. McNeill states that in 1500, Western
Europe began to extend influence to other parts of the world, resulting in
a revolution in world relationships, in which the West was the principal
beneficiary. History professor Philip D. Curtin states that the amount of
control the West had over the rest of the world was mitigated by the
European colonial process and the reaction it engendered throughout
the world.

Introduction

The Study of World History
Volume I

What Is History?

History is a dialogue between the past and the present. As we respond to events in our own world, we bring the concerns of the present to our study of the past. What seems important to us, where we turn our attention, how we approach a study of the past—all these are rooted in the present. It has been said that where you stand determines what you see. This is especially the case with history. If we stand within the Western tradition exclusively, we may be tempted to see its story as the only story or the only one worth telling. And whose perspective we take is also critical. From the point of view of the rich and powerful, the events of history take one shape; through the lens of the poor and powerless, the same events can appear quite different. If we take women, or non-Western cultures, or the ordinary person as our starting point, the story of the past may present us with a series of surprises.

Tools of the Historian

Much of the raw material of history consists of written sources. Original sources— from a period contemporary with the events or ideas described—are called **primary sources.** These may include documents of all kinds, including official records as well as personal letters and diaries. The writings of historians reflecting on the past are called **secondary sources.** It is important to keep in mind that primary sources may not automatically be assumed to be free from bias. Each contains historical and personal perspectives. Their principal limitation, however, is that they record what people considered noteworthy about their own age and not necessarily what would most interest us today. As the concerns of the present evolve, the questions we bring to our study of the past will also change. Much of what you read in this book will reflect differences in focus between one historian and another. As Edward Hallett Carr points out, the historian constructs a working model that enables him or her to understand the past. It would be a great mistake to confuse this working model with a photocopy.

Traditional History

Only recently has history considered itself a social science and striven for a kind of scientific accuracy in speaking about the past. For much of human history, until perhaps the late nineteenth century, history was considered a branch of literature rather than a kind of science. It was concerned first of all with narrative, with the telling of a compelling story, and its focus was on the fascinating characters whose lives shaped and defined the past.

Biography, the recounting of the life and times of a powerful man, was regarded as one of the most reliable windows on the past. The so-called "great man" was credited with shaping and defining his own time. As a result, studying Alexander the Great, Martin Luther, or Justinian and Theodora was assumed to offer one of the most reliable keys to unlocking a specific historical time period.

And, traditional history looked relatively uncritically at the great men from the past. Military heroes, for example, were lauded for their conquests with little or no focus on the carnage that made those conquests possible. Another unspoken assumption was the dominance and superiority of the West as the creator and bearer of human civilization. Divine power was sometimes seen as directing or, at least, approving the actions of powerful nations and men.

The traditional areas of focus for the historian have been political, diplomatic, and constitutional: Political history considers how power has been organized and enforced by the state within human societies. Diplomatic history looks at what has influenced the power struggles between states as they continually struggled for dominance. Constitutional history examines the evolution of national states with special attention to who rules and who or what confers the right to rule.

A related domain of the traditional historian has been that of intellectual history or the history of ideas—in the fields of politics, economics, sociology, theology, and science. Probing the power of Christianity or Zen Buddhism, tracing the roots of the modern university, examining the influence of a worldview on a nation's commercial enterprises—all these are the province of intellectual history. Taking this approach to its widest scope, one might explore the intellectual climate of an entire age, such as the Renaissance, the Reformation, or the Scientific Revolution. Which ideas shaped and defined each of these distinct historical periods? And, what marked the change from one age to another?

Revisionism

However, history is not a once-and-for-all enterprise. Each generation formulates its own questions and brings new tools to the study of the past resulting in a process called revisionism. Much of what you will read in this book is a product of revisionism as historians reinterpret the past in the light of the present. One generation values revolutions; the next focuses on their terrible costs. One generation assumes that great men shape the events of history; the next looks to the lives of ordinary people to illuminate the past. There is no final answer, but where we stand will determine which interpretation seems more compelling to us. Issues 4, 7, 14, and 15 introduce the tension between traditional and revisionist views of Alexander the Great, Justinian and Theodora, Christopher Columbus, and Martin Luther.

As new tools of analysis become available, our ability to understand the past improves. Bringing events into clearer focus can change the meaning we assign to them. Many of the selections in this book reflect new attitudes and new insights made possible by the tools that historians have borrowed from other social sciences. For instance, finding and deciphering long-hidden manuscripts can shed new light on belief systems such as Christianity, studied in Issue 5. And, physical artifacts can help us decode elements of language and culture as, for instance, Issue 8 looks at conflicting theories in determining why the civilization of the Mayas collapsed.

Presentism

While we stand in the present, we must be wary of what historians call presentism, that is, reading the values of the present back into the past. If we live in a culture that values individualism and prizes competition, we may be tempted to see these values as good even in a culture that preferred communalism and cooperation. And, we may miss a key component of an ancient civilization because it does not match what we currently consider worthwhile. Issue 18 questions whether we can, any longer, deny the role of non-Europeans in shaping the modern world. We cannot and should not avoid our own questions and struggles. They will inform our study of the past; and yet, they must not warp our vision. Ideally, historians engage in a continual dialogue in which the concerns but not the values of the present are explored through a study of the past.

At the same time, though, we might bring the moral standards of the present to bear on the past. Cultural relativism, pioneered in the field of anthropology, has made us sensitive to the many and varied ways in which civilizations define what is "normal" and what is "moral." So, we remain appropriately reluctant to judge individuals from other times and places by our standards since they were or are, in fact, behaving perfectly normally and morally by the standards of their own time and place. However, from the perspective of the present, we do not hesitate to condemn slaveholding, genocide, or even the zealotry that leads to what the modern world calls "ethnic cleansing."

Changing Historiographical Focuses

All cultures are vulnerable to the narrow-mindedness created by ethnocentrism— the belief that my culture is superior to all others. From inside a particular culture, certain practices may seem normative—that is, we may assume that all humans or all rational humans must behave the way we do or hold the attitudes we hold. When we meet a culture that sees the world differently from ourselves, we may be tempted to write them off as inferior or primitive. As an alternative to ethnocentrism, we might want to enter the worldview of another and see what we can learn from expanding our perspective. These issues will offer you many opportunities to try this thought experiment.

Stepping outside the Western tradition has allowed historians to take a more globocentric view of world events. Accusing their predecessors of

Eurocentrism, some historians have adopted an Afrocentric view of world history that emphasizes Africa's seminal role in cultural evolution, which we explore in Issue 2. Within the Western tradition, women have challenged the male-dominated perspective that studied war but ignored family. Including additional perspectives complicates our interpretation of past events but permits a fuller picture to emerge. We must be wary of universalism—assuming, for example, that patriarchy or the nuclear family has always existed. If patriarchy, for example, has a historical beginning, then there was a time when some other pattern existed; Issue 2 on Sumerian civilization explores this possibility. If cultures other than the West have been dominant or influential during the past, what did the world look like under those circumstances?

Social History

Some historians have moved beyond political, diplomatic, and constitutional history to explore economics and demographics as well as to study social processes. Moving from a focus on nations and rulers to a close examination of forces that can be studied analytically has opened up the realms of business and the family to the historian. Proponents of the so-called new social history rejected what they called history from the top down. Instead of the great man whose influence shaped his age, they looked to the lives of ordinary people and called what they were doing history from the bottom up. The previous generation of historians, they claimed, had sometimes acted as if only the influential had a role in shaping history. Social history assumes that all people are capable of acting as historical agents rather than being passive victims to whom history happens. With this shift in attitude, the lives of slaves, workers, women of all kinds, and children, too, become worthy subjects of historical investigation.

Because the poor and powerless seldom leave written records, other methods must be used to understand their lives. Applying the methods of social scientists to their own discipline, historians have broadened and deepened their field of study. Archaeological evidence, DNA analysis, the tools of paleoanthropology, computer analysis of demographic data—all these have allowed the voiceless to speak across centuries. Fossil evidence, for instance, and the analysis of mitochondrial DNA—the structures within cells we inherit only from our mothers—may each be employed, sometimes with strikingly different results, to trace the migrations of preliterate peoples. The debate between these two conflicting interpretations shapes Issue 1, which considers an African origin for *homo sapiens*.

What historians call material culture reveals the everyday lives of people by analyzing what they discarded as well as the monuments and other material objects they intended to leave as markers of their civilizations. At certain points in human history, owning a plow made the difference between merely surviving and having some surplus food to barter or sell. What people leave to their heirs can tell us how much or how little they had to brighten their lives while they lived. As we continue to dig, we may find our assumptions confirmed or denied by the fossils of once-living organisms. Evidence of sea life on the top of a mountain lets us know that vast geologic changes have taken place. And, in another example, our genetic material has information we are just now learning to decode and interpret that may settle important questions of origin and migration as we learn to read the data locked inside our DNA.

The high-speed comparative functions of computers have allowed the historian to analyze vast quantities of data and look at demographic trends. How old are people when they marry for the first time, have a child, or die? Only with the expanded life expectancy made possible by the modern world has it been possible for people to see their children's children—to become grandparents. Looking at the time between marriage and the birth of a first child can help us calculate the percentage of pregnant brides and gain some insight into how acceptable or unacceptable premarital sex may have been in the context of an expected future marriage. If we study weather patterns and learn that certain years were periods of drought or that the glacier receded during a particular time period, we will know a little more about whether the lives of people who lived during these times were relatively easier or more difficult than those of their historical neighbors in earlier or later periods.

Race, Class, and Gender

The experience of being a historical subject is never monolithic. That is, each of us has a gender, a race, a social class, an ethnic identity, a religion (even if it is atheism or agnosticism), an age, and a variety of other markers that color our experiences. At times, the most important factor may be my gender and what happens may be more or less the same for all members of a particular gender. Under other circumstances, however, race may be predominant. Being a member of a racial minority or of a powerful racial majority may lead to very different experiences of the same event. At other times social class may determine how an event is experienced; the rich may have one story to tell, the poor another. And, other factors, such as religion or ethnic identity, even age, can become the most significant piece of a person's identity, especially if prejudice or favoritism is involved. Historians try always to take into account how race, class, and gender (as well as a host of other factors) intersect in the life of a historical subject. Issue 16 asks this question: Were those accused as witches of a different social class and gender than their accusers? And, were these differences significant?

Issues Involved in Historical Interpretation

Often historians will agree on what happened but disagree about why or how something occurred. Sometimes the question is: Were internal or external causes more responsible? Both may have contributed to an event but one or the other may have played the more significant role. Looking at differing evidence may lead historians to varying interpretations. Issue 6 looks at the fall of the Roman Empire from two points of view—internal factors, such as the weakness of emperors and declining support for the military or external factors, such as the unity among Germanic tribes provoked by the Huns and the frictions that erupt across a shared border. Similarly, Issue 8 explores the demise of the Maya civilization in the context of both internal (environmental and social conditions) and external (military) factors.

A related question is: Was it the circumstances that changed or only the attitudes of those who experienced them? If we find less protest, for instance, can we conclude that things have gotten better or only that people have found a way to accommodate themselves to a situation beyond their control? Does the increasing invisibility of the early Christian women, discussed in Issue 5, indicate their lack of interest or their marginalization? How deeply can we hope to penetrate attitudes within Sumerian, Egyptian, or Maya civilizations? Can the archaeological record and writings about long-dead peoples open their lives to us or must we acknowledge that our interpretations will always remain provisional rather than definitive?

Periodization

Even more basically, the student of the past must wonder whether the turning points that shape the chapters in our history books are the same for all historical subjects? The process of marking turning points is known as periodization. It is the more or less artificial creation of periods that chunk history into manageable segments by identifying forks in the road that took people and events in a new direction. Using an expanded perspective, we may learn that the traditional turning points hold for men but not for women or reflect the experiences of one ethnic group but not another. And, if periodization schemes conflict, which one should we use? Issues 10, 11 and 17 examine questions of periodization. If Europe was experiencing a "dark age" while the Islamic world enjoyed a "golden age," which one more accurately describes the time period? Issue 10 looks at the rise of the university from within the context of this question. And, was there a distinct break at the periods we designate the Renaissance (Issue 11) and the Scientific Revolution (Issue 17)? If so, did women and men experience these breaks identically?

It is also important to keep in mind that people living at a particular moment in history are not aware of labels that later historians will attach to their experience. People who lived during the Middle Ages were surely not aware of living in the middle of something. Only much after the fact were we able to call a later age the Renaissance. To those who lived during what we call the Middle Ages or the Renaissance, marriage, childbirth, work, weather, sickness, and death were the real concerns, just as they are for us. Our own age will certainly be characterized by future historians in ways that might surprise and shock us. As we study the past, it is helpful to keep in mind that some of our assumptions are rooted in a traditional periodization that is now being challenged.

Continuity or Discontinuity?

A related question concerns the connection or lack of connection between one event or set of events and another. When we look at the historical past, we must ask ourselves whether we are seeing continuity or discontinuity. In other words, is the event we are studying part of a normal process of evolution or does it represent a break from a traditional pattern. Questions of continuity vs. discontinuity are the fundamental ones on which the larger issue of periodization rests. Did the Industrial Revolution take the lives of workers in wholly new directions? Were the periods we refer to as the Renaissance and the Scientific Revolution really more discontinuous with the past than continuous with it? And, if some elements shift while others constitute a seamless web, which is the more significant element for the historian?

Sometimes events may appear continuous from the point of view of one group and discontinuous from the point of view of another. Issue 9, for example; looks at the Crusades through Muslim and Christian memories. Suppose that factory owners found their world and worldview shifting dramatically, whereas the lives and perspectives of workers went on more or less as they had before. When this is the case, whose experience should we privilege? Is one group's experience more historically significant than another's—and how should we decide? Issue 14 reveals the struggle with these questions, as the voices of America's original inhabitants compete with those praising Columbus's voyages of discovery.

The Power of Ideas

Can ideas change the course of history? People have sometimes been willing to die for what they believe in and revolutions have certainly been fought, at least in part, over ideas? Some historians believe that studying the clash of ideas or the predominance of one idea or set of ideas offers the best key to understanding the past. Issue 12 looks at the roles of Zen, Confucianism, and Shinto in defining the bushido code of the Samurai warrior. And, Issue 13 examines whether it was China's view of itself and the world or more practical considerations that brought a halt to its commercial and maritime voyages during the Ming dynasty

What do you think? Do ideas shape world events? Would devotion to a political or religious cause you to challenge the status quo? Or, would economic conditions be more likely to send you to the streets? Historians differ in ranking the importance of various factors in influencing the past. Do people challenge the power structure because they feel politically powerless, or because they are hungry, or because of the power of ideas?

The Timeliness of Historical Issues

When we read the newspaper, check breaking news online, or listen to the evening news, there are a confusing number of present-day political, economic, religious, and military clashes that can be understood only by looking at their historical contexts. The role of the United States in world events, the perennial conflicts in the Middle East, China's emerging role as an economic superpower, the threat posed by religious fundamentalism, Africa's political future, the question of whether revolutions are ever worth their costs—these concerns of the global village have roots in the past. Is it helpful, for instance, to look at Islamic revivalism in the context of the Crusades or of the bloody religious wars of the Reformation? Understanding the origins of conflicts gives us the possibility of envisioning their solutions. The issues in this book will help you think through the problems facing our world and give you the tools to make an informed decision about what you think is the best course of action.

In a democracy, an informed citizenry is the bedrock on which a government stands. If we do not understand the past, the present will be a puzzle to us and the future may seem out of our control. Seeing how and why historians disagree can help us determine what the critical issues are and where informed interpreters part company. This, at least, is the basis for forming our own judgments and acting upon them. Looking critically at clashing views also hones our analytic skills and makes us thoughtful readers of all our textbooks as well as magazines and newspapers.

Why Study World History?

You may be wondering why this book deals with world history rather than exclusively with Western Civilization. At times the West has felt its power and dominance in the world made only its own story worth studying. History, we are sometimes told, is written by the winners. For the Chinese, the Greeks, the Ottoman Turks, and many other victors of the past, the stories of other civilizations seemed irrelevant, unimportant, not nearly as valuable as their own triumphal saga. The Chinese considered their Middle Kingdom the center of the world; the Greeks labeled all others barbarians; and the Ottoman Turks expected never to lose their position of dominance. From our perspective in the present these stories form a tapestry. No one thread or pattern tells the tale and all seem to be equally necessary for a complete picture of the past to emerge.

Any single story—even that of a military and economic superpower—is insufficient to explain the scope of human history at a given moment in time. Our story is especially interesting to us and you will find issues specific to Western Civilization in this book. However, as we are learning, our story achieves its fullest meaning only when it is told in concert with those of other civilizations that share an increasingly interconnected planet with us. As communications systems shrink the Earth into a global village, we may be ignoring the rest of the world at our own peril. At the very least the study of civilizations other than our own can alert us to events that may have worldwide implications. And, as we are beginning to learn, no story happens in isolation. The history of the West can perhaps be accurately told only within a global context that takes into account the actions and reactions of other civilizations as they share the world stage with the West. As you read the issues that concern non-Western civilizations, stay alert for what you can learn about your own.

Your textbook may take a global focus or it may be restricted to the study of Western Civilization. In either case, the readings in this book will enrich your understanding of how the peoples of the world have understood themselves and their relationships with others. As we become a more clearly multicultural society, we have an additional reason for studying about other civilizations that have blended with our own through immigration. Perhaps the biggest challenge for an increasingly diverse United States of America is to understand its own role in world affairs and its relationship with other countries, which may have different histories, value systems, and goals.

On the Internet . . .

Becoming Human

Using a documentary film, learning center, news and features, and resources sections, this site covers all aspects of human origins.

http://becominghuman.org

Materials for the Study of Women and Gender in the Ancient World

Provides lists of Web site materials in areas such as bibliography, essays, and images; also contains a useful search engine.

www.stoa.org/diotima

Olmec Art

Art is key to the argument for African influence on Olmec civilization. Using these images along with the essays, will help students evaluate this issue.

www.latinamericanstudies.org/olmec-colossal-heads-1.htm

Alexander the Great

A cradle-to-grave treatment of Alexander's life and accomplishments in small segments; includes some interesting visuals.

http://1stmuse.com/frames/project.html

From Jesus to Christ: The First Christians

Based on a six-part PBS/FRONTLINE series, one of which is devoted to "The Roles for Women." It contains the raising of important questions on the subject, which are subsequently answered by a noted expert in the field.

**http://www.pbs.org/wgbh/pages/frontline/
shows/religion/**

The Illustrated History of the Roman Empire

A multifaceted site that contains valuable information, some of it visual, on the Roman Empire in general and its decline and fall in particular.

http://www.roman-empire.net/

PART 1

The Ancient World

*B*eginning with the question of the origins of humankind, this section covers the development of the world's earliest civilizations, and crosses over into the classical era. It analyzes and evaluates the origins and development of the world's oldest civilizations, the challenges they faced, and how they responded to them. Conquerors such as Alexander the Great rose and fell; the Roman Empire did the same. Christianity emerged as a world religion. With written history came the never-ending process of historical revisionism.

- Did *Homo Sapiens* Originate in Africa?

- Was Sumerian Civilization Exclusively Male Dominated?

- Was Mesoamerica's Olmec Civilization Influenced by African Sources?

- Does Alexander the Great Deserve His Reputation?

- Did Christianity Liberate Women?

- Were Internal Factors Responsible for the Fall of the Roman Empire?

ISSUE 1

Did *Homo Sapiens* Originate in Africa?

YES: Stephen Oppenheimer, from "The First Exodus," *Geographical* (July 2002)

NO: Milford Wolpoff and Rachel Caspari, from *Race and Human Evolution* (Simon & Schuster, 1997)

ISSUE SUMMARY

YES: Professor and researcher Stephen Oppenheimer states that genetic, archaeological, and climatic evidence proves that modern humans first developed in Africa and then spread to other parts of the world, referred to as the "out of Africa" theory.

NO: Paleoanthropologists Milford Wolpoff and Rachel Caspari claim that scientific evidence proves that humans developed simultaneously in different parts of the world, now called the "multiregional" theory.

Where did we come from? This question strikes at the heart of human existence. For each individual, its answer provides an identity which gives us a uniqueness that no one else can share. When it is applied universally to all humankind, it can provide answers to questions which go back to the origin of the species: How did we get here? From whom are we descended? To what extent are we all related?

In the twentieth century, the origin of our ancestors was determined by the most recent fossilized discovery. With each time period, the location shifted from one part of the world to another until the last generation's pioneering work placed humankind's origins firmly in East Africa. But this answers only the origins part of the human puzzle. When did these "ancestors" evolve into *Homo sapiens*, and where did this occur?

Answers to these questions have come within the domain of scientists known as **paleoanthropologists**. Relying on fossil discoveries and the latest tools and methodologies used to analyze and evaluate them, these scientists have done much to provide information regarding the origins of humankind. But, recently, they have been joined in the quest by another group of scientists— **molecular biologists** (or molecular geneticists)—who have used advances in the study of DNA in their search for answers to the same questions.

In 1987, the latter group published their findings, thus firing the opening shots in what would become an interdisciplinary conflict within the scientific community. By examining the mitochondrial DNA, taken from the placentas of women representing every identifiable racial and ethnic group possible, they concluded that approximately 200,000 years ago, our earliest traceable ancestor existed in Africa. This species migrated throughout the world, thus making Africa the birthplace of *Homo sapiens*. This is known as the "out of Africa" theory.

The popular media quickly picked up this debate: articles in *Time, Newsweek, The New York Times*, and many other publications publicized the new findings, naming our common ancestor "Eve" and proclaiming her to be "the mother of us all".

For a time, the DNA proponents seemed to dominate the world's attention with "Eve." But it didn't take long for some paleoanthropologists to fire back. Claiming the reasoning of the DNA disciples to be flawed, they offered evidence to support a multiregional approach to the evolution of humankind, in which prehistoric creatures originated in Africa, migrated to other parts of the world, and then separately evolved into *Homo sapiens*. This is referred to as the "multiregional" theory in regard to the origins of humankind.

Although the media has made this seem like a battle between the old school paleoanthropologists and the new school molecular biologists, there are fundamental differences in the arguments developed by both sides that require further research and evaluation. In the April 1992 edition of *Scientific American*, the two sides squared off for a page-by-page debate on the subject. This was followed by the publication of several books on the subject, as each side attempted to gain the upper hand in this academic dispute.

For a few years, the "African Eve" side seemed to have the upper hand in the courts of academic and public opinion. However, scrutiny of their analysis of mitochondrial DNA and the conclusions drawn from it exposed weaknesses in their methodology and interpretations. The criticism was so damaging that it caused Milford Wolpoff to claim, "It's all over for Eve." (*Science*, volume 259, p. 1249).

The anouncement of Eve's demise, however, proved to be "greatly exaggerated," as evidence supporting the "out of Africa" theory began to surface. A combination of improvements in the gathering and interpretation of DNA evidence, advancements in the ability to date fossilized materials, and new evidence emphasizing climate and its influence on early migrations have moved "Eve" back on the front burner.

But this will not be the last word on the subject. The debate will continue, and it will be a while (if ever) before one side "cries uncle". Within the scientific world, a theory is only as strong as the latest evidence which supports it. Another interesting circumstance is the recent appearance of books and articles which attempt to glean the best arguments from both sides to produce a consensus opinion. Stay tuned!

In the following selections, Stephen Oppenheimer argues for the "out of Africa" theory by using genetic, archaeological, and climatic evidence to support his assertions. Milford Wolpoff and Rachel Casperi contend that the "multiregional" theory is more accurate by presenting what they perceive are flaws in the "out of Africa" theory.

YES

Stephen Oppenheimer

The First Exodus

We have all wondered why it is that people in different parts of the world look so different and what possible ancestral relationships exist between people like Europeans, Chinese, Africans or Australian aborigines. Do all the human 'races' derive from several geographic sources or just one? If there was one source, where was that, and how, if we are all related, did we get to be where we are today? Such questions are at the heart of our sense of identity, and are well summarised by the Pacific Island proverb: "To know where we are going, first we have to know who we are and where we came from".

Although some see our 'races' as very ancient divisions, the dominant view today is that the ancestors of all modern humans expanded recently from Africa to replace all archaic human types throughout the world (see Human Ancestry, below). The Out-of-Africa theory was originally based on study of anatomical features, but recent genetic study has provided a scientific foundation for the hypothesis.

The Past in Our Genes

The genes we carry in our cells define each of us as individuals and are inherited from both our parents. Since this insight over a hundred years ago, geneticists have dreamed of using genetic markers to classify human 'races' and establish how they are related, and thus determine where we all come from. One of the earliest attempts to mine our genetic present in order to trace our geographic past involved the study of blood groups among different peoples. This study, conducted over 80 years ago, foundered in a morass of absurd links, such as Russians with Madagascans. But in recent years, geneticists have succeeded in building 'family trees' of individual genes and their variants, using technology that sequences our DNA. Their research was based on the fact that two tiny elements of our DNA pass intact from generation to generation without mixing—the Y Chromosome through the male line from our fathers, and 'mitochondrial DNA' (mtDNA) through the female' line by our mothers.

The first major breakthrough in using genetics to trace prehistory was made 15 years ago by Hawaiian geneticist Rebecca Cann and colleagues who published the first mtDNA tree showing that all modern humans traced back to a single African female ancestor, named 'Eve' by the media. The mtDNA finding was subsequently mirrored for the Y Chromosome.

From *Geographical* by Stephen Oppenheimer, vol. 74, no. 7 July 2002, pp. 32–36. Copyright © 2002 by Campion Interactive Publishing Ltd. Reprinted by permission.

Since mutations occur at a constant—though random—rate, it was then possible to date not only the branches, but the base of the tree. The age of the latter was less than 200,000 years. This confirmed the 'Garden of Eden' theory that modern humans, arising in Africa, had only recently replaced all earlier human species throughout the world.

The 'Adam' and 'Eve' trees also have the power to answer more detailed geographic questions of how we came out of Africa; which exit route we took, how many exits there were and where we went from there. For these questions, the most important advance in the past five years was the fine resolution of the mtDNA tree by English geneticist Dr Martin Richards and colleagues from Britain, New Zealand and Germany. This showed only one of the multiple African mtDNA branches peopling the whole of the rest of the world. Geneticists have confirmed a similar finding for several other gene trees, including the Y Chromosome. Logically this single branch pattern makes it extremely unlikely there was more than one exodus. In other words, only one band successfully made it out of Africa to colonise the rest of the world.

The implications of only one exodus are enormous. First, it means all non-African peoples, including Europeans, Indians, Chinese, Australians and Native Americans, are related, and are recent descendants of that one small family band. Secondly we can now begin to get an idea of the genetic trail from Africa, which could tell us not only when and where they went, but how each modern regional group is related to the others.

It is not quite as easy as that, however. A mitochondrial genetic tree put on the wall does not just read like a management chart and divide into regional 'races'. Regional populations as in India, Europe and China are not the same as single branches of gene trees. The 'tree' is, in reality, more like several strands of creeping ivy spreading and branching over the Earth. Multiple genetic lines migrated in parallel, thus eroding, even further, out-moded concepts of 'race'. One region will share strands of different genetic branches with neighbouring regions; but each region has its own unique new growth. It is the new twigs and leaves that grew on the older strands in different regions that tell us where people migrated to and where they went after that. Genetic branches, however, only have approximate dates while climatic and archaeological events can be better dated; so the reconstruction of these ancient migrations has to be matched with archaeology, the dramatic effects of changing climate and natural geographic corridors and barriers.

I believe we can take this reconstruction right back to Africa's doorstep. There are only two routes out of sub-Saharan Africa to Asia, one up the Nile corridor, through Egypt and the Suez to the Levant, and the other in the south across the mouth of the Red Sea and along the Arabian coast to Yemen and Oman. For most of the past 100,000 years, the Syrian and Arabian deserts separated southern Asia from the Levant and Europe. So, taking the northern route meant that emigrants could only go farther north to Europe and the Caucasus. Taking the southern route meant continuing along the coast of the Indian Ocean to India, the Far East and Australia. With these constraints in mind, if there was only one exodus, we can compare the evidence for each of the two routes and then focus on dates.

Southern Exit

Archaeology and climate both favour the southern route. Australia was colonised at least 20,000 years before Europe. If there was only one exodus through the northern route, Europe should have been colonised earlier. My argument for the late colonisation of Europe is that the ancestors of West Eurasians had to wait somewhere in southern Asia, such as the Arabian Gulf, until the climatic amelioration after 50,000 years ago allowed them to make their way north to the east coast of the Mediterranean. From there, they could enter Europe. The genetic evidence is consistent with this delay.

A Drier World

There are other elements, too. Between 80-50,000 years ago the world was much drier than today. Sea levels were lower and the short crossing of the mouth of the Red Sea directly from sub-Saharan Africa would have been less hazardous than crossing the Sahara desert to get to North Africa. Evidence for systematic beachcombing has recently been found, near the mouth of the Red Sea on the west coast, as far back as 125,000 years ago. So, a means of survival along the Arabian coast was definitely available to southern migrants. Increasing salinity of the Red Sea as a result of falling sea levels, a shallow mouth and increased evaporative loss may have prompted the move 80,000 years ago.

The clincher is the genetic evidence. Reasonably we might suppose that our emigrant band from Africa would leave a trace of their early genetic branches at the start of their trail. There is no evidence for this in the northern route through North Africa, to the Levant or Europe. Instead, in these places, we only see derivative genetic branches from after 50,000 years ago, agreeing with the archaeological evidence for a later colonisation. Furthermore, one of the two earliest mtDNA branches outside Africa, 'Asian M', is virtually absent here. In India, by contrast, the first major dispersal point along the southern route, we find all the earliest genetic branches outside Africa and at great diversity and antiquity.

Date of Departure

Dating the exodus is another matter. Increasing genetic evidence from East Asia and the Antipodes suggests the exodus could be as old as 80,000 years, but the genetic clock lacks precision. Here the archaeology may help in the synthesis. A picture is growing of a single exit by the southern route and a rapid spread of beachcombers round the Indian Ocean over land-bridges through Indonesia to Bali. From there a few short island hops took our migrants to Timor. The final stretch was more of a problem. Today there are 500 kilometres of sea between Timor and Australia. But 70,000 years ago a severe glaciation briefly locked up enough water to lower the sea level by 80 metres, taking the coast of Timor to within 160 kilometres of Australia. Archaeological evidence for the earliest occupation of Australia by modern humans suggests this is the only time they could have got across.

Other dates further back on the trail support this 80,000-year exodus. There is increasing consensus that certain pebble tools only appear in Southeast Asia with the arrival of modern humans over 70,000 years ago. One group of these tools was found in Kota Tampan in the Malay Peninsula, encased in volcanic ash from the great Toba eruption. The latter has now been accurately dated to 74,000 years, indicating the presence of modern humans—already halfway to Australia. Arriving in Malaysia 74,000 years ago and Australia by 70,000 years ago makes an 80,000-year exit from Africa look very reasonable.

Later events—such as the peopling of the Americas and the last Ice Age— are also illuminated by the new genetic tools. Archaeological preconceptions, such as the size of neolithic expansions, can now be held up to the scrutiny of the tree that tracks people. The study of archaeology is changing forever.

Human Ancestry: The Two Views

Two opposing views of human ancestry are based on physical comparisons. One of these surfaced 60 years ago at the time of World War II. Now labelled 'multiregionalism', this theory argued for multiple sources of the different human races, claiming that they had evolved slowly from previous regional archaic species. Thus Neanderthals (Homo neanderthalensis) were ancestors of Europeans, Orientals derived from Peking Man (Homo erectus), and Australians from Java Man (Homo erectus).

The alternative view, originally hinted at by Darwin, began to gain ground less than 30 years ago. Now called 'Garden of Eden' or 'Out-of-Africa', this theory held that all human species, including the archaic types, had arisen in Africa, but that modern humans, being the most recent group to emerge, had physically replaced all the others. Genetics has now vindicated the Out-of-Africa idea and the multiregionalists have become a dwindling persuasion regarded by some geneticists as akin to flat-earthers.

There remains the question whether our ancestors might still have interbred with the archaic humans, since modern Europeans co-existed with Neanderthals for over 10,000 years. It is possible for the genetic tree to give a provisional answer on this. Neanderthal mtDNA has now been sequenced from several bones, revealing at least 18 mutational differences from our African genetic Eve. If there had been mixing with Neanderthal mtDNA, their mtDNA would have continued into modern times. Such a great difference in sequence should easily have been detected among the thousands of modern people whose mtDNA has been sampled—and it has yet to be found. Absence of evidence does not, however, prove conclusively that interbreeding did not occur.

The Gene Key

Genes are made up of a long string-like molecule, DNA, which carries a sequence of coded instructions to build and maintain our bodies. Over many generations harmless mutations build up in the DNA code. These mutations can be detected in the laboratory by sequencing the code. Since the new mutations are then passed on down the generations, they each act as markers to identify new branches of a family tree for that gene or locus—the small stretch of DNA.

The problem is that most of our DNA has the tendency to get shuffled up and spliced after fertilisation of the ovum at every generation, thus blurring the family tree. Two small parts of our DNA do not suffer this shuffling process and are passed intact through the generations. One of these is the Y Chromosome which is only passed down the male line through our fathers. The other is 'mitochondrial DNA' (mtDNA) which we all have in our cells, but is only transmitted down the female line by our mothers. By studying Y Chromosomes and mtDNA from thousands of living people, geneticists have built two family trees which trace back to one single common ancestor for the whole modern human species.

Since these represent the male and female parts of our DNA heritage they have been called the 'Adam' and 'Eve' gene trees. These genetic trees have revolutionised our view of our past. However, while they enable us to peer far back in the vertebrate tree, these two small parts of the human genome represent a fraction of our genetic heritage. We may have thousands of common ancestors corresponding with the 30,000 other genes in our genome.

Milford Wolpoff and
Rachel Caspari

 **NO**

Multiregional Evolution and Eve: Science and Politics

What Is Multiregional Evolution?

The fundamental question that has been asked historically is how people all over the world could evolve in the same way, all becoming modern humans, and yet maintain some regional differentiation for long periods of time. This is an observation, and the fundamental problem is how to resolve the contradiction that seems to lie at its heart. The genic exchanges between populations that would seem critical for one would seem equally destructive of the other. Confronted with compelling similarities between Australasian specimens separated by three quarters of a million years, and somewhat different similarities across perhaps an even longer time span in China, patterns of details not shared by fossils from other regions, Milford [Wolpoff], Alan [Thorne], and Wu [Xinzhi] developed a model to explain these sets of seemingly contradictory observations that have puzzled paleoanthropologists for close to a century—evidence of longstanding regional differences between human groups in the face of evidence of important global similarities in the direction of evolution. . . .

Multiregional evolution provides resolution of the contradictions between genetic exchanges and population differentiations in a broad-based theory that links gene flow and population movements, and natural selection, and their effects on populations both at the center and at the peripheries of the geographic range of the human species. In a nutshell, the theory is that *the recent pattern of human evolution has been strongly influenced by the internal dynamics of a single, far-flung human species, internally divided into races. Human populations developed a network of interconnections, so behavioral and genetic information was interchanged by mate exchanges and population movements. Gradients along these interconnections encouraged local adaptations. These and other sources of population variation that depended on population histories developed, and stable adaptive complexes of interrelated features evolved in different regions. But, at the same time, evolutionary changes across the species occurred as advantageous features appeared and dispersed because of the success they imparted. These changes took on different forms in different places because of the differing histories of populations reflected in their gene pools, and the consequences of population placements in terms of habitat and their relations to other populations. Some evolutionary changes happened everywhere, because of these processes and because of common aspects of selection created by the extra informa-tion exchanges allowed by the evolving cultural and communications systems. Consequently, throughout the past 2 million years humans have been a single widespread polytypic species, with multiple, constantly evolving, interlinked popu-lations, continually dividing and merging. Because of these internal divisions and the processes that maintain them, this species has been able to encompass and maintain adaptive variations across its range without requiring the isolation of gene pools. This pattern emerged once the Old World was colonized, and there is no evidence of speciations along the human line since then that would suggest there were different evolutionary processes, such as complete replacement, at work.*

Over the past decade Multiregional evolution has itself evolved into a broad and malleable frame. It is a *general* explanation for the pattern and pro-cess of human evolution within which virtually any hypothesis about dynam-ics between specific populations can be entertained, from the mixture, even replacement, of some populations to the virtual isolation of others. To be valid, the model must be able to incorporate a wide range of population dynamics, from expansion to extinction, leaving paleoanthropologists room to derive more detailed understandings of specific evolutionary patterns for particular times and places. Various groups of people behave in different ways that affect their demographic structure (that is, the specific attributes of their population, such as its size, mortality rates, sex ratios, age profiles). If you are trying to predict patterns of evolutionary change, this demographic informa-tion is absolutely essential, since the major evolutionary forces of natural selection and genetic drift operate differently on populations with diverse demographic structures. As with all social animals, every human population has a different evolutionary story, with its own historical, biological, and social constraints that affect its evolution. The human evolutionary pattern is even more dynamic than that of other species, because cultural and linguistic factors are added to the list of constraints, even as they expand the different ways in which populations can exchange and share information. Culturally prescribed marriage systems, trading networks, religious practices, likes and dislikes, all affect reproduction, death, and breeding group size and therefore the evolution of these populations. Consequently, *detailed* understanding of the course and processes of human evolution is unusual, and can be obtained only for small temporal and geographic windows, where many ecological, demographic, and cultural variables are known. Multiregional evolution can be thought of as the structure in which these windows sit. It is compatible with all the windows we've looked through so far, a structure that allows them all to exist together. In other words, it is a model that fits the skeletal and genetic data we have today, and we also think it works in the past, where the information is much less precise, and there is much less of it.

Using the Multiregional model for interpreting the past assumes that the modern pattern of human evolution is the best model for interpreting the human condition ever since the first colonizations of the world outside of Africa began. If this assumption is valid, the present can be used as a model for explaining the past; this is the principle of "uniformitarianism" that the geologist Charles Lyell so successfully applied during the last century to interpreting the geological and paleontological record, work that was critical to Darwin's emerging theory of evolution. We consider this the most logical approach to understanding the recent pattern of human evolution, and treat it as the null hypothesis (the hypothesis of no difference, or no change, is the hypothesis to disprove, or try to disprove, with ongoing research and discoveries) for interpreting the past. It is the simplest hypothesis, one that models the evolutionary patterns of our behaviorally complex, geographically widespread predecessors after the living species most like them: our own.

We are quite aware that people have not always been the same. The evolutionary dynamics of modern humans are far from fully understood, and there are many factors in modern human populations that cannot be applied to the past. People have changed dramatically in recent times—their cultures have become incredibly complex, their demographics have altered remarkably, populations have expanded dramatically—and there is no way that evolutionary processes at work today can be expected to be identical with those of the past, just as the evolutionary processes at work today vary from population to population. But stepping away from the details, there is a frame of conditions these processes work within, and it is here that we draw the basis for applying the uniformitarian principle. It seems to us that the bases for approaching the past this way are twofold: we recognize no biological species formation in humanity once *Homo sapiens* appeared some 2 million years ago, and the fundamental shift from a solely African scavenging/gathering species to a colonizing species taking place at *Homo sapiens* origins or early in their evolution set up the conditions of polytypism across a broad geographic range that allowed Multiregionalism to work.

Thus Multiregional evolution is a gradualist model, with the primary tenet that humans *are* a single polytypic species and *have been* for a very long time into the past. It interprets the fossil record to show that human beings— that is, our species *Homo sapiens* and its main attribute *humanity*—happened only once, and once on the scene they evolved without a series of speciations and replacements. No speciation events seem to separate us from our immediate ancestors, and cladogensis, the splitting of one species into two, last characterized our lineage at the origin of *Homo sapiens* some 2 million years ago, when members of what we once called *"Homo erectus"* first appeared in East Africa. For 2 million years, from the end of the Pliocene until now, ancient and modern *Homo sapiens* populations are members of the same species. This doesn't mean they didn't change—*au contraire*—but we think these changes neither led to nor required a speciation. The broad-based evolutionary processes proposed in Multiregional evolution are formulated to explain patterns of variation *within* a polytypic species: the same evolutionary processes shown to be important in other polytypic species have shaped our patterns of diversity in the past and do so in the present.

The ability to account for all the data it is supposed to explain is only one hurdle for a hypothesis. It also must, at least in principle, be refutable. Multiregional evolution would be wrong, a disproved and invalid hypothesis, if the evolutionary changes it accounts for and the contradiction between genic exchanges and local continuity of features it resolves were explained instead by a series of successive speciations and replacements. Multiregional evolution would also be wrong if the pattern of human evolution it describes never existed—that is, if the interpretation of long-standing polytypism in the human fossil record is incorrect, since the explanations would then be elucidating a pattern that did not exist. Evidence of multiple speciations, indicating a different *pattern* of human evolution and, in particular, a recent speciation for modern humans, could provide this refutation, and the Eve theory claimed to rest on just such evidence.

So Eve came as a wake-up call for Multiregionalism. Although not particularly aimed that way at first, it was soon correctly perceived by all as the first serious attempt at its disproof, and for "Popperian" scientists, refutation is the key way that science proceeds. Milford is a deductionist, strongly influenced by the philosopher of science Karl Popper and most concerned with refuting hypotheses. The role of deduction comes after a hypothesis is framed; what matters most is whether it is explanatory, is testable, and requires the least number of assumptions. Multiregional evolution is our null hypothesis, the simplest and most explanatory hypothesis that covers the pattern of Pleistocene human evolution. But it was just recently developed, at least in its modern form, and until the Eve theory there were no significant attempts to disprove it.

After the publication of the 1984 paper, Alan, Wu, and Milford didn't think too much about Multiregional evolution in a theoretical way. Prior to the marketing of Eve, they had each proceeded to treat Multiregional evolution as a working hypothesis. Many others accepted the hypothesis as well, and research was initiated within a Multiregional paradigm, which in itself was not the focus of the investigations. As Multiregionalists studied human evolution, they were consciously aware of geographic variation and its confounding effects in understanding human evolution as a whole; Multiregional scholars were, and are, careful to view temporal trends as potentially regional phenomena and cautious not to generalize too quickly between one region and another, often avoiding a kind of ethnocentrism applied to the fossil record.

Before Eve, the few attempts to show species change in the recent human fossil record were focused on the seemingly unending Neandertal issue and were unconvincing to most scientists. Nothing effectively challenged the explanatory value of Multiregionalism as an explanation for worldwide change. As Alan made movies all over the world, the patterns of variation in the people he visited fit the Multiregional model. He collected and bred snakes, and the patterns of their variation fit the Multiregional model. Wu struggled with the long-awaited completion of his monograph on the Dali skull. Milford returned to focused, problem-oriented research. Always interested in patterns and causes of variation, he wrote papers on allometry, on sexual dimorphism, and on biomechanics, seeking explanations for trends that extended across broad periods of human evolution. But they all returned to issues of Multiregional evolution after the 1987 publication announcing what was soon widely called the Eve theory, and several publications following in the next year cited evidence that could refute the Multiregional model and our entire understanding of the human fossil record.

NO / Wolpoff and Caspari

The Eve theory played *the* lead role in what quickly became a confrontation between paleontological and molecular genetic interpretations of the past. The development of Multiregionalism owes a great deal to her. When the Eve publications emerged, the Multiregional camp quickly responded to them, pointing out several problems that prevented them from refuting the Multiregional hypothesis. The Eve debates made us very introspective about our proposals and their implications. We were forced to think about Multiregionalism's development and testability and the things we think make it a good hypothesis. . . .

The Politicization of Eve

Eve was new. Eve was modern. Eve was glamorous and sexy. Eve was a simple theory that made science reporting easy and fun. Eve gave answers and represented 20th-century technology providing answers—telling us about our origins. Eve implied the brotherhood of all humankind and was politically correct. Eve was perfect in every way, actually too good to be true. How is it that a theory so flawed could be embraced by so many? Why was she so uncritically accepted? The answer incorporates politics, and Eve gained political favor two ways: first by the appeal of new science, new technology, and new ideas replacing old-fashioned ones. It was a demonstration that public tax dollars were not really being misspent, that the results tell us something new about ourselves and something we can all understand. Second, it underscored the genetic unity of the human species, something we all need to be reminded of in the face of so many factious elements in our world. Both factors contributed to Eve's appeal to the public, and both entered the scientific discourse because science, in the end, is a human activity.

Unlike many scientific debates, where different sides may write quiet (or not so quiet) articles back and forth in professional journals for decades, the Eve debate quickly became politicized for a variety of reasons. . . . As the science of human origins has always been, this debate is public. It is sometimes pitched as a battle between the paleontologists (using archaic science) and the geneticists (modern scientists, exploiting the advantages of new techniques and modern technology), although this is far from true. Much hay is made over personal differences between the investigators in the different disciplines and even more over the differences in technology used. In a sense the fuss over Eve is an appealing topic because it illustrates the advantages of the modern age. Images are fostered of bright young geneticists using modern techniques the doddering old fossil hunters, ill prepared to understand, let alone participate in real science, cannot hope to. This is actually actively promoted by a few of the Eve researchers in statements such as those of [Allan] Wilson and [Rebecca] Cann in *Scientific American*, no less, where they contrast paleoanthropologists with "biologists trained in modern evolutionary theory" who "reject the notion that fossils provide the most direct evidence of how human evolution actually proceeded." Cann then held paleoanthropology in especially low regard, once saying "it is too much to hope the trickle of bones from fossil beds would provide a clear picture of human evolution any time soon." The paleoanthropologists themselves are portrayed as poor scientists engaged in circular reasoning. For instance Wilson and Cann quipped in *Scientific American*, "fossils cannot, in principle, be interpreted objectively . . . [paleoanthropologists'] reasoning tends to circularity."

In fact, there is nothing particularly difficult to understand about mitochondrial genetics, or the Eve position. We find the fuss over technology something less than relevant, since quality of science is not measured by the level of technology employed, but by the design of questions asked and testing methodology (not technology). Many people seem to believe something seen with the naked eye is less valid or scientific than something seen with a microscope, and the more powerful the microscope the more valuable the observation. But microscopes "showed" scientist after scientist that humans had 48 chromosomes, when they actually have only 46.

Scientists working today do have great advantages over their historical counterparts, and some of the advantage comes from technology and its applications in research. Advances in instrumentation are extremely beneficial, but by themselves do not make "good" science. In fact, there has been a real tendency for the technologies themselves to drive the direction of scientific research, as they become techniques in search of questions to answer. Real advantages we enjoy come from our recognition of the understandings arrived at by our predecessors and their incorporation into our consciousness, our world view. As Newton said of himself, "If I see so far, it is because I stand on the shoulders of giants." Multiregional evolution was only derived now, in spite of age-old grappling with many of the same problems, not because of the advance of technology, but because our world view has changed. The triumph of Darwinian thinking and an appreciation of population dynamics are actually very recent. Whatever insights we may have into the evolution of humans as a polytypic species are due to the influence on our thinking, both conscious and unconscious, of the prior work of others.

Misconceptions about the power of technology are generated by the press, not the geneticists (with one or two notable exceptions). For the most part, there are very good feelings between geneticists and paleontologists, two groups of scientists who study different data bases, but who sometimes ask the same questions of them. Both kinds of data can give us information about evolutionary history and relationships. One kind of data, whether from genes or bones, is not "better" than the other, and if data from different, independent sources seem to bring totally conflicting evidence to bear on a single question, it is not time to choose between them, but rather to see what is wrong with our hypotheses and methods of analysis.

There are other, far more serious ways than the technology issue in which the public aspects of the debate have influenced it, the positions taken by its participants, and its perceived outcome. These evolved over the question of political correctness. It is possible, as the late Glynn Isaac reportedly said, that Multiregional evolution holds the high ground on the political correctness issue because by positing an ancient divergence between races it implies that the small racial differences humans show must have evolved slowly and therefore are insignificant. But the high ground is widely perceived to be held by the Eve theory, not Multiregional evolution, and in any event Multiregional evolution does not mean that the modern *races* are particularly ancient: groups of features, not groups of populations, are ancient according to this model.

Even as the debate was first joined, Eve theorists claimed the high moral ground for themselves. In 1987 S. J. Gould wrote: "We are close enough to our African origins to hope for the preservation of unity in both action and artifacts." In 1988 he proclaimed: "Human unity is no idle political slogan . . . all modern humans form an entity united by physical bonds of descent from a recent African root." Of course, if the Eve theory means the *unity* of humankind, what could Multiregional evolution mean? And why should either side be more politically correct? A paper read by Fatimah Jackson at the 1994 meetings of the American Anthropological Association tars all of the modern human origins theories with typology and racism in one form or another. As she sees the debate, it begins with the presumption that there are typologically distinct races. She believes that this assumption is a reflection of Eurocentrism: the races must be distinct for Europeans to be distinct from the others. Writing with L. Lieberman, she goes on to conclude of all the theories, "Each . . . relies to varying degrees on static, typological definitions of human biological variation at some point in its analysis, and this reliance limits the explanatory power and utility of each model for understanding the origins and maintenance of human diversity."

Although there is much truth in what she says, Dr. Jackson misses a fundamental point. Far from having the same view on race and human variation, different views on these topics underscore the various theories of modern human origins. The different origins theories hold very different positions on how to model human variation, or race, and therefore on evolutionary pattern. Or perhaps it is the other way around: proponents of different origins theories have different ideas about evolutionary pattern, and this influences their views on race and modern human variation. Whatever the case, the two issues (race and modern human origins) are inextricably related. Multiregional evolution is clearly tied to race: it was developed to explain regional continuity which, given our own views of race, *should not exist*. But by accepting the existence of regional continuity, we recognize morphology that has been interpreted to both elevate and rank the importance of human differences, we believe incorrectly, with horrendous consequences. In order to understand the nature of the mutual influences of race and human evolution we need to examine how these mutual influences developed. . . . There, we can also find clues to the origins of modern predispositions toward one theory or another.

POSTSCRIPT

Did *Homo Sapiens* Originate in Africa?

A good starting place for a general search in human origins could begin with a Special Edition Magazine, "New Look at Human Evolution," *Scientific American* (13: 2, 2003), which contains articles by some of the leading scholars in the field, and some interesting and pertinent graphics. Two video series, each in three parts, would also be helpful: "In Search of Human Origins," PBS/NOVA (1997); and "Dawn of Man: The Story of Human Evolution," *British Broadcasting Corporation* (2000).

The role Neanderthals played in human evolution has become a timely topic and which raises many questions. What were their chief characteristics? How did they compare with Homo sapiens? Did the two species co-habitate? Were they genetically related? And, most importantly, what happened to them and why? Answers to these questions are important to the study of human evolution, and some books useful to questions raised above would be: James Shreeve, *The Neanderthal Enigma: Solving the Mystery of Human Origins* (Avon Books, 1995); Christopher Stringer and Clive Gambee, *In Search of the Neanderthals: Solving the Puzzle of Human Origins* (Thames & Hudson, 1995); Paul Mellars, *The Neanderthal Legacy* (Princeton University Press, 1995); Ian Tattersall, *The Last Neanderthal: The Rise, Success, and Mysterious Extinction of Our Closest Human Relatives* (Westview Press, 1999); Paul Jordan, *Neanderthal Man and the Story of Human Origins* (Sutton Publishing, 2000). There are also many articles on the subject available from various Internet providers.

Of course, the central question raised by this issue is where Homo sapiens originated, shaped by the differing opinions espoused by the molecular scientists and their "Out of Africa" theory, and the paleoanthropologists with their "Multiregional" one. Two of the first general accounts of the subject, each supporting one side of this issue are: Christopher Stringer and Robin McKie, *African Exodus: The Origins of Modern Humanity* (Henry Holt and Company, 1996); and, *Race and Human Evolution* by Milford Wolpoff and Rachel Caspari (Simon and Schuster, 1997).

In recent years, "Eve" has been featured in many works, among them: Bryan Sykes, *The Seven Daughters of Eve: The Science That Reveals Our Genetic Ancestry* (W.W. Norton, 2001); Stephen Oppenheimer, *The Real Eve: Modern Man's Journey Out of Africa* (Carroll & Graf, 2003); and Lee R. Berger, *In the Footsteps of Eve: The Mystery of Human Origins* (National Geographic, 2000). The latter presents an interesting twist in the human origins story by locating it in Africa, but in South Africa and not East Africa.

A book that presents both sides of the debate, and also explores other issues relevant to the human origins debate is Geoffrey A. Clark and C.M.

Willermet, eds., *Conceptual Issues in Modern Human Research* (Wayne State University Press, 1997). Their use of articles by many scholars well known in the field makes this a most useful tool.

When pursuing this subject, be aware that every piece of new evidence may alter the framework of the debate.

ISSUE 2

Was Sumerian Civilization Exclusively Male Dominated?

YES: Chester G. Starr, from *A History of the Ancient World* (Oxford University Press, 1965)

NO: Samuel Noah Kramer, from "Poet and Psalmists: Goddesses and Theologians: Literary, Religious, and Anthropological Aspects of the Legacy of Sumer," in Denise Schmandt-Besserat, ed., *The Legacy of Sumer: Invited Lectures on the Middle East at the University of Texas at Austin* (Undena Publications, 1976)

ISSUE SUMMARY

YES: Historian Chester G. Starr finds Sumerian society to be male dominated, from the gods to human priests and kings, and he barely acknowledges the status of women in either the heavenly or the earthly realm.

NO: Museum curator Samuel Noah Kramer relies on much of the same data as Starr, but finds powerful goddesses and earthly women to have played prominent roles in both cosmic and every-day Sumerian life.

T his issue rests on a difference in interpretation rather than on a clearly stated topic debate. Each writer makes assumptions about what ancient Sumerian society was like and each finds evidence to support those assumptions. As you read the following two selections, notice that both cite remarkably similar findings. The difference is that for Chester G. Starr they are asides, whereas, for Samuel Noah Kramer they are the focus. For centuries the story of life in the Fertile Crescent has been told as if only men were actors in the drama. If royal queens received splendid burials, does it make sense to refer to rulers exclusively as kings? If women in a particular culture exhibited what historians like to call *agency*, acting on their own behalf to shape their own lives, is it accurate to term that culture male dominated? Much will depend on interpretation, on whose perspective seems to you more accurate. Was Inanna a "fertility goddess" as Starr assumes or "Queen of Heaven" and goddess of everything as

Kramer implies? Although Kramer's perspective is gaining acceptance, your textbook may continue to make Starr's assumptions.

Since the sophisticated civilization at Sumer is one of the earliest in human history, it has become a model for our understanding of human behavior. If men have always dominated women, then arguments that this arrangement is "natural" have greater strength. If, on the other hand, women played more active roles, then perhaps our understanding of what is by nature and what is by custom needs to be rethought. Virtually all of Kramer's evidence is present in Starr's essay. Is Starr correct to downplay or ignore most of it in favor of male-centered givens? As you read the first essay, pay particular attention to every mention of women as a group and to particular royal and divine women. When you find these female characters more fully developed in the second essay, ask yourself which viewpoint you question.

One of the dangers that historians must constantly be aware of is called *presentism*. We all have a tendency to judge whatever we read about the past in terms of our present values. If we assume that our ways of doing and being are best, we may judge the past in terms of what makes sense for us. Those who find it proper and even natural for men to dominate social, cultural, and religious life may assume that the past generated this pattern and fit existing evidence into these assumptions. Those who question patriarchal dominance may be inclined to look for and find evidence of strong, contributing, and empowering women. The historian's task is to take the evidence on its own terms and let it tell its own story, whether or not that story meshes with the present one.

In 1970 virtually all world history books would have told the story of Sumer as Professor Starr has done. Thirty years later new understandings have led a growing number of scholars to take a fresh look at all of the past and question its archaeological and literary records, making as few assumptions as possible. Curator Kramer represents this new breed of scholars. He does not assert that women dominated Sumerian society, but he finds areas in which women seem to have held as exalted positions as men and he discovers female deities who refuse to be demoted. Their authority and enduring inspiration suggest that women were not seen as outsiders to power. Indeed, the idea of "sacred marriage" suggests that the vital acts of creation and sustenance flowed from a blending of male and female energies.

Try to set aside your own assumptions about how women and men should behave and your own early-twenty-first-century way of looking at the world. Try to see only the evidence as it has come to us in cylinder seals, burial chambers, and texts. Based purely on what both selection authors agree is there, what conclusions can we draw about Sumerian society? Being able to critically evaluate what we learn permits us to make our own judgments and frees us from dependence on the theories of others.

The First Civilization of Mesopotamia

The Mesopotamian Outlook

Sumerian civilization.   The Sumerians, who were in the forefront of early Mesopotamian progress, are linguistically a puzzle, for their agglutinative, largely monosyllabic speech cannot be connected with any of the major groups of languages. By about 3500 B.C. they had begun to draw conventionalized pictograms (representations of physical objects) on clay tablets, found at Kish and Uruk, and perhaps on other, less enduring materials. Three hundred years later, about 3200, tablets show that the scribes of Sumer took a tremendous step, which we do not know ever to have occurred independently elsewhere; that is, they advanced to a mixture of ideograms (marks representing concepts such as "day") and phonograms (symbols expressing syllabic phonetic values, as we might draw a bee for the sound be). Since some symbols expressed more than 1 phonetic value and, on the other hand, 1 single sound could be expressed by up to 14 different marks, sometimes "determinatives" were prefixes to indicate the class to which the word in question belonged, as deity, bird, and so on. These elements came to be wedge-shaped marks impressed in the clay by a stylus; from the Latin word *cuneus* for wedge the Mesopotamian script is called "cuneiform."

From this stage onward cuneiform script could be employed to set down languages of any type; both Semitic dialects like Akkadian and Indo-European tongues like Hittite and Old Persian were so written. Due to the mixture of ideograms, syllabic phonograms, determinatives, and other complications the number of individual signs was much larger than in an alphabetic form of writing. The earliest Sumerian script had perhaps 2000 symbols, but eventually about 500-600 sufficed. Each of these, though considerably simplified over the years, remained so complicated that only professional scribes commonly wrote in the ancient Near East. Writing was an arcane mystery down to Greek times.

The earliest Sumerian tablets are very difficult to comprehend. Largely, though not entirely, they are temple accounts: "so many sheep, so many goats"; or "to so-and-so, beer and bread for one day." If we place them against the much larger bulk of written documents which had appeared by the end of the third millennium, it is nonetheless possible to gain precious light upon early Sumerian thought. The main characteristics of this outlook appeared very swiftly and were essentially fixed as the main lines of Mesopotamian civilization over the next 2500 years. Yet we can also observe that the structure of this outlook became ever more complicated and advanced. The "black-headed people," as the Sumerians called themselves, affected greatly their Semitic neighbors and followers, reaching on up through the Fertile Crescent, and were in turn influenced from the outside.

To a modern observer the pattern of thought which developed in third millennium Mesopotamia is marked by its formal, outwardly static, and religious qualities. In the Sumerian view their arts and crafts had been "revealed" to them by the gods above and were unchanging. Everything must have its name to assure its place in the universe, and one who knew the true name of something had a power over it. Among the earliest Sumerian documents are lists of stones, animals, plants, and the like, classified on their outward characteristics. Yet these lists, which students probably learned by heart, reflect the fact that men were deliberately analyzing and imposing abstract order upon the materials of nature. We must not make the mistake of underestimating the tremendous achievements of these first civilized thinkers merely because their approach was so different from our own; indeed, they created many of the basic tools of thought and concepts we take for granted.

It was now, for instance, necessary to count and to write down numbers; Mesopotamian arithmetic was based sometimes on units of 10, sometimes on units of 60. The latter style, which through its fractions gives us our division of the hour and of the circle, was eventually used especially in astronomy, where men charted the major constellations still marked on modern sky-charts. By the first millennium Mesopotamian scholars began a tradition of ever more refined, precise, and abstract thinking and evolved a concept of place-value notation which was the root of our number system. Civilization also required the measurement and weighing of quantities of grain and metals; the chief weight, a talent of 60 minas, remained the standard quantity on down through the Greek era. Geometry began in the measurement of fields and the requirements of building. The year was solar but was defined in 12 lunar months, with an intercalary month inserted about every 3 years, to fix the great religious festivals and so to regulate agricultural activity.

The arts also progressed. The use of mudbrick and baked brick produced heavy, massive architecture, in which true arches were developed. To cover the ugly brick walls the Sumerians decorated their temples with bands of colored clay cones rammed into the walls and semi-columns; painted frescoes appeared later.

The gods were now visualized in human shape and were represented in statues which are, as it were, the gods themselves; for any transcendental quality was lacking. In some temples there were placed before the gods statues of the rulers, commemorating their devout piety in an equally straightforward, factual, yet reverent manner. The technical problem that stone was hard to come by forced sculptors often to create seated figures and almost always to exaggerate the size of the head. Although some pieces are sharply conceived, they do not exhibit in general an intense interest in nature or a sense of human individuality. Equally significant are the many cylinder seals of men of property, carved with a representation of gods, imaginary animals, or myths. The demonic or bestial motifs that developed in this field were a rich repertoire of great influence on other Near Eastern and Greek art forms, but a modern rationalist will often feel disturbed by their suggestion that man did not yet recognize the distinctiveness of his own nature.

Early Mesopotamian religion.   Man's failure fully to recognize himself is reflected in the religious aspect of the early Mesopotamian outlook. Sumerian civilization had a very strong religious imprint. Only in the confidence born of their common belief in divine support could these men have endured the hardships and unremitting toils necessary to assure a firm foothold in the valley. Their greatest building, the temples, are a mighty testimonial to a human ideal; the priests who clustered about these temples were so important that one may almost call an early Sumerian city-state a theocracy.

The character of this religious system becomes more apparent once there are written copies of Mesopotamian myths and artistic representations of the gods and heroes. To the inhabitants of Mesopotamia the gods were many, for they represented the forces which drove mankind; and in primitive thought these forces were many, distinct in origin. Yet the gods were grouped in a regular pantheon.

Highest was An, the divine force, which could be visualized in the over-arching bowl of Heaven; his name meant "sky" or "shining." Then came Enlil, the active force of nature, who at times manifested himself in the raging storms of the plains, and at other times aided men. The goddess of earth was worshiped as Nin-khursag and under other names. Last of the four creator gods came Enki, the god of waters who fertilized the ground, and by extension became the patron of the skills of wisdom. To these were added 50 "great gods" who met in the assembly of the gods, the Annunaki; a host of other deities, demons, and the like also floated in the Mesopotamian spiritual world.

To the Sumerians their physical environment had come into being from a primordial chaos of water, whence the forces Tiamat and Abzu arose and, by processes of procreation, created the gods. Thereafter came the sky, the earth, and finally mankind. In the spring of each year occurred the greatest religious festival of the land, known as the Akitu in later Babylonia. This was the New Year's feast, an 11-day ceremony of gloom and purification and then of joy, which ended as the gods set the lots for mortal men during the coming year. On the fourth day of the festival the priests recited a myth of the creation called from its opening words *enuma elish*:

> When on high the heaven had not been named,
> Firm ground below had not been called by name . . .
> No reed hut had been matted, no marsh land had appeared.

Beside this ritual myth many other tales evolved to explain the nature of life. The underlying scheme of thought expressed therein postulated that the world was the product of conscious divine action for divine purposes; obvious, too, is the feeling that the world was all animate. Throughout ancient times, down to and past the rise of Christianity, mankind could not quite divest itself of the idea that trees, springs, and the like were endowed with human character- istics or were directed by manlike immortals. In Mesopotamia, as elsewhere, religion not only bound together society but also assured to man the fertility of his fields, his flocks, and himself. One of the greatest figures in Mesopotamian myth was the goddess of human fertility, Inanna (later Ishtar), who may in root have gone back to the Neolithic female figurines found in Halafian levels. Her descent to the underworld and then her return symbolized the renewal of agri- cultural life; her husband Dumuzi (later Tammuz), went permanently to the nether regions as a substitute for her. Each year he was mourned, and his mar- riage with Inanna was celebrated at the New Year's feast.

To modern men, who approach these early myths from a scientific point of view, the tales of the gods are neither sensible nor logical, and the view of life which they express in their repetitious verse is basically a primitive one of gross action and elemental passions. In explaining the nature of the universe men translated into divine terms their own earthly concepts of personal clash and procreation. Yet in early civilized societies these tales were so satisfying that people all over the Near East accepted them. Mesopotamian stories thus passed into the early chapters of the Book of Genesis, where they continued to answer men's curiosity about the Creation down to the past century.

Place of man.   The gods, though human in appearance, paid little attention to mortal men as they drank and made merry, and also wrangled and abused each other in the divine assemblies. Men feared and honored the gods; each city-state was but the earthly domain of certain divine forces on high, for whose ease men toiled throughout their lives. Once dead, men and women could expect only to go to a shadowy, gray land of departed spirits. Such views befitted a land that had recently raised itself to the level of civilization by hard labor, where the climate was severe, where the dangers of flood and sudden disease were ever present, inexplicable, and incurable by human means.

Yet two further reflections may be made. In the first place, the spiritual world of early Mesopotamia was an orderly structure, within which men could operate in a rational fashion; the gods could be propitiated by their human servants through the creation of divine ceremonies. Again, mankind could not quite forget that *it* was the agent that built and tilled, even though human society was far from perfect. In part this hidden realization led to a nagging fear that men might be upsetting an order laid down by the gods. One myth thus depicted the gods, angered by the clamor of men, sending down the Flood; other myths seem akin to the Hebrew story of the Fall of Man from a primitive grace and leisure through his own unwillingness to be pas- sive. In part, however, men were proud of their achievements. A prime reflec- tion of this point of view is the myth of Gilgamesh.

The Gilgamesh epic.   The tale of the hero Gilgamesh, two-thirds god in origin, had Sumerian roots but was more fully formulated into a continuous epic about 2000 B.C. Then it spread all over the Near East and long exercised men's imagination; one artistic symbol drawn from it, that of Gilgamesh strangling a lion, was handed down age after age until it appeared on medieval cathedrals in Western Europe.

Unlike the other myths, which were largely theological creations associated with certain rituals, this epic was centered on human figures. Essentially it was a mighty reflection on the nature of man, who strives and creates but in the end must die. Gilgamesh himself was a legendary king of Uruk, who built its great wall but treated his subjects so harshly that the gods created a wild man, Enkidu, to subdue him. Gilgamesh, wily as well as harsh, did not meet Enkidu head-on, but sent out a harlot, who by her arts tamed Enkidu—this taming we may perhaps take as an exemplification of the passage of mankind to civilization. "Become like a man," Enkidu put on clothing and went forth to protect the cattle against lions and wolves. The bulk of the epic then recounts the heroic adventures of Gilgamesh and Enkidu against various inhuman monsters:

> Who, my friends, [says Gilgamesh] is superior to death?
> Only the gods live forever under the sun.
> As for mankind, numbered are their days;
> Whatever they achieve is but the wind!

So, while they lived, let them at least make a name for themselves.

During the course of these exploits Enkidu offended the gods (especially Ishtar), and died after a long death-bed scene of recrimination against divine decrees. Gilgamesh first lamented, then set out to seek the plant of eternal life so that he might bring his friend back to life. Eventually Gilgamesh made his way to Ut-napishtim, the original Noah, who told him the story of the Flood and advised him how to get the miraculous plant under the sea. Although Gilgamesh succeeded in his quest, on his return journey he lost the plant to a snake. The dead, in sum, cannot be brought back to life.

When later we come to Greek civilization we shall meet another half divine hero, Achilles, who fought in the war against Troy and there lost his friend Patroclus; and at that point we shall be able to compare the essential qualities of two different civilizations, the Greek and the Mesopotamian, as reflected in their great epics, the tale of Gilgamesh and the *Iliad*. Here it may be observed that in the earlier tale the story is balder and has less artistic unity; it is more naive, far earthier (especially in the harlot scenes). Monsters are prominent in the plot of Gilgamesh's adventures, and the appeal is rather to emotion and passion than to reason, as is that of the *Iliad*.

In both epics the divine plane determines earthly events, though men have freedom to oppose the gods; but the heroes of the *Iliad* are more strongly characterized and far more optimistic. Mesopotamian pride in human achievements went hand in hand with fear for human audacity. Men must cling closely to their fellow men on earth and must appease the jealous gods carefully. The individualism of Homer's heroes, their ability to accept human fate while yet enjoying life, their passionate curiosity and delight in the physical world—these were qualities which did not exist in early, god-fearing Mesopotamia. Yet in saying so much, in an effort to relate the alien world of Gilgamesh to a world that most of us know far better, we must not depreciate the earlier epic too much. Poetically it was a magnificent creation, and psychologically it reflects a truly civilized meditation upon the qualities of mankind.

The Results of Civilization

Rise of classes (3000-2000 B.C.*).*   That the early Mesopotamian outlook had at times a gloomy cast the modern historian can well understand. Not only did the fabrication of civilization itself impose terrific social burdens upon its human creators, but also the subsequent developments during the third millennium resulted in disturbing changes.

This evolution must be considered, if only briefly, in any sketch of early Mesopotamian civilization, for the structure of society had been greatly elaborated by the time of Hammurabi (1700); therewith, inevitably, the outlook of the Mesopotamian world was modified in important particulars. Although the documents available at the present time are not yet adequate to trace the political history of the third millennium in detail, it is amazing—and instructive—to see even dimly the rise of many critical problems which have been enduring issues in all subsequent civilized societies. Social classes, for example, became differentiated. Economic exploitation and social unrest inevitably followed hard upon this differentiation; law developed both to regulate social and economic relationships and to prevent undue oppression. Interstate warfare appeared and led to imperialism, which in turn produced military classes and bureaucratic systems to run the larger states born of conquest.

The first cities seem to have been masses of relatively undifferentiated fellow workers who were tightly grouped in an economic and spiritual unity. Separate classes, however, evolved rather quickly. Toward the top were the priests, who also worked in the early days but tended to become managers on behalf of the gods; the temples grew into powerful economic centers, which owned much of the land and absorbed a large part of the product in rents and temple dues. The records of Baba, divine consort of the main god of Lagash, show that her priests directed about one-sixth of the farm land of the city-state in the Early Dynastic period. Half of this domain was rented out to peasants, who paid their dues at the rate of one-third to one-sixth of the yield and also owed sums in silver, which they obtained by selling other parts of their produce in the city. The second half of her domain was cultivated by the labor of the peasants, organized in guilds under foremen. The goddess also controlled large flocks, shipping craft, fishermen, brewers, bakers, and spinners of wool; the growth in industrial production in Early Dynastic times, which was remarkable, was largely for purposes of cult as well as for military use and for the kings and their henchmen. The raw materials needed from outside Mesopotamia were obtained by merchants, who trafficked by sea, by river, and by land for stone, metals, wood incenses, and jewels.

Beside and above the priests rose the king or *lugal*. In later views kingship "was lowered from heaven by the gods" as a guarantee of earthly order.

Palaces began to appear; the tomb of one queen of Ur, about 2500 B.C., astounded the modern world with its wealth of delicate jewelry, its harps, and the masses of sacrificed servants. To conclude that the kings and priests were simply parasites would be unjust, for these upper elements held together the state, harbored its reserves, and expanded its strength. Yet they did draw profit from their superior position, and the rest of society now fell into a dependent status.

One mark of this situation is the appearance of slavery. Some men were forced to sell themselves or their children into bondage through the workings of debt; others were captives, especially from the hilly country to the east. While the reduction of human beings to the legal level of chattels always has a distorting influence upon social relationships, morals, and general views of human nature, its effects must be assessed soberly. In the present case, the institution of slavery was but the extreme edge of the fact that the leisure of the upper classes and the great monuments of early times rested upon the forced labor of the multitude and otherwise would have been impossible. In other words, civilization was not lightly bought and did not directly benefit all men alike. Most of the labor force, however, in Mesopotamia as in other slave-holding societies of the ancient world consisted of technically free men. Slaves were rarely used in agriculture, the main occupation of mankind throughout the ancient world; rather, slaves lived in cities, where they were domestic servants, concubines, and artisans. As valuable pieces of capital, slaves were usually accorded a minimum standard of human needs, and at times were able to rise again into freedom through hard work. . . .

Conclusion.   If we look back, rather than forward, the story of man's advance in Mesopotamia from the first Neolithic villages of the valley down to the age of Hammurabi must strike us as one of the most amazing achievements of mankind. Despite the difficulties of climate and terrain the settlers had harnessed their energies toward a remarkable physical progress, and the compact masses of population which now dotted lower Mesopotamia were far larger than had ever before been possible.

 **NO**

Poets and Psalmists:
Goddesses and Theologians

Introductory

Let us now turn . . . to an anthropological inquiry relating to the Sumerian counterpart of one of modern man's more disturbing social ills: the victimization of woman in a male-dominated society. At the *XVIII Rencontre assyriologique internationale* held in Munich in 1970, I read a paper entitled "Modern Social Problems in Ancient Sumer," that presented evidence in support of the thesis that Sumerian society, not unlike our own rather tormented society, had its deplorable failings and distressing shortcomings: it vaunted utopian ideals honored more in the breach than in observance; it yearned for peace but was constantly at war; it preferred such noble virtues as justice, equity and compassion, but abounded in injustice, inequality, and oppression; materialistic and shortsighted, it unbalanced the ecology essential to its economy; it was afflicted by a generation gap between parents and children and between teachers and students; it had its "drop-outs," "cop-outs," hippies and perverts.

This highly competitive, and in some ways hypocritical, unjust, oppressive, genocidal Sumerian society, resembled our own sick society in one other significant aspect—it was male dominated: men ran the government, managed the economy, administered the courts and schools, manipulated theology and ritual. It is not surprising to find therefore, that by and large, women were treated as second-class citizens without power, prestige, and status, although there are some indications that this was predominantly true only of later Sumerian society, from about 2000 B.C. on; in earlier days the Sumerian woman may have been man's equal socially and economically, at least among the ruling class. Moreover, in the religious sphere, the female deity was venerated and worshipped from earliest times to the very end of Sumer's existence; in spite of some manipulative favoritism on the part of the male theologians, God in Sumer never became all-male.

From Samuel Noah Kramer, "Poet and Psalmists: Goddesses and Theologians: Literary, Religious, and Anthropological Aspects of the Legacy of Sumer," in Denise Schmandt-Besserat, ed., *The Legacy of Sumer: Invited Lectures on the Middle East at the University of Texas at Austin* (Undena Publications, 1976). Copyright © 1976 by Undena Publications. Reprinted by permission of The Estate of Samuel Noah Kramer.

Woman in Early Sumer

We begin our inquiry with the little that is known about women's rights and status in early Sumer. Some time about 2350 B.C., a king by the name of Urukagina reigned for a brief period in Lagash, one of Sumer's important city-states. Many of his inscriptions were excavated by the French almost a century ago and have since been deciphered and translated. Among them is a "reform" document in which Urukagina purports to depict the evil "of former days," that is, of the times preceding his reign, as well as the measures he introduced to alleviate them. One of these reforms reads as follows: "The women of former days used to take two husbands, but the women of today (when they attempted to do this) were stoned with stones inscribed with their evil intent." To judge from this rather strident boast, women in pre-Urukagina days practiced polyandry, which hardly smacks of a male-dominated society.

Or, take the case of Baranamtarra, the wife of Urukagina's predecessor, Lugalanda. Quite a number of administrative documents concerned with this lady have been uncovered, and these indicate that she managed her own estates, and even sent diplomatic missions to her counterpart in neighboring city-states, without consulting her husband.

Even Urukagina who, because of his uptight reaction to polyandry, might perhaps be stigmatized as the first "sexist" known to history, was not all anti-feminine. His wife Shagshag, for example, like her predecessor Baranamtarra, was the mistress of vast estates, and ran her affairs every bit her husband's equal. In fact Urukagina might well be acclaimed as the first known individual to favor "equal pay for equal work" regardless of sex. One of the remedial measures he proudly records in the above-mentioned reform document, concerns the bureaucratic gouging of the bereaved by officials in charge of a funeral. In pre-Urukagina days, reads the document, when a citizen was brought to rest "among the reeds of Enki," a cemetery that was deemed more desirable than an ordinary burial ground, there were on hand three male officials who received a considerable amount of beer, bread, and barley, as well as a bed and a chair, as compensation for their services. But Urukagina decreed that the food rations of the three male attendants be reduced considerably and that the furniture "bonus" be eliminated altogether. At the same time he ordered that a woman designated as *nin-dingir*, "Lady Divine," who formerly had received no remuneration, be given a headband and a *sila*-jar (about one-fifth of a gallon) of scented ointment as compensation for her services—a payment that compared not unfavorably with that received by her male colleagues.

Enheduanna: The First Woman Poet on Record

Nor was the *nin-dingir* the only priestess who played a significant role in the cult. A more prominent and important lady was the *en*, a Sumerian word that may be rendered "high priestess" as well as "high priest." According to Sumerian religious practice, the main temple in each large city had its *en* who was male if the deity worshipped in that temple was female, and was female if the deity worshipped there was male. Quite a number of these high-priestesses are known to us by name, beginning with about 2300 B.C., a generation or two after the days of Urukagina. The first of these is Enheduanna, the daughter of Sargon the Great, one of the first empire-builders of the ancient world, whom her father appointed to be high-priestess of great moon-god temple in the city of Ur. But not only was she the spiritual head of one of Sumer's largest temples, she was also a poet and author of renown. Quite recently it has been demonstrated that at least three poetic compositions—a collection of temple hymns and two hymnal prayers to the Goddess Inanna, are at least in part, the imaginative literary creation of this Enheduanna. Here, in Sumer, therefore, some 4300 years ago, it was possible for a woman, at least if she was a princess, to hold top rank among the literati of the land, and to be a spiritual leader of paramount importance.

Woman in Later Sumer

From the three centuries following the days of Enheduanna, little is known about Sumerian society and the status of woman. But from about 2000 B.C. there have been recovered legal documents and court decisions of diverse content, and from these we learn that the role of woman had deteriorated considerably, and that on the whole it was the male who ruled the roost. Marriage, for example, was theoretically monogamous, but the husband was permitted one or more concubines, while the wife had to stay faithful to her one and only spouse. To be sure, a married woman could own property and other possessions, could sometimes buy and sell without consulting her husband, and on rare occasions, could even set special conditions in her marriage contract. In case of divorce, however, the husband had very much the upper hand—he could divorce his wife virtually at will, although if he did so without good cause, he had to pay her as much as *mina* (about a pound) of silver, no mean sum in those days.

Female Deities: Victimization and Resentment

But it was not only on the human plane that women had lost some of their rights and prerogatives in the course of the centuries—it also happened on the divine plane. Some of the female deities that held top rank in the Sumerian pantheon, or close to it, were gradually forced down the hierarchical ladder by the male theologians who manipulated the order of the divinities in accordance with what may well have been their chauvinistic predilections. The goddesses, however, were no "pushovers"; more determined and aggressive than their human counterparts, they struggled to hold or regain at least part of their deprived supremacy to the very end of Sumer's existence. What is more, at least one of the goddesses, Inanna, "Queen of Heaven," continued to be predominant and preeminent to the very last, although the theologians ranked her only seventh in the divine hierarchy. The available texts are not explicit on the subject, but with a bit of between-the-lines reading and burrowing, it is possible to follow the struggling career of at least two important female deities, and to trace some of their ups and downs in myth and cult.

Nammu, Goddess of the Primeval Sea

The female deity that seems to have suffered the sharpest decline was Nammu, the goddess of the primeval sea who, according to several texts, was the creator of the universe and the mother of all the gods. By all genealogical rights, therefore, had the theologians played it fair, she should have had top billing in the pantheon. But in the god-lists where the deities are arranged in hierarchical order, she is rarely mentioned, and never at the head of the list. Moreover, her vast powers as goddess of the sea were turned over to the male deity Enki, who was designated by the theologians as the son of Nammu, in an apparent attempt to mitigate and justify this bit of priestly piracy. Even so, the king who founded the Third Dynasty of Ur, and ushered in a political and cultural Sumerian renaissance about 2050 B.C., chose as his royal name *Ur-Nammu*, "Servant of Nammu," which indicates that the goddess was still worshipped and adored by the mighty of the land.

Ki, Mother Earth

But it is Nammu's daughter Ki, "(Mother) Earth," whose gradual decline can be followed almost step by step with the help of the ancient texts. As noted above, the sea-goddess Nammu was conceived as the creator of the universe. Now the Sumerian word for universe is the compound *an-ki*, where *an* means both "heaven," and "(Father) Heaven," and *ki* means both "earth," and "(Mother) earth." It was the sexual union of Father Heaven with Mother Earth, that according to the Sumerian theologians, ushered in the birth of the gods unto their generations. The first to be born of this Heaven-Earth union, was the airgod Enlil, "Lord Air," and it was he who, by making use of his atmospheric power, succeeded in separating Heaven from Earth, thus preparing the way for the creation of vegetation and all living things including man. In view of these theological premises and postulates, the leading deities of the pantheon, once Nammu had been deprived of her supremacy, should have been ranked by the theologians in the order An (Heaven), Ki (Earth), and Enlil (Lord Air), and this may have been so in very early times. But by 2400 B.C., when the relevant inscriptional evidence first becomes available, we find the leading deities of the pantheon usually arranged in the order An (Heaven), Enlil (Lord Air), Ninhursag (Queen of the Mountain), and Enki (Lord of the Earth). What had evidently happened was, that the theologians, uncomfortable and unhappy with a female deity as the ruler of so important a cosmic entity as earth, had taken this power away from her and transferred it to the male deity Enlil who, as one poet puts it, "carried off the earth," after he had separated it from heaven. Moreover, after taking away from the goddess the rulership over the earth, the theologians also deprived her of the name *Ki*, (Mother) Earth," since it no longer accorded with her reduced status. Instead they called her by one of her several epithets, Ninhursag, that means "Queen of the Mountain," and demoted her to third place in the pantheon.

But the worst was yet to come—even third place was deemed too high by male "chauvinistic" theologians, and she was finally reduced to fourth place, third going to Enki, "Lord of the Earth." This god's name was actually a misnomer, since he had charge only of the seas and rivers, and even this power, as noted earlier, he usurped from the Goddess Nammu. But the theologians of Eridu, a city not far from Ur, which was the God's main seat of worship, were consumed with ambition. As the name "Lord of the Earth" indicates, the devotees of this God were really out to topple the God Enlil who had become the ruler of the earth after he had separated it from heaven. To achieve their goal, they went so far as to have their God Enki confound the speech of man and turn it into a "babel" of tongues, in order to break up Enlil's universal sway over mankind that worshipped him "in one tongue." In spite of this, however, they failed to dethrone Enlil from second place, since his bailiwick was Nippur, Sumer's holy city, whose priests were too powerful to overcome. Disappointed and frustrated the Eridu theologians turned upon the female deity Ninhursag (originally named Ki) whose devotees were evidently too weak to prevent her victimization. And so, by 2000 B.C., when the pertinent texts become available once again, the order of the four leading deities of the pantheon is no longer An, Enlil, Ninhursag, Enki, but An, Enlil, Enki, and Ninhursag.

Still, as already noted, the Sumerian goddesses did not take male-domination "lying down," and not infrequently, according to the mythographers, they registered their resentment in no uncertain terms, and showed the male "victors" who was really "boss." As of today, for example, we have two myths in which Ninhursag and Enki are the main protagonists, and in both it is Ninhursag who dominates the action, with Enki "playing second fiddle."

The scene of one of these myths is Dilmun, the Sumerian "Paradise" land, where both Ninhursag and Enki are at home. Here, after considerable maneuvering, Ninhursag contrived to make eight different plants sprout. But when Enki sees them, they tempt his appetite, and he sends his vizier to pluck them and bring them to him. After which, he proceeds to eat them one at a time. This so enrages Ninhursag that she pronounces against him the "curse of death." And mighty male though he was, eight of his organs become sick, one for each of the plants he had eaten without permission from the goddess. The failing Enki would surely have died in due course, had not the goddess finally taken pity on him, and created eight special deities, each of whom healed one of Enki's ailing organs.

In the other available myth, we find Ninhursag and Enki acting as partners in the creation of man from the "clay that is over the Deep." In the course of a banquet of the gods, however, the two deities become tipsy, and the partnership turns into a competition. First Ninhursag fashions six malformed creatures whom Enki dutifully blesses and for whom he even finds useful "jobs" in spite of their handicaps. Then it was Enki's turn. But the creature he fashions displeased Ninhursag who proceeds to rebuke Enki bitterly for his clumsy effort, a reproach that the god accepts as his due, in language that is obsequious and flattering.

Prestigious Female Deities

Nor was Ninhursag the only female deity who, in spite of occasional victimization by the theologians, continued to be revered and adored in the land. There was Nidaba, the patroness of writing, learning, and accounting, whom the theologians provided with a husband by the name of Haia, who seemed to be no more than a shadowy reflection of the goddess. There was the goddess of medicine and healing who was worshipped in Lagash under the name of Bau, and in Isin under the name of Ninisinna. In Lagash, it is true, the theologians did succeed in making her husband Ningirsu paramount in cult and adoration. Even so, there are indications that originally Bau was of higher rank than her spouse. Moreover, when it came to the naming of their children, the people of Lagash preferred by far to include Bau rather than Ningirsu in the chosen theophoric name—clear evidence of the popularity of the goddess, no matter what the theological dogma. As for Ninisinna, it was she who was venerated as the heroic tutelary deity of Isin, while her husband Pabilsag is a far less impressive figure. Most interesting is the case of the Lagashite goddess Nanshe who was acclaimed and adored as Sumer's social conscience, and who was depicted as judging mankind every New Year. Her spouse Nindara, a far less significant figure, did not participate in this solemn and fateful procedure; it was her bailiff, the male deity Hendursagga, who carried out obediently and faithfully the verdict of his deeply revered mistress.

Inanna, "Queen of Heaven"

But the goddess that should be soothing balm to the resentful wounds of liberated women the world over, is the bright, shining Inanna, the brave, crafty, ambitious, aggressive, desirable, loving, hating "Queen of Heaven," whose powers and deeds were glorified and extolled throughout Sumer's existence in myth, epic, and hymn. No one, neither man nor god, dared oppose her, stand in her way, or say her nay. Early in her career, perhaps about 3000 B.C., she virtually took over the divine rulership of the important city, Erech, from the theoretically and theologically all powerful heaven-god An. In an effort to make her city Erech the center of civilized life, she braved a dangerous journey to the *Abzu*, "the Deep," where the cosmic and cultural divine laws were guarded by its King Enki. When this same Enki organized the universe and somehow failed to assign her the insignia and prerogatives she felt were her due, he had to defend himself apologetically and contritely against her angry complaint. When the rebellious highland, Ebih, failed to show her due honor, she virtually destroyed it with her fiery weapons, and brought it to its knees. Raped by the gardener Shukalletuda while sleeping wearily after a long cosmic journey under one of his shade-trees, she pursued him relentlessly and finally caught up with him and put him to death, but was gracious enough to console him with the promise to make his name endure in story and song.

The role that no doubt delighted Inanna most, one that guaranteed her the affection and veneration of every Sumerian heart, was that which she played in the New Year "Sacred Marriage" rite, that celebrated her sexual union with the King of Sumer in order to ensure the fertility of the soil and the fecundity of the womb. The first king whom the goddess selected as her mortal spouse was Dumuzi (Biblical Tammuz), who reigned early in the third millennium B.C. From then on, many, if not most of the rulers of Sumer, celebrated their marriage to the goddess as avatars, or incarnations of Dumuzi. Throughout the "Sacred Marriage" ceremony, it was the goddess who was the active, dominant protagonist; the king was but the passive, ecstatic recipient of the blessings of her womb and breasts, and of just a touch of her immortality. And when—so tell the mythographers—Dumuzi, with typical male arrogance, became weary of being subordinate to the goddess, and, in her absence, began to play high and mighty, she fastened upon him her "eye of death," and had him carried off to the Nether World. There he would have remained forever, had not his loving sister offered herself as his substitute, thus allowing him to return to earth for half the year.

Monotheism: Death-Knell of the Female Deity

So much for the Goddess Inanna, the feared and beloved "Holy Terror" of the ancients. The female deity, as is clear from what was said above, had her ups and downs in Sumerian religion, but she was never really licked or totally eclipsed by her male rivals. Even in much later days, when Sumer had become generally known as Babylonia, and the Sumerian language was superseded by the Semitic Akkadian, the poets continued to compose hymns and psalms to the female deities, and especially to the Goddess Inanna under her Semitic name Ishtar. The death-knell of the female deity in Near Eastern religious worship came with the birth of monotheism, and especially the Jahwistic monotheism propagated by the Hebrew prophets. For them, Jahweh was the one and only, omniscient, omnipotent and all-male—there was no room for any goddess no matter how minimal her power, or how irreproachable her conduct. Still, even in Jahwistic Judaism there are faint echoes of the female divinities of earlier days, and it is not altogether surprising to find that the Hebrew mystics, the Kabbalists, spoke of a feminine element in Jahweh designated as the "Shekinah," opposed to a masculine element designated as the "Holy One, Blessed Be He." And at least one passage in the renowned Kabbalistic book, the Zohar, states that Moses, the son of God, actually had intercourse with the "Shekinah,"—a distant but not so faint reminder of the "Sacred Marriage" between Dumuzi and Inanna, that provides us with one more example of the far, gossamer, reach of the "legacy of Sumer."

POSTSCRIPT

Was Sumerian Civilization Exclusively Male Dominated?

Because humans make assumptions about race and gender and then find evidence to support these assumptions, it is not surprising that Starr and Kramer reach different conclusions. Among Kramer's many books is *Sumerian Mythology: A Study of Spiritual and Literary Achievement in the Third Millennium B.C.* (Peter Smith Publisher, 1980). Sir C. Leonard Woolly discovered and excavated the Royal Cemetery of Ur; his *The Sumerians* (Oxford at the Clarendon Press, 1928, 1929) is a classic in the field. William W. Hallo, who participated with Kramer in the Invited Lectures, which produced the book from which the No-side selection is taken, is a prolific and compelling chronicler of this period. His recent *Origins: The Ancient Near Eastern Background of Some Modern Western Institutions* (E. J. Brill, 1996) contains three chapters concerning women—in law, in public life, and as authors.

Has patriarchy—the rule of society by men—always existed? Or, as historian Gerda Lerner argues in *The Creation of Patriarchy* (Oxford University Press, 1986), was this pattern created as a historical event? Erich Newman's *The Great Mother: An Analysis of the Archetype* (Princeton University Press, 1963) broke new ground in explaining the goddess archetype as did Elizabeth Gould Davis's *The First Sex* (Putnam, 1971); Merlin Stone's *When God Was a Woman* (Dorset Press, 1976); and Marija Gimbutus's *Goddesses and Gods of Old Europe* (University of California Press, 1982). All of these books explore goddess cultures and the earthly women who lived within them. *Engendering Archaeology: Women and Prehistory*, Joan M. Gero and Margaret W. Conkey, eds. (Basil Blackwell, 1991) examines the archaeological record for gender-based approaches and assumptions. In that work, see Susan Pollack's "Women in a Man's World: Images of Sumerian Women." Also see Pollack's book entitled *Ancient Mesopotamia: The Eden That Never Was* (Cambridge University Press, 1999).

For a look at assumptions challenged, students may enjoy Elaine Morgan's anthropological study *The Descent of Woman* (Bantam, 1972). Playing on the title of Charles Darwin's *The Descent of Man*, Morgan assumes that the mother/ child dyad rather than the male/female pair-bond is the basis of evolution. What brought about the worldwide transition to patriarchy? Leonard Shlain's *The Alphabet Versus the Goddess* (Viking/Penguin, 1998) states that the widespread acquisition of alphabet literacy changes the way we perceive the world and rewires the brain. In each world civilization, Shlain finds this transition from image to word leading to the demise of goddess worship, a plunge in women's status, and the advent of harsh patriarchy and misogyny.

Inanna's enduring fascination is captured in two recent books, both based on the poems dedicated to the goddess. Kim Echilin's *Inanna: From the*

Myths of Ancient Sumer (Groundwood, 2003), which credits the priestess Enheduanna mentioned in the No-side selection, explores the amorous and warlike aspects of the goddess and follows her descent into the underworld. In *Inanna: Queen of Heaven and Earth* (Point Foundation, 1992), storyteller and folklorist Diane Wolkstein has taken the goddess's words form "Inanna's scribe" [Samuel Noah Kramer] and, in her own words, "I have sung them as best I can."

ISSUE 3

Was Mesoamerica's Olmec Civilization Influenced by African Sources?

YES: Ivan Van Sertima, from "Van Sertima's Address to the Smithsonian," in Ivan Van Sertima, ed., *African Presence in Early America* (Transaction Publishers, 1995)

NO: Gabriel Haslip Viera, Bernard Ortiz de Montellano, and Warren Barbour, from "Robbing Native American Cultures: Van Sertima's Afrocentricity and the Olmecs," *Current Anthropology* (June 1997)

ISSUE SUMMARY

YES: History professor Ivan Van Sertima argues that Mesoamerica's Olmec civilization was influenced by African sources that date back to both ancient and medieval civilization.

NO: Scholars Gabriel Haslip Viera, Bernard Ortiz de Montellano, and Warren Barbour counter that Mesoamerica's Olmec civilization developed on its own, with little, if any, influences from African sources.

Issue 1 in this volume deals with the origins of humankind and the possibility of its African roots. The "out of Africa" theory states that approximately 200,000 years ago, our ancestors left Africa. They spread throughout the world where they provided a link to our prehistoric past. To scholars who have been arguing that Africa's place in history has been ignored or distorted by Western scholars, this news was like a breath of fresh air. They sought to make connections between Africa and the world in order to rectify the omissions and errors of the past. Some of them who see Africa as the center of world development have been referred to as "Afrocentrists."

In 1976, Ivan Van Sertima published a book entitled, *They Came Before Columbus: The African Presence in Ancient America* (Random House, 1976), in which he attempted to prove the connections between ancient Egypt (which he considers to be a black African civilization) and the Olmecs of ancient

Mesoamerica (now Central America). Examining the presence of pyramids, sculptures, mummification, metallurgy, and textile techniques found there, he claims their roots can be traced to ancient Egypt. These first made their way to Central America when the ancient Egyptians, with the assistance of their sea-faring Phoenician neighbors, were exploring the coast of West Africa and were taken off course by prevailing winds and currents and eventually came to the land of the Olmecs in Mesoamerica. There the cultural exchanges took place, which Van Sertima states resulted in the permanent presence of African sources as a part of Olmec civilization.

Van Sertima also states that this cultural diffusion was repeated in the 14th century A.D., when traders from the west African Kingdom of Mali, explored and made contact with the Native American civilizations of Mesoamerica that had succeeded the Olmecs. He claims that there are numerous examples of African influences in their technology, religion, art, and everyday lives (crops, utensils, pipes, etc.) to prove this cultural diffusion took place.

As with any historical work that postulates a radical new theory, Van Sertima has had his share of critics as well as supporters. The former, some of whom are Mesoamerican scholars, fault him not only for his theory but for the methodology he uses to support it; the latter support him for promoting the cause of Afrocentrism and redressing past grievances that African Americans received from the historical profession.

One group that has begun to speak out against Van Sertima and his work has been Latin American scholars themselves, who find in his work a denial of the complex nature of Mesoamerican cultures that they see as a home-grown one, rather than the diffused one postulated by Van Sertima. If he can develop a theory that promotes his own race and culture, they believe an equal right to do the same with theirs.

The readings used here offer diametrically opposed opinions regarding who and what influenced the development of the Olmec civilization. Ivan Van Sertima sees it as influenced by African contacts, while Gabriel Haslip-Viera, Bernard Ortiz de Montellano, and Warren Barbour state that it developed free from any sources other than its own.

YES

Ivan Van Sertima

African Presence in Early America: Van Sertima's Address to the Smithsonian

So far we have been talking about African voyages in fourteenth and fifteenth centuries. But there was a visit or visits which occurred much earlier, in the pre-Christian are, in fact . . . I shall shift now to the slides. I would like you to follow in images what I am saying.

First, examine the map of the Gulf of Mexico. This is the terminus or end-point of the currents that sweep from Africa towards the Americas. Those diamond-points on the map are the points where we find sculptural and skeletal evidence of an African presence in early America.

This Gulf Coast area was occupied and dominated by the Olmec, the first major high-culture or civilization that we know of in North America. It is considered the mother-culture of America. It was, in my opinion, as in the opinion of most Americanists, a home-grown civilization. But I think only a very closed mind would assume that it developed in total isolation. As the International Congress of Americanists declared in 1964, "There cannot now be any doubt but that there were visitors from the Old World to the New before 1492." America is no laboratory for the study of virginal culture. It shows not only traces of an alien presence but of an alien penetration.

In 1858, peasants at Tres Zapotes found an enormous stone head which was described as having pronounced Africoid features. But in 1862 came an even more significant discovery.

Look at the front and side of this head. A very broad nose, pronounced prognathism, very full-fleshed lips. But you cannot be sure of its Africanness just by examining the front because some anthropologists will argue to the death that it is just a plain clear case of an Asiatic. As Bernard Ortiz de Montellano would say, this ancient stone head in America is a "spitting image" of the people living there. Aguirre Beltran will tell us that these are human-jaguar combinations. That accounts, he claims, for the "snarling lips." Some have even claimed that these are "baby faces" and that is why they are so pug-nosed and heavy-jowled. Michael Coe, author of ancient Mexico, claims that the reason they have such broad noses and thick lips is because the tools the carvers used were blunt and they could not make the features any thinner. Ignacio Bernal argues that they could not be African because Africans do not have epicanthic folds (I shall come back to the problem of the epicanthic fold a little later). But now look at the back of the head.

Look at it very closely. You are seeing something hidden from public view for fifty years. Probably the most well-kept secret in Mesoamerican archeology. This head, although covered by a helmet (as most of them) shows the hair. The carver or carvers went to the trouble of representing the hair against the helmeted dome. Note the unique, extraordinary braids. There is no evidence before this, or since, of any native American with a seven-braided hairstyle. Beatrice de la Fuente, in *Las Cabezas Colosales Olmecas*, comments on this head.

> If in some moment one appeared to ponder on the existence of negroes in [early] Mesoamerica, such a thought would surely occur after you have seen the head at Tres Zapotes (Tres Zapotes 2) the most remote in physiognomy from our indigenous ancestors. The elevated position of this personage is revealed in the headdress, from the back of which dangles seven bands which figure braids that taper off into rings and tassels (translated from the Spanish).

No one who was on that site when the discovery was made doubted that they were seeing something very different from the native. Even the natives themselves felt they were in the presence of something foreign. José Melgar, who excavated this head, wrote the first essay on an African presence in pre-Columbian Mexico. Yet the head disappeared from photographic collections. It reappeared in my anthology *Nile Valley Civilizations* in 1984 because of the photo-research done by Wayne Chandler and Gaynell Catherine. I had not seen it when I wrote *They Came Before Columbus*. Alexander Von Wuthenau, who had done the most exhaustive work of excavation and classification of terracotta in ancient America, had never seen it. Rafique Jairazbhoy, one of the most meticulous scholars on cross-cultural diffusion, who has done a microscopic examination of ritual correspondences between the world's civilizations, had never seen it. National Geographic never published it. This photograph was kept in the dark (and I think the blackout was deliberate) for about fifty years. . . .

. . . [A]nother head, not far from where José Melgar found the one with braids. It is known as Tres Zapotes F. It is even more "amazingly Negroid" in its physiognomy (to use Matthew Stirling's phrase for a La Venta head). Most unusual of all, the stone from which it is carved is of a jet black color. Unlike most of the heads, too, it has no helmet, so that the tuft of close-cropped hair is exposed. . . . [T]he art historian Alexander von Wuthenau compares this head with that of a Nuba chief. You feel you are looking at members of the same family, in fact at twin brothers. Now study the helmet in the next slide. Note the main features of this helmet (probably made of leather). Note the parallel incised lines, the straps falling along the side of the face, the circular ear plug. Rafique Jairazbhoy has shown the same features on helmets which cap colossal heads at Tanis, the sea-going port in the Egyptian delta. Compare it with this slide showing obvious similarities to the headgear of the Egyptian military in the same period. Look also at this other helmeted Africoid head in Egypt, probably a Nubian.

Here is a spectacular new stone head found only a few years ago. It is staring up at us from the belly of a swamp. Nobody would move it. The federal government of Mexico, I have been made to understand, feels it is the responsibility of the state in which it was found to take care of it. The locals feel it is not their responsibility but that of the federal government. I have sometimes had a secret overwhelming urge to hire a helicopter and lift it out of the swamps under the shadow of night. But this phenomenal thing weighs, as the other stone heads do, between ten to forty tons. Brood on that fact! For the nearest quarry, rich in this basalt stone, is 60–80 miles downriver and the stone can only be transported by water to the ceremonial platform where they were found. There is a twenty-two foot wide gorge that makes the overland route from the quarry to La Venta an impassable nightmare.

Now we are not in the least suggesting that the Egyptians taught native Americans their portrait art. But we are faced with some facts here that do not fit neatly within the conventional isolationist model. For early Olmec art shows no transition from the beautiful little pieces of fully-formed humans or jungle cats, demonic masks or fierce were-jaguars, to this monumental concentration, this fascination, this obsession with bodiless heads, heads so colossal that, were bodies attached to them, they would rise fifty feet or more above the earth. Second, the heavy transport techniques used by the Egyptians and Nubians to move colossi across the waters on barges and rafts are unique in the ancient world. The Japanese found in the 1970's that they could not replicate this technology. Barges carrying much lighter balls of stone sank or capsized. Yet Robert Heizer, who was no diffusionist, tells us that there were startling identities between the unique heavy transport techniques of the ancient Americans and Egyptians. We search in vain for antecedents for this development in the American archeological record. Although San Lorenzo has occupation datings centuries before La Venta (where the experts agree that the first in the sequence of stone heads appear) we have absolutely nothing like it. The stone heads found on the San Lorenzo site appear there much later than at La Venta. Coe and Bernal and all the dating experts, I repeat, are agreed on this.

Now we come to the question of the epicanthic fold raised by Ignacio Bernal, who claims that Africans do not have the epicanthic fold. Those who have never studied Africa do not know of its many types. Meek and Seligman and Evans-Pritchard have all shown us examples of unmixed Africans from Nigeria and Ethiopia who have the epicanthic fold. But that is not the only answer to this objection since the migrants could not all have come in with epicanthic folds. We must consider too the habitual and standardized representation of the eye in ancient American art. The Buddha looks half-Indian, half-Greek, in Hellenistic art. But most importantly, we are not dealing just with pure Africans but with migrants who are intermarrying with the native population. Let me use an illustration from my own family. My uncle, Alick Van Sertima, married a Chinese woman and my first cousins, Sheila and Anita, have the epicanthic fold. You can acquire this feature in nine months.

To conclude the panorama of stone heads, let us look at two more of these. They were found within the same area where the head with seven braids was found.

But the sculptural evidence does not merely lie in the stone heads, some of which, as I have indicated, are racial mixtures, as indeed they should be. There are many terracotta figurines which represent Africoid types. Some are rather stylized and we can dismiss them with a contemptuous wave of the hand but some are so startlingly realistic that we ignore them at the peril of an objective vision of history. My good friend, Alexander von Wuthenau, who has excavated and classified more of these terracotta than any other investigator, presents at least a hundred of these in *The Art of Terracotta Pottery in Pre-Columbian America* and *Unexpected Faces in Ancient America.*

Comas said there were no such terracotta, that no image in American sculpture looked like anything other than the typical Mongoloid type that came across the Bering Straits from Asia. His latter-day disciple, de Montellano, sings the same tune. They are all "spitting images of the native." Michael Coe told the *Science Digest* in 1981 that he had never seen any terracotta in Mexico that looked African. This is not necessarily dishonesty on the part of Comas and Coe. They may have never, in their earlier studies, had a chance to be expose to the range and variety of ancient American terracotta. The Museum of Anthropology in Mexico City, for example, puts on display less than half a dozen of these among their thousands of exhibits, and the references to them are designed to give the public the impression that they are post-Columbian. For those who would like to follow this official line, let me warn them. A few of these have been subjected, at Von Wuthenau's expense, to thermino-luminescence dating. His organization of these into specific time-frames or historical periods, therefore, is not mere guesswork. It is related not only to stratigraphy and typology but, in some cases, to the most advanced methods of dating. You can visit the finest collection of these Africoid heads at his chateau and studio at San Angel. . . .

Here is a naked Olmec woman from Xochipala in pre-Christian Mexico. Observe her again. Unlike the mask, you are dealing now with the faithful portrayal of a human, skillfully carved. I have held this doll-like marvel in my hands in Von Wuthenau's studio at San Angel. It is about 3000 years old, yet it looks today as it did before Christ. Perfect in its proportions. The mouth, the teeth, the eyes, the African coiffure, the ear-pendants. Everything is detailed— all of her front teeth, every one of her ten fingers and toes, the fluid curve of her arms, the delicate bulb of her nipples, and when she turns, the voluptuously sculptured cheeks of her buttocks. It is rare in ancient American art.

Here is another woman from Xochipala. Very Africoid features and hairstyle, in a sitting position. And here is an acrobat from the Diego Rivera museum with superbly detailed Africoid hair, mixed Afro-Asiatic features, sculpted in charcoal black clay. Finally, two Africoid heads with beards, one from Tabasco the other from Guerrero, all from the Olmec world and time.

But the iconographic evidence cannot and does not stand alone. Even the most stunning visual witnesses will elicit the cry: These are just "spitting images of the native." They merely look African, our detractors will say, because of stylization. Hence, it is necessary to show a corroboration of the sculptural evidence by an equally meticulous examination of the skeletal remains in the graveyards of the Olmec.

This seemed at first a problematic proposition since the corrosive humidity of the soil destroyed the bones in the humid capitals of the Olmec. But in the drier centers—Tlatilco, Cerro de las Mesas and Monte Alban—the Polish craniologist Andrez Wiercinski found ample and indisputable evidence of an Africoid presence. Wiercinscki, in 1972, assessed the presence of a negroid pattern of traits on the basis of a detailed multivariate analysis of a large set of skill traits which differentiate between Africoid, Mongoloid and Caucasoid racial varieties. The traits analyzed included "degree of prognathism, prominence of nasal bones, height of nasal roof, width of nasal root, shape of nasal aperture, position of nasal spine, prominence of nasal spine, shapes of orbits, depth of canine fossa and depth of maxillary incisure." Wiercinski sees the colossal heads as representing individuals with "negroid" traits predominating but with an admixture of other racial traits. That is what I have said.

The work of A. Vargas Guadarrama is an important reinforcement of Wiercinski's study. Guadarrama's independent analysis of Tlatilco crania revealed that those skulls described by Andrez Wiercinski as "negroid" were radically different from the other skulls on the same site. He also noted similarities in skull traits between these "negroid" finds in the Olmec world and finds in West Africa and Egypt. . . .

Mummification among the Olmec is another claim that has been made but the evidence is scanty. This may be due to the fact that the corrosive humidity of the soil destroyed much of the skeletal material. But, as we have shown, there are significant centers where crania were found in good enough condition to be analyzed. There are mummified remains in Mexico, to be sure, but no hard evidence, it seems, that the manner of the mummification or the formula for mummification is close enough to suggest an influence. In Peru, however, Professor Ruetta has cited such evidence. In Olmec Mexico Rafique Jairazbhoy presents a very unusual sculpture from Oaxaca with rib cages outlined as those of a dead man and arms folded in exactly the same way as in some Egyptian mummies—arms crossed over chest, fingers open.

Certainly unusual in the ritual of the ancient world was the plucking out of the human heart. Here is a representation of it in Egypt where the enemies of the sun-god have their hearts plucked out. This was simply symbolic in Egypt but it became terrifyingly real in Mexico, where human hearts (often from the breasts of subject tribes) were torn out and fed to the sun-god. It can be argued, however, that the idea blossomed independently, by sheer coincidence, among these two peoples and cultures, although one would be hard put to show its parallel elsewhere in the ancient world.

But here is another so-called coincidence that is much harder to explain. Let us look at the ceremonial platform at La Venta where the first sequence of stone heads appear. Here, in spite of earlier centuries of occupation of Olmec sites like San Lorenzo, (as early as 1500 B.C.) we are witnessing the very first pyramidal construction at La Venta (948–680 B.C.). Not just the conical pyramid but the step-pyramid. And further, the first use in America of a north-south axial orientation for ceremonial structures. This axial orientation for pyramids is not only unique to Egypt and Nubia. It has an indisputable antecedence.

Now. what have the isolationists said about this? They have ducked this one rather awkwardly. The large construction at one end of the platform is not a pyramid at all, they say, but "a fluted cone." This is meant to represent, they claim, "a volcano." This explanation ignores two very important things.

First, that it was built of clay, not stone, as in the Old World prototype. Also, it was built in a swampy area. The sides would inevitably collapse inwards with time, as do all earthen hills, and the construction would naturally lose the sharpness of its original slopes. All formations of this nature, not set in natural rock or man-made stone, suffer the same fate.

Second, how can we ignore the miniature step-pyramid at the other end of the platfom, which is clearly and undeniably related? Is this then a baby volcano? Come on. If our critics are going to be absurd, let them be absurd logically.

Now, I have never claimed that Africans built this pyramid or any other pyramid in America. It would have been most unlikely. This is about 103 feet high. It is three and a half million cubic feet in volume. It is estimated that it took 18,000 men one million man-hours to construct. There could not have been that many foreign migrants to the Olmec world. What we are talking about is a stimulus, an influence. The natives had never built a full, blown pyramid before. They had never placed a miniature step-pyramid on a ceremonial platform before. They had never carved colossal stone heads before. They had never transported 10–40 tons of basalt on rafts or barges before. They had never used a north-south axial orientation before. Earlier sites tell us this. San Lorenzo was occupied half a millennium before La Venta. Yet none of these things are evidence. It needs repeating once again, for those who find it difficult to separate occupation-phase datings from datings of structures on a site, that the stone heads at San Lorenzo appear much later than those at La Venta. None of the structures at San Lorenzo observe any axial orientation. They are slipshod, poorly planned, irregular and uneven. We are facing something *new* at La Venta, something both native and foreign. How can we insist categorically that this is a virginal culture when we have a corroboration of iconographic and skeletal evidence and such provocative ritual identities and correspondences?

Now we return to the question of boats. Here is a representation of the typical African dugout. But the dugout is a mere template or building block for extension and expansion techniques. Africans had many other types of boats. Apart from 3000 years of shipping on the Nile, we find a considerable range of watercraft on the Niger, a marine highway that is two thousand, six hundred miles long. On this highway one could find reed boats with sails, like the reed boats of ancient Egypt and Ethiopia; log-rafts lashed together; enormous dugouts as wide-berthed, long and sturdy as Viking ships; double-canoes connected catamaran fashion like the Polynesian; lateen-rigged dhows, as used by the Arabs and African maritime peasants on the Indian Ocean; rope-sewn plank vessels with cooking facilities in the hold; jointed boats fitted out with woven straw cabins.

Here is the famous reed-boat, RA I. This is the boat the Buduma people rebuilt for Thor Heyerdahl. It is an ancient pre-Christian vessel. In 1969 the Africans set out from Safi in North Africa and crossed the Atlantic, getting as far as Barbados. They had crossed 2,000 miles of ocean using a vessel they had at their disposal even as early as Olmec times. Bear in mind that Africa, at its nearest point, is only 1500 miles away. Europe, by the way, is twice as far from America as is Africa and it does not have the advantage of the currents off the Atlantic coast of Africa. But there are even more important experiments with African boats than those attempted by Heyerdahl. Dr. Alain Bombard took an African raft in 1952 and sailed from Casablanca in North Africa to Barbados. Hannes Lindemann made the journey from Africa to America in an African dugout in 52 days. Vespucci took 64 days to do this, not counting the days travelling from Europe. He actually set out from an advantageous position in Africa in 1502 in a Portuguese caravel and yet Lindemann's African dugout beat him by 12 days. Bombard did it without a crew, without any stored food or water, with only a cloth net for small sea fauna, a fishing line with hook for tunny, and two spears. Lindemann did the same in the African dugout but, in addition to a fishing kit, he look along an instrument to squeeze liquids out of fish in case no rain fell on the ocean. Both men survived in perfect health.

Here is an African ship also built before Christ—on the opposite side of the continent. This is the *mtepe,* used by the Swahili on the Indian Ocean. There is also the *dua la mtepe,* which has banks of oars as well as a sail. Africans were not a boatless people. The Chinese report Africans transhipped an elephant to the court of China two hundred years before Columbus. You cannot ship elephants to China in a dugout.

Now look at the map of currents which leave Africa for the Americas. This is a United States oceanographic map. It shows you clearly three powerful currents which, like marine conveyor belts, take everything that remains afloat to the Americas. It is at the termini of these currents that we have found the African presence.

Here now is a map which is the most extraordinary piece of evidence that Africans crossed the Atlantic in early times. This map is, beyond the shadow of a doubt, pre-Columbian. It was redrawn in 1513 from pre-Christian maps found in the sacked library of Alexandria. It is called the Piri Reis map from the Turkish admiral who found it. It has its meridian in Egypt, in the area later called Alexandria by the Greeks, later called Cairo by the Arabs. It definitely precedes them. Their maps do not show these things. The mid-Atlantic islands are shown with remarkable accuracy. The Cape Verde, Madeira Islands, and the Azores are shown in perfect longitude. The Canary islands are only off by 1 degree longitude. The Andes are shown on this map. This was only seen by Europeans in 1527 when Pizarro claimed to have "discovered" it. The Atrata River in Columbia is shown for a distance of 300 miles from the sea. The Amazon River is shown, the actual course of the river, while the 16th century European maps bear no resemblance to its real course. Even more remarkable is the near-accuracy of the longitudinal and latitudinal coordinates between the African and, the American coasts. No European map came even close to this until the eighteenth century. 150 years after the death of Columbus, European encyclopedias declared that longitude had not been discovered and was probably undiscoverable.

So far we have been looking at faces from the pre-Christian world in Mexico. There were obviously descendants of these Africans and, on some occasions, new arrivals, not just in the later Mandingo voyages of the fourteenth and fifteenth centuries. The African image can be seen in various periods—pre-Classic, Classic, post-Classic. I shall present just a dozen of these visible witnesses. Observe this African figure from Vera Cruz with turban and ritual scarification, this African drummer from Colima, this African woman from the Pyramid of Teotihuacan. Observe the startling realism of this piece, down to the headkerchief, the ear pendants, the blackness of the skin. Compare with the next slide where Von Wuthenau shows us a near identical counterpart from the African continent, both in facial form and cultural accoutrements. Look at the bearded African with the topknot hair style from Tabasco and what is perhaps the finest representation of an African in pre-Columbian art, a Mandingo type found among the Mixtecs at Oaxaca.

Here is another African from the Mandingo period. This is from the Josue Saenz collection in Mexico City. As realistic in every detail as the previous one, which is now in the Stavenhagen collection in Germany. Here, heavily tattooed, in roughly the same period, is an African from the province of Guanacaste, Costa Rica. Here is another in a portrait vessel from Oaxaca. Another, now in the National Museum in Mexico City. Von Wuthenau says that this figure was worshipped by Aztecs in the province where it was found because it had the right ritual color of one of their gods, Tezcatlipoca. This has nothing to do (please do not misunderstand) with them mistaking it for a god. It was just an appropriate image for that ritual purpose. The next, however, is the black god of jewelers, Na-ua-pilli. Stylized though he may be, everything is done to emphasize his Negroid or Africoid element. It is hard to dismiss this as purely accidental or arbitrary since the Mandingo traders were associated with the gold trade. According to Ramon Pane, as I mentioned before, they are called the "black guanini," the black gold merchants. The final selection is of a black in the Mexican marketplace. A red-skinned native is standing by a stall where the trader, his Africoid features heavily emphasized down to the painted exaggeration of his lips, is offering his wares.

We shift now to something that came about as a result of the Smithsonian find of African skeletons in a pre-Columbian grave in the Virgin Islands. The skeletons could not be dated and so the matter remains inconclusive, at least where the bones are concerned. But not far from Hull Bay, where these skeletons were found, at the bottom of the Reef Bay Valley on St. John's, something unusual has emerged.

This script is found at the bottom of a waterfall in the Reef Bay Valley and it is reflected in the water. The unusual regularity of the dot and crescent formation is what attracted me to it and away from the relatively meaningless carvings of animals further up the rock-face. It has been deciphered by Barry Fell, professor emeritus of Harvard. Fell has got into a lot of trouble over some of his decipherments but this has been carefully checked out. Scholars in the Libyan Department of Antiquities arrived at the same decipherment as he did. It has been identified as the Tifinagh Branch of the Libyan script. This was used not only by Southern Libyans but by people in some parts of medieval Mali and by the Tamahaq Berbers which, in the period of which we speak, were not the heavily mixed Euro-African people they are today. The inscription reads: "Plunge in to cleanse yourself. This is water for purification before prayer."

The African presence is also found in South America. The heads that now follow clearly show Africans in Ecuador and Peru. These are far too realistic to be brushed aside. But we cannot deal with that chapter of the African presence in this lecture. There is one, however, which we must comment upon as we close. That is this remarkable portrait of the sons of African governors in South America. These Africans are chieftains from Esmeraldas in what is now Ecuador. They visited Quito in 1599. They are shown here in Spanish dress and Indian ornaments but were descendants of a group of 17 shipwrecked Africans who gained political control of an entire province of Ecuador in short order.

Let me close by saying, this is not all diffusionist fantasy and all I ask is that there should be a little more tolerance and openness to discussion and examination of this subject. It will take a lot of time and study by many experts, in many fields, to settle upon the validity of some of the data and to distinguish an apparent influence from a mere coincidence, but we cannot approach the study of shattered worlds like Africa and America the way we approach the study of Europe. We are forced to venture into several disciplines today because of destruction of documents, in order to grasp the true complexity of these vanished worlds. But America was not the tidy, closed world we would like to think it was. The Negroid or Africoid type, depicted in the terracotta and in the bones and stones, was not the result of local microevolution but hybridization through migration. The Atlantic was never an impassable sea of darkness. Its currents were living, moving roads, marine conveyor belts. The only cultures in the world that we have found, built up over millennia in almost pure, impervious bubbles of glass, are the cultures of jungle primitives.

No great civilization, be it African, Asian, or European, developed in total isolation. Why should America then? Why should we assume that a world, so vast and various, that the peoples in Mexico alone spoke fourteen languages, rotated away from the rest of humanity for tens of thousands of years, until a little gold-hungry adventurer, Christopher Columbus, suddenly discovered that the people here were really living in India, that Cuba was the continent, South America an island, and the Caribbean Sea the Gulf of the Ganges?

Gabriel Haslip Viera, Bernard Ortiz de
Montellano, and Warren Barbour

 **NO**

Robbing Native American Cultures: Van Sertima's Afrocentricity and the Olmecs

According to Van Sertima's hypothesis, the Nubian rulers of ancient Egypt (25th dynasty, 712–664 B.C.) organized an expedition with the help of the Phoenicians to obtain various commodities, including iron, from sources on the Atlantic coast of North Africa, Europe, and the British Isles during the late 8th or early 7th century B.C. This expedition allegedly sailed from the Nile Delta or the Levant across the Mediterranean, through the Pillars of Hercules, and down the Atlantic coast of North Africa, where it was caught in some current or storm that sent it across the Atlantic to the Americas. Following the prevailing wind and ocean currents, the expedition allegedly sailed or drifted westward from some unspecified location in the eastern Caribbean or the Bahamas to the Gulf Coast of Mexico, where it came into contact with the receptive but inferior Olmecs. According to the scenario at this point, the Olmecs presumably accepted the leaders of the Nubian/Egyptian expedition as their rulers ("black warrior dynasts"), and these individuals, in turn, created, inspired, or influenced the creation of the Olmec civilization, which in turn influenced Monte Alban, Teotihuacan, the Classic Maya, and all the other Mesoamerican civilizations that followed.

In Van Sertima's scenario, the Nubians became the models for the colossal stone heads which the Olmecs produced in the years that followed the alleged contact. They also presided over a mixed crew of voyagers that included Egyptians, Phoenicians, and "several women." The Nubians subsequently provided the impetus for the building of pyramids and ceremonial centers and introduced a number of technological innovations and practices (mummification, cire-perdue metallurgy, the symbolic use of purple murex dye, weaving, etc.) which presumably influenced Mesoamerican religion, mythology, customs, and even the calendar. This is an enormous number of claims, and several large volumes would be needed to deal with all of them. In this essay we will discuss the evidence that would be most significant if it were true. We will deal elsewhere with Van Sertima's historical methodology, his use of sources, and his writings on iconography and linguistics.

Van Sertima occasionally says that the Olmecs were not pure Africans or that the African voyagers only influenced and were not the main catalyst for

From *Current Anthropology,* Vol. 38, No. 3, June 1997, pp. excerpt 420, 421, 422, 423, 425, 426, 427, 428, 430, and 431. Copyright © 1997 by University of Chicago Press. Reprinted by permission.

the rise of civilization in the Americas, but these disclaimers are merely pro forma. The cumulative total of his claims amounts to a decisive influence on most aspects of the Olmec culture (religion, language, pyramids, customs, weaving, metalworking, dyeing, etc.). If the Nubians were not "godlike" or superior, why would the Olmecs on short acquaintance put forth the herculean efforts required to transport and carve their likenesses in basalt? If the Nubians were not superior, why would most of Van Sertima's followers attribute the "sudden" rise of the Olmecs to Egypto-Nubian influences?

Van Sertima also claimed that "black Africans" made other journeys to the Americas at various times after the 7th century B.C. The most important of these alleged voyages was that of Abu-Bakari II, the Mandingo emperor of Mali, in A.D. 1311. According to Van Sertima, Abu-Bakari embarked from some unspecified location on the western coast of his dominions (Senegambia) with a large fleet of ships and sailed across the Atlantic to the Gulf Coast of Mexico, where his expedition came into contact with the peoples of the Vera Cruz region, the Valley of Mexico, and the Valley of Oaxaca. These peoples were profoundly influenced by Abu-Bakari and his Mandingo agents in the areas of technology, religion, and the arts in the period after contact was established.

In the years since the publication of *They Came Before Columbus,* Van Sertima has revised his hypothesis only slightly and with great reluctance. For example, in the early 1980s he pushed back the date for the earliest possible contact between the Olmecs and the Egypto-Nubians to the early 10th century B.C. in an attempt to account for the revised dates established for the origins of Olmec civilization at that time. The revised chronology was also used by Van Sertima to claim that the Nubians had had a strong influence over the Egyptians from the early 11th to the middle of the 7th century B.C. More recently, he has grudgingly accepted the Olmec chronology by emphasizing the alleged importance of the "black-Egyptian" in pharaonic society and by claiming that "the black African . . . played a dominant role in the Old World at either end of the dating equation, be it 1200 B.C. or 700 B.C."

Van Sertima has nurtured a coterie of enthusiastic supporters among the Afrocentrists and the cultural nationalists in general. These individuals are inclined to promote his concepts as historical truths. They have also launched impassioned attacks against the academic establishment for not supporting Van Sertima's and other questionable theories. The recent publication of one of his essays by the Smithsonian Institution Press has conferred some academic respectability on his views, and he has heen praised by St. Clair Drake and Manning Marable, two non-Afrocentric scholars with considerable reputations. His hypothesis has become almost an article of faith within the African-American community. It is taught across the country in African-American and Africana studies programs that use Maulana Karenga's *Introduction to Black Studies* (1993) and similar texts. It is taught in the large urban school districts that have adopted Afrocentric curricula. The presumably "Negroid" Olmec heads have become staples of African-American historical museums and exhibitions. It is therefore no wonder that students in colleges and universities across the country are mystified by the dismissive statements occasionally uttered by academic professionals when Van Sertima's ideas are discussed. African-American students, in particular, have not been impressed by the abbreviated critiques that have been published thus far. They are also generally suspicious of the academic establishment, with its record of "neglect" and "distortion" with regard to Africa, and have called for a detailed response to Van Sertima's ideas. This article is an attempt to address the issues articulated by students and concerned educators with regard to the validity of Van Sertima's hypotheses and the failure of the academic establishment to confront them in a systematic way. It is important for anthropologists and archaeologists to deal with this question because of its prevalence and because it diminishes the real accomplishments of Native American cultures. As Robert Sharer and Wendy Ashmore put it, "Archaeology has a responsibility to prevent pseudo-archaeologists from *robbing* humanity of the real achievements of past cultures." This essay will examine Van Sertima's claims to determine whether they have any validity or foundation in the evidence that has been collected thus far by scholars in the humanities and the social and physical sciences.

It is necessary to limit our discussion here to the most important claims and the most convincing types of evidence. Authentic artifacts found in controlled archaeological excavations provide absolute proof of contact; however, *no such artifact of African origin has ever been found in the New World.* The archaeological discovery of nonnative plants can also provide good evidence of contact. Van Sertima's crucial claim deals with the influence of the alleged Nubian/Egyptian visitors of the 25th dynasty on the Olmec culture, because at this time and in this culture a number of definitive Mesoamerican traits presumably appear. If Van Sertima and others are correct, Mesoamerican civilization owes a great debt to Egypt. If the idea of Egyptian contact with the Olmecs is invalid, then other claims by Van Sertima and his colleagues are greatly weakened. For example, the proposed A.D. 1311 expedition from Mali to Mexico, even if it were true, would be less meaningful because the most significant Mesoamerican cultural traits (worldview, calendars, deities, etc.) can clearly be shown to have been present prior to that time, and this violates a cardinal rule in the classic diffusionist argument—that the diffused traits must be present in the donor culture and absent in the recipient culture prior to the presumed contact.

For the most part, our arguments will deal with this presumed earliest contact, because only contact at this stage of development might have been able to have a real impact on Mesoamerican cultures. . . .

The Colossal Olmec Heads

The main pieces of evidence presented by Van Sertima are the monumental carved basalt Olmec heads. To a lay observer, it seems at first glance that these grey, "black"-looking heads, with their thick lips and flat noses, *must* be images of Africans. This impression makes the other claims appear to be support for an obvious conclusion. However, this is a fundamental error. The people claimed by Van Sertima and other Afrocentrists to have influenced the Olmecs (and to be the models for the heads) are Nubians or Egyptians, that is,

North and East Africans, whereas the slave ancestors of African-Americans came primarily from tropical West Africa. These groups are very different and do not look alike. Flat noses are particularly inappropriate as racial markers, because the shape of the nose is primarily a function of climatic factors such as the ambient temperature and the moisture content of the air. One of the functions of the nose is to moisten the air before it goes to the lungs. In areas where the air is very dry, such as deserts, a larger mucous area is required to moisten inspired air, and this necessitates a longer and narrower nose. Both the Olmecs and the West African ancestors of African-Americans have short, flat noses because they lived in wet, tropical areas; Nubians and Egyptians have longer, thinner noses because they have lived in a desert. Comparison . . . reveals that although these two groups differ in the shape of the nose and the lips, both are dolichocephalic and prognathous. Most of the colossal Olmec heads are not; only 3 of the 16 Olmec heads show a degree of prognathism. . . . [These] heads do not resemble Nubians (having flat noses, thick lips, and epicanthic-folded eye-lids and lacking dolichocephaly or prognathism) or, for that matter. West Africans (having epicanthic folds and lacking dolichocephaly or prognathism). The people represented in the Olmec sculptures had short, round, flat faces with thick lips, flat noses, and epicanthic folds; that is, they resembled people who still live in the tropical lowlands of Mexico. . . .

Archaeological Evidence

Some Olmec heads are dark not because they represent black people but because they were made of dark stone. If Luckert is correct and the Olmecs associated volcanoes with rain and fertility, then volcanic rocks (basalt, jade, and serpentine) would have had symbolic importance and would have been appropriate for important sculptures. These heads represent an enormous amount of work, having been transported from quarries as much as 70 kilometers away without the use of wheels or beasts of burden and then carved with stone tools, bronze and iron being unknown. The implication that Afrocentrists draw from this is that the Egyptian civilization was so superior that the Olmecs regarded its "black" representatives almost as gods and dropped whatever they were doing to devote enormous effort over many years to quarrying, transporting, and carving their likenesses.

Van Sertima's description of the contact between the Nubian-Egyptians and the Olmecs makes it appear as if the Olmec civilization arose suddenly after the period in question. However, the civilization of the Olmecs had a long period of gestation in situ. San Lorenzo was occupied from the beginning of the Formative, 1793 B.C., and La Venta was occupied from 1658 B.C. onward. San Lorenzo flourished from 1428 to 1011 B.C. (1200–900 B.C.), a period characterized by three-dimensional monumental sculptures including the colossal heads. There was also a San Lorenzo phase at La Venta, 1150–800 B.C., during which monumental sculpture was produced. La Venta rose to prominence during the Middle Formative, 905–400 B.C., a period characterized by low-relief sculptures.

Although the exact dating of the colossal heads is a complex matter, they pose a serious chronological problem for Van Sertima's hypothesis. To date, 17 heads have been found, 10 in San Lorenzo, 4 in La Venta, 2 in Tres Zapotes, and 1 in Cobata. The majority of the heads in San Lorenzo were found in a ravine where they were deposited by erosion, have no clear stratigraphic association, and were dated by iconographic cross-ties. However, 16 other monuments had stratigraphic associations placing them in the final stages of the San Lorenzo B phase (1011 B.C.), and therefore Coe and Diehl conclude that these heads cannot be younger than 1011 B.C. However, San Lorenzo heads 6, 7, and 8 have original placements. Ann Cyphers has radiocarbon-dated the undisturbed context of head 7 and found it to be older than 1011 B.C. She concludes on the basis of the uniformity of sculpting technique and style that all these heads fall within the Early Formative (personal communication, 1995). A number of Olmec heads may be even older than they seem. Porter (1989) has good evidence that many were made by recarving massive thrones and speculates that a ruler's throne was recarved into his image after his death.

The excavators of La Venta also considered the heads to belong to the Early Formative, that is, earlier than 1011 B.C. although this cannot be proven because they were relocated to a Middle Formative context. Lowe states that many Olmec specialists consider most or all of the colossal heads (at San Lorenzo, La Venta, Tres Zapotes, Cobata) to have been made in the Early Formative. De la Fuente speaks of "a point that everyone who has dealt with the problem agrees on: all the heads were carved during a relatively short period that varies between one hundred and, at the most, two hundred years." Because it is impossible to date all the heads unequivocally, one cannot prove that the San Lorenzo, La Venta, and Tres Zapotes heads were contemporaneous. They might have been sequential, and carving might have extended into the Middle Formative. However, Cypher's definitive dating of San Lorenzo head 7 proves that "Negroid-looking" heads were being carved, mutilated, and buried between 1428 and 1011 B.C., that is, prior to 1200 B.C. and centuries before the alleged arrival of Van Sertima's Nubian voyagers.

Van Sertima's postulated crew included Phoenicians because of their sailing expertise and because he had identified a carved portrait of a "Phoenician merchant captain" on a stela at La Venta. Unfortunately, this "Phoenician" could not have been a shipmate of the Nubians (in 1200 or 700 B.C.), because sculpted stela were produced during the Middle Formative period, several hundred years later than the colossal heads.

In addition to seeing "Negroid" traits in the Olmec stone heads, Van Sertima tries to establish parallels between the pyramid complexes of the Nile Valley and the mounds or platform structures at La Venta. References are made to the "north-south" orientation of "pyramids," to "step pyramids," to their astronomical alignment, to the dual function of "pyramids" as both "tomb and temple," to a system of drains, moats, and "sacred pools," to the complex of walls which surrounded the ceremonial precincts, and to the "fact" that the Olmec "pyramid" complexes appear for the first time during the alleged contact period. In drawing these parallels Van Sertima is suggesting that the Olmecs were influenced by Egyptian and Nubian architecture, but the evidence from the archaeological sites themselves fails to support this assertion in several important ways.

For example, large pyramids were not being built in Egypt or in Nubia at the end of the 13th century B.C.; the great age of pyramid building had ended much earlier. The last step pyramid was built in 2680 B.C., and the last large regular pyramid was Khenjefer's (ca. 1777 B.C.). In 1200 B.C. the Egyptians either buried their dead in secret, as was the case with all the pharaohs of this period, or constructed small tombs that might incorporate small, pointed pyramids into their overall design. All of these tombs, such as those at Deir el Medina, were quite small, and none of them were more than about 20 ft. in height.

The evidence for Van Sertima's other presumed contact period (the late 8th and early 7th century B.C.) is likewise problematical or nonexistent. The Egyptians continued to bury their dead in secret or constructed the same kinds of diminutive tombs with small pointed pyramids that they had built in the 13th century B.C. In Nubia pyramids were built for the first time at El Kurru in 751 B.C., but these structures were also quite small and bore no resemblance to the rectangular, oval, or conical mounds or platform structures built by the Olmecs. Like their Egyptian counterparts of the same period, the Nubian pyramids were generally tall and pointed, with an average slope of 60–70 and an average base of 30–40 sq. ft. The Nubian pyramids were also connected to small Egyptian-style mortuary temples, which faced southeast, in contradiction to Van Sertima's claim that all such structures had a "north-south" orientation. The Nubian pyramids were also built with "gravel," "sandstone," and "solid stone masonry" and contained burial chambers in which were found figurines, painted mortuary scenes, written texts, and other artifacts in the Egyptian and Egypto-Nubian style. In contrast, the Olmec structures were built of different layers of carefully selected earth and clay in various colors and were apparently used primarily for ceremonial and religious rituals rather than for the burial of the dead. They also lack any evidence of figurines, painted mortuary scenes, written texts, or any other artifact in the Egyptian or Egypto–Nubian style.

The Olmec mounds or platform structures of the Middle Formative were relatively large compared with the Nubian pyramids of the same period. At La Venta they were mostly 200–400-sq. ft. rectangular structures with sloping sides and flat tops, which apparently served as platforms for temples and other structures made of thatch or some other perishable material. There were also courtyards, plazas with palisades, and circular, oval, or pentagonal mounds, but none of these structures resembled the Nubian pyramids and their affiliated buildings. The La Venta stepped pyramid, although deeply eroded and conelike, is 120 ft. high and has a base diameter of 420 ft. Van Sertima continues to use an old photograph of an outdated reconstruction of this edifice to insist that it was a four-sided pyramid comparable to those built by the ancient Egyptians and Nubians. . . .

Mummification

Van Sertima continues to claim that the Egyptians brought mummification to the New World. His only sources for this claim are the discredited hyperdiffusionist authors of the early 20th century, whom he quotes from Mackenzie

(1923). All of his citations except for those that refer to Palenque ultimately derive from Grafton Elliot Smith, a prolific hyperdiffusionist who believed that all civilization derived from Egypt, or his disciple W. J. Perry. Elliot Smith proposed that this "Heliolithic" culture had first spread to Asia and was taken from there to America. The diffusion of mummification from Egypt to the rest of the world was central to his thesis. This thesis was thoroughly demolished in 1928 by Roland B. Dixon's *The Building of Cultures*—a problem that Van Sertima ignores.

Citing no original sources, Van Sertima claims:

> We have indisputable proof of Mexican mummification. . . . one of the best examples is the mummified figure in the sarcophagus at Palenque. Three features of this Palenque burial indicate an Egyptian influence. The jade mask on the face of the dead, the fact of mummification itself, and the flared base of the sarcophagus. . . . Egyptians made sarcophagi with a flared base to enable them to stand it up because their burials were vertical. . . . The Mexicans, like the Nubians, buried in a horizontal position, yet at Palenque the flared base is retained, although it serves no function. The retention of such a non-functional element . . . is among the clearest indications of an influence. A borrowed artifact often goes through an initial period of "slavish imitation" before it is restructured to suit local needs.

Van Sertima is wrong on all counts. Every basic text on the Maya states that the sarcophagus contained a *skeleton* not a mummy. Any interested party can verify this by looking at the photograph of Pacal's skeleton in the sarcophagus, the photograph has been published in this text since 1956). From this or any other picture of the open sarcophagus one can also verify that the "flared base" is, in fact, a widening of the open interior of the slab, not the bottom of the sarcophagus or a "slavish imitation" of an Egyptian prototype. For Van Sertima's claim to be true, it would have required the Mesoamericans to imitate the Egyptians from 800 B.C. until A.D. 683 (almost 1,500 years) without any evidence of an intervening culture transmitting any trait. It should also be noted that jade death masks were never used by the ancient Egyptians.

Finally, if the source of diffusion is the oldest place where the practice is found, perhaps travelers from the New World went to Egypt and taught them how to mummify the deceased. The oldest mummies in the world are those associated with the Chinchorro culture of Chile. The oldest mummy there is dated 5050 ± 135 B.C. This is 2,000 to 3,000 years earlier than in Egypt, where artificial preservation of corpses began in the Old Kingdom.

Conclusion

There is hardly a claim in any of Van Sertima's writings that can be supported by the evidence found in the archaeological, botanical, linguistic, or historical record. He employs a number of tactics commonly used by pseudoscientists, including an almost exclusive use of outdated secondary sources and a reliance on the pseudoscientific writing of others. One finds very few references to primary sources, to archaeological site reports, or to up-to-date publications by scholars who have actually done original research or who have dug in the field. One might get the impression that there had been no research in Mesoamerica since 1920. He claims linguistic and cultural influences between peoples and cultures that existed thousands of years apart without any evidence of an intermediate transmitting culture. Chronologies and sequences are completely disregarded; for example, the use of purple in Mixtec codices of the 15th century A.D. is said to prove that Egyptians brought Tyrian purple to the Olmecs in 800 B.C. The chronology offered produces contradictions to the arguments he advances. If Egyptians contacted the Olmecs around 1200 B.C. in accordance with Jairazbhoy's chronology and with the carving of the colossal heads, there is a problem with claiming that pyramids were imported, since none had been built in Egypt for years. If instead the time of contact is said to be 700 B.C., in agreement with the renewal of pyramid building in Nubia, there is the problem of the colossal "portrait" heads' having been carved hundreds of years prior to the supposed contact. Van Sertima uses photographs to support racial stereotypes in the portrayal of sculptured heads and other types of figurative art, and his work substitutes assertion and scenarios for evidence.

For the most part, the Afrocentrists and the other cultural nationalists have heartily endorsed Van Sertima's thesis despite its obvious weaknesses in methodology and evidence. Although they have called for an Afrocentric history that is accurate and well-intentioned, they seem to be more concerned with the need to raise the "self-esteem" of African-Americans, regardless of the impact on other groups. By endorsing Van Sertima's writings, the Afrocentrists and cultural nationalists have accepted a hegemonic and racialist view of pre-Columbian America that is completely lacking in historical accuracy. They have also accepted a theory and a methodological approach that grossly distort the historical record at the expense of Native Americans. Despite vehement protestations to the contrary, Van Sertima has, in effect, trampled on the self-respect or self-esteem of Native Americans by minimizing their role as actors in their own history, denigrating their cultures, and usurping their contributions to the development of world civilizations.

POSTSCRIPT

Was Mesoamerica's Olmec Civilization Influenced by African Sources?

This issue represents a case study in how different interpretations of his-torical artifacts—art, architecture, metallurgy, burial practices—can produce historical controversy. Van Sertima's assertion that Africans may have influ-enced the Olmec civilization based on his interpretation of the sources is challenged by Haslip Viera, Ortiz de Montellano, and Barbour who claim Olmec civilization to have been native bred. Whose interpretation is closer to the truth will be the determining factor in the outcome of this historical-archaeological debate. This reliance on the physical evidence makes viewing that evidence an important part of the debate. Consult the Web site recom-mended on the "On the Internet" page preceding Part 1 of this book for the visuals it provides.

Race, ethnicity, and historical-archaeological controversy seem to be common themes within today's academic disciplines. Issue 1 in this volume, "Did *Homo Sapiens* Originate in Africa," is one such example. Another centered around Martin Bernal's thesis, represented in his *Black Athena* volumes, which stated that Greek civilization was influenced by diffusion from Africa and Asia and therefore created the same kind of stir within academic circles. Race and ethnicity can be volatile factors that should not cloud the search for academic truth, which must always based on the available evidence.

For further information, consult Van Sertima's first book on the subject, *They Came Before Columbus: The African Presence in Ancient America* (Random House, 1976). Compare his work with the speech given almost twenty years later that provides an opportunity to see if there has been any modification in his interpretation. The aforementioned Martin Bernal provided support for Van Sertima and called for a calm, reasoned approach to the subject, free from emotionalism, in "On 'Robbing Native American Cultures,'" *Current Anthropology* (August–October 1998). *Current Anthropology* (June 1997), which provided the NO side of this issue, also included comments on the subject by other archaeologists.

ISSUE 4

Does Alexander the Great Deserve His Reputation?

YES: N. G. L. Hammond, from *The Genius of Alexander the Great* (University of North Carolina Press, 1997)

NO: Ian Worthington, from "How 'Great' Was Alexander?" *The Ancient History Bulletin* (April–June 1999)

ISSUE SUMMARY

YES: Professor emeritus of Greek N. G. L. Hammond states that research has proven that Alexander the Great is deserving of his esteemed historical reputation.

NO: Professor Ian Worthington counters that Alexander's actions were self-serving and eventually weakened his Macedonian homeland; therefore, he does not merit the historical reputation he has been given.

From 431–404 B.C.E. Greek city-states (polei) were destroying themselves in a needless but predictable series of wars that have become known as the Peloponnesian Wars. Chronicled by Thucydides (460–400 B.C.), an eyewitness and participant, these wars showed the Greek states at their worst—selfish, contentious, avaricious, and power-hungry. The result was a series of conflicts in which one side, Sparta and its allies, was able to defeat its traditional enemy, Athens and its Delian League allies. Both sides suffered heavy losses and learned no lessons from the prolonged conflict. In their weakened, unenlightened state, they were easy prey to a strong, united Greek kingdom from the north—the Macedonians and their powerful king Philip.

The Macedonians were considered by the Greek city-states of the south to be barbaric. However, they had unification and military prowess on their side, and soon all of Greece was under their control. Philip was deprived of his chance for a more exalted place in history when he was assassinated by a bodyguard while attending a wedding festival in 336 B.C.E. He was succeeded by his son Alexander, then a young man of 19 years.

Alexander seemed to be destined for greatness. At an early age he displayed strong leadership and military skills, and to complement these,

Philip hired the noted Greek philosopher Aristotle as a tutor to help develop Alexander's intellectual side. Although it is difficult to pinpoint specific contributions that Aristotle made to the development of his pupil, some general ones were a passion for Greek culture, a strong affinity for intellectual pursuits, and a keen interest in Greek literature and art.

Given the volatile nature of Macedonian politics and Alexander's lack of experience, accession to his father's crown was not guaranteed. But he did succeed, and within 14 years he conquered most of the then-known world. This earned him a place in history with the sobriquet—Alexander the Great.

Alexander's place in history was created immediately after his death. There were some who spoke of him as a divinity, even while he was alive, and Alexander did nothing to discourage it. This glorification process continued through the next few centuries. The Romans, who featured likenesses of him in many of their art works, saw themselves in him as they began to follow in his footsteps, conquering much of the known world. The apex of his Roman reputation occurred when Plutarch (42–102 C.E.) wrote glowingly of him in his *Lives*, claiming that Alexander was descended from Hercules. A few of the historical figures who engaged in Alexandrine worship included Julius Caesar, Napoleon Bonaparte, and U.S. World War II general George Patton. Alexander's persona has also been featured in literary works by writers too numerous to mention.

What is the basis of Alexander's glowing historical reputation? Obviously, his conquests form its essence—but it is based on more than territorial accumulation. It is the story of the "philosopher-king," the cultured leader who attempted to create a cultural synthesis by fusing the best of the East and the West. It is the saga of an attempt by a man to create a "one world" ideal, a man trying to achieve the "impossible dream" and coming close to it.

For most of recorded history, humankind's story has been told through the words and deeds of its great men, and occasionally, great women. This is known as the "heroic" approach to the study of history. In the first part of the twentieth century, this version of history dominated, and historical figures such as Alexander still received favorable press. But the repetitive violence of the twentieth century influenced people to interpret history in a less militaristic vein, and the positive assessment of Alexander the Great began to change. How much it will change remains to be seen.

N. G. L. Hammond, who has written three books about Alexander, still finds much to admire in him, especially his love of Greek culture and his strong intellectual qualities. To Hammond, Alexander is worthy of his historical appellation. On the other hand, Ian Worthington states that Alexander's historical reputation may be undeserved due to the death and suffering caused by his military campaigns, and how they weakened the Macedonian state at home.

YES

N. G. L. Hammond

The Plans and Personality of Alexander

Arrangements Affecting the Macedonians and Macedonia

After the reconciliation in late summer 324 Alexander [the Great] offered his terms for any Macedonians who might volunteer to go home. They would be paid the normal wage up to their arrival in Macedonia, and each man would receive a gratuity of one talent. They were ordered to leave their Asian wives and children in Asia, where Alexander undertook to bring up the boys "in the Macedonian manner in other respects and in military training"; and he said he would send them thereafter to their fathers in Macedonia. He made provision also for orphans of Macedonian soldiers in Asia. Some 10,000 Macedonians accepted these terms. "He embraced them all, with tears in his eyes and tears in theirs, and they parted company." They were being released from the campaign in Asia, not from military service. In summer 323 they reached Cilicia, where Alexander intended that they should winter. In spring 322 they were to be transported to Macedonia by his newly built fleet. By then Alexander expected to have completed his Arabian campaign and to be in Egypt or Cilicia. He was to be joined there by 10,000 Macedonians "in their prime," who would be replaced in Macedonia by the returning veterans. . . .

Arrangements Affecting the City-States

Alexander respected the sovereignty of the Greek Community in the settlement of affairs after the defeat of Agis and his allies, and he continued to do so, for instance by sending captured works of art to the states in the Greek Community. His conduct in these years indicates that the allegations of exceeding his powers as *Hegemon*, which were made in a speech "On the Treaty with Alexander" in 331, were groundless. Within the Greek Community only one breach of the charter was reported in our sources, the expulsion of the people of Oeniadae from their city by the Aetolians. It happened perhaps in 325; for Alexander said that he himself would punish the Aetolians, presumably on his return to the West. In the years of peace a large number of Greek allies went east to serve in Alexander's army, and no doubt others emigrated to trade or settle in Asia. At Athens Phocion was re-elected general repeatedly as the advocate of compliance with the Charter, and Lycurgus used the prosperity which Athens enjoyed under the peace to complete the construction in stone of the auditorium of the theatre of Dionysus and to improve the naval shipyards.

In June 324, when Alexander was at Susa, one of his financial officers, Harpalus, fled to Greece in order to escape punishment for misconduct. He came to Cape Sunium with 5,000 talents, 6,000 mercenaries and 30 ships, and as an Athenian citizen (for he had been honoured earlier by a grant of citizenship) he proceeded to Athens and asked for asylum and in effect alliance against Alexander. The Assembly rejected his request. He and his forces went on to Taenarum in the Peloponnese, but he returned as a suppliant with a single ship and a large amount of money. The Assembly then granted him asylum as an Athenian citizen. Although he gave bribes freely in Athens, he did not win over the leading politicians. Meanwhile Antipater [general "with full powers"] and Olympias [handler of religious and financial affairs] made the demand that Athens as Macedonia's ally should extradite Harpalus; and envoys from Alexander came from Asia with a similar demand. On the proposal of Demosthenes the Assembly voted to arrest Harpalus, confiscate his money, and hold him and his money "for Alexander." . . .

When his forces were assembled at Susa, Alexander announced to them that all exiles, except those under a curse and those exiled from Thebes, were to be recalled and reinstated. . . . The wording was as follows: "Alexander to the exiles from the Greek cities . . . we shall be responsible for your return . . . we have written to Antipater about this, in order that he may compel any states which are unwilling to restore you." . . . The purpose of Alexander was twofold: to resettle the floating population of exiles (we may call them refugees today), which caused instability and often led to mercenary service; and to reconcile the parties which had fought one another and caused the vicious circle of revolutionary faction.

Such an act of statesmanship was and is unparalleled. It affected almost all Greek city-states to varying degrees, and it hit Athens and Aetolia hardest. For Athens had expelled the population of Samos in 365 and occupied the island herself; and now, forty years later, she would have to restore the island to its proper owners. And Aetolia had to hand back Oeniadae to the Acarnanians she had expelled. At the time Alexander could not be accused of restoring his own partisans; for the bulk of the exiles had been opponents of the pro-Macedonian regimes in power. According to Hieronymus, an objective historian born around 364, "people in general accepted the restoration of the exiles as being made for a good purpose." In many states the restoration had taken place at the time of Alexander's death, but Athens and Aetolia were still making objections. . . .

Alexander's Beliefs and Personal Qualities

Alexander grew up in a kingdom which was continually at war, and he saw it as his duty to lead the Macedonians in war not from a distance but in the forefront of the fighting. He saw the destiny of Macedonia as victory in war, and he and his men made military glory the object of their ambitions. Thus he spoke of the victorious career of Philip [king of Macedonia (359–336 B.C.) and father of Alexander] as conferring "glory" both on him and on "the community of Macedonians." His own pursuit of glory was boundless. As he declared to his Commanders at the Hyphasis, "I myself consider that there is no limit for a man of spirit to his labours, except that those labours should lead to fine achievements." He made the same demand on his Commanders and his men. They had committed themselves to following him when they had sworn the oath of allegiance (*sacramentum pietatis*), to be loyal and have the same friend and enemy as their king. If a man should be killed in his service, Alexander assured them that his death would bring him glory for ever and his place of burial would be famous.

Life was competitive for boys in the School of Pages and for boys being trained for the militia in the cities, and thereafter in civilian affairs and in the services. No Macedonian festival was complete without contests in such arts as dramatic performance, recitation of poetry, proclamation as a herald, and musicianship, and in athletic events which on occasion included armed combat. Alexander was intensely competitive throughout his life. He would be the first to tame Bucephalus [a wild horse], to attack the Theban Sacred Band [an army of the boldest Theban warriors, organized to fight the Spartans in 371 B.C.], to mount a city wall or climb an impregnable rock. He was the inspirer and often the judge of competition in others. He alone promoted soldiers and officers, awarded gifts for acts of courage, bestowed gold crowns on successful Commanders, and decided the order in the hierarchy of military rank up to the position of Senior Friend and Leading Bodyguard. Competitions between military units and between naval crews were a part of training and of battle. Alexander himself believed that he must compete with Philip, Cyrus the Great, Heracles and Dionysus and surpass them all, and as Arrian remarked, "if he had added Europe to Asia, he would have competed with himself in default of any rival."

His belief in the superiority of Greek civilisation was absolute. His most treasured possession was the *Iliad* of Homer, and he had the plays of the three great tragedians sent to him in Asia, together with dithyrambic poems and the history of Philistus. They were his favourite reading. He admired Aristotle as the leading exponent of Greek intellectual enquiry, and he had a natural yearning (*pothos*) for philosophical discussion and understanding. His mind was to some extent cast in the Aristotelian mould; for he too combined a wide-ranging curiosity with close observation and acute reasoning. His belief in the validity of the Greek outlook of his time was not modified by his acquaintance with Egyptian, Babylonian and Indian ideas. One mark of Greek civilisation was the vitality of the city, both in Europe and in Asia, and Alexander believed that the best way to spread Greek culture and civilisation was by founding cities throughout Asia. At the outset the leaders in these cities were the Macedonians and the Greek mercenary soldiers, who conducted the democratic form of self-government to which they were accustomed. At the same time the future leaders were being educated "in Greek letters and in Macedonian weaponry" in the schools which Alexander established. The process was already well under way before Alexander died, as we see from a passage in Plutarch's *Moralia*: "When Alexander was civilising Asia, the reading was Homer and the boys (*paides*) of the Persians, Susianians and Gedrosians used to chant the tragedies of Euripides and Sophocles . . . and thanks to him Bactria and Caucasus revered the Greek gods." Egypt has yielded a teaching manual of the late third century, which was designed to teach Greek as a foreign language and included selections from Homer and the tragedians. The excavations at Ai Khanoum in Afghanistan have revealed Greek temples, theatre and odeum (for music) alongside a very large Asian temple in the late fourth century. Alexander was the standard-bearer of Greek civilisation. His influence in education and so in civilisation has been profound, extending even into our own age.

Faith in the orthodox religion of Macedonia was deeply implanted in Alexander's mind. He sacrificed daily, even in his last illness, on behalf of himself and the Macedonians and on innumerable other occasions. He organised traditional festivals in honour of the gods in the most lavish fashion. He believed as literally as Pindar had done in the presence in our world of the Olympian gods, in the labours of heroes such as Heracles and the exploits of Achilles, both being his ancestors. The deities made their wishes or their warnings manifest to men through natural phenomena and through omens and oracles, which were interpreted and delivered by inspired men and women. It was an advantage of polytheism that the number of gods was not limited, and Alexander could see Zeus in the Libyan Ammon and in the Babylonian Belus, and Heracles in the Tyrian Melkart or the Indian Krishna. His special regard for Ammon was probably due to the prophetic oracles which he received at Siwah and which were evidently fulfilled *in toto* when Alexander reached the outer Ocean. He gave thanks time and again to "the usual gods" (the twelve Olympians) for the salvation of himself and his army, and he must have thought that he owed his charmed life to them. Even in his last illness he believed that his prayers in the course of sacrifices would be heard and that he would live. For he died without arranging for the transition of power.

Of the personal qualities of Alexander the brilliance, the range and the quickness of his intellect are remarkable, especially in his conduct of warfare. At Gaugamela and at the Hydaspes he foresaw precisely the sequence of moves by his own units and the compulsion they would place on his enemies. As Ptolemy, himself a most able commander, observed of the first campaign, "the result was as Alexander inferred that it would be," and after the last campaign "not a one of the operations of war which Alexander undertook was beyond his capability" (*aporon*). In generalship no one has surpassed him. Arrian wrote that Alexander had "the most wonderful power of grasping the right course when the situation was still in obscurity." Thus he knew on his landing in Asia that he must set up his own Kingdom of Asia and obtain the willing cooperation of his subjects. Already at Sardis he began the training of boys who would become soldiers of that kingdom. The orginality of his intellect was apparent in his development of the Indus, the Tigris and the Euphrates as waterways of commerce and his reorganisation of the irrigation of Mesopotamia. The boldness of his calculations was rewarded with success in many engagements and especially in the opening of navigation between the Indus Delta and the Persian Gulf.

His emotions were very strong. His love for his mother was such that one tear of hers would outweigh all the complaints of Antipater. He sent letters and gifts to her constantly, and he said that he would take her alone into his confidence on his return to Macedonia. His loyalty to the friends of his own generation was carried sometimes to a fault, and his passionate grief for Hephaestion [his closest friend from childhood days] was almost beyond reason. He loved his soldiers and they loved him; he and his veterans wept when they parted company; and he and they acknowledged that love in his last moments. When he killed Cleitus [an old-fashioned noble in a drunken brawl], his remorse was desperate. His compassion for the Theban Timoclea and for the family of [Persian ruler] Darius and his love for [wife] Roxane were deeply felt and led to actions which were probably unique in contemporary warfare.

As King of the Macedonians and as King of Asia he had different roles to fill. His way of life was on the same level as that of the Macedonians on campaigns and in leisure. As he said at Opis, his rations were the same as theirs and he shared all their dangers and hardships; and he enjoyed the same festivals and drinking parties as they did. He led them not by fiat but by persuasion, and a crucial element in that persuasion was that he should always tell them the truth, and they should know that he was telling them the truth. Thus he respected the constitutional rights of the Macedonians, and his reward was that he was generally able to convince them in their Assemblies that they should accept his policies. His role as King of Asia was almost the opposite. His court, like that of the Persian King of Kings, was the acme of luxury and extravagance. He gave audience in a huge pavilion which rested on fifty golden columns, and he himself sat on a golden chair, surrounded by so many richly-dressed guardsmen that "no one dared approach him, such was the majesty associated with his person." He accepted obeisance, and he ruled by fiat. The wealth at his command was beyond belief; for he had taken over the accumulated treasure of the Persian monarchy, and he received the fixed tribute which was paid by his subjects over a huge area. His expenditure was extraordinary by Greek standards, for instance on memorials commemorating Hephaestion, but it was in proportion to his wealth as King of Asia. The strength of his personality was such that he was able to keep the two roles separate in his mind and in his behaviour, and Ptolemy and Aristobulus were correct in seeing the real Alexander as Alexander the Macedonian.

Alexander combined his extraordinary practicality with a visionary, spiritual dimension which stemmed from his religious beliefs. As a member of the Temenid house he had a special affinity with his ancestors Heracles and Zeus, and he inherited the obligation to rule in a manner worthy of them and to benefit mankind. His vision went beyond Macedonia and the Greek Community. When he landed on Asian soil, his declaration, "I accept Asia from the gods," and his prayer, that the Asians would accept him willingly as their king, were expressions of a mystical belief that the gods had set him a special task and would enable him to fulfil it. This spiritual dimension in his personality created in him the supreme confidence and the strength of will which overrode the resistance of the Macedonians to his concept of the Kingdom of Asia, and which convinced the Asians of the sincerity of his claim to treat them as equals and partners in the establishment of peace and prosperity. The power of his personality was all-pervading. It engaged the loyalty of Persian commanders and Indian rulers after defeat in battle and the loyalty of Asian troops at all levels in his service. It inspired *The Alexander Romance* in which Asian peoples adopted Alexander as their own king and incorporated his exploits into their own folk-lore. We owe to Plutarch [Greek writer and historian (45 A.D.–125 A.D.)], drawing probably on the words of Aristobulus, an insight into this spiritual dimension in Alexander.

> Believing that he had come from the gods to be a governor and reconciler of the universe, and using force of arms against those whom he did not bring together by the light of reason, he harnessed all resources to one and the same end, mixing as it were in a loving-cup the lives, manners, marriages and customs of men. He ordered them all to regard the inhabited earth (*oikoumene*) as their fatherland and his armed forces as their stronghold and defence.

How "Great" Was Alexander?

Why was Alexander III of Macedon called 'Great'? The answer seems relatively straightforward: from an early age he was an achiever, he conquered territories on a superhuman scale, he established an empire until his times unrivalled, and he died young, at the height of his power. Thus, at the youthful age of 20, in 336, he inherited the powerful empire of Macedon, which by then controlled Greece and had already started to make inroads into Asia. In 334 he invaded Persia, and within a decade he had defeated the Persians, subdued Egypt, and pushed on to Iran, Afghanistan and even India. As well as his vast conquests Alexander is credited with the spread of Greek culture and education in his empire, not to mention being responsible for the physical and cultural formation of the hellenistic kingdoms—some would argue that the hellenistic world was Alexander's legacy. He has also been viewed as a philosophical idealist, striving to create a unity of mankind by his so-called fusion of the races policy, in which he attempted to integrate Persians and Orientals into his administration and army. Thus, within a dozen years Alexander's empire stretched from Greece in the west to India in the far east, and he was even worshipped as a god by many of his subjects while still alive. On the basis of his military conquests contemporary historians, and especially those writing in Roman times, who measured success by the number of body-bags used, deemed him great.

However, does a man deserve to be called 'The Great' who was responsible for the deaths of tens of thousands of his own men and for the unnecessary wholesale slaughter of native peoples? How 'great' is a king who prefers constant warfare over consolidating conquered territories and long-term administration? Or who, through his own recklessness, often endangered his own life and the lives of his men? Or whose violent temper on occasion led him to murder his friends and who towards the end of his life was an alcoholic, paranoid, megalomaniac, who believed in his own divinity? These are questions posed by our standards of today of course, but nevertheless they are legitimate questions given the influence which Alexander has exerted throughout history—an influence which will no doubt continue.

The aims of this [selection] are to trace some reasons for questioning the greatness of Alexander as is reflected in his epithet, and to add potential evidence dealing with the attitude of the Macedonians, Alexander's own people,

From Ian Worthington, "How 'Great' Was Alexander?" *The Ancient History Bulletin*, vol. 13, no. 2 (April–June 1999). Copyright © 1999 by Ian Worthington. Reprinted by permission of *The Ancient History Bulletin*. Notes and references omitted.

in their king's absence. It is important to stress that when evaluating Alexander it is essential to view the 'package' of king as a whole; i.e., as king, commander and statesman. All too often this is not the case. There is no question that Alexander was spectacularly successful in the military field, and had Alexander only been a general his epithet may well have been deserved. But he was not just a general; he was a king too, and hence military exploits form only a percentage of what Alexander did, or did not do—in other words, we must look at the 'package' of him as king as a whole. By its nature this [selection] is impressionistic, and it can only deal rapidly with selected examples from Alexander's reign and discuss points briefly. However, given the unequalled influence Alexander has played in cultures and history from the time of his death to today, it is important to stress that there is a chasm of a difference between the mythical Alexander, which for the most part we have today, and the historical.

Alexander died in 323, and over the course of time the mythical king and his exploits sprang into being. Alexander himself was not above embellishing his own life and achievements. He very likely told the court historian Callisthenes of Olynthus what to say about his victory over Darius III at the battle of Issus in 333, for example. Contemporary Attic oratory also exaggerated his achievements, and so within a generation of his death erroneous stories were already being told.

As time continued we move into the genre of pulp fiction. In the third or second century BC Alexander's exploits formed the plot of the story known as the *Alexander Romance*, which added significantly to the Alexander legend and had such a massive influence on many cultures into the Middle Ages. Given its lifespan, deeds were attributed to Alexander which are unhistorical, such as his encounters with the tribe of headless men, his flying exploits in a basket borne by eagles, and the search for the Water of Life, which ended with his transformation into a mermaid. These stories became illustrative fodder for the various manuscripts of the *Alexander Romance*—one of the most popular episodes is Alexander's ascent to heaven, inspired by the myth of Bellerephon to fly to Mount Olympus on Pegasus, which is found in many Byzantine and later art-works, sculptures and paintings. As a result of the *Romance* Alexander astonishingly appears in the literature of other cultures: in Hebrew literature, for example, he was seen as a preacher and prophet, who even becomes converted to Christianity. In Persian literature he is the hero Sikandar, sent to punish the impure peoples. In the West he appears as a Frank, a Goth, a Russian and a Saxon.

Then there is Plutarch, writing in the late first and second century AD, who has probably done the most damage to our knowing the historical Alexander. In his treatise *On The Fortune or The Virtue of Alexander*, Plutarch was swayed (understandably) by the social background against which he was writing and especially by his own philosophical beliefs, and he portrayed Alexander as both an action man and a philosopher-king, whose mission was to impose Greek civilisation on the 'barbarian' Persians. Plutarch's work is essentially a rhetorical exercise, but as time continued the rhetorical aspects were disregarded in favour of a warrior-king who was more than the stuff legends were made of; this was a warrior who was seen to combine military success with wisdom and unification. And so Alexander emerges as the promoter of the brotherhood of man in Tarn's 1948 biography, which was greatly influenced by what Plutarch wrote.

The Alexander legend was a ready feeding ground for artists throughout the centuries as well. When Alexander invaded Persia in 334 he detoured to Troy to sacrifice at the tomb of his hero Achilles. This was a stirring story, which became a model for heroic piety in the Renaissance and later periods; thus, for example, we have Fontebasso's painting of Alexander's sacrifice at Achilles' tomb in the eighteenth century. In modern Greece Alexander became both an art-work and a symbol, as seen in the painting by Engonopoulos in 1977 of the face-less Alexander standing with his arm around the face-less Pavlos Melas, a modern hero of the struggle for Macedonian independence.

Thus, we can see how the historical Alexander has faded into the invincible general, the great leader, explorer and king, as time continued, especially in the Middle Ages with its world of chivalry, warriors and great battles: a superb context into which to fit Alexander, even if this meant distortion of the truth, and history subsumed to legend. Indeed, during the Middle Ages he was regarded as one of the four great kings of the ancient world. Let us now consider some specific aspects of Alexander's reign in support of this.

⋅◦❀◦⋅

In 334 Alexander III left home for Asia, entrusting to Antipater as guardian . . . a stable—for a while—Greece and Macedon. The king also unilaterally made Antipater deputy hegemon in the League of Corinth. Alexander's 'mandate' or prime directive, as inherited from his father Philip II and endorsed by the League of Corinth, was to pursue his father's plan of punishing the Persians for their sacrilegious acts of 150 years ago and to 'liberate' (whatever that meant) the Greek cities of Asia Minor. In other words, a panhellenic mandate. After he had fulfilled it, people quite rightly would have expected him to return home. People were wrong: the king would soon disregard the prime directive for personal reasons, causing discontent amongst the army with him and also, even more ominously, with his countrymen back home.

We have a fair amount of information for events in mainland Greece, especially Athens, during the reign of Alexander, however events in Macedon in this period are undocumented and largely unknown. We certainly cannot say that there was a hiatus in Macedonian history, for Antipater kept Macedon powerful and united while Alexander was absent, so much so that there was economic growth, and education and military training, for example, remained at a high standard. However, appearance is not likely to reflect reality. Macedon in this period may well have been fraught with discontent, and it provides insights into the Macedonians' attitude to their king and he to them. At the same time a consideration of the Macedonian background also lends further weight to questioning the aptness of Alexander's title 'Great'.

Alexander's military successes throughout his reign were spectacular to a very large degree—and certainly manufactured by the king to be great—and we should expect his people back home to feel proud of their king at the head of his panhellenic mission of punishment and liberation, and to proclaim his victories to all and sundry. His deeds and the geographical extent of his conquests were certainly known for we have references to them in contemporary Attic oratory. However, the impression which strikes us about the Macedonians themselves is that Alexander was far from their idea of an ideal king. Why might they feel this way? In addressing this, we can begin with the vexed question of Macedonian manpower. Did Alexander's demands for reinforcements from the mainland seriously deplete the fighting strength of the army under Antipater? Did he make these demands regardless of the pressure under which he was putting Antipater and without regard for the lives of his people and the security of his kingdom from external threat? And if so, how did the people feel and how did they react? . . .

Alexander's generalship and actual military victories may be questioned in several key areas. For example, after the battle of Issus in 333 Darius fled towards Media, but Alexander pressed on to Egypt. He did not pursue Darius, as he surely ought to have done and thus consolidate his gains, especially when so far from home and with the mood of the locals so prone to fluctuation, but left him alone. He was more interested in what lay to the south: the riches of Babylon and then Susa, or as Arrian describes them the 'prizes of the war'. However, a war can hardly be seen as won if the opposing king and commander remains at large and has the potential to regroup. Alexander's action was lucky for Darius, then, as he was able to regroup his forces and bring Alexander to battle again almost two years later, at Gaugamela (331). It was not lucky for Alexander, though, and especially so for those men on both sides who fell needlessly that day in yet another battle.

We have also the various sieges which Alexander undertook and which were often lengthy, costly, and questionable. A case in point is that of Tyre in 332 as Alexander made his way to Egypt after his victory at Issus. In Phoenicia Byblos and Sidon surrendered to Alexander, as did the island town (as it was then) of Tyre until the king expressed his personal desire to sacrifice in the main temple there. Quite rightly considering his demand sacrilegious, the Tyrians resisted him and Alexander, his ego affronted and refusing to back down, laid siege to the town. The siege itself lasted several months, cost the king a fortune in money and manpower, and resulted in the slaughter of the male Tyrians and the selling of the Tyrian women and children into slavery. There is no question that control of Tyre was essential since Alexander could not afford a revolt of the Phoenician cities, given their traditional rivalries, as he pushed on to Egypt. Nor indeed, if we believe his speech at Arrian, could he allow Tyre independence with the Persian navy a threat and the Phoenician fleet the strongest contingent in it. However, there was no guarantee that the destruction of Tyre would result in the Phoenician fleet surrendering to him as he only seems to have *expected* it would. Moreover, laying siege to Tyre was not necessary: he could simply have left a garrison, for example, on the mainland opposite the town to keep it in check. Another option, given that the Tyrians had originally surrendered to him, would have been the diplomatic one: to recognise the impiety of his demand in their eyes and thus relinquish it, thereby continuing on his way speedily and with their goodwill. Ultimately no real gain came from his siege except to Alexander on a purely personal level again: his damaged ego had been repaired; the cost in time, manpower and reputation mattered little.

Alexander's great military victories over his Persian and Indian foes which have so long occupied a place in popular folklore and been much admired throughout the centuries are very likely to have been embellished and nothing like the popular conceptions of them. A case in point is the battle of Issus in 333. Darius threw victory away at that battle and he was, to put it bluntly, a mediocre commander—the battle might have been very different if Alexander had faced a more competent commander such as Memnon, for example. Alexander was lucky, but this does not come in the 'official' account we have of the battle, probably since he told Callisthenes, the court historian, what to write about it.

. . . [W]ord would filter through to the Macedonians back home. Alexander's growing orientalism, as seen in his apparent integration of foreigners into his administration and army, was a cause of great discontent as the traditional Macedonian warrior-king transformed himself into something akin to a sultan. He began to change his appearance, preferring a mixture of Persian and Macedonian clothing, despite the obvious displeasure of his troops, and he had also assumed the upright tiara, the symbol of Persian kingship. Some saw the writing on the wall and duly pandered to the king. Thus, Peucestas, the Macedonian satrap of Persis, was well rewarded by the king for adopting Persian dress and learning the Persian language. However, he was the only Macedonian to do so according to Arrian.

Significant also was Alexander's attempt to adopt the Persian custom of *proskynesis*—genuflection—at his court in Bactra in 327, and his expectation that his men would follow suit. *Proskynesis* was a social act which had long been practised by the Persians and involved prostrating oneself before the person of the king in an act of subservience, and thereby accepting his lordship. The custom however was regarded as tantamount to worship and thus sacrilegious to the Greeks—worship of a god or a dead hero was one thing, but worship of a person while still alive quite another. Callisthenes thwarted Alexander's attempt, something which the king never forgot and which would soon cost Callisthenes his life in sadistic circumstances.

Why Alexander tried to introduce *proskynesis* is unknown. Perhaps he was simply attempting to create a form of social protocol common to Macedonians, Greeks and Persians. However, he would have been well aware of the religious connotations associated with the act and hence its implications for his own being. It was plain stupidity on his part if he thought his men would embrace the custom with relish, and his action clearly shows that he had lost touch with his army and the religious beliefs on which he had been raised. Evidence for this may be seen in the motives for the Pages' Conspiracy, a serious attempt on Alexander's life, which occurred not long after Alexander tried to enforce *proskynesis* on all. A more likely explanation for the attempt to introduce *proskynesis* is that Alexander now thought of himself as divine, and thus *proskynesis* was a logical means of recognising his divine status in public by all men.

Indeed, Alexander's belief that he was divine impacts adversely on any evaluation of him. History is riddled with megalomaniacs who along the way suffered from divine pretensions, and the epithet 'Great' is not attached to them. Regardless of whether his father Philip II was worshipped as a god on his death, Alexander seems not to have been content with merely following in his footsteps but to believe in his own divine status while alive. . . .

Was Alexander using his own people for his own personal ends now? Philip II risked the lives of his men as well, but for his state's hegemonic position in international affairs, not for his own selfish reasons or a *pothos* which might well jeopardise that position of Macedon. Others saw the danger, even from early in his reign. Thus in 335, after the successful termination of the Greek revolt, which broke out on the death of Philip II, Diodorus says that Parmenion and Antipater urged Alexander not to become actively involved in Asia until he had produced a son and heir. Alexander opposed them for personal reasons: he could not procrastinate at home waiting for children to be born when the invasion of Asia had been endorsed by the League of Corinth! In the end, says Diodorus, he won them over. Then in 331 Darius III offered *inter alia* to abandon to Alexander all territories west of the Euphrates and to become the friend and ally of the king. Parmenion thought the Persian king's offer to be in the Macedonians' best interests, but Alexander refused to accept it (in a famous exchange in which Parmenion is alleged to have said that if he were Alexander he would accept the terms, and a displeased Alexander is alleged to have replied that if he were Parmenion he would, but instead he was Alexander). . . .

Alexander's autocratic nature and its adverse impact on his army have been illustrated many times, but it extended beyond the men with him to the Greeks back on the mainland. One example is his Exiles Decree of 324, which ordered all exiles to return to their native cities (excluding those under a religious curse and the Thebans). If any city was unwilling, then Antipater was empowered to use force against it. The context was no doubt to send home the large bands of mercenaries now wandering the empire and which posed no small military or political danger if any ambitious satrap [subordinate official] or general got his hands on them. The decree was technically illegal since it clearly flouted the autonomy of the Greek states, not to mention the principles of the League of Corinth, but Alexander cared little about *polis* autonomy or the feelings of the Greeks. Although the Athenians refused to receive back their exiles, resistance, to coin a phrase, was futile: Alexander was king, the Macedonians controlled Greece, and the final clause of the decree on coercing Greek cities would not be lost on them. The flurry of diplomatic activity to the king over the decree proves this, even though outright rebellion was not planned at that stage. His death altered the situation dramatically, and only one state, Tegea, actually implemented the decree.

There is no need to deal in great detail with the notion which originates in Plutarch's treatise on Alexander, and has found its way into some modern works (such as Tarn's biography), that Alexander pursued an actual policy to promote a unity of mankind. In other words, that Alexander is deserving of the title 'Great' for these ideological reasons. The belief is 'founded' on such factors as his integration of foreigners into his army and administration, the mass mixed marriage at Susa (324), and Alexander's prayer for concord amongst the races after the Opis mutiny (also 324). The belief is quite erroneous, and Alexander, as with everything else, was acting for purely political/military, not ideological, purposes. For one thing, it is important to note that in the army foreigners were not peppered consistently amongst existing units, and when this did happen the instances are very few and far between. Thus, a few Persians are found incorporated in the *agema* [the Royal squadron] of the Companion cavalry, and Persians and Macedonians served together in a phalanx at Babylon, but Alexander's motive in both cases was military.

While Alexander did use Persians and Orientals in his administration it was always Macedonians and Greeks who controlled the army and the treasury. For example, at Babylon Alexander appointed as satrap the Persian Mazaeus, who had been satrap of Syria under Darius and commander of the Persian right at the battle of Gaugamela. However, Apollodorus of Amphipolis and Agathon of Pydna controlled the garrison there and collected the taxes. In a nutshell, the natives had the local knowledge and the linguistic expertise. The conscious policy on the part of Alexander was to have the different races working together in order to make the local administration function as efficiently as possible, and had nothing to do with promoting racial equality.

Then there is the mass wedding at Susa, also in 324, at which Alexander and 91 members of his court married various Persian noble women in an elaborate wedding ceremony (conducted in Persian fashion too), which lasted for five days. The symbolism as far as a fusion of the races is concerned is obvious, but again too much has been made of this marriage: it is important to note that no Persian men were given honours at Alexander's court or in his military and administrative machinery. Moreover, no Macedonian or Greek women were brought out from the mainland to marry Persian noble men, which we would expect as part of a fusion 'policy'. A closer explanation to the truth is probably that Alexander could not afford these noble women to marry their own races and thus provide the potential for revolt, something mixed marriages with his own court might offset. That the marriages were forced onto his men is proved by the fact that all apart from Seleucus seem to have divorced their wives upon the king's death. Once again, however, Alexander seems to have ignored the displeasure of his men, ultimately at great cost to himself and his empire.

Finally, the great reconciliation banquet at Opis in 324 (after the second mutiny), in which Macedonian, Greek, Persian and Iranian sipped from the same cup, and Alexander significantly 'prayed for various blessings and especially that the Macedonians and Persians should enjoy harmony as partners in the government'. Yet, *inter alia* it is important to remember that Alexander had played on the hatred between the Macedonians and the Persians in ending the mutiny, and that the Macedonians were seated closest to him at the banquet, thereby emphasising their racial superiority and power. Moreover, we would expect a prayer to future concord after such a reconciliation since dissension in the ranks was the last thing Alexander needed given his plans for future conquest, which involved the invasion of Arabia in the near future! Thus, we may reject the notion of a 'brotherhood of mankind', and divorce it from any objective evaluation of Alexander.

In conclusion, the 'greatness' of Alexander III must be questioned, and the historical Alexander divorced from the mythical, despite the cost to the legend. There is no question that Alexander was the most powerful individual of his time, and we must recognise that. For sheer distance covered, places subdued, battle strategy, and breadth of vision he deserves praise. In just a decade he conquered the vast Persian empire that had been around for two centuries, and he amassed a fortune so vast that it is virtually impossible to comprehend. Alexander also improved the economy of his state (to an extent) and encouraged trade and commerce, especially by breaking down previously existing frontiers (of major importance in the hellenistic period), and an off-shoot of his conquests was the gathering of information on the topography and geography of the regions to which he went, as well as new and exotic flora and fauna. However, at what cost? Was the wastage in human lives, the incalculable damage to foreign peoples, institutions, livelihoods, and lands, not to mention the continuation of the dynasty at home, the security of Macedon, the future of the empire, and the loyalty of the army worth it?

That Alexander did not endear himself to his own people and that they grew discontented with him, has significant implications for his ultimate objectives and how he saw himself. The move to establish a kingdom of Asia with a capital probably at Babylon is significant. Given his disregard of the feelings of his own people (as evidenced by his lack of interest in producing a legal and above-age heir to continue the dynasty and hegemonic position of Macedon), we can only surmise that his belief in his own divinity and his attempts to be recognised as a god while alive—including the attempt at *proskynesis*—are the keys to his actions and motives. As Fredricksmeyer has so persuasively argued, Alexander was out to distance himself as far as possible from the exploits and reputation of Philip II since his attitude to his father had turned from one of admiration and rivalry, from one warrior to another, to resentment. He strove to excel him at all costs and he could not handle praise of Philip. . . . Military conquest was one thing, but simple conquest was not enough: Alexander had to outdo Philip in other areas. Deification while alive was the most obvious way. Everything else became subordinated to Alexander's drive towards self-deification and then his eventual and genuine total belief in it.

Therefore, it is easy to see, on the one hand, why Alexander has been viewed as great, but also, on the other hand, why that greatness—and thus his epithet—must be questioned in the interests of historical accuracy.

POSTSCRIPT

Does Alexander the Great Deserve His Reputation?

Someone once stated, "Pity the nation that has no heroes!" Someone else wryly replied, "Pity the nation that needs them!" To what extent have national desires created the aura of Alexander the Great? How many historical figures were so inspired by his story that they sought to emulate it? And what were the results of such actions? Military historian John Keegan, in *The Mask of Command* (Jonathan Cape, 1987), contends that Alexander's "dreadful legacy was to ennoble savagery in the name of glory and to leave a model of command that far too many men of ambition sought to act out in the centuries to come." But should Alexander be held responsible for the actions of those who have attempted to emulate him?

Also contributing to future analyses of Alexander might be a reaction against the experiences of many in what was the most violent century in the history of the world. The twentieth century saw two world wars and countless smaller ones. Words such as *Holocaust* and *genocide* were created to describe some of the century's barbarities. It saw the names of Hitler, Stalin, and Mao Zedong become infamous for the millions of deaths they have caused, many in their own countries. Noted Holocaust historian Yehuda Bauer sums up the world's propensity for violence and war—and its consequences—in *Rethinking the Holocaust* (Yale University Press, 2001), pp. 40, "Napoleon. . . won the Battle of Austerlitz—but was he there alone? Was he not helped a little bit by a few tens of thousands of soldiers whom he (and others) led into battle? How many soldiers were killed on both sides? . . . And what about the civilians near the roads that the armies traveled on? What about the dead, the wounded, the raped, and the dispossessed? We teach our children about the greatness of the various Napoleons, Palmerstons, and Bismarcks as political or military leaders and thus sanitize history." Should Alexander's name be added to this list?

As one can imagine, books about Alexander are numerous. The late Ulrich Wilcken's classic biography, *Alexander the Great*, first published in 1931, has been reissued in 1997 (W. W. Norton). It contains an insightful chapter entitled, "Introduction to Alexander Studies" by Eugene N. Borza of Pennsylvania State University. Other Alexander biographies that are worth reading are A. B. Bosworth, *Conquest and Empire: The Reign of Alexander the Great* (Cambridge University Press, 1993) and Peter Green, *Alexander of Macedon: A Historical Biography* (University of California Press, 1991). Michael Wood's *In the Footsteps of Alexander the Great* (University of California Press, 1997) is a recent book/television series that is worth recommending. Since the book contains the program narration, rent the videos and get the visual images along with the words. Ian Worthington has made two recent contributions to Alexandrine Scholarship: *Alexander the Great: A Reader* (Routlegde, 2003); and *Alexander the Great: Man and God* (Pearson Longman, 2003).

ISSUE 5

Did Christianity Liberate Women?

YES: Karen L. King, from "Women in Ancient Christianity: The New Discoveries," A Report from *FRONTLINE* (April 6, 1998)

NO: Lisa Bellan-Boyer, from "Conspicuous in Their Absence: Women in Early Christianity," *Cross Currents* (Spring 2003)

ISSUE SUMMARY

YES: Professor of New Testament Studies and the History of Ancient Christianity Karen L. King presents evidence from biblical and other recently discovered ancient texts to illuminate women's active participation in early Christianity—as disciples, apostles, prophets, preachers, and teachers.

NO: Art historian Lisa Bellan-Boyer uses mimetic theory to explain why women's richly diverse roles were severely circumscribed in the name of unity and in order to make the new religion of Christianity acceptable in the Greco-Roman world.

Have women been excluded from leadership roles in the Christian Church from the beginning? The ordination of women as ministers and priests during the twentieth century sometimes gave the impression that new ground was being broken by women who sought to lead congregations. Some charged that these women were carrying the movement for women's liberation in civil society inappropriately into churches and defying a two thousand year tradition that had properly excluded them. Radical, however, means "from the roots" and a return to ancient sources may link modern claims with ancient practices.

It is deeply challenging to our modern notions of progress to think that, even by present standards, women may have been more "liberated" two thousand years ago than they are today. Our greatest challenge might come from trying to imagine how early Christian women regarded their own status in what was frequently called the Jesus Movement. Did they feel liberated from the more patriarchal world of first century Palestinian Judaism and Hellenistic paganism? And, regardless of how they felt, does our assessment of their status merit claiming that Christianity liberated them?

Before the Christian Church became institutionalized and before a theology was clearly defined, early converts acted out of intense personal conviction and met informally to share their faith. Most churches were based in people's homes and some state that it was this private dimension that made women's leadership possible. Gender conventions of the time declared the public sphere male and confined the woman's sphere of influence to the home. An outcast sect because its followers refused to worship the Emperor, Christianity remained an underground religion until the early fourth century when Constantine, the Roman Emperor, forbade government persecution and, eventually, made Christianity the state religion.

Missionaries converted many Greeks to Christianity, resulting in more Gentile or non-Jewish Christians than Jewish Christians by the third century. The Greek-speaking world, where many of the women in these selections lived, was the first to accept Christianity in large numbers. If Christian women in both Jewish and Gentile environments during the early centuries enjoyed equality with men, what happened to create the climate of misogyny or hatred of women during later centuries?

In the sixth century a Christian Church Council actually debated whether or not women had souls. The question seemed to be whether women were made in the image and likeness of God, as men were, or merely in the image and not in the likeness. Women are still barred from the Roman Catholic priesthood, primarily using a theological argument introduced by Thomas Aquinas in the thirteenth century. He stated that women are inferior by nature and incapable of assuming leadership positions. If only males can "image" God to their congregations, women must be barred from the priesthood.

How did this happen? The Yes-side emphasizes the evidence we have for the truly radical character of the early Jesus movement. The No-side chronicles the process by which Christianity became mainstream and details the sacrifices that were made to reach this state. According to mimetic theory, as uncovered by Rene Girard, we begin by imitating and envying those we admire. As the process unfolds, we sacrifice what gets in the way and unconsciously become what we originally opposed. According to the No-side, this mimetic process can help us understand how Christianity, which began as anti-establishment, could become, within a few centuries, the state religion of the Roman Empire.

Karen L. King, who teaches in the Divinity School at Harvard University, is widely regarded as a leading authority on women in ancient Christianity. Using both the scrolls included in the Bible and newly-discovered texts from the same period, she reconstructs the enthusiastic and welcome participation of women in every aspect of the early Christian Church. Once Christianity moved from house churches to public meeting places and became the state religion of the Roman Empire, however, women's roles were restricted in a bid for legitimacy and in conformity with prevailing gender conventions.

Art historian Lisa Bellan-Boyer describes how the full and equal participation of early Christian women has been eclipsed by forcing them into a pre-existing honor/shame system, based in Greco-Roman goddess attributes and social expectations For example, the many Marys in the gospels were sorted into one good Mary (the mother of Jesus) and one bad Mary (Mary Magdelene). The latter, a disciple, apostle, and missionary, has been merged and then identified with the repentent prostitute. According to Bellan-Boyer, we become what we profess to hate; and Christianity abandoned its radical beginnings in order to fit into an existing set of gender conventions. Women, Bellan-Boyer claims, were the sacrifice that got the early church to a state the victorious called "unity."

YES

Karen L. King

Women in Ancient Christianity: The New Discoveries

In the last twenty years, the history of women in ancient Christianity has been almost completely revised. As women historians entered the field in record numbers, they brought with them new questions, developed new methods, and sought for evidence of women's presence in neglected texts and exciting new findings. For example, only a few names of women were widely known: Mary, the mother of Jesus; Mary Magdalene, his disciple and the first witness to the resurrection; Mary and Martha, the sisters who offered him hospitality in Bethany. Now we are learning more of the many women who contributed to the formation of Christianity in its earliest years.

Perhaps most surprising, however, is that the stories of women we thought we knew well are changing in dramatic ways. Chief among these is MaryMagdalene, a woman infamous in Western Christianity as an adulteress and repentant whore. Discoveries of new texts from the dry sands of Egypt, along with sharpened critical insight, have now proven that this portrait of Mary is entirely inaccurate. She was indeed an influential figure, but as a prominent disciple and leader of one wing of the early Christian movement that promoted women's leadership.

Certainly, the New Testament Gospels, written toward the last quarter of the first century CE [Christian Era], acknowledge that women were among Jesus' earliest followers. From the beginning, Jewish women disciples, including Mary Magdalene, Joanna, and Susanna, had accompanied Jesus during his ministry and supported him out of their private means (Luke 8:1–3). He spoke to women both in public and private, and indeed he learned from them. According to one story, an unnamed Gentile woman taught Jesus that the ministry of God is not limited to particular groups and persons, but belongs to all who have faith (Mark 7:24–30; Matthew 15:21–28). A Jewish woman honored him with the extraordinary hospitality of washing his feet with perfume. Jesus was a frequent visitor at the home of Mary and Martha, and was in the habit of teaching and eating meals with women as well as men. When Jesus was arrested, women remained firm, even when his male disciples are said to

From Karen L. King, "Women in Ancient Christianity: The New Discoveries," a Report from *FRONTLINE* (April 6, 1998), From Jesus to Christ: The First Christians. Copyright © 1998 by PBS and WGBH/FRONTLINE. Reprinted by permission of WGBH. http://www.pbs.org/wgbh/pages/frontline/shows/religion.

have fled, and they accompanied him to the foot of the cross. It was women who were reported as the first witnesses to the resurrection, chief among them again Mary Magdalene. Although the details of these gospel stories may be questioned, in general they reflect the prominent historical roles women played in Jesus' ministry as disciples.

Women in the First Century of Christianity

After the death of Jesus, women continued to play prominent roles in the early movement. Some scholars have even suggested that the majority of Christians in the first century may have been women.

The letters of Paul—dated to the middle of the first century CE—and his casual greetings to acquaintances offer fascinating and solid information about many Jewish and Gentile women who were prominent in the movement. His letters provide vivid clues about the kind of activities in which women engaged more generally. He greets Prisca, Junia, Julia, and Nereus' sister, who worked and traveled as missionaries in pairs with their husbands or brothers (Romans 16:3, 7, 15). He tells us that Prisca and her husband risked their lives to save his. He praises Junia as a prominent apostle, who had been imprisoned for her labor. Mary and Persis are commended for their hard work (Romans 16:6, 12). Euodia and Syntyche are called his fellow-workers in the gospel (Philippians 4:2–3). Here is clear evidence of women apostles active in the earliest work of spreading the Christian message.

Paul's letters also offer some important glimpses into the inner workings of ancient Christian churches. These groups did not own church buildings but met in homes, no doubt due in part to the fact that Christianity was not legal in the Roman world of its day and in part because of the enormous expense to such fledgling societies. Such homes were a domain in which women played key roles. It is not surprising then to see women taking leadership roles in house churches. Paul tells of women who were the leaders of such house churches (Apphia in Philemon 2; Prisca in I Corinthians 16:19). This practice is confirmed by other texts that also mention women who headed churches in their homes, such as Lydia of Thyatira (Acts 16:15) and Nympha of Laodicea (Colossians 4:15). Women held offices and played significant roles in group worship. Paul, for example, greets a deacon named Phoebe (Romans 16:1) and assumes that women are praying and prophesying during worship (I Corinthians 11). As prophets, women's roles would have included not only ecstatic public speech, but preaching, teaching, leading prayer, and perhaps even performing the eucharist meal. (A later first century work, called the Didache, assumes that this duty fell regularly to Christian prophets.)

Mary Magdalene: A Truer Portrait

Later texts support these early portraits of women, both in exemplifying their prominence and confirming their leadership roles (Acts 17:4, 12). Certainly the most prominent among these in the ancient church was Mary Magdalene. A series of spectacular 19th and 20th century discoveries of Christian texts in Egypt dating to the second and third century have yielded a treasury of new information. It was already known from the New Testament gospels that Mary was a Jewish woman who followed Jesus of Nazareth. Apparently of independent means, she accompanied Jesus during his ministry and supported him out of her own resources (Mark 15:40–41; Matthew 27:55–56; Luke 8:1–3; John 19:25).

Although other information about her is more fantastic, she is repeatedly portrayed as a visionary and leader of the early movement.(Mark 16:1–9; Matthew 28:1–10; Luke 24:1–10; John 20:1, 11–18; Gospel of Peter). In the Gospel of John, the risen Jesus gives her special teaching and commissions her as an apostle to the apostles to bring them the good news. She obeys and is thus the first to announce the resurrection and to play the role of an apostle, although the term is not specifically used of her. Later tradition, however, will herald her as "the apostle to the apostles." The strength of this literary tradition makes it possible to suggest that historically Mary was a prophetic visionary and leader within one sector of the early Christian movement after the death of Jesus.

The newly discovered Egyptian writings elaborate this portrait of Mary as a favored disciple. Her role as "apostle to the apostles" is frequently explored, especially in considering her faith in contrast to that of the male disciples who refuse to believe her testimony. She is most often portrayed in texts that claim to record dialogues of Jesus with his disciples, both before and after the resurrection. In the Dialogue of the Savior, for example, Mary is named along with Judas (Thomas) and Matthew in the course of an extended dialogue with Jesus. During the discussion, Mary addresses several questions to the Savior as a representative of the disciples as a group. She thus appears as a prominent member of the disciple group and is the only woman named. Moreover, in response to a particularly insightful question, the Lord says of her, "You make clear the abundance of the revealer!" (140.17–19). At another point, after Mary has spoken, the narrator states, "She uttered this as a woman who had understood completely"(139.11–13). These affirmations make it clear that Mary is to be counted among the disciples who fully comprehended the Lord's teaching (142.11–13).

In another text, the Sophia of Jesus Christ, Mary also plays a clear role among those whom Jesus teaches. She is one of the seven women and twelve men gathered to hear the Savior after the resurrection, but before his ascension. Of these only five are named and speak, including Mary. At the end of his discourse, he tells them, "I have given you authority over all things as children of light," and they go forth in joy to preach the gospel. Here again Mary is included among those special disciples to whom Jesus entrusted his most elevated teaching, and she takes a role in the preaching of the gospel.

In the Gospel of Philip, Mary Magdalene is mentioned as one of three Marys "who always walked with the Lord" and as his companion (59.6–11). The work also says that Lord loved her more than all the disciples, and used to kiss her often (63.34–36). The importance of this portrayal is that yet again the work affirms the special relationship of Mary Magdalene to Jesus based on her spiritual perfection.

In the Pistis Sophia, Mary again is preeminent among the disciples, especially in the first three of the four books. She asks more questions than all the rest of the disciples together, and the Savior acknowledges that: "Your heart is directed to the Kingdom of Heaven more than all your brothers" (26:17–20). Indeed, Mary steps in when the other disciples are despairing in order to intercede for them to the Savior (218:10–219:2). Her complete spiritual comprehension is repeatedly stressed.

She is, however, most prominent in the early second century Gospel of Mary, which is ascribed pseudonymously to her. More than any other early Christian text, the Gospel of Mary presents an unflinchingly favorable portrait of Mary Magdalene as a woman leader among the disciples. The Lord himself says she is blessed for not wavering when he appears to her in a vision. When all the other disciples are weeping and frightened, she alone remains steadfast in her faith because she has grasped and appropriated the salvation offered in Jesus' teachings. Mary models the ideal disciple: she steps into the role of the Savior at his departure, comforts, and instructs the other disciples. Peter asks her to tell any words of the Savior which she might know but that the other disciples have not heard. His request acknowledges that Mary was preeminent among women in Jesus' esteem, and the question itself suggests that Jesus gave her private instruction. Mary agrees and gives an account of "secret" teaching she received from the Lord in a vision. The vision is given in the form of a dialogue between the Lord and Mary; it is an extensive account that takes up seven out of the eighteen pages of the work. At the conclusion of the work, Levi confirms that indeed the Saviour loved her more than the rest of the disciples (18.14–15). While her teachings do not go unchallenged, in the end the Gospel of Mary affirms both the truth of her teachings and her authority to teach the male disciples. She is portrayed as a prophetic visionary and as a leader among the disciples.

Other Christian Women

Other women appear in later literature as well. One of the most famous woman apostles was Thecla, a virgin-martyr converted by Paul. She cut her hair, donned men's clothing, and took up the duties of a missionary apostle. Threatened with rape, prostitution, and twice put in the ring as a martyr, she persevered in her faith and her chastity. Her lively and somewhat fabulous story is recorded in the second century Acts of Thecla. From very early, an order of women who were widows served formal roles of ministry in some churches (I Timothy 5:9–10). The most numerous clear cases of women's leadership, however, are offered by prophets: Mary Magdalene, the Corinthian women, Philip's daughters, Ammia of Philadelphia, Philumene, the visionary martyr Perpetua, Maximilla, Priscilla (Prisca), and Quintilla. There were many others whose names are lost to us. The African church father Tertullian, for example, describes an unnamed woman prophet in his congregation who not only had ecstatic visions during church services, but who also served as a counselor and healer (On the Soul 9.4). A remarkable collection of oracles from another unnamed woman prophet was discovered in Egypt in 1945. She speaks in the first person as the feminine voice of God: Thunder, Perfect Mind. The prophets Prisca and Quintilla inspired a Christian movement in second century Asia Minor (called the New Prophecy or Montanism) that spread around the Mediterranean and lasted for at least four centuries. Their oracles were collected and published, including the account of a vision in which Christ appeared to the prophet in the form of a woman and "put wisdom" in her (Epiphanius, Panarion 49.1). Montanist Christians ordained women as presbyters and bishops, and women held the title of prophet. The third century African bishop Cyprian also tells of an ecstatic woman prophet from Asia Minor who celebrated the eucharist and performed baptisms (Epistle 74.10). In the early second century, the Roman governor Pliny tells of two slave women he tortured who were deacons (Letter to Trajan 10.96). Other women were ordained as priests in fifth century Italy and Sicily (Gelasius, Epistle 14.26).

Women were also prominent as martyrs and suffered violently from torture and painful execution by wild animals and paid gladiators. In fact, the earliest writing definitely by a woman is the prison diary of Perpetua, a relatively wealthy matron and nursing mother who was put to death in Carthage at the beginning of the third century on the charge of being a Christian. In it, she records her testimony before the local Roman ruler and her defiance of her father's pleas that she recant. She tells of the support and fellowship among the confessors in prison, including other women. But above all, she records her prophetic visions. Through them, she was not merely reconciled passively to her fate, but claimed the power to define the meaning of her own death. In a situation where Romans sought to use their violence against her body as a witness to their power and justice, and where the Christian editor of her story sought to turn her death into a witness to the truth of Christianity, her own writing lets us see the human being caught up in these political struggles. She actively relinquishes her female roles as mother, daughter, and sister in favor of defining her identity solely in spiritual terms. However horrifying or heroic her behavior may seem, her brief diary offers an intimate look at one early Christian woman's spiritual journey.

Early Christian Women's Theology

Study of works by and about women is making it possible to begin to reconstruct some of the theological views of early Christian women. Although they are a diverse group, certain reoccurring elements appear to be common to women's theology-making. By placing the teaching of the Gospel of Mary side-by-side with the theology of the Corinthian women prophets, the Montanist women's oracles, Thunder Perfect Mind, and Perpetua's prison diary, it is possible to discern shared views about teaching and practice that may exemplify some of the contents of women's theology:

- Jesus was understood primarily as a teacher and mediator of wisdom rather than as ruler and judge.
- Theological reflection centered on the experience of the person of the risen Christ more than the crucified savior. Interestingly enough, this is true even in the case of the martyr Perpetua. One might expect her

to identify with the suffering Christ, but it is the risen Christ she encounters in her vision.

- Direct access to God is possible for all through receiving the Spirit.
- In Christian community, the unity, power, and perfection of the Spirit are present now, not just in some future time.
- Those who are more spiritually advanced give what they have freely to all without claim to a fixed, hierarchical ordering of power.
- An ethics of freedom and spiritual development is emphasized over an ethics of order and control.
- A woman's identity and spirituality could be developed apart from her roles as wife and mother (or slave), whether she actually withdrew from those roles or not. Gender is itself contested as a "natural" category in the face of the power of God's Spirit at work in the community and the world. This meant that potentially women (and men) could exercise leadership on the basis of spiritual achievement apart from gender status and without conformity to established social gender roles.
- Overcoming social injustice and human suffering are seen to be integral to spiritual life.

Women were also actively engaged in reinterpreting the texts of their tradition. For example, another new text, the Hypostasis of the Archons, contains a retelling of the Genesis story ascribed to Eve's daughter Norea, in which her mother Eve appears as the instructor of Adam and his healer.

The new texts also contain an unexpected wealth of Christian imagination of the divine as feminine. The long version of the Apocryphon of John, for example, concludes with a hymn about the descent of divine Wisdom, a feminine figure here called the Pronoia of God. She enters into the lower world and the body in order to awaken the innermost spiritual being of the soul to the truth of its power and freedom, to awaken the spiritual power it needs to escape the counterfeit powers that enslave the soul in ignorance, poverty, and the drunken sleep of spiritual deadness, and to overcome illegitimate political and sexual domination. The oracle collection Thunder Perfect Mind also adds crucial evidence to women's prophetic theology-making. This prophet speaks powerfully to women, emphasizing the presence of women in her audience and insisting upon their identity with the feminine voice of the Divine. Her speech lets the hearers transverse the distance between political exploitation and empowerment, between the experience of degradation and the knowledge of infinite self-worth, between despair and peace. It overcomes the fragmentation of the self by naming it, cherishing it, insisting upon the multiplicity of self-hood and experience.

These elements may not be unique to women's religious thought or always result in women's leadership, but as a constellation they point toward one type of theologizing that was meaningful to some early Christian women, that had a place for women's legitimate exercise of leadership, and to whose construction women contributed. If we look to these elements, we are able to discern important contributions of women to early Christian theology and praxis. These elements also provide an important location for discussing some aspects of early Christian women's spiritual lives: their exercise of leadership, their ideals, their attraction to Christianity, and what gave meaning to their self-identity as Christians.

Undermining Women's Prominence

Women's prominence did not, however, go unchallenged. Every variety of ancient Christianity that advocated the legitimacy of women's leadership was eventually declared heretical, and evidence of women's early leadership roles was erased or suppressed.

This erasure has taken many forms. Collections of prophetic oracles were destroyed. Texts were changed. For example, at least one woman's place in history was obscured by turning her into a man! In Romans 16:7, the apostle Paul sends greetings to a woman named Junia. He says of her and her male partner Andronicus that they are "my kin and my fellow prisoners, prominent among the apostles and they were in Christ before me." Concluding that women could not be apostles, textual editors and translators transformed Junia into Junias, a man.

Or women's stories could be rewritten and alternative traditions could be invented. In the case of Mary Magdalene, starting in the fourth century, Christian theologians in the Latin West associated Mary Magdalene with the unnamed sinner who anointed Jesus' feet in Luke 7:36–50. The confusion began by conflating the account in John 12:1–8, in which Mary (of Bethany) anoints Jesus, with the anointing by the unnamed woman sinner in the accounts of Luke. Once this initial, erroneous identification was secured, Mary Magdalene could be associated with every unnamed sinful woman in the gospels, including the adulteress in John 8:1–11 and the Syro-phoenician woman with her five and more "husbands" in John 4:7–30. Mary the apostle, prophet, and teacher had become Mary the repentant whore. This fiction was invented at least in part to undermine her influence and with it the appeal to her apostolic authority to support women in roles of leadership.

Until recently the texts that survived have shown only the side that won. The new texts are therefore crucial in constructing a fuller and more accurate portrait. The Gospel of Mary, for example, argued that leadership should be based on spiritual maturity, regardless of whether one is male or female. This Gospel lets us hear an alternative voice to the one dominant in canonized works like I Timothy, which tried to silence women and insist that their salvation lies in bearing children. We can now hear the other side of the controversy over women's leadership and see what arguments were given in favor of it.

It needs to be emphasized that the formal elimination of women from official roles of institutional leadership did not eliminate women's actual presence and importance to the Christian tradition, although it certainly seriously damaged their capacity to contribute fully. What is remarkable is how much evidence has survived systematic attempts to erase women from history, and with them the warrants and models for women's leadership. The evidence presented here is but the tip of an iceberg.

Lisa Bellan-Boyer

 **NO**

Conspicuous in Their Absence:
Women in Early Christianity

In recent decades, a great deal of work has been done to reconstruct our understanding of the ancient world and the early church, particularly in regard to the women who participated in early Christian communities. Enriched by interdisciplinary collaboration with cultural and social anthropologists, the findings of archeologists and the interpretations of art historians, we can visualize a fuller, more colorful picture of women's lives in the late Classical period than we have had available to us heretofore.

There was a much greater diversity of ministries available to early churchwomen than we have been led to think by the historiography of the past. It is now clear that the "open commensality" of Jesus was absolutely scandalous; the nearly infinite implications of women and men actually eating together are hard for modern people to grasp. Contemporary and interdisciplinary biblical scholarship has helped widen our knowledge of what open commensality meant in that social context. Psychology has brought some insight into the shadowy corners in the divided minds of the men of the early church, immersed in a deeply honor/shame-based culture and desiring social acceptability for the sake of church growth. Mimetic theory, as it has germinated following the work of Rene Girard, can provide some further tools to analyze and interweave the historical fragments in order to discern wider systemic patterns at work.

Other than the well-known statement of Caiaphas, in the Gospel of John's passion narrative, that "It is better for one man to die for the people than that the whole nation should perish" (John 11:50), there is no more concise formulation of the scapegoat mechanism in action than the sentence that is placed in the mouth of Simon Peter in the last part of the Gospel of Thomas: "Make Mary (Magdalene) leave us, for women are not worthy of life."

A close friend of mine, with a long record of church-based social activism, recently reminded me that: "The Orthodox are the Orthodox not because they are fight, but because they won." My understanding of what Girard has brought to our ability to see into our cultural shadows makes it imperative that we look at history and myth, as written by those who won, with deep suspicion and an ever-present concern for what has been silenced and covered. This is the process of normalizing a view; relentlessly pursued by what Walter Wink calls "the domination system." I ask you to suspend what you think you may know about some cherished church traditions.

My approach uses both art history and mimetic theory, learned from the community of scholars working with tools uncovered by Rene Girard, to compose a picture of what happened during the long mystification and traditionalizing process. Art history can play an important part in helping clarify what affect the early church battles over dogma had on people and culture in the long centuries that followed. Simplistically depicted as a struggle of true-believing Orthodoxy over a bewildering assortment of heresies unhelpfully labeled "gnosticism," the history of the early church, as it is most commonly written, bears the perduring stain of mimetic rivalry.

I contend that women were the sacrifice that got the early church to a state that the victorious called "unity." This can be read in the surviving texts, both in and between the lines, and also in the visual tradition. Who is and is not present or absent in the icons, frescoes, woodcuts, and canvasses? What do these compositions say about their subjects as cultural objects? Given all the knowledge now available about the lives of women in the early church, who is conspicuous by their absence?

Contemporary scholars of the early Christian communities, such as Margaret MacDonald and Luise Schottroff, have offered practical and convincing circumstantial evidence for the robust presence and activity of women from all livelihoods and class levels in fostering the new religion. Women were often very successful as evangelists precisely because they could permeate barriers between the "inside" realm of women and the "outside" realm of men, either by the power-behind-authority of matriarchs in noble households (a la the present-day examples of Barbara and Laura Bush) or through the intermediary functions of craftswomen and tradeswomen who staffed the workshops associated with wealthy houses. Schottroff, in particular, has emphasized the stark necessity that women had to work alongside their husbands in trades and agriculture, and that there was no such thing as a stay-at-home farm wife or fish wife. Raw economics precluded such a luxury.

Women's tending of home and children was so much of an expectation that no special mention or commendation of it was thought of; and by the time of the Roman occupation of Palestine and the displacement of the peasantry off the land, the outside labor of women for supplementary income meant the difference between living or starving to death. So there were many peasant women working in the fields as hired laborers and shepherds, in workshops of all sorts, and as fisherwomen.

Women lived their lives in the tension between social standards that required women to stay indoors and hidden away as the coveted symbols of honor and shame-based cultural systems; and economic forces driving them out and into the fields and the streets of the city. Women in the Dustbowl era had to do sharecropping and migrant picking to secure their families' survival. In the Ellis Island immigration period, it was sweatshops and piece work at home in their tenement kitchen—all the while cooking meals, raising children, and caring for the sick and elderly. It was no different from the state of economic desperation so common to the majority of the women living in first- and second-century Palestine. Incorporating this understanding changes the way we exegete passages such as the Parable of the Lost Coin or the way we picture life on the shore of the Galilean Sea. This is fundamental to expanding our understanding of women in the time of Jesus.

Women could function as fluid intermediaries in part, because they "didn't count." As a consequence, they could escape notice, or "fly under the radar" in conducting house churches, catechizing converts in pagan households, seeing to the needs of prisoners, and acting as "look-outs." Margaret MacDonald's insightful mining of Greco-Roman records provides a vivid description of how valuable these ministries must have been in fostering the early church. The orders of widows provided the believing community with a safety net that was even commended by Christianity's pagan critics: well-off widows took in poor widows, who looked after orphans, thus forming viable and sustaining "family."

The patronage of wealthy widows accounts for much travel under sponsorship for both female and male evangelists, as for other types of emissaries, and it is well known that travel was extremely important in nurturing the early church. The Deacon, Phoebe, is one example of a traveling woman, and the Ethiopian eunuch traveling as the emissary of Candace are some examples from canonical texts. Mary Magdalene, the "Apostle to the Apostles" and John the Evangelist are said, in Eastern Church tradition, to have traveled together as partner-evangelists.

This may have been a model of partnership ministry that was not uncommon in the early church, and might well account for Paul's reference to "sister-wives" in First Corinthians. It would have been a very effective model in that time and place, as well as many others: the men more able, in terms of social acceptability, to speak in public places and proselytize on the streets, and the women able to go places denied to the men: in the confines of private, family space, and in the workshops and warehouses of those who supplied the material needs of large households.

Roman critics slandered early Christians by spreading rumors having to do with this cult of wicked, home-wrecking women under the spell of evil men: they will insinuate themselves inside your honorable household and subvert it, with their sexual immorality, hysteria, witchcraft, incest, and cannibalism. Later, orthodox churchmen concerned with fostering church growth and assimilation used these very same languages of contagion and scandal about fellow Christians in putting down the groups of heretics and "Gnostics" in which women played significant roles, controlling and subduing the "house churches" in the process. The perennial reappearance of these coded attributes of sin and scandal should sound a bell for those with an ear for the mimetic processes at work, as they lead up to acts of sacrificial violence.

In both the first and second centuries, the radical hospitality and table culture of the house churches, following the example of Jesus, was an invitation to scandal: Uncovered women, eating and talking with men-teaching men! They could be nothing else but prostitutes and courtesans. Celibate women—in particular-were thought of as sexual deviants and outlaws, because of their defiance of the enforced convention. They rebelled against the state, which imposed strict marriage and childbearing requirements on women, backed up by severe punishments written into the Roman law codes. The very existence of Christian women who had deliberately chosen a life of celibacy posed an embarrassment to the honor of the law-abiding, paternalistic Roman household. It is instructive to recall a twentieth-century example of similar marriage and childbearing requirements for women: Nazi Germany.

"Holy in body and spirit," they challenged the cultural structures of the honor/shame system, which MacDonald has succinctly described with the sentence: "Men defend honor, women embody shame." Sadly, it is not hard to find this system hard at work in our own historical period, fuelling millions of episodes of domestic violence, perhaps most dramatically illustrated by the prevalence of "honor killings" in the Middle East.

The Pastoral Epistles, especially 1st and 2nd Timothy and Titus, reveal the ambivalent position of celibate women in the church community. Paul and his followers endorsed celibacy, but this led to many dilemmas of practical theology: believing women married to pagan husbands, the legally mandated remarriage of young widows (under sixty), Christian women who defied their paterfamilias by refusing arranged marriages to pagans, etc. As the ideal of celibacy placed into practice began to impact public opinion about Christians, churchmen revealed what Luise Schottroff calls a "divided mind" toward women who embraced celibacy as a way to an independent, spiritually free way of life. This "divided mind" is evident in the second-century text: The Acts of Paul and Thecla, sometimes known as just The Acts of Paul. Hmm. . . .

Thecla becomes a follower of Paul after hearing him preaching outside her window, where she is transfixed by his words. Leaving family and fiance, she becomes active in a house church and lives under the protection of the wealthy widow, Tryphaena. She travels and evangelizes, eventually becoming a spiritual teacher in her own right, independent of Paul. As a result of this boldly public ministry, several attempts are made to kill her. Celibate Thecla is accused of sorcery and adultery. In an echo of Peter's denial, Paul stands weakly by as Thecla is stripped in public. Accused of being shameless, she is ritually shamed. As she is traveling with Paul in Antioch, a Syrian named Alexander sexually assaults her, but she escapes and causes him to be ridiculed. For this mortal blow to his honor, she is sent to the beasts in the arena.

Why has Thecla disappeared? Saint Thecla was removed from the Vatican's list of official Saints in the 1960s, when St. Christopher and many others were also removed. There is a continuing tradition about her in the Eastern Churches, though it is but a glimmer.

Looking at Church hagiographies about early Christian female martyrs shows that conflicted, ambivalent thinking about their sister Christians continued in the minds and hearts of the Christian men who set down their stories.

The medieval repression of the Beguines is only one later example of how this ambivalence carried on. In the hagiographies, female saints who resisted the patronal systems of Mediterranean household law by clinging to celibacy and dying as martyrs are generally depicted in the most passive, meek, and mild terms—like sacrificial lambs. Their roll call is a long one: St. Ursula and the 11,000 Virgins, St. Barbara, St. Catherine, St. Agatha, St. Lucia, et al.

Women of the early church who were known to not be purely virginal were even more problematic to the honorable status of the men in the community. Female slaves were expected to be sexually available to their owners, and former slaves came with this in their (often immediate) past. How did the church's valuation of celibacy work for them? How easy for them to declare themselves a "born-again virgin by choice" in the wording of today's faith-based sexual abstinence for teens movement? That female slaves were active participants in church communities, and even bore some leadership authority is attested to by the correspondence of Pliny the Younger to the Emperor Trajan, circa 112 G.E., in which he reports on the torture of two female slaves (ancilla) who are called deacons (ministra). Pliny states that these two deacons had been turned in by an informant. MacDonald posits the likelihood that they either annoyed the pagan patriarch of the household they belonged to and were simply dumped on Pliny, or sacrificed in order to deflect suspicion from a Christian master or mistress.

All the major objections against "Gnostic" groups mimicked pagan criticisms of early Christians, and included all the major headings from the list of archaic accusations familiar to mimetic theorists. As orthodox doctrine developed in the Byzantine era, it distinguished itself from the horde of heretics by claiming that their theology was more incarnational, thereby affirming the true humanity of Christ. While the centuries wore on, however, Greco-Roman goddess attributes and social conventions migrated onto churchwomen to reflect social systems of honor/shame, "good girl/bad girl" dualities. This was calcified into the culture of the Roman Church by Pope Gregory (for whom the chant form is named) in the sixth century, in a famous series of sermons that merely made official what had been a popular trend for some time.

This was to conflate all the women who supported and participated in the life and ministry of Jesus into as few women as possible, making the many Marys into one honorable Mary and one Mary who bore the mark of shame. Mary, the Mother of Jesus, like her son, become less and less Jewish and more and more divinized. She became increasingly separated from all other women, "blessed among women" so as to become ostracized from them, or they from her. One can never be as good as the Blessed Virgin Mary, no matter how unassailable one's bodily purity may be or how selfless a mother. You could be "as good" as Mary Magdalene, though.

Mary Magdalene's reputation as a prostitute, however undeserved, clings to her today, despite having been officially rescinded by the Vatican in 1969 and thoroughly deconstructed by New Testament scholars and historians of church art such as Jane Schaberg and Susan Haskins. The stain of a reputation is a hard thing to lose even now—clearly impossible for the women who embodied the shame and honor of their house church communities. By the Medieval period, Magdalene Houses all over Western Europe provided the public with a steady supply of designated penitents who enacted the community's shame, functioning as female versions of the Spanish colonial orders of Penitente. Interestingly, while the Beguinage where independent communities of women lived and worked were violently suppressed, the Magdalene Houses for public penitents were officially fostered and supported. (1)

The casting of Mary Magdalene as a prostitute happened concurrently with the development of the Cult of the Virgin Mary, and this is no coincidence at all. Gradually, pagan goddess attributes sorted themselves out between the "good" girl and the "bad" girl with astonishing continuity: portraits of Mary, the Mother of Jesus, were decorated with starry crowns and crescent moons, attributes of the ever-virgin Athena/Diana. Pomegranates and vineyards, attributes of Demeter and Persephone and the Syrian Mother Goddess, become associated with Mary Magdalene. Many of the clues to this syncretic divination process have their roots and ruins at Ephesus, the great temple city dedicated to the Mother Goddess centuries before the Greek conquest. A city that was, of course, a center of Paul's ministry. It is said, in the Eastern Church's tradition, to be a place where Mary, the Mother of Jesus spent time in her later years. It is also the place where Mary Magdalene is said to have been buried.

White doves were an attribute of the Syrian Mother Goddess, and of Venus to the Romans. So familiar to Christians as the symbol of the Holy Spirit: in the classical period, white doves were strongly associated with this then-ancient Temple at Ephesus. Demolished in the Byzantine era, the great columns of the Temple to the Mother Goddess at Ephesus were transported to Constantinople by Justinian to become the great columns in the Cathedral of Hagia Sophia, or Holy Wisdom. They are still there today.

Between the time when Christianity became a state-sponsored religion and the period of the schism between the Eastern and Roman Churches, the Cult of the Virgin gradually crystallized into its own form of inherently anti-incarnational "Gnostic" heresies, and the process of "becoming what you profess to hate," a basic principle of mimetic theory, had come full circle. The "law of anti-idolatry" spoken of so eloquently by Sandor Goodhart calls us to unpack this history, to look at what kinds of sacrifices women and their friends have had to make in order for the domination system to ensure that the repetitive duality of who can wear the white dress and who must wear the red dress will be preserved.

Theologies of Mary's immaculate conception and emphases on "pure vessel" and "ever virgin" language about her isolates and denatures her in a way not far distant from the kind of Goddess who is spawned from the forehead of her Father. Because this "blessed among women" is said in legends to have visited Mount Athos in Greece, for centuries the Orthodox monasteries there have dedicated themselves to barring female humans and domestic animals from the place of pilgrimage, calling this an honor to Mary. Of course, the monks have no way of preventing Holy Sophia from sending female flora and fauna there, anyway. And a question, for me, hangs in the air: Wouldn't this way of being "honored" make a real flesh-and-blood Mary feel lonely? When she had her important news to tell, the Mary of the text sought out the company of other women—her cousin, Elizabeth, and the circle of women that were certainly a big part of her cousin's village life.

"Pure vessel" theology has been the subject of long dispute between the Eastern and Roman Churches, and then the Roman Church and the Protestant

Reformers and secular Enlightenment. These rivalries reached a climax in the middle of the nineteenth century with the declaration of the Doctrine of the Immaculate Conception and were closely tied to the declaration of the Doctrine of Papal Infallibility. These are intimately related to the idea of Mary as a cosmic "Beatrix Mundi," of which John Paul II is so fond. What does it mean for a Church hierarchy that refuses to even consider the ordination of women, to call Mary "The Queen of Priests" in the ordination liturgy?

It is critically important to pay attention to language about the Church, who genders it, and how it is done. Hearing Cardinals talk about how the Church is working to uphold Her honor is quite instructive in this era of sexual scandal.

The "true-believing" (as the term "orthodox" is commonly translated) leadership of the Church became what they professed to hate. This can be detected in the phenomenon of "reversing the text." This is something the early Church "fathers" accused opposing groups of doing on a regular basis—turning a text inside out and standing it on its head so that it means the opposite of what it says, solely for the evil purpose of spreading chaos and confusion.

As concerns the place of women in the faith community, two texts come immediately to mind as nominations for orthodoxy's "text reversal." First is Matthew 23:9, where Jesus says: "Call no man on earth your father, for you have one Father who is in Heaven." Structuring that title as a necessary resume requirement for Churchly office has proven to be a reversal of this instruction from Jesus, turning away from his radical re-visioning of what it could mean to be family to one another, and back toward the old paternalistic domination system of the pagan world.

The second text is the frequently ignored (excluded from the common lectionary) passage in Luke 11:27, a scene which also appears in the Gospel of Thomas 79:1-2. When Jesus is on the street, a woman calls out to him: "Blessed is the womb that bore you and the breasts that nursed you!" He answers: "Blessed rather are those who hear the word of God and obey it!" Beyond virginity, honor/shame based patriarchal systems value women primarily for their fertility, especially for being "fruitful" in bearing strong sons. I read this text as a rebuke of the woman for her admiration (envy'?) of Mary as a particularly blessed mother. Jesus tells her that is not what it's about: in the realm of God, biology is not destiny.

The missing pieces of history surrounding the family life of this woman of first-century Palestine (and all the other women of her era); and the structures of the sacred that have been erected to fill those pieces in still have power to provoke the honor/shame reflex today. Lest you doubt this, I remind you of Mayor Giuliani's rage at the Brooklyn Museum over the Chris Ofili painting/collage of the Madonna, adorned with pictures clipped from pornographic magazines and elephant dung.

The overarching cultural motifs clarified by mimetic theory are evident in this history. It is a history in which real women lived out their lives in social systems where their roles were largely circumscribed, as symbols of family honor and social acceptability. Their passion and commitment still shine through, if we will not neglect to keep their lamps faithfully filled. In their time, the women of the early church were sacrificial victims to a rivalry over honor and "true belief." Let them now be inspired and inspiring "Sheroes for Christ"—models of resistance and reform.

Notes

1. On Sunday, January 19, 2003, ABC "World News Tonight" aired a segment on the Magdalene Houses of Ireland. Terry Moran, the anchor introduces the segment by relating how this has become yet another variety of scandal in the Roman Catholic Church, and with a few phrases about the history of the Magdalene House system. The news writers for the network provided him with this sentence: "These workhouses in Ireland were named after Mary Magdalene, who is identified as a repentant prostitute in the Gospel of Saint Luke."(?!) The broadcast went on to talk about the recent coverage of this story on BBC-TV, and shows clips from a BBC docudrama about the Magdalene Houses, titled: "Sinners." Operated as profit-making convent laundries, they were actually prisons, dumping places for "wayward" girls and unwed mothers, some of whom spent their entire lives in these dismal places. Told that they must remain there to "wash away their sins," the girls and women were called by numbers, not names. Hilary Brown, the correspondent reporting from County Cork, interviewed two of the surviving witnesses to the cruelties of the Magdalene Houses, Sadie Williams and Mary Norris, who have campaigned for a memorial to the women who died in the Magdalene House system, known as the "Irish Gulag." The last Magdalene House was closed seven years ago, in 1996. There was at least one in every city in Ireland.

POSTSCRIPT

Did Christianity Liberate Women?

The Bible provides ample evidence of women's active roles during the early years of what would later be called Christianity. For a look at this early period, see *First Converts: Rich Pagan Women and the Rhetoric of Mission in Early Judaism and Christianity* (Stanford University Press, 2001). Eusebius (263–339 C.E.), a Greek Christian and intimate friend of Emperor Constantine, mentions women by name and identity in his account of the first 300 years, *The History of the Church* (Dorset Press, 1984). Fifth-century historians often omitted names and changed narratives in the process depersonalizing and shaming the women, according to Anne Jensen in *God's Self-Confident Daughters: Early Christianity and the Liberation of Women* (Knox, 1996).

During the first centuries of Christianity, different schools of what would later become theology existed side by side. One of these was Gnosticism, a mystical worldview that predominated in Greece and Rome. Remarkable for its androgynous view of God as father and mother, Gnosticism was the first heresy condemned by the Christian Church because some of its views clashed with what had become orthodoxy. Four Gnostic Gospels, part of what scholars call the Nag Hammadi library, found in Egypt in the 1940s, are available in Marvin W. Meyer's translation in *The Secret Teachings of Jesus* (Vintage Books, 1986). Elaine Pagels, an authority in this field, has written a useful guide to Gnosticism in *The Gnostic Gospels* (Vintage Books, 1989). Her more recent *Beyond Belief: The Secret Gospel of Thomas* (Random House, 2004) contrasts the canonical gospel of John, in which salvation comes only through belief in Jesus, with the Gnostic Gospel of Thomas, in which each person is encouraged to know God directly, through the divinely-given capacity, granted to all who are created in the image of God. See also the PBS/Frontline website recommended for this issue on the On the Internet page for Part I.

Karen Jo Torjesen's *When Women Were Priests* (Harper-San Francisco, 1995) highlights women as deacons, priests, prophets, and bishops and documents their exclusion from many of these roles as the Christian Church joined the establishment and worship moved from private to public space. During the Patristic Age, holy women paid a high price for their piety, energy, and talent. Gilian Close captures this time in *'This Female Man of God': Women and Spiritual Power in the Patristic Age, AD 350–450* (Routledge, 1995). Any woman holy enough to be an exemplar of the faith must be spiritually male. Finally, former Boston College theologian Mary Daly in *The Church and the Second Sex* (Beacon Press, 1985) follows up on Simone de Beauvoir's feminist classic *The Second Sex* by documenting sexism in Christian Church history and the "otherness" of women.

ISSUE 6

Were Internal Factors Responsible for the Fall of the Roman Empire?

YES: Antonio Santosuosso, from *Storming the Heavens: Soldiers, Emperors, and Civilians in the Roman Empire* (Westview Press, 2001)

NO: Peter Heather, from "The Huns and the End of the Roman Empire in Western Europe," *The English Historical Review* (February 1995)

ISSUE SUMMARY

YES: History professor Antonio Santosuosso states that the Roman Empire's inability to cope with demands involving the defense of the empire was responsible for its demise.

NO: Professor of history Peter Heather claims that the invasion of the Huns forced other barbarians to use tribal unity as a survival technique and to seek safety within the confines of the Roman Empire, thus permitting the invasion of the Huns to bring about the fall of the Roman Empire.

Periodization illuminates the past by delineating significant changes in humanity's progress from one time period to another. The European Renaissance, which marks the transition from the medieval to the modern world, is one such example. The decline and fall of the Roman Empire is another, because it notes the end of the Greco-Roman classical era and the beginning of the Middle Ages. Greek and Roman cultures provided Western civilization with some of its greatest historical and cultural endowments. Thus, the demise of these cultures continues to interest Western historians.

Not until the Italian Renaissance, with its renewed interest in classical antiquity, did the fall of Rome, along with its antecedent causes, earn an official place in the world of scholarship. Humanist scholar Francesco Petrarca (Petrarch) (1304–1374) blamed internal problems for the empire's demise. In the next century, however, Niccolo Machiavelli (1469–1527), perhaps the first modern political scientist, blamed the constant attacks of neighboring barbarians, which eventually wore down the empire and caused its collapse.

Modern historical scholarship on the fall of Rome began with Edward Gibbon (1737–1794), who injected another variable into the mix. In his multivolume work *The Decline and Fall of the Roman Empire* (first published between 1776 and 1782), Gibbon stated that the rise of Christianity may have played an significant role in Rome's collapse. Because he was a product of Europe's Enlightenment era and shared its skepticism regarding the effects of organized religion on a civilization's progress, many modern historians consider his focus on Christianity to be overemphasized. In general, he took a more fatalistic approach to the empire's demise, stating that "the decline of Rome was the natural and inevitable effect of immoderate greatness."

More recently, countless reasons have been given for Rome's fall: the disintegration of the imperial economy, agricultural problems caused by climatic changes, manpower shortages due to lead poisoning from the empire's water pipes, destruction of the leadership class through imperial executions and civil wars, racial mixing that diluted the old Roman stock, the drain of gold and silver, widespread slavery that made the rich richer and the poor poorer, and a class war waged by peasant soldiers against the ruling class. This list is not complete, but it does testify to the interest historians have taken in the fall of Rome.

While recognizing the probability of multiple causation in most historical events, twenty-first-century historians continue to debate the reasons for Rome's demise by analyzing and evaluating the effects of internal and external forces. By applying the Roman experience to the rise and fall of other civilizations—past and present—contemporary historians continue to revitalize the debate.

Our two historians reflect this internal/external dialogue. Peter Heather stresses the role of the barbarians in the empire's downfall, but offers a different spin. The 4th century C.E. invasion of Europe by the Huns was key to the fall of the Roman Empire, in his view, because it forced Germanic tribes to seek safety within the empire's boundaries where they developed a sense of unity, which ultimately gave them the power to supplant it. Antonio Santosuosso provides a new spin for the internal side of the argument. He states that internal disintegration within the Roman army, caused by a variety of factors, made it impossible for the legions to resist the barbarian pressures. If these weaknesses had not existed, the Empire might have been able to survive this crisis.

YES

Antonio Santosuosso

Storming the Heavens:
Soldiers, Emperors, and Civilians
in the Roman Empire

Introduction

Storming the Heavens begins in the second century B.C., when the Romans established clear supremacy over most of the Mediterranean world, and ends with the melancholic collapse of the empire in the fifth century A.D. I have tried to view this fascinating, dramatic tale from different angles, treasuring especially the voices of those who lived when the empire existed. My goal has been to integrate the emperor—the manager of war—and the military forces within the social, economic, religious, and symbolical context. Several powerful themes have emerged: the monopoly of military power in the hands of a few, whether an oligarchy or the emperor as the embodiment of the oligarchy; the connection between the armed forces and the most cherished values of the state; the manipulation of the lower classes so that they would accept the oligarchy's view of life, control, and power; the absence of real class conflicts; and imperialism's subjugation and dehumanization of people and the arrangements that made possible their subjugation, whether they were Gauls, Britons, Germans, Mideasterners, or Africans.

As enemies were cowed into submission, Rome, after a century, faced an internal situation that endangered its supremacy throughout the empire: social turmoil in the very heart of the Roman territories among an increasing number of dispossessed farmers; a scarcity of manpower for the army; and inevitable conflict with allies who had fought side by side with Romans to establish Rome's dominion in the Italian peninsula and elsewhere.

In the later half of the second century B.C., once the land redistribution reforms of the Gracchi (Tiberius and Gaius Gracchus) had failed, the ruling order had no alternative but to open the army's ranks to all citizens regardless of background. Although necessary, this measure soon became a harbinger of destruction and chaos. The rank and file, now mostly from the lower classes, switched allegiance from the abstract entity of the state to the commanders who provided a living and the loot. The army was democratized—but not the leadership. The highest order—the senatorial aristocracy—still retained its function as the manager of Roman war, for the soldiers never translated their struggle into class terms. Yet the upheaval was immense. Ambitious aristocrats fed on one another; in the process their troops became armies of pillagers, their targets citizens like them. All this played out on a stage where other violent events had long been taking place. First, non-Roman allies from central Italy and the peninsular south took the field against Rome upon being refused citizenship yet again; then an army of slaves, led by the Thracian gladiator Spartacus, became so dangerous that the primacy of the state and its security verged on collapse.

By the middle third of the first century B.C., the allies had finally been accepted as citizens and the slaves were crushed, but the Civil Wars ended only when Augustus (63 B.C.–A.D. 14) finally defeated, in 31 B.C., the last contenders to the supreme power: Marcus Antonius (a fellow Roman popularized as Marc Anthony) and Cleopatra, the queen of Egypt. Earlier, under Julius Caesar (100–44 B.C.), Augustus's granduncle, the rank and file were acclimating themselves to a new ideal as defenders of Rome's best values. It was an ideal that Augustus cherished and then enforced by bringing fundamental changes to the army and the empire. Augustus became the sole manager of war: He cut the legions from about sixty total to twenty-eight and then twenty-five; established a fund providing troops with a secure source of income; and centralized, in his own hands, the administration of the provinces where most of the armed forces were posted. The soldiers, except for the imperial guard and the units in charge of public duties (policing and fire fighting, for instance), went to man the frontiers or the most dangerous internal spots of the empire.

Augustus's dominion seemed to restate the values of old, for he tried to preserve the arrangement of the past, wherein the commoners were in a subordinate position while the highest orders—senatorial aristocrats and equestrians—maintained their prestige and at least the semblance of political power in their hands. In reality, however, the changes were profound. The center of power was still apparently in the Senate, but in truth it had passed to the emperor or his delegates. He also retained the might of the sword, for he was the armed forces' paymaster; he, not the Senate, controlled most of the resources and legions stationed at the frontiers. The process was sanctioned ideologically and religiously. Literary works, visual creations, and religious rituals became an integral part of the imperial image.

During the same period, Roman supremacy extended to the whole Mediterranean, and to all lands west of the Rhine and south of the Danube, while Emperor Claudius (10 B.C.–A.D. 54) completed the conquest of Britain. Before he died in A.D. 14, Augustus instructed the Roman people to be satisfied with and defend what they had already acquired. It was an ideal he had come to accept only after the destruction of three legions in the Teutoburg Forest in A.D. 9, but this did not guarantee that his successors would adopt a defensive stance. Aggression remained the fundamental principle of Roman policy until well into the third century A.D.; it was assumed that legionaries should not only confront any invader that approached imperial lands but also enter enemy territories, retaliate against those left behind, and punish those who had escaped destruction during the invasion.

Rome's supremacy was never in danger during most of the first two centuries A.D. The situation started to change in the latter part of the second century, but thanks to Marcus Aurelius (161–180) and Septimius Severus (193–211) Rome still managed to push back the barbarian threat at the frontier. Still, the more serious danger emerged from within. In the last years of the second century and for a good part of the next, most emperors became the puppets of soldiers, especially of the pretorians, the emperor's personal guard. The pretorians kept their role as bloodied emperor-makers even after Septimius Severus disbanded them in A.D. 193, for the newly formed pretorian guard reacquired the power of its predecessor.

The army that emerged from Septimius onward was forged from a new mold: Its pay was raised; the permanent legions were increased; more troops were stationed in Italy (there was even a legion located a few kilometers from Rome—a radical departure from tradition); and aristocrats began to be elbowed out of command positions. But probably the most influential novelty was the erosion of the central position of Rome and of the Italian-born in the army. For instance, the new pretorian guard was formed with legionaries coming from the frontier, whereas before it had been almost a complete monopoly of native Italians. During the subsequent decade more changes were implemented. The influx of Italian-born soldiers had steadily declined since Augustus's time; now they almost disappeared except (for the most part) in command posts. Moreover, a troubling situation developed at the frontier under pressure mainly from the Germanic tribes in Europe. Emperor Diocletian (c. 245–313?) tried to stop the threat with stronger fixed defenses, but when that did not work Constantine (c. 272 or 273–337) adopted a defense in depth, that is, fortifications in stages that slowed the enemy so that a mobile army could face it in a decisive encounter. Probably beginning with Severus or more likely with Gallienus (d. 268; emperor 253–268), the Roman troops were being divided between those who served at the frontier—usually less paid and less qualified—and those in the mobile field armies—better paid and better qualified; the task of the latter was to face the invaders after they had pierced the frontier. In the process, the role of the infantry—the backbone of earlier Roman armies—eroded and was taken up by the cavalry.

The empire survived, though sometimes in tatters, frequently pierced but more often repositioned in a menacing stance. The end came in the fifth century A.D. not because of Adrianople 378—when Emperor Valens fell before the Visigoths who crossed the Danube—and the barbarian populations who were permitted to settle within the imperial territory, but because by the second half of the fourth century there were not enough resources for a relentless war effort, especially in the western region (the territories had been divided into the Western Empire and the Eastern Empire since Diocletian's time). This was so because the Germanic tribes relentlessly poured across the borders, undaunted by defeats and always hoping to lay hands on the rich spoils of the empire. In the meantime, an oppressive taxation system, and a society with privileges for the few and burdens for the rest, were among the ails that would eventually bring death to the empire. The eastern region of the empire, richer and less menaced, lasted another thousand years (its capital,

Constantinople, finally fell to the Turks in 1453). In A.D. 476 the last emperor of the West, Romulus Augustulus—the "little Augustus" in more ways than one—was deposed. Roman supremacy had ended.

Rome Is No More: The End of the Empire

In 410, about eight centuries after it was sacked by the Gauls, Rome fell again to barbarians. This time, Gothic troops broke through the gate, having taken imperial lands about three decades earlier. As Jerome lamented from Palestine, the whole world perished in one city. But this event was not the beginning of the age of troubles. The troubles had begun three decades earlier, but after the sack of Rome the political landscape in western Europe would shift. Fifteen years afterward, Britain was no longer part of the empire. Barbarian kingdoms under the Vandals, Suebians, Visigoths, and Burgundians would be established throughout western Europe and North Africa. Rome was lucky to keep a tenuous hold on the Italian peninsula and the Balkans, but these territories would also fall to the invaders. Forty-five years later a new barbarian army—the Vandals—would sack the city again; twenty-one years after that—in A.D. 476—the Western Roman Empire came to its official end. . . .

The Illnesses of the Empire

In one of history's surprises, an empire as powerful as Rome raised an army of only a half-million (with mobile armies in support) to guard an enormous frontier and was unable to meet the barbarians' concerted attacks. The truth is that the empire could recruit no more than 600,000–650,000 men. The total recruiting pool was relatively small, the mortality rate was high, and financing and administration were a crushing burden. Any tax increase could not be implemented unless the state taxed the people that tradition, power, and prestige made untouchable. Even maintaining this army on the field disrupted society and stressed the Western Empire so much that it fell to the barbarians.

Although the figures are debatable, there are several factors indicating a demographic decline in the Late Empire. Cultivated lands decreased as much as 50 percent in Africa and perhaps 10–15 percent elsewhere due to lack of manpower, land erosion, deforestation, soil exhaustion, and a logical tendency to abandon areas prone to barbarian attack. The Roman Empire was essentially a primitive subsistence peasant society. The lower classes must have been weakened by chronic malnutrition, which prevented prodigious childrearing. The economic situation was so dire that peasants and the urban poor sold their children. Plagues struck the Roman Empire under Marcus Aurelius and Commodus in the second century and then in repetition in the third century (251, 261, and 271) before subsiding in the fourth century. Farmers abandoned their lands under the tax burden, unable to make a living. The "landlords were perennially short of tenants to cultivate their land," and the government tried to meet the demand by tying agricultural workers to their occupation by law—a policy implemented for most essential activities, including the armed forces. All this limited the labor force and thus the ability to recruit more soldiers. Even worse, the state and the rigid class and religious structure excluded many adults from serving in the army.

Roman technology was low, and the manpower (i.e., the lower classes) had to provide for consumers who paid either no or few taxes. The senatorial order, which continued even after being spoiled of most political power, was one of the wealthiest groups of the empire; besides gaining enormous wealth and building large estates, this class was able to avoid fiscal obligations by way of privilege. The civil service was another group that was supported by the state and thus sucked resources from the economy with minimal benefits to the rest. The Christian Church created a new group that provided spiritual guidance but no economic gain. The situation became more serious because; the new church accumulated wealth to a degree unknown in pagan religions. The 600,000–650,000 soldiers cost too much but created no new wealth once being placed on the defensive for more than a century. (The last large territorial acquisition had been the brief control of Mesopotamia under Septimius Severus.) Finally, the soldiers (who could barely hold their own against the increasing waves of barbarians) needed a large administrative machine that was inefficient, corrupt, and nonproductive

A decline in civic spirit spread throughout the social system and touched all classes. The official defenders of the state, the soldiers, became isolated from the civilian population, the butt of ridicule and scorn or the object of fear. As Jean-Michel Carrié points out, the situation had reversed since the first two centuries A.D. The new army was divorced from society because so many soldiers came from behind the frontiers, spoke languages that the rest could not understand, brought alien customs that were reprehensible, and were considered as barbaric as those who pressed at the gates.

Christianity, in the words of Friedrich Nietzsche, "was the vampire of the *imperium Romanum*—in a night it shattered the stupendous achievement of the Romans." But surely he exaggerates. The old pagans and the new Christians were attached to the empire just the same. And both looked in horror at the "savage nations" pressing the empire's defenses. In any case, Christianization of the military was a slow process, and those who subscribed to the Christian God could hardly be viewed as inferior soldiers. Yet it is hard to deny that Christianity emphasized peace, not war, and that several reluctant recruits tried to avoid military service for religious reasons. The old gods were part and parcel of the army and the state; the Christian God praised peace and brotherhood and encouraged many new believers to choose a life removed from the battlefield. The Christian God would provide a martial function in time in the form of the Crusades.

The major problem was the lack of manpower. More than 50 percent of the soldiers became "second-class troops"; the recruits were men of inferior quality organized under the greatest administrative abuses. Even if we downplay this negative interpretation, the *limitanei* seemed undisciplined and undermanned in comparison to their fighting peak under Diocletian. The elite was the mobile field army, and the idea behind it was effective. Even the later development, when mobile armies were stationed in the west and the east, was a step forward, for a single mobile army could not hope to cover the length of the frontier. Then regional reserves mushroomed in the Western Empire, Africa, Spain, and Britain, and the huge army in the Eastern Empire remained idle, poised against Persia while providing no relief to the Rhine and the Danube frontiers. The Roman empire was fragmented, stretched, and about to break down.

In time the problem would become insurmountable. Enemies roamed about at will. Stopping one threat was not enough, for another would emerge; if that new threat was pushed back, another popped up elsewhere. This was an epidemic of violence, yet contenders to the throne fought one another as much as they fought the enemy. Invasions often took advantage of civil war in the empire. As with the German tribes during the first two centuries A.D., the empire had fractured into factions that were impossible to unite in common cause. The Western Empire was a "nursery" of pretenders to the throne, and the armies of Britain and Gaul were the real threat to the security of the emperors. This meant that Roman generals sometimes had to rely more on barbarian soldiers. They were cheaper and more trustworthy than Roman citizens, who were quick to back a different pretender to the throne. The emperor and the pretenders alike did not hesitate to employ recruits from across the northern frontier to attack their rivals.

Still, the Eastern Empire—the "Romans of Constantinople"—continued for another thousand years. Why did they remain so strong? The western frontiers were too long, the resources too few, the coffers empty, the population smaller, civil wars more common, the enemy more intrusive and persistent. But the Roman army created the stresses, throwing society and the economy off balance. It required huge taxation, which in turn caused a decline in agriculture and population. It also required the establishment of a large civil service to gather and administer the tax revenues. But the real key was the decision of the Eastern Empire not to support the Western Empire. When the emperors of Constantinople like Justianian had a mind to, they successfully defeated the barbarians in the west. By that time, however, it was too late. Rome lay in pieces.

Epilogue

Melancholy pervaded the last years of the Roman Empire and it never disappeared. The Empire gave future generations their sense of destiny. It survived for another thousand years in the East, it was ever-present in most of the barbarian kingdoms. New people emerged, the borders were different.

Rome shaped the past and the future of western Europeans and through them most of the world. After a dramatic entrance following the Second Punic War, Rome would teeter on the edge of collapse but always reemerged. The first century B.C. would set Rome down another path. Marius's reform of 107 B.C. made sense, for the ranks of the army were difficult to replenish as long as the old eligibility requirements were maintained. Marius opened the army to everyone as long as they held Roman citizenship. But over time this would upset the republic's stability. For the next seven decades or so, until Augustus's victory at Actium in 31 B.C. against the fleet of Marcus Antonius and Cleopatra, the glorious armies of the past became hosts of pillagers.

With the military ranks opened to all, the new army no long longer served as the depository of values for upper-class and propertied families; potentially it could become the representative of the poor. In reality, however, the leadership core was unchanged. And the new soldiers—the rank and file—simply wanted to improve their lot, to gain immediate wealth, material goods and improve their condition. Overthrowing the privileged classes was not on their mind, and the "war managers" of the past—the aristocrats—remained in command. If one can identify any innovation, it was probably in the appearance of the new leader, the obvious case being Marius. But even he did not come from the dregs of society; he was an equestrian who had married into a distinguished family. The most radical change was seen in the soldiers' behavior. The troops became the enemy within; pillage and slaughter of fellow citizens was indiscriminate; loyalty was pledged not to the republic but to their leaders—as long as they provided the booty.

All this played out amid external and internal disorder. New invaders, the Cimbri and the Teutones, had to be thwarted; then the *socii* (non-Roman Italian allies) united and requested citizenship; finally Spartacus and the slaves threatened the very idea of Roman domination. It is remarkable that the slave rebellion never mushroomed into class warfare, with the lower classes making common cause with Spartacus and his men. Even the *socii* episode was not a class conflict for, with few exceptions, all social orders shared similar goals—to have the same rights, not just the duties of Roman citizens. In spite of the immense bloodshed that it caused, the integration of all peninsular Italians south of the Rubicon, that is, central and southern Italy (not the islands, however), made Rome stronger and laid the basis for extending its power even farther. Yet for decades afterward Romans slaughtered Romans, and troops felt little loyalty to society. The situation changed during the last stages of the Roman Civil Wars, and certain events made the reestablishment of social harmony mandatory: In part it was the work of a remarkable individual—Julius Caesar; in part it was the realization among the generals and their followers that killing friends and enemies alike led nowhere; and in part it was the massacre of members of the highest aristocratic order—the senators.

The new army, forged under Caesar and refined by his successor, Augustus, reacquired the traditional sense of destiny. It was Rome's duty to conquer all and to bring civilization to all corners of the earth. But it was also a matter of material gain and the fulfillment of a sense of violence and lust for power that had distinguished the men of Rome from the very beginning. Caesar and Augustus were pivotal in shaping the Roman Empire that followed. By Augustus's time the borders had reached almost their farthest expansion; the army finally was brought under control.

But Augustus went much further than did Julius Caesar (his great-uncle). The army finally received fair rewards for its services, but he also ensured that the emperor was the one who held the purse strings. This made the army reluctant to listen to anyone other than the commander in chief, it spoiled the troops from any political ascendancy that they may have acquired in the last stages of the civil wars. Augustus monopolized military power by controlling most of the far-flung provinces where the army was stationed, leaving the

Senate to control few soldiers. Moreover, he made certain that generals kept military control only for short periods to prevent the emergence of rivals to the throne. The imperial forces were his army, his soldiers, his fleet.

The reorganization of the state went hand in glove with a reformulation of the "Roman man" and its symbols. As the republic neared its final days and the army's rank and file transformed, Roman intellectuals, foremost Cicero, felt it necessary to restate the traditional virtues first articulated following the Second Punic War. The highest orders—senators and equestrians—were depicted as separate from the lower classes and provincials just as they were making their impact on society felt. This attitude was reflected in the emergence of the Principate: The emperor became the highest symbol of the state through Roman literature, art, and architecture, and the capital became his city. Soon this became the deliberate policy of the emperor, his family, and his troops and was mirrored in places throughout the frontier.

Augustus also added a new dimension to the commander in chief. Like his great-uncle Caesar, he would become worshipped as a god. Scipio Africanus was the first to undertake a process toward divine status, but Augustus perfected it. The idea that the supreme commander was a deity in death if not in life became a fixture of imperial power. Beginning with Diocletian, the association with the gods became stronger. Before him, the emperor's selection was based on merit and reflected the will of the people through the Senate. It was not a hereditary right (even though succession was often kept in the family). As we move toward the end of the third century A.D., however, it was understood that imperial authority rested in the will of the gods, a policy repeated under Constantine a few decades later (although the pagan gods of the past had given way to the Christian God).

Like all emperors, Augustus realized that his power rested on the support of his soldiers, for the emperor had become the exclusive manager of war. Yet he kept them at a distance from the center of power, a policy that worked for about two centuries (excepting a brief period in the aftermath of Nero's death). In the waning years of the second century A.D. things changed, ironically in the aftermath of the death of the ideal emperor, Marcus Aurelius, under his son Commodus. The praetorians, the emperor's guard formed by Augustus and stationed in and near Rome, became, sometimes with soldiers stationed at the frontier, the makers of emperors.

The third century A.D. was a most turbulent period. Barbarian tribes—more numerous, better organized, and more proficient in the art of war than in the past—pierced the empire's border (although this was a problem that Marcus had to face already in the second half of the second century A.D.). Emperor Septimius Severus, who finally brought some order to the anarchy following Commodus's death, was compelled to deal with this threat. And where Marcus and Septimius succeeded, others did not, and the remainder of the third century saw a series of barbarian strikes and Roman defeats.

Septimius was the greatest reformer since Augustus. He increased the number of legions and opened their ranks to more and more non-Romans. By then the armed forces had changed their nature. Senators were apparently discouraged from serving—a policy that became permanent about half a century later under Gallienus; Italian-born men, except in moments of great emergency, practically disappeared from the rank and file (although they still held higher commands); the old praetorian guard, the exclusive reserve of Italians, was disbanded and then refashioned using the best legionnaires from the frontier. This weakened the central tenet of the imperial army: Rome's dominance. Yet the soldier-citizen ideal would be renewed in 312 A.D when the next emperor, Caracalla (Septimius's son), extended citizenship to all freemen within the Roman Empire. By extending such privileges to practically all imperial subjects, this policy diluted the Roman military ideal.

Disorder followed. After Septimius, every ruler and pretender (except for three emperors) fell victim to the sword until Diocletian in 284 A.D. returned stability to the center; no emperor was murdered during the next seventy years.

Augustus made certain that legions were never located within Italy. Nearly all of them would be stationed in the most dangerous frontier hot spots—the Rhine, the Danube, and the Euphrates. Despite Augustus's last instructions, neither he nor his successors intended to switch over to a defensive policy, for the Roman mind believed in aggression. All territories, even those beyond the Roman posts, were considered to be part of the Roman dominion. If Roman lands were threatened, then the enemy had to be met before it pierced the frontier; it was then harshly punished inside its own territory. Supremacy extended to any place where Rome could in theory extend its military force.

The policy worked well until the end of the second century A.D. Dangers were met as they arose, with commanders moving troops from one frontier to the next as attacks progressed. It did not work in the third century, however, as enemy strikes became more common and were carried out simultaneously at times. The solution was to create a mobile field army (later several mobile armies were created). In varying forms, this strategy appeared first under Gallienus, then Diocletian, and finally Constantine (although one can argue that the troops Septimius Severus stationed in Italy were the nucleus of the Roman field army). The strength of the new army was its mobility. Thus the foot soldier, once the pride of the Roman military, gave way to cavalry. This also meant that the border troops were relegated to second-class status. Service in the mobile field army meant prestige, rewards, and promotion.

This emphasis on mobility led to important changes in frontier policy. Diocletian had strengthened the frontier borders with fortifications, adopting an elastic defense to hold the enemy in check at the frontier. Constantine abandoned the idea of stout border defense and instead sought to slow invaders by constructing a series of obstacles within the imperial territories. This strategy of defense in depth placed frontier troops and populations in great danger and eroded the principle that peace reigned throughout the Roman Empire.

By then, however, Roman power was clearly on the wane. And although the Roman armies were still powerful, their outright superiority slowly disappeared after Constantine. Under Augustus and his successors, the armed forces combined superior strategic skill with effective tactics. But this was not necessarily the case thereafter. The suppression of Boudicca's Rebellion, the capture of Masada, and the see-saw struggle against the German tribes are good examples. By the second half of the fourth century A.D. things would be different. The Romans could still hold their own and often defeated their opponents, as at Strasburg in 357. But as the quality of the troops declined, the onslaught from outside and the struggles within became in the long run impossible to restrain. Roman armies, especially the infantry, became the victims of disaster (e.g., Adrianople) and attrition (e.g., Ad Salices). And the traditional core elements of the Roman army practically disappeared. Friends and enemies greeted Rome from the same corners of the world.

The end of the Roman Empire coincided with population decline, polarization of society (many individuals took from but did not give back to the community), corruption at the highest levels, disappearance of the civic sense, and perhaps even the appearance of Christianity, which emphasized peace over military glory. As in the past, the key was the army: It was too small to patrol the border; was too expensive to maintain (even with heavy taxes); and was badly led by incompetent emperors. The final blow was the bifurcation into the Western Empire and Eastern empire, begun under Diocletian and completed after Theodosius. Practically abandoned by their eastern brethren, the westerners were overrun by the German tribes. The Romans in the east would last for another millennium.

The Huns and the End of the Roman Empire in Western Europe

Based on the Mediterranean, the Roman Empire forged Europe as far as the rivers Rhine and Danube—and, for lengthy periods, extensive lands beyond those boundaries—together with North Africa and much of the Near East into a unitary state which lasted for the best part of 400 years. The protracted negotiations required to bring just some of this area together in the European Community put the success of this Empire into perspective. Yet since the publication of Gibbon's masterpiece (and long before), its very success has served only to stimulate interest in why it ended, 'blame' being firmly placed on everything from an excess of Christian piety to the effect of lead water pipes. The aim of this paper is to reconsider some of the processes and events which underlay the disappearance of the western half of the Roman Empire in the fifth century AD. This was an area encompassing essentially modern Britain, France, Benelux, Italy, Austria, Hungary, the Iberian Peninsula, and North Africa as far east as Libya, whose fragmentation culminated in the deposition of Romulus Augustulus on or around 4 September 476. That groups of outsiders—so-called 'barbarians'—played an important role in all this has never been doubted. A full understanding of the barbarians' involvement in a whole sequence of events, taking the best part of a hundred years, lends, however, an unrecognized coherence to the story of western imperial collapse.

There are two main reasons why this coherence has not been highlighted before. First, most of the main barbarian groups which were later to establish successor states to the Roman Empire in western Europe, had crossed the frontier by about AD 410, yet the last western Roman emperor was not deposed until 476, some sixty-five years later. I will argue, however, that the initial invasions must not be separated from the full working-out of their social and political consequences. Not just the invasions themselves need to be examined, but also the longer-term reactions to them of the Roman population of western Europe, and especially its landowning elites. While the western Empire did not die quickly or easily, a direct line of historical cause and effect nonetheless runs from the barbarian invasions of the late fourth and early fifth centuries to the deposition of Romulus Augustulus. The second reason lies in modern understandings of what caused the different groups of outsiders to cross into the Empire in the first place. These population movements did not happen all at once, but were stretched out over about thirty-five years, c 376–410. Here again, however, a close re-examination of the evidence reveals that the years of invasion represent no more than different phases of a single crisis. In particular, the two main phases of population movement—c. 376–86 and 405–8—were directly caused by the intrusion of Hunnic power into the fringes of Europe.

The Huns were very much a new factor in the European strategic balance of power in the late fourth century. A group of Eurasian nomads, they moved west, sometime after AD 350, along the northern coast of the Black Sea, the western edge of the great Eurasian Steppe Illiterate, and not even leaving a second-hand account of their origins and history in any Graeco-Roman source, they remain deeply mysterious. Opinions differ even over their linguistic affiliation, but the best guess would seem to be that the Huns were the first group of Turkic, as opposed to Iranian, nomads to have intruded into Europe. Whatever the answer to that question, the first half of this study will reconsider their impact upon the largely Germanic groups of central and eastern Europe which had previously been the main focus of Roman foreign policy on Rhine and Danube.

⋅◈⋅

This fundamental change in the nature of political activity from regimes independent of the immigrant groups to regimes which included them—a direct result of the disappearance of the Huns as an outside 'force—had important consequences. No group of supporters was ready (nor previously had any of the more traditional power-blocks ever been ready) to back a regime without some kind of pay-off. One effect of including immigrants in governing coalitions, therefore, was to increase the numbers of those expecting rewards, most obviously involvement in the running of the Empire. Burgundian kings took Roman titles, for instance, while the Visigoth Theoderic II attempted to order affairs in Spain. The Vandals' intervention in Italy in 455 should likewise be read as an attempt to stake their claim in the new political order. That they sacked the city of Rome has naturally received most attention; but Geiseric, the Vandal leader, also took back to North Africa with him Eudoxia and Eudocia—respectively wife and daughter of Valentinian III—and married the daughter to his son and heir Huneric. The two had been betrothed but not married under the treaty of 442, yet in 455 Petronius Maximus married her to his son, the Caesar Palladius. Thus Geiseric intervened in Italy at least partly out of fear that a match which should have cemented the Vandals' status within the western Empire was not going to take place. Subsequent years, similarly, saw Geiseric forward the imperial claims of Olybrius who married Placidia, the younger daughter of Valentinian, and was thus his relative by marriage.

Involvement in imperial affairs carried great prestige, and had been sought, as we have seen, since the time of Alaric and Athaulf. The western Empire only had this prestige, however, because it was, and was perceived to be, the most powerful institution of the contemporary world. Prestige certainly incorporates abstract qualities, but the attraction of the living Empire for immigrant leaders was firmly based upon its military might and overall wealth. They wished to avoid potentially dangerous military confrontations with it, while its wealth, when distributed as patronage, could greatly strengthen a leader's position. By the 450s, however, the real power behind the western imperial facade was already ebbing away. As we have seen, Britain, parts of Gaul and Spain (at different times), and above all North Africa had removed themselves or been removed from central imperial control. The rewards—money or land, such wealth being the basis of power—which were given after 454 to new allies from among the barbarian immigrants therefore only depleted further an already shrunken base.

Take, for example, Avitus. Under him, the Goths were sent to Spain to bring the Suevi to heel. Unlike the 410s, however, Theoderic II's troops seem to have operated by themselves, and according to Hydatius' account basically ransacked northern Spain, including loyal Hispano-Romans, for all the wealth they could muster. This benefited the Goths, but not the Roman state; there is no indication that Roman administration and taxation were restored. Likewise the Burgundians: after participating in Spain, they received new and better lands in Savoy, which, an enigmatic chronicle entry tells us, they divided with local senators. Another prosperous agricultural area no longer formed part of central imperial resources.

After 454, there thus built up a vicious circle within the western Empire, with too many groups squabbling over a shrinking financial base. In political terms, this meant that there were always enough groups left out in the cold, after any division of the spoils, which wanted to undermine the prevailing political configuration. Moreover, with every change of regime, there had to be further gifts to conciliate supporters anew. Having been granted a free hand in Spain under Avitus, the Goths then received the city of Narbonne and its territory (especially, one supposes, its tax revenues) as the price of their support for Libius Severus, Majorian's successor, in the early 460s. Even worse, this concentration on the internal relations of the established power-blocks allowed the rise of other more peripheral forces, which would previously have been suppressed, and whose activities took still more territory out of central control. Particularly ominous in this respect was the expansion of the Armoricans, and, above all, the Franks in northern Gaul from the 460s, as increasingly independent leaders gathered around themselves ever larger power-bases.

There were only two possible ways to break the circle. Either the number of political players had to be reduced, or the centre's financial base had to expand. This clarifies the logic behind the policies pursued by the only effective western regimes put together after the death of Aetius: those of Majorian (457–61) and Anthemius (467–72). Majorian's regime combined the sufferance of all the western army groups with the support of Italian aristocrats and a careful courting of the Gauls who had previously backed Avitus. He also won at least the temporary acquiescence of the Goths and Burgundians, and Constantinople seems eventually to have recognized him. Anthemius was son-in-law of the former eastern Emperor Marcian, and came to Italy with an army and a blessing from the reigning eastern Emperor, Leo. His leading general was Marcellinus, commander in Dalmatia; Ricimer accepted him in Italy (they forged a marriage alliance); Gallic landowners were again carefully courted;

and, at the start of his reign at least, the major immigrant groups deferred to him. The central policy of both these regimes was to reconquer Vandal Africa, Majorian making his bid in 460, Anthemius in 468. Victory in either of these wars would have renewed imperial prestige, but, more important, would have removed from the political game one of its major players, and, perhaps above all, restored to the rump western Empire the richest of its original territories.

Both Vandal expeditions failed, and as a result both regimes fell apart. But what if either had succeeded? Particularly in 468, a really major expedition was put together and the later success of Belisarius shows that reconquering North Africa was not inherently impossible. There was, so to speak, a window of opportunity. Buoyed up by victory and the promise of African revenues, a victorious western emperor could certainly have re-established his political hold on the landowners of southern Gaul and Spain, many of whom would have instinctively supported an imperial revival. Sidonius, and the other Gallic aristocrats who organized resistance to Euric, for instance, would have been only too happy to reassert ties to the centre. Burgundians, Goths, and Suevi would have had to be faced in due course, but victory would have considerably extended the active life of the western Empire. The failure of the expeditions foreclosed the possibility of escaping the cycle of decline. With the number of players increasing rather than diminishing, as the Franks in particular grew in importance, and with the Empire's financial base in decline, the idea of empire quickly became meaningless, since the centre no longer controlled anything anyone wanted. In consequence, the late 460s and 470s saw one group after another coming to the realization that the western Empire was no longer a prize worth fighting for. It must have been an extraordinary moment, in fact, when it dawned on the leaders of individual interest groups, and upon members of local Roman landowning elites, that, after hundreds of years of existence, the Roman state in western Europe was now an anachronism.

The first to grasp the point seems to have been Euric the Visigoth. After the Vandals defeated Anthemius, he quickly launched a series of wars which, by 475, had brought under his control much of Gaul and Spain. There is a striking description of his decision to launch these campaigns in the Getica of Jordanes:

> Becoming aware of the frequent changes of [western] Roman Emperor, Euric, King of the Visigoths, pressed forward to seize Gaul on his own authority.

This extract captures rather well what it must have been like suddenly to realize that the time had come to pursue one's own aims with total independence. The correspondence of Sidonius Apollinaris likewise shows members of the Roman landowning elite of southern Gaul transferring their allegiance piecemeal to Euric's colours at much the same time: some had taken stock of the terminal decline of the Empire as early as the 460s; others, like Sidonius himself, did not accept the situation until the mid-470s. Euric's lead was followed at different times by the other interested parties.

The eastern Empire, for instance, abandoned any hope in the west when it made peace with the Vandals, probably in 474. As we have seen, Constantinople had previously viewed North Africa as the means of reinvigorating the western Empire. Making peace with the Vandals was thus a move of huge significance, signalling the end of attempts to sustain the west; diplomatic recognition as western emperor was subsequently granted to Julius Nepos, but he never received any practical assistance. That the western Empire had ceased to mean anything dawned on the Burgundians at more or less the same time. Gundobad, one of the heirs to the throne, played a major role in central politics in the early 470s; a close ally of Ricimer, he helped him defeat Anthemius, supported the subsequent regime of Olybrius, and, after Ricimer's death, even persuaded Glycerius to accept the throne in 473. Sometime in 473 or 474, however, he 'suddenly' (as one chronicler put it) left Rome. Possibly this was due to his father's death, or perhaps he just gave up the struggle; either way, he never bothered to return. Events at home were now much more important than those at the centre, which now, of course, was the centre no longer.

The army of Dalmatia made one final attempt to sponsor a regime when Julius Nepos marched into Italy in 474, but one year later he left again—definitively—in the face of the hostility of Orestes and the army of Italy. Fittingly, it was the army of Italy which was the last to give up. In 475, its commander Orestes proclaimed his son Romulus Emperor, but within a year lost control of his soldiers. Not surprisingly, given all the resources which had by now been seized by others, it was shortage of money which caused the unrest. Odovacar was able, therefore, to organize a putsch, murder Orestes, and depose Romulus Augustulus. He then sent an embassy to Constantinople which did no more than state the obvious: there was no longer any need for an emperor in the west. With this act, the Roman Empire in western Europe ceased to exist.

That the Huns and other outside, 'barbarian', groups were a fundamental cause of western imperial collapse is not a novel conclusion. The real contribution of this paper to scholarly debate, outside matters of detail, lies in three main lines of argument. First, the invasions of 376 and 405–8 were not unconnected events, but two particular moments of crisis generated by a single strategic revolution: the emergence of Hunnic power on the fringes of Europe. This was not a sudden event, but a protracted process, and the movements of the Huns provide a real unity and coherence to thirty-five years of instability and periodic invasion along Rome's European frontiers in the later fourth and early fifth centuries.

Second, while some sixty-five years separate the deposition of Romulus Augustulus from these invasions, they are, nonetheless, intimately linked. The regular crises for the Empire in intervening years represent no more than the slow working-out of the full political consequences of the invasions, with the events of 476 marking the culmination of the process whereby the aftereffects of invasion steadily eroded the power of the western Roman state. The loss of territory to the invaders—sometimes sanctioned by treaty, sometimes not—meant a loss of revenue, and a consequent loss of power. As the state lost power, and was perceived to have done so, local Roman landowning elites came to the realization that their interests would best be served by making political accommodations with the outsiders, or, in a minority of cases, by taking independent responsibility for their own defence. Given that the Empire had existed for four hundred years, and that the east continued to prop up the west, it is not surprising that these processes of political erosion, and of psychological adjustment to the fact of erosion, took between two and three generations in the old Empire's heartlands of southern Gaul, Italy, and Spain (even if elites in other areas, such as Britain, were rather quicker off the mark). Despite the time-lag, the well-documented nature of these processes substantiates a very direct link between the period of the invasions and the collapse of the Empire. There was no separate additional crisis. Simply, the overwhelming consequences of the arrival, inside the body politic of the western Roman state, of new military forces, with independent political agendas, took time to exert their full effect.

A third line of argument has concerned the paradoxical role of the Huns in these revolutionary events. In the era of Attila, Hunnic armies surged across Europe from the Iron Gates of the Danube towards the walls of Constantinople, the outskirts of Paris, and Rome itself. But Attila's decade of glory was no more than a sideshow in the drama of western collapse. The Huns' indirect impact upon the Roman Empire in previous generations, when the insecurity they generated in central and eastern Europe forced Goths, Vandals, Alans, Suevi, Burgundians across the frontier, was of much greater historical importance than Attila's momentary ferocities. Indeed, the Huns had even sustained the western Empire down to c. 440, and in many ways their second greatest contribution to imperial collapse was, as we have seen, themselves to disappear suddenly as a political force after 453, leaving the west bereft of outside military assistance.

I would like to finish by trying to place these lines of argument in broader historical perspective. Taken together, they indicate firmly, of course, that it was a foreign policy crisis which brought down the western Empire, and thus cast further fuel on long-raging fires of debate over whether it was internal or external factors which caused the fall of Rome. Indeed, there exists a vast secondary literature—what Peter Brown once labelled the 'sacred rhetoric'— which would argue precisely the opposite, seeing internal social, economic, and psychological developments as fully explaining imperial collapse. According to this view, the balance of power on the frontier was broken by progressive Roman enfeeblement, rather than by developments in areas beyond Rome's control.

Transformations within the Roman world must obviously be taken into account when we look at the ability of outside groups to create increasing mayhem inside its borders. Despite possible appearances, the argument of this paper is itself very far from monocausal, since internal and external factors obviously interrelate. On a very basic level, the economic, demographic and other resources of a society fundamentally explain its success or failure in the face of outside threat. If the Empire had a sufficiently large and wealthy population, it would have been able to resist even the new forces unleashed by the Huns. More particularly, as we have seen, the appearance of barbarian powers actually within the Empire's borders, in the fifth century, opened up a pre-existing fault line in the relationship between imperial centre and local Roman landowning elites. The centre relied on a mixture of constraint and reward to focus the loyalties of landowners, some of them many hundreds of miles distant, upon the Empire. The new barbarian powers of the fifth century undermined the ability of the Empire to prop up the position of its local supporters, to reward them, or even to constrain their loyalty. The Empire thus fell apart as local landowners found alternative methods to guarantee their elite status, making accommodations with the new powers in the land.

Even so, it remains very much to the point to ask a hypothetical question. What would have happened had barbarians not invaded the Empire en masse in the face of the Hunnic threat? Despite continued attempts of late to stress the importance of internal factors, there is still not the slightest sign that the Empire would have collapsed under its own weight. Indeed, a great body of recent (and not so recent) research in two separate areas would collectively support the contention of this paper, derived from a close examination of the sequence of events, that it was developments beyond, rather than within, the imperial frontier which upset the prevailing balance between Rome and its neighbours. There is no space here to deal with either fully, but brief summaries can at least set an agenda for further debate.

First, there have been substantial reappraisals of different aspects of the later Roman Empire, whose cumulative effect, to my mind, has been to overturn the 'sacred rhetoric'. The fourth-century Empire was not socially rigid, economically stagnant, culturally dead, or politically dislocated to an obviously greater degree than earlier Roman societies. Much, of course, was problematic about the late Roman world, but perfect societies exist only in historians' imaginations. Recent studies have revealed that there was no fundamental dislocation in the rural economy, the power-house of the Empire; that trade was flourishing in a far from demonetarized economy; and that local elites were participating in imperial structures in unprecedented numbers. Traditional classicists' prejudice has also given way—in some cases, at least—to a fuller appreciation of the cultural dynamism generated by the incorporation of Christianity within the existing political and social edifice.

On a second front, archaeological investigations have also revealed a total transformation in the nature of Germanic societies in the first three centuries or so AD. Causes are still a matter for debate, but agricultural output and economic sophistication both grew exponentially, generating in their wake profound social change. In particular, differentiation in status and wealth expanded markedly, creating much more pronounced social hierarchies. All this is consonant with the literary evidence, which shows the existence of much larger political entities and of real dynasties among at least some Germanic groups of the fourth century. Demonstrably true of Goths on the Danube, it also seems to be the case with the Franks and Alamanni of the Rhine frontier. Fourth-century Alamannic society threw up a succession of leaders with pre-eminent power—Chnodomarius, Vadomarius, and Macrianus being described as such by Ammianus—and Roman policy was precisely directed towards containing the threat they posed: kidnapping them at banquets being a preferred approach. These new, larger entities, as might be expected, acted more assertively towards the Roman state. In the aftermath of a Roman civil war, for instance, Chnodomarius actually attempted to annex Roman territory (and was matched in this by some Frankish groups), and the later 360s and early 370s saw both Alamannic and Gothic groups demand (and succeed in establishing) less subservient diplomatic relationships.

Taken together, these entirely separate areas of research suggest that any substantial change in the strategic balance of power was prompted by the growing strength and cohesion of Germanic groups, not the enfeeblement of the Roman Empire. Even so, the effects of those changes should not be overstated. Germanic groups were stronger in the fourth century; but when it came to direct confrontation, the Roman Empire was still overwhelmingly victorious in the vast majority of cases. And this, perhaps, finally allows us to bring the role of the Huns in the destruction of the western Empire into clear focus. Individually, the new Germanic powers were still no match for the Roman state in the fourth century. By themselves, they could generate some adjustment in relations along the frontiers, but were not about to pull the Empire apart. The most important effect of the Huns, therefore, was to make sufficient numbers of these new Germanic powers, which were not themselves politically united, act in a sufficiently similar way at broadly the same time. If ambition had prompted just one new dynast to invade the Empire on his own, his fate would have been the same as that of Chnodomarius, crushed by Julian at Strasbourg (or, indeed, of Radagaisus). The Huns, however, induced too many of these more substantial groups to cross the frontier in too short a space of time for the Roman state to be able to deal with them effectively. The balance of power on the frontier was already swinging away from the Empire, but only within a limited arc. By creating an accidental unity of purpose among Rome's neighbours, the Huns shattered frontier security, and set in motion processes which generated—out of unprecedented combinations of outside military power and existing local Roman elites—a new political order in western Europe.

POSTSCRIPT

Were Internal Factors Responsible for the Fall of the Roman Empire?

Most historians studying the fall of Rome agree that neither internal nor external forces can be ignored, yet many continue to produce works that emphasize one side of the debate. E. A. Thompson, *Romans and Barbarians: The Decline of the Western Empire* (University of Wisconsin Press, 2002, reprint) has been a standard source on the external forces side for decades. Arthur Ferrill's *The Fall of Rome: The Military Explanation* (Thames & Hudson, 1986) is a more recent account of the role played by the barbarians in Rome's collapse. Hugh Elton, *Warfare in Roman Europe, A.D. 350–425* (Oxford University Press,1998) brings the subject up-to-date. In *Warfare in the Classical World* (Salamander Press, 1998), John Warry surveys the role of wars and their effects on Greco-Roman civilization, titling a concluding chapter, "The Coming of the Barbarians." Derek Williams, in *Romans and Barbarians: Four Views From the Empire's Edge, First Century*, A.D. (St. Martin's Press, 1998), and Thomas S. Burns, *Rome and the Barbarians, 100 B.C.–A.D.* 400 (John Hopkins University Press, 2003) offer two more contemporary updates.

A. H. M. Jones's *The Decline of the Ancient World* (Oxford University Press, 1964) and Peter Brown's *The World of Late Antiquity* (Thames & Hudson, 1971) are classics on the internal factors side of the debate. Averil Cameron, *The Later Roman Empire: A.D. 284–430* (Harvard University Press, 1993) surveys the centuries before the empire's fall. Geza Alfoldy's *The Social History of Rome* (Johns Hopkins University Press, 1988) is a short but well-packed volume on Rome's social history that sets the stage for the fall of Rome. Jaroslav Pelikan, *The Excellent Empire: The Fall of Rome and the Triumph of the Church* (Harper & Row, 1987) gives a religious spin to the question.

Despite its age, one should not ignore Gibbon's classic, *The History of the Decline and Fall of the Roman Empire*, republished recently in many new editions. Its lasting value is more evident today when scholars and politicians are currently debating the pros and cons of the "New American Empire."

There has been renewed interest in the role of the barbarians in the process. Many historians are now willing to credit them with helping to establish the Middle Ages, viewing that era as emerging from Greco-Roman, Christian, and barbarian influences. Perhaps it's time to put the term "barbarians" to rest. For more information on the barbarians and their contributions, see Peter S. Wells, *The Barbarians Speak: How the Conquered Peoples Shaped Roman Europe* (Princeton University Press, 1999), and, Richard Fletcher, *The Barbarian Conversion: From Paganism to Christianity* (Henry Holt and Company, 1997).

On the Internet . . .

Justinian, Theodora, and Procopius

This site contains 150 links organized and described, including the complete *Secret History* of Procopius; biographies and other articles about Justinian and Theodora, Procopius, and Belisarius; art images; and general histories.

http://www.isidore-of-seville.com/justinian/

Lost King of the Maya

Site based on a 2001 PBS special, which contains a guided tour of important Maya sites, a historical account of their first discovery, a map of the Maya world, an exercise in reading Maya hieroglyphs, and a list of related resources.

http://www.pbs.org/wgbh/nova/maya/

The Crusades

This Crusades and Medieval information links Web site is a United Kingdom-based site that contains 18 links to a wealth of information about the Crusades.

http://www2.prestel.co.uk/church/chivalry/crusades.htm

High Medieval Europe

University Web site with an outline of the Middle Ages based on various themes, one of which is entitled "Medieval Universities and Intellectual Life." Makes use of links to other sites.

http://www2.sunysuffolk.edu/westn/highmed.html

Biographies of Notable Medieval and Renaissance Women

Contains biographical sketches of many notable women who lived during the Middle Ages and Renaissance periods. Each one provides valuable links to more information on each subject, as well as for the Renaissance in general.

http://womenshistory.about.com/od/medieval

Bushido: The Way of the Warrior

A site with brief but useful information on the samurai which include: origins, their creed, Bushido, and Web sites related to the subject.

http://mcel.pacificu.edu/as/students/bushido/bindex.html

PART 2

The Medieval/Renaissance Worlds

*I*n this section we find the world's civilizations building upon what the ancients created, struggling to survive in some cases and moving in new directions in other cases. In their personal lives, the exciting environment of the university, the demands of the Samurai code, we see individuals struggling to define themselves and their culture. Contact with Islam brought Europeans into a wider and more complex world. With the Renaissance, they also rediscovered their Greek and Roman roots.

- Did the Byzantine Empire Benefit from the Rule of Justinian and Theodora?
- Did Environmental Factors Cause the Collapse of Maya Civilization?
- Could the Crusades Be Considered a Christian Holy War?
- Does the Modern University Have Its Roots in the Islamic World?
- Did Women Benefit from the Renaissance?
- Was Zen Buddhism the Primary Shaper of the Samurai Warrior Code?

ISSUE 7

Did the Byzantine Empire Benefit from the Rule of Justinian and Theodora?

YES: Paolo Cesaretti, from *Theodora: Empress of Byzantium* (The Vendome Press, 2004)

NO: Procopius, from *Secret History,* trans. by Richard Atwater (P. Covici, 1927; Covici Friede, 1927; University of Michigan Press, 1961)

ISSUE SUMMARY

YES: Professor of Byzantine studies, Paolo Cesaretti, presents a balanced view of the accomplishments of Justinian and Theodora in the Byzantine Empire of the sixth century.

NO: Procopius, a contemporary of the Byzantine rulers, offers a "secret history" of their personal and administrative failings.

Accurate and reliable historical accounts depend on good sources. In this issue we confront the dilemma posed by an "insider's" account that was kept secret by its author and that contrasts sharply with published historical accounts by the same author. Which more accurately reflects reality—the open or the secret history of the Byzantine Empire, both written by Procopius?

The Roman Emperor Constantine had established an eastern capital on the strait of Bosporus, where Europe and Asia meet, in 330. Endowed with his name, Constantinople was a fortress city, built to repel attacks from land and sea. After the fall of Rome and the elevation of a Germanic ruler in 476, power shifted to the eastern capital, which had been built on the ancient Greek city of Byzantium. The Byzantine emperors claimed succession from their counterparts in ancient Rome, and their Christian empire had preserved both the brilliance of Greek culture and the administrative genius of the Romans.

Justinian, who had been groomed by his uncle Justin I, became emperor in 527. He codified the laws of ancient Rome, preserving principles of reason and justice. However, he did press Justin to amend the law forbidding a patrician to marry an actress, when he fell in love with Theodora, a former actress who would become the empress. Byzantine emperors claimed divine right of sovereignty, and the emperor had a quasi-priestly role in some religious services. Justinian and Theodora used the ancient Roman term, referring to themselves as Augusti (plural of Augustus), the absolute rulers of Byzantium.

Under the leadership of his able general Belisarius, Justinian reclaimed North Africa from the Vandals, part of southern Spain from the Visigoths, and Italy from the Ostrogoths. Procopius was advisor to Belisarius, accompanying the general on many military campaigns. His eight-volume *History of the Wars* is ambitious, adopting a sophisticated tone of impartiality and hinting at criticisms of the royal sovereigns. A later commentary *On the Buildings* was filled with praise for the emperor, as builder of magnificent sacred and secular edifices.

The *Secret History,* begun at the same time as his published works [the 550s], was intended by Procopius to be published after the death of Justinian. Unfortunately for Procopius, he pre-deceased his emperor. It purports to be the history of "what really happened," and he fears that disparities between this work and the public ones might cause future generations to "think me a writer of fiction." Both the Augusti are portrayed in the *Secret History* as ambitious, cruel, arrogant, and two-faced. He presents "evidence" that both were "fiends" in the literal sense of demonically driven. Little wonder then that he feared discovery of this work would merit him "a most horrible death."

Virtually all biographies of Justinian and Theodora, as well as histories of the Byzantine Empire of this period, have relied on this first-hand account, at least since 1623 when it was found in the Vatican Library and published for the first time. Professor Cesaretti quotes extensively from Procopius, although he offers a balanced portrayal of both Justinian and Theodora. And, Procopius is the source for Theodora's dramatic speech, during the Nika rebellion. As events unfold in the Hippodrome, where the Blue and Green factions contend in chariot races, imagine 100,000 people engrossed in, sometimes, 24 races in a single day, interspersed with wild animal acts. Theodora's father had been a bear trainer and her early life in the theatre was probably by necessity, to put food on the family table. As you read these two accounts, ask yourself whether it is possible to have an "unbiased" historical account.

YES

Paolo Cesaretti

Theodora: Empress of Byzantium

Like every great story, the events of the Nika rebellion have been told an infinite number of times; each retelling prompts new interpretations and debates. . . . The Nika rebellion actually sprung from the grass roots of society, and it was prompted not by nostalgia for the past but by present needs; as was always the case in Constantinople, the truth was a complex mosaic of elements.

Some dignitaries of the empire had already likened Justinian to a sea monster that sucked up water and money. Others criticized his policies regarding the many nomadic tribes that moved along the dangerous borders of the empire from the Danube to Arabia: he had purchased their nonbelligerence at too high a price, they said. Even Khosrow I, the new king of Persia, demanded gold before he would consider the possibility of peace along the eastern frontier. In addition, the emperor's imitation of God did not seem to be particularly welcome "in the high heavens." The tragic Antioch earthquake of 526 was followed by a second one in 528. In 530, yet another earthquake had shaken Antioch's historical rival, Laodikeia, one of the best ports of the Levant and the capital of the new province of Theodorias (recently established in honor of Theodora Augusta).

The two sovereigns had dug deep into the imperial coffers to help with post-earthquake reconstruction, displaying dedication and generosity, but their actions had not served to dispel concerns and suspicions aroused by the behavior of some of their closest collaborators. It was rumored, for example, that the jurist Tribonian, who supervised the great project of rewriting the body of laws and was quaestor of the sacred palace (a sort of minister of justice), "was always ready to sell justice for gain." The perception of judicial disarray enraged the masses, who were already bitter about John the Cappadocian's fiscal policies. Capping a swift series of promotions, John had become praetorian prefect of the East, the most influential of ministers. Justinian relied heavily on his skills, and for ten years, from 531 to 541, John exerted great power throughout the empire.

John the Cappadocian did not have a classical education, but he knew accounting very well. Justinian expected him to generate the income, or the savings, which he needed to pursue his "Great Idea" of renewal and restoration, and John met his expectations. He made sure that fiscal laws were obeyed. He supervised the landowners, the merchants, and the shopkeepers. Revenues were routed directly to him by his inspectors, instead of passing through the provincial élites, the curiae, as they once had. John the Cappadocian was pivotal in the process of centralization required by Justinian's plan. A manager with a sharp eye for cutting costs, John reduced and even eliminated part of the postal service, which is the essential glue of any polity. The post had been among the empire's traditional glories—one of the services that set the Roman civilized world "of the thousand cities" apart from the "barbarian" no-man's-lands.

. . . The public post not only guaranteed speedy communications, but also affected the supply of all kinds of raw materials and staples. The results of its elimination were disastrous for rural industry, a productive base that contributed food and tax revenue to the empire. The owners of large estates, who had been accustomed to "sell[ing] their excess crops," now saw "their crops rotting on their hands and going to waste." The small landowners bore the brunt of the new situation, since they supplied the city markets. Unable to afford the cost of private transportation, the farmers (both men and women) trudged along the roads of the empire carrying their crops on their backs. . . . Overcome by fatigue, many lay down and died on the road. Others abandoned their crops and moved to the city, trusting in some form of Providence, whether divine or imperial.

When the food supply is irregular, life gets harder in a capital overcrowded with mouths to feed. Besides, hungry people talk. . . . And so before long John the Cappadocian was being blamed on moral and Christian grounds, instead of being judged simply by bureaucratic or political criteria. It was rumored that he was an evil man who kept Roman citizens in secret chambers, forcing them to pay taxes he claimed were overdue by threatening them with the same humiliating torture inflicted on slaves or highway robbers. All this, to channel money into Justinian's coffers. Or was it for personal gain?—some swore that John embezzled most of the taxes that the citizens believed they were contributing to the welfare of the empire.

The slanderous rumors intensified: John was getting rich; John was a drunk; John had an infamous retinue of jesters and prostitutes both male and female; he was a heathen who pretended to say Christian prayers while actually reciting magical pagan formulas. The rumors and accusations were not so different from those that once circulated about Theodora. In time, John and the empress would grow to be enemies, but they were both victims (for different reasons) of hostile preconceptions among those who considered themselves decent and upright citizens.

Because the factions were so active in the Hippodrome, that place became a natural sounding board for economic and political tensions. After the violent urban riots of 523–24, after Justinian's arbitrary protection of the Blue radical fringe, the Greens had even chanted:

> Would that Sabbatius [Justinian's father] had never been born! That he might not have a murderer [Justinian] for a son!

The year 532 began with new trouble between the Blues and the Greens. Now focused on military issues in the west, Justinian ordered that the situation be brought under control with the same measures he had used in 524 against *his* Blues; such measures were now to be applied impartially to the extremists of both factions. Eudaemon, the city prefect, ordered the militia to arrest anyone engaged in violence, no matter what faction they belonged to. The Greens saw this as a continuation of the unjustified persecution of their group, while the Blues felt betrayed by their longtime patron, especially when they heard that the investigations and arrests were culminating in death sentences for members of *both* factions. Four rebel leaders, both Green and Blue, were sentenced to be hanged.

The scaffold where the sentences were carried out was in Sykae (Galata), beyond the Golden Horn, in a square near one of the many monasteries where religious men tried to merge heavenly and earthly life through prayer and exercise, without meddling in politics. Tensions were running high, and the hangman's hand was unsteady: two of the prisoners, one Blue and one Green, survived the first attempt. The noose was wound more tightly, but the two men fell from the scaffold still alive. Shouting, the public proclaimed it a miracle, a sign of God's favor.

With the help of the nearby monks, the two prisoners were ferried over to the city and brought to a church that had the right of asylum. Eudaemon stationed a circle of militiamen around the edifice, while the crowd demanded freedom for the two men who had been saved by the hand of God. It was Saturday, January 10, 532.

A few days later, Tuesday, January 13, was a day for the emperor to preside over chariot races at the Hippodrome. Both factions took the floor: the spokesman for the Greens talked with devout respect, but the Blues' spokesman had a more colloquial tone. They both asked for pardons, but Justinian rejected their pleas with the customary arrogance of the potentate who receives a supplication. He may have wanted to show how firm he was, but his stubbornness seemed unjustified and arrogant more than authoritative.

After twenty-two chariot races, the short winter day was coming to a close. It was then that an unheard-of, new shout rose from the Hippodrome crowd:

Long live the benevolent Greens and Blues!

It was shocking to hear the two names pronounced together: never before had one faction recognized the other's "benevolence" or humanity (*philanthropia*). Indeed, this virtue had always been considered a uniquely imperial prerogative. So here was a brand-new situation: the established power no longer appeared to be completely sacred.

For their part, the emperors of the past had always set the factions against each other so as to avoid potentially threatening coalitions. They simply applied the divide-and-conquer strategy learned from that ancient Roman culture whose glory Justinian sought to renew. But now events were conspiring against him. His great vision of the Mediterranean scenario had neglected some essential elements of the urban scene right under his nose. Meanwhile, the Greens and Blues were setting aside their reciprocal hostility and turning jointly against the palace. Maybe it was good medicine for healing the "disease of the soul" that affected them.

Justinian's ears ("donkey ears," according to his critics) heard the acclamation that was being shouted over and over, louder and louder. It rose like thunder, shouted by tens of thousands of voices. The emperor, the "Chosen One," could not bear it. He left the Kathisma and retreated to the sacred palace, the glorious public institution that was also his personal haven.

Now a new shout was heard in the Hippodrome, terrifying in its brevity:

Nika! Nika! Nika!

"May you win! May you win! May you win!" *Nika* was the Greek version of the Latin *Tu vincas*, the cheer from the crowds that usually greeted the Augustus in his role as military chief. The crowd's change of language signaled a change in meaning. The phrase no longer exhorted the emperor to prevail over an enemy; now one faction was exhorting the other, one citizen wishing another, "may *you* be victorious!" Thus, the emperor was no longer "benevolent" and "humane" or "victorious." Strengthened by its size and its everyday language, the crowd had seized those prerogatives for itself, without any partisan distinctions. Being able to speak out meant being able to act.

The emperor did not lower himself to a verbal confrontation, for it would have meant recognizing the opposing party. Just as Asterius gave no answer when the little girls pleaded with him in the Kynêgion years before, the prefect Eudaemon, who was in charge of public order, gave no answer to the crowds that flocked to his palace to hear the fate of the two men who had survived the hanging. His refusal was the legendary straw that broke the camel's back. The crowd went on a rampage: it killed soldiers and officers, set fire to the prefecture, and threw open the jail doors. The factions joined against one common enemy, one oppressor: Eudaemon. (Ironically, the Greek root of his name refers to happiness.)

Then the crowd attacked the doors of the sacred palace. The elegant and decorative guards were not warriors: they put up no opposition. The crowd set fire to the palace vestibule (the Chalkê), to the senate building, and to the basilica of the Holy wisdom (Hagia Sophia). These were some of the most distinctive building of Constantine's city: the palatial symbol of power; the home of the senate that had raised up the second Rome to equal the first; and the church that kept the city under God's protection were all lost in a single night of fire. . . .

On Sunday, January 18, the emperor made an appearance in the imperial box at the Hippodrome. In his hands he reportedly carried the Gospel, and in his mind must have been two political, personal precedents. The first was from the time of the civilian uprising against Anastasius. In response to his critics, Anastasius had provocatively appeared in public without the imperial crown and invited the arena to choose a new monarch. Taken by surprise, the crowd did nothing but reconfirm his position and their trust in him. The second precedent was from Easter 527, when for the first time Justinian had blessed the crowd as the Augustus.

As he had done on that occasion, he now assumed a priestly role. Then he made himself into a sacrificial lamb, saying, "I forgive you the offense you have committed against me. I shall order no arrests as long as calm returns. You are not to blame for what happened. I am, for my sins." . . . [T]he Christian reference to his sins backfired, for the crowd grasped his weakness. . . . The jeering grew, and the emperor began descending the stairs of the Kathisma.

The doors closed behind him, hiding him again in the protective shell of his palace. Instead of a possible arbiter and moderator in the dispute between ministers and factions, he had become an enemy, the greatest enemy. . . .

．．０．．

The right gesture might be taken as a sign, so Justinian's secret council considered all kinds of possible actions. A "true Roman male" in ancient times—even someone as abominable as Nero—would have killed himself to save his honor, but suicide was an unsuitable choice for a Christian. Flight seemed to be the only option left. The southern coast of the Black Sea (or Pontos Euxeinos) offered a safe haven, with lands and palaces still faithful to the crown. This would be a good temporary solution, a fine place from which to later recapture the city. But Justinian knew his ancient history, and he knew that such a solution was rarely successful.

Like a great ship, the *restitutio* seemed to have run aground even before setting sail; the restoration seemed to be sunk, and it looked as if the Augusti would never reach their glorious destination. But a real boat was at the palace quay, waiting to take the sovereigns on a far shorter crossing, to safety.

At this point—according to Procopius, who probably got an eyewitness account from Belisarius—Theodora stepped in. Her speech to the emperor's secret council is the longest one of hers ever recorded, and while her biographer may have polished it and added erudite allusions to suit his rhetorical purpose, it remains unique. It may not reflect the actual form of speech, but it testifies to Theodora's intentions and her logical argument. She took the floor before the highest dignitaries of the empire and said:

> As to the belief that a woman ought not to be daring among men or to assert herself boldly among those who are holding back from fear, I consider that the present crisis most certainly does not permit us to discuss whether the matter should be regarded in this or in some other way.
>
> For in the case of those whose interests have come into the greatest danger nothing else seems best except to settle the issue immediately before them in the best possible way.
>
> My opinion then is that the present time, above all others, is inopportune for flight, even though it bring safety.
>
> For while it is impossible for a man who has seen the light not also to die, for one who has been an emperor it is unendurable to be a fugitive. May I never be separated from this purple, and may I not live that day on which those who meet me shall not address me as mistress.
>
> If, now, it is your wish to save yourself, O Emperor, there is no difficulty. For we have much money, and there is the sea, here the boats. However, consider whether it will not come about after you have been saved that you would gladly exchange that safety for death.
>
> For as for myself, I approve a certain ancient saying that royalty is a good burial-shroud.

She was not speaking in abstractions, in general statements for the whole group; she spoke to Justinian, her preferred interlocutor. She looked only into the eyes of God's "Chosen One." The other characters had suddenly fallen to the back of the stage; they were mere extras, and the close-up was now on the two rulers.

They were separated from the group, and Theodora—in a move worthy of an Attic tragedy—separated her destiny from that of the emperor. The emperor could save himself if he chose: there was no dearth of money, the sea was open, the ships were ready to welcome whoever wanted to flee. But Theodora saw flight not as salvation but as a "second death," in the words of the Gospel—a fate even worse than death.

She was accustomed to defying the world's customs and conventions: she would not run. Should Justinian choose to retreat, she would not share his fate; he would prove himself unworthy of the throne. In spite of his ego, his studies of antiquity, even his concept of messianic power, he might choose to flee, doing something that no Roman emperor had ever considered suitable or possible. *She* would remain faithful to her purple. She would carry on the traditions of antiquity, in the present, in her deeds—not just in words, not just in plans for the future. She would do so by resisting, even dying, because there was no life without the purple cloak of power. To avoid being separated from her purple, Theodora was saying, she was even willing to lose Justinian and marry death instead, to choose the purple over the man who had granted it to her.

≈◉≈

Belisarius entered the Hippodrome from the western gate, which had direct access to the Blues's section; Mundus and his men used the entrance ominously called the "Deadman's Gate." The large crowd assembled in the huge arena was armed with only primitive weapons and it could not resist the two select corps of military professionals. A ferocious slaughter ensued; this was perhaps the bloodiest Sunday of the first Christian millennium.

The palace guard, which had been hesitating between the rebels and the legitimate ruler, opened the doors of the imperial gallery and easily captured the frightened Hypatius and his followers, including his brother Pompeius. There was no resistance.

The uprising was defined as a crime of high treason, which was punished by beheading. The rebels were immediately led before the emperor. Hypatius told Justinian that he had given him proof in writing of his fealty.

"Your message never reached us," was the answer.

He added that he had been forced to act under duress.

"But you did not have to wait such a long time to show your loyalty to the emperor."

At this point Hypatius began begging for his life.

Since the two men knew each other well, the emperor was inclined to spare Hypatius in a generous act of clemency. Justinian may have thought about all the Christian blood had already been shed that day; he may have considered the lofty concept of "benevolence" that the rebels had wanted to grab away from the emperor. And, of course, he may have recalled the recent blame over his treatment of Vitalian. He was not eager to hear the same accusations again in the future.

Just as in the previous council, when debating between resistance and fight, the emperor's thinking was worlds away from the blunt realism of the daughter of the Hippodrome. She knew the arena habitat all too well. Theodora knew that a wounded beast has to be killed immediately.

Letting the two brothers live would be seen as proof of weakness, she argued; it would undermine the continuity of power, dim the splendor of the emperor's majesty, and rekindle the conspiracies. A few hours earlier, the emperor had appeared before the rebels with the Gospels in his hand–and what had been the result? Theodora insisted that the law be applied. She disregarded her family ties to Hypatius and Pompeius (through her daughter, who had married into the house of Anastasius). Theodora put aside her private life and reacted to public events. And in one stroke she implicitly shifted Justinian's personal, private position: from that moment on, he had to acknowledge that *he* owed his purple to *her*.

⚜

Like a meridian, Easter Day, 542, marked fifteen years of Justinian and Theodora's reign. They must have reviewed a list of their accomplishments and of the other initiatives still in the planning stage or already under construction, from the most remote borders of the empire to the heart of Constantinople. After the destruction wrought by the Nika rebellion, they had completely rebuilt Constantinople in just ten years, transforming it from a city of late antiquity into an imperial capital. A jewel of the Byzantine age, it was to be admired by medieval visitors from both West and East (the Slavs called it Tsargrad), raided by invaders in the second millennium (the Crusaders first, then the Ottoman Turks), and celebrated by poets such as W. B. Yeats. All of this made Constantinople a universal city of the soul. None of this would have transpired without Theodora's unforgettable speech on that bloody Sunday in 532, in the midst of the raging rebellion.

The emperors' architectural and urban planning policy did not aim to revive the art of previous centuries. Constantine's and Theodosius's achievements inspired Justinian's politics, but their art and architecture did not inspire his. The Augusti leaned toward the new and the grandiose, fusing classical elements with oriental seduction, three-dimensional naturalism with geometric abstraction, urban tradition with Christian touches; they even indulged in personal whims. They rediscovered the daring, insouciant, light-hearted quality that had blessed their early years together, the boldness of those intricate laws that seemed to be written for everyone but were really conceived only for the two of them. They were inimitable. There were no other comparable patrons of art and architecture until the Renaissance.

After the Nika—which was a political phenomenon that impacted the urban fabric—Justinian and Theodora focused on secular architecture, starting with a redefinition of the facade of power: the facade of the palace. They totally redesigned the vestibule, the Chalkê or "bronze house" (a little building with a golden bronze roof). From the palace, the Chalkê opened onto the imperial square (the Augustaeum), with access to the basilica of the Holy Wisdom—the celebrated Hagia Sophia. The Chalkê was the visual threshold of power, its projection upon the city. After the fires of the rebellion, Justinian and Theodora set out to make the new incarnation of the Chalkê more splendid and precious. So the interior of the new dome was decorated with mosaics celebrating Belisarius's victories over the Vandals and the Goths. Nearby were the baths of Zeuxippus and the Senate palace; they were also destroyed in the flames of 532. Now they were rebuilt "in more beautiful form" than before.

But the emperor and empress did not stop here. They had inherited a complex metropolis with an urban administration and police force of more than a thousand men. This required premises for the supply and management of food staples and the channeling of water through aqueducts that still astonish us fifteen hundred years later. Like the ancient provincial benefactors of the earliest pagan tradition (the "Euergeti"), the two emperors undertook other initiatives "for the welfare of their subjects." Some, like the hospitals and almshouses, were Christian institutions; but the porticoed streets, roads, and cisterns were secular public works that stand to this day as masterpieces of ancient architecture (the Basilike Cistern is one shining example). The rulers who commissioned them, and the skilled engineers and architects, both knew how to "enhance the monumental significance even of those buildings that had a purely functional purpose." Edward Gibbon was wrong to disparage this period: it was not a time dominated simply "by the darkest shadows of shame." . . .

The Augusti intended the church of the Holy Apostles to be their final resting place; they poured their deepest feelings into the church of Saints Sergius and Bacchus; but their pride and joy—especially the emperor's—was the Holy Wisdom. Fifteen hundred years after it was built, after acting as a mosque and then a museum, it is still among the most famous and admired buildings in the world—though, paradoxically, it is famous for what it was *not* meant to be: an architectural space, a temple of light, the final wonder of Christian antiquity.

Medieval visitors might have come closest to the spirit of the place since they recognized Constantinople as the Mother of all cities. Admiring the Holy Wisdom, they found renewed faith in Paradise; they were surrounded by objects, colors, visions, and scents (lost to us now) that they perceived as promises and prefigurations. If the city rebuilt by the emperor and the empress in the light of Christianity was a sacred shell, then the Holy Wisdom was its pearl. It was the most visible, most flaunted treasure of Justinian and Theodora.

The two rulers used the Holy Wisdom to express their power fully. They were not building but *re*building a city that had risen against them. They wanted the result to be a total redemption, a gesture of great daring that would fully display their personal and institutional arrogance. Perhaps because of this, there is no great church less mystical than the Holy Wisdom. It was not meant to be the church of a monastic order or a district or a guild, nor was it built by an individual suppliant. It was the basilica where the emperor of Constantinople, the thirteenth apostle, the Viceroy of Christ on Earth, the highest, noblest man of all, attended sacred ceremonies. In the symmetrical, inverted projection of roles between imperial Constantinople and papal Rome, the only worthy comparison is the basilica of Saint Peter's at the time of the universalist popes of the Renaissance.

Procopius of Caesarea: The Secret History

Character and Appearance of Justinian

As soon as he took over the rule from his uncle, his measure was to spend the public money without restraint, now that he had control of it. He gave much of it to the Huns who, from time to time, entered the state; and in consequence the Roman provinces were subject to constant incursions, for these barbarians, having once tasted Roman wealth, never forgot the road that led to it. And he threw much money into the sea in the form of moles, as if to master the eternal roaring of the breakers. For he jealously hurled stone breakwaters far out from the mainland against the onset of the sea, as if by the power of wealth he could outmatch the might of ocean.

He gathered to himself the private estates of Roman citizens from all over the Empire: some by accusing their possessors of crimes of which they were innocent, others by juggling their owners' words into the semblance of a gift to him of their property. And many, caught in the act of murder and other crimes, turned their possessions over to him and thus escaped the penalty for their sins.

Others, fraudulently disputing title to lands happening to adjoin their own, when they saw they had no chance of getting the best of the argument, with the law against them, gave him their equity in the claim so as to be released from court. Thus, by a gesture that cost him nothing, they gained his favor and were able illegally to get the better of their opponents.

I think this is as good a time as any to describe the personal appearance of the man. Now in physique he was neither tall nor short, but of average height; not thin, but moderately plump; his face was round, and not bad looking, for he had good color, even when he fasted for two days. To make a long description short, he much resembled Domitian, Vespasian's son. He was the one whom the Romans so hated that even tearing him into pieces did not satisfy their wrath against him. . . .

Now such was Justinian in appearance; but his character was something I could not fully describe. For he was at once villainous and amenable; as people say colloquially, a moron. He was never truthful with anyone, but always guileful in what he said and did, yet easily hoodwinked by any who wanted to deceive him. His nature was an unnatural mixture of folly and wickedness.

From SECRET HISTORY, 1927. Chicago: Covici, 1927; reprinted University of Michigan Press, 1961.

What in olden times a peripatetic philosopher said was also true of him, that opposite qualities combine in a man as in the mixing of colors. I will try to portray him, however, insofar as I can fathom his complexity.

This Emperor, then, was deceitful, devious, false, hypocritical, two-faced, cruel, skilled in dissembling his thought, never moved to tears by either joy or pain, though he could summon them artfully at will when the occasion demanded, a liar always, not only offhand, but in writing, and when he swore sacred oaths to his subjects in their very hearing. Then he would immediately break his agreements and pledges, like the vilest of slaves, whom indeed only the fear of torture drives to confess their perjury. A faithless friend, he was a treacherous enemy, insane for murder and plunder, quarrelsome and revolutionary, easily led to anything evil, but never willing to listen to good counsel, quick to plan mischief and carry it out, but finding even the hearing of anything good distasteful to his ears.

How could anyone put Justinian's ways into words? These and many even worse vices were disclosed in him as in no other mortal nature seemed to have taken the wickedness of all other men combined and planted it in this man's soul. And besides this, he was too prone to listen to accusations; and too quick to punish. For he decided such cases without full examination, naming the punishment when he had heard only the accuser's side of the matter. Without hesitation he wrote decrees for the plundering of countries, sacking of cities, and slavery of whole nations, for no cause whatever. So that if one wished to take all the calamities which had befallen the Romans before this time and weigh them against his crimes, I think it would be found that more men had been murdered by this single man than in all previous history.

He had no scruples about appropriating other people's property, and did not even think any excuse necessary, legal or illegal, for confiscating what did not belong to him. And when it was his, he was more than ready to squander it in insane display, or give it as an unnecessary bribe to the barbarians. In short, he neither held on to any money himself nor let anyone else keep any: as if his reason were not avarice, but jealousy of those who had riches. Driving all wealth from the country of the Romans in this manner, he became the cause of universal poverty.

Now this was the character of Justinian, so far as I can portray it.

How Theodora, Most Depraved of All Courtesans, Won His Love

He took a wife: and in what manner she was born and bred, and, wedded to this man, tore up the Roman Empire by the very roots, I shall now relate.

Acacius was the keeper of wild beasts used in the amphitheater in Constantinople; he belonged to the Green faction and was nicknamed the Bearkeeper. This man, during the rule of Anastasius, fell sick and died, leaving three daughters named Comito, Theodora and Anastasia: of whom the eldest was not yet seven years old. His widow took a second husband, who with her undertook to keep up Acacius's family and profession. But Asterius, the dancing master of the Greens, on being bribed by another removed this office from them and assigned it to the man who gave him the money. For the dancing masters had the power of distributing such positions as they wished.

When this woman saw the populace assembled in the amphitheater, she placed laurel wreaths on her daughters' heads and in their hands, and sent them out to sit on the ground in the attitude of suppliants. The Greens eyed this mute appeal with indifference; but the Blues were moved to bestow on the children an equal office, since their own animal-keeper had just died.

When these children reached the age of girlhood, their mother put them on the local stage, for they were fair to look upon. . . .

. . . Now Theodora was still too young to know the normal relation of man with maid, but consented to the unnatural violence of villainous slaves who, following their masters to the theater, employed their leisure in this infamous manner. And for some time in a brothel she suffered such misuse.

But as soon as she arrived at the age of youth, and was now ready for the world, her mother put her on the stage. Forthwith, she became a courtesan, and such as the ancient Greeks used to call a common one, at that: for she was not a flute or harp player, nor was she even trained to dance, but only gave her youth to anyone she met, in utter abandonment. Her general favors included, of course, the actors in the theater; and in their productions she took part in the low comedy scenes. For she was very funny and a good mimic, and immediately became popular in this art. There was no shame in the girl, and no one ever saw her dismayed: no role was too scandalous for her to accept without a blush. . . .

Thus was this woman born and bred, and her name was a byword beyond that of other common wenches on the tongues of all men.

But when she came back to Constantinople, Justinian fell violently in love with her. At first he kept her only as a mistress, though he raised her to patrician rank. Through him Theodora was able immediately to acquire an unholy power and exceedingly great riches. She seemed to him the sweetest thing in the world, and like all lovers, he desired to please his charmer with every possible favor and requite her with all his wealth. The extravagance added fuel to the flames of passion. With her now to help spend his money he plundered the people more than ever, not only in the capital, but throughout the Roman Empire. As both of them had for a long time been of the Blue party, they gave this faction almost complete control of the affairs of state. . . .

How Justinian Created a New Law Permitting Him to Marry a Courtesan

Now as long as the former Empress was alive, Justinian was unable to find a way to make Theodora his wedded wife. In this one matter she opposed him as in nothing else. . . . But finally her death removed this obstacle to Justinian's desire.

Justin, doting and utterly senile, was now the laughing stock of his subjects . . . but Justinian they all served with considerable awe. His hand was in everything, and his passion for turmoil created universal consternation.

It was then that he undertook to complete his marriage with Theodora. But as it was impossible for a man of senatorial rank to make a courtesan his wife, this being forbidden by ancient law, he made the Emperor nullify this ordinance by creating a new one, permitting him to wed Theodora, and consequently making it possible for anyone else to marry a courtesan. Immediately after this he seized the power of the Emperor, veiling his usurpation with a transparent pretext: for he was proclaimed colleague of his uncle as Emperor of the Romans by the questionable legality of an election inspired by terror.

So Justinian and Theodora ascended the imperial throne three days before Easter, a time, indeed, when even making visits or greeting one's friends is forbidden. And not many days later Justin died of an illness, after a reign of nine years. Justinian was now sole monarch, together, of course, with Theodora.

Thus it was that Theodora, though born and brought up as I have related, rose to royal dignity over all obstacles. For no thought of shame came to Justinian in marrying her, though he might have taken his pick of the noblest born, most highly educated, most modest, carefully nurtured, virtuous and beautiful virgins of all the ladies in the whole Roman Empire: a maiden, as they say, with upstanding breasts. Instead, he preferred to make his own what had been common to all men, alike, careless of all her revealed history, took in wedlock a woman who was not only guilty of every other contamination but boasted of her many abortions.

I need hardly mention any other proof of the character of this man: for all the perversity of his soul was completely displayed in this union; which alone was ample interpreter, witness, and historian of his shamelessness. For when a man once disregards the disgrace of his actions and is willing to brave the contempt of society, no path of lawlessness is thereafter taboo to him; but with unflinching countenance he advances, easily and without a scruple, to acts of the deepest infamy.

However, not a single member of even the Senate, seeing this disgrace befalling the State, dared to complain or forbid the event; but all of them bowed down before her as if she were a goddess. Nor was there a priest who showed any resentment, but all hastened to greet her as Highness. And the populace who had seen her before on the stage, directly raised its hands to proclaim itself her slave in fact and in name. Nor did any soldier grumble at being ordered to risk the perils of war for the benefit of Theodora: nor was there any man on earth who ventured to oppose her.

Confronted with this disgrace, they all yielded, I suppose, to necessity, for it was as if Fate were giving proof of its power to control mortal affairs as malignantly as it pleases: showing that its decrees need not always be according to reason or human propriety. Thus does Destiny sometimes raise mortals suddenly to lofty heights in defiance of reason, in challenge to all outcries of injustice; but admits no obstacle, urging on his favorites to the appointed goal without let or hindrance. But as this is the will of God, so let it befall and be written.

Now Theodora was fair of face and of a very graceful, though small, person; her complexion was moderately colorful, if somewhat pale; and her eyes were dazzling and vivacious. All eternity would not be long enough to allow one to tell her escapades while she was on the stage, but the few details I have mentioned above should be sufficient to demonstrate the woman's character to future generations.

What she and her husband did together must now be briefly described: for neither did anything without the consent of the other. For some time it was generally supposed they were totally different in mind and action; but later it was revealed that their apparent disagreement had been arranged so that their subjects might not unanimously revolt against them, but instead be divided in opinion.

Thus they split the Christians into two parties, each pretending to take the part of one side, thus confusing both, as I shall soon show; and then they ruined both political factions. Theodora feigned to support the Blues with all her power, encouraging them to take the offensive against the opposing party and perform the most outrageous deeds of violence; while Justinian, affecting to be vexed and secretly jealous of her, also pretended he could not openly oppose her orders. And thus they gave the impression often that they were acting in opposition. Then he would rule that the Blues must be punished for their crimes, and she would angrily complain that against her will she was defeated by her husband. However, the Blue partisans, as I have said, seemed cautious, for they did not violate their neighbors as much as they might have done.

And in legal disputes each of the two would pretend to favor one of the litigants, and compel the man with the worse case to win: and so they robbed both disputants of most of the property at issue.

In the same way, the Emperor, taking many persons into his intimacy, gave them offices by power of which they could defraud the State to the limits of their ambition. And as soon as they had collected enough plunder, they would fall out of favor with Theodora, and straightway be ruined. At first he would affect great sympathy in their behalf, but soon he would somehow lose his confidence in them, and an air of doubt would darken his zeal in their behalf. Then Theodora would use them shamefully, while he, unconscious as it were of what was being done to them, confiscated their properties and boldly enjoyed their wealth. By such well-planned hypocrisies they confused the public and, pretending to be at variance with each other, were able to establish a firm and mutual tyranny.

How the Defender of the Faith Ruined His Subjects

As soon as Justinian came into power he turned everything upside down. Whatever had been before by law, he now introduced into the government, while he revoked all established customs: as if he had been given the robes of an Emperor on the condition he would turn everything topsy-turvy. Existing offices he abolished, and invented new ones for the management of public affairs. He did the same thing to the laws and to the regulations of the army; and his reason was not any improvement of justice or any advantage, but simply that everything might be new and named after himself. And whatever was beyond his power to abolish, he renamed after himself anyway.

Of the plundering of property or the murder of men, no weariness ever overtook him. As soon as he had looted all the houses of the wealthy, he looked around for others; meanwhile throwing away the spoils of his previous robberies in subsidies to barbarians or senseless building extravagances. And when he had ruined perhaps myriads in this mad looting, he immediately sat down to plan how he could do likewise to others in even greater number.

As the Romans were now at peace with all the world and he had no other means of satisfying his lust for slaughter, he set the barbarians all to fighting each other. And for no reason at all he sent for the Hun chieftains, and with idiotic magnanimity gave them large sums of money, alleging he did this to secure their friendship. This, as I have said, he had also done in Justin's time. These Huns, as soon as they had got this money, sent it together with their soldiers to others of their chieftains, with the word to make inroads into the land of the Emperor: so that they might collect further tribute from him, to buy them off in a second peace. Thus the Huns enslaved the Roman Empire, and were paid by the Emperor to keep on doing it.

This encouraged still others of them to rob the poor Romans; and after their pillaging, they too were further rewarded by the gracious Emperor. In this way all the Huns, for when it was not one tribe of them it was another, continuously overran and laid waste the Empire. For the barbarians were led by many different chieftains, and the war, thanks to Justinian's senseless generosity, was thus endlessly protracted. Consequently no place, mountain or cave, or any other spot in Roman territory, during this time remained uninjured; and many regions were pillaged more than five times. . . .

Proving That Justinian and Theodora Were Actually Fiends in Human Form

Now the wealth of those in Constantinople and each other city who were considered second in prosperity only to members of the Senate was brutally confiscated, in the ways I have described, by Justinian and Theodora. But how they were able to rob even the Senate of all its property I shall now reveal.

There was in Constantinople a man by the name of Zeno, grandson of that Anthamius who had formerly been Emperor of the West. This man they appointed, with malice aforethought, Governor of Egypt, and commanded his immediate departure. But he delayed his voyage long enough to load his ship with his most valuable effects; for he had a countless amount of silver and gold plate inlaid with pearls, emeralds and other such precious stones. Whereupon they bribed some of his most trusted servants to remove these valuables from the ship as fast as they could carry them, set fire to the interior of the vessel, and inform Zeno that his ship had burst into flames of spontaneous combustion, with the loss of all his property. Later, when Zeno died suddenly, they took possession of his estate immediately as his legal heirs; for they produced a will which, it is whispered, he did not really make.

In the same manner they made themselves heirs of Tatian, Demosthenes, and Hilara, who were foremost in the Roman Senate. And others' estates they obtained by counterfeited letters instead of wills. . . .

I could hardly catalogue all the other people whose estates these two chose to inherit. However, up to the time when the insurrection named Nika took place, they seized rich men's properties one at a time; but when that happened, as I have told elsewhere, they sequestrated at one swoop the estates of nearly all the members of the Senate. On everything movable and on the fairest of the lands they laid their hands and kept what they wanted; but whatever was unproductive of more than the bitter and heavy taxes, they gave back to the previous owners with a philanthropic gesture. Consequently these unfortunates, oppressed by the tax collectors and eaten up by the never-ceasing interest on their debts, found life a burden compared to which death were preferable.

Wherefore to me, and many others of us, these two seemed not to be human beings, but veritable demons, and what the poets call vampires: who laid their heads together to see how they could most easily and quickly destroy the race and deeds of men; and assuming human bodies, became man-demons, and so convulsed the world. And one could find evidence of this in many things, but especially in the superhuman power with which they worked their will.

For when one examines closely, there is a clear difference between what is human and what is supernatural. There have been many enough men, during the whole course of history, who by chance or by nature have inspired great fear, ruining cities or countries or whatever else fell into their power; but to destroy all men and bring calamity on the whole inhabited earth remained for these two to accomplish, whom Fate aided in their schemes of corrupting all mankind. For by earthquakes, pestilences, and floods of river waters at this time came further ruin, as I shall presently show. Thus not by human, but by some other kind of power they accomplished their dreadful designs. . . .

Deceptive Affability and Piety of a Tyrant

Justinian, while otherwise of such character as I have shown, did make himself easy of access and affable to his visitors; nobody of all those who sought audience with him was ever denied: even those who confronted him improperly or noisily never made him angry. On the other hand, he never blushed at the murders he committed. Thus he never revealed a sign of wrath or irritation at any offender, but with a gentle countenance and unruffled brow gave the order to destroy myriads of innocent men, to sack cities, to confiscate any amount of properties.

One would think from this manner that the man had the mind of a lamb. If, however, anyone tried to propitiate him and in suppliance beg him to forgive his victims, he would grin like a wild beast, and woe betide those who saw his teeth thus bared!

The priests he permitted fearlessly to outrage their neighbors, and even took sympathetic pleasure in their robberies, fancying he was thus sharing their divine piety when he judged such cases, he thought he was doing the holy thing when he gave the decision to the priest and let him go free with his ill-gotten booty: justice, in his mind, meant the priests' getting the better of their opponents. When he himself thus illegally got possession of estates of people alive or dead, he would straightway make them over to one of the churches, gilding his violence with the color of piety—and so that his victims could not possibly get their property back. Furthermore he committed an inconceivable number of murders for the same cause: for in his zeal to gather all men into one Christian doctrine, he recklessly killed all who dissented, and this too he did in the name of piety. For he did not call it homicide, when those who perished happened to be of a belief that was different from his own.

So quenchless was his thirst for human blood; and with his wife, intent on this end, he neglected no possible excuse for slaughter. For these two were almost twins in their desires, though they pretended to differ: they were both scoundrels, however they affected to oppose each other, and thus destroyed their subjects. The man was lighter in character than a cloud of dust, and could be led to do anything any man wished him to do, so long as the matter did not require philanthropy or generosity. Flattery he swallowed whole, and his courtiers had no difficulty in persuading him that he was destined to rise as high as the sun and walk upon the clouds. . . .

There remained, while he ruled the Romans, no sure faith in God, no hope in religion, no defense in law, no security in business, no trust in a contract. When his officials were given any affair to handle for him, if they killed many of their victims and robbed the rest, they were looked upon by the Emperor with high favor, and given honorable mention for carrying out so perfectly his instructions. But if they showed any mercy and then returned to him, he frowned and was thenceforth their enemy.

Despising their qualms as old-fashioned, he called them no more to his service. Consequently many were eager to show him how wicked they were, even when they were really nothing of the sort. He made frequent promises, guaranteed with a sworn oath or by a written confirmation; and then purposely forgot them directly, thinking this summary negligence added to his importance. And Justinian acted thus not only to his subjects, but to many of the enemy, as I have already said.

He was untiring; and hardly slept at all, generally speaking; he had no appetite for food or drink, but picking up a morsel with the tips of his fingers, tasted it and left the table, as if eating were a duty imposed upon him by nature and of no more interest than a courier takes in delivering a letter. Indeed, he would often go without food for two days and nights, especially when the time before the festival called Easter enjoins such fasting. Then, as I have said, he often went without food for two days, living only on a little water and a few wild herbs, sleeping perhaps a single hour, and then spending the rest of the time walking up and down.

If, mark you, he had spent these periods in good works, matters might have been considerably alleviated. Instead, he devoted the full strength of his nature to the ruin of the Romans, and succeeded in razing the state to its foundation. For his constant wakefulness, his privations and his labors were undergone for no other reason than to contrive each day ever more exaggerated calamities for his people. For he was, as I said, unusually keen at inventing and quick at accomplishing unholy acts, so that even the good in him transpired to be answerable for the downfall of his subjects.

POSTSCRIPT

Did the Byzantine Empire Benefit from the Rule of Justinian and Theodora?

Whatever else it might be, the rule of Justinian and Theodora is also a love story. From her humble and unsavory beginnings, Theodora rose to become the partner of her husband Justinian, during one of the most interesting chapters in the history of the Byzantine Empire. Procopius's *Secret History* is available in English translation on the Internet, as are his published works on the wars and buildings. All were written after Theodora's death in 548.

Even to Procopius's jaundiced eye, she was beautiful and clever. When Belisarius took back Italy, a western capital was established at Ravenna, in northeastern Italy. In the church of San Vitale, built during the sixth century, mosaics of Justinian and his entourage cover the left wall of the sanctuary, while mosaics of Theodora and her attendants cover the right. Most histories of Western art will have photos of these magnificent purple, green, and gold portraits, created from drawings the royal couple posed for in Constantinople.

In addition to the excellent biography of Theodora that forms the "yes" election, see also James Allan Evans, *The Emperor Justinian and the Byzantine Empire* (Greenwood Press, 2005) and *The Empress Theodora: Partner of Justinian* (University of Texas Press, 2002). On the magnificent structures, especially the churches of Hagia Sophia [Holy Wisdom], the Basilica of the Holy Apostles, and the church of Saints Sergius and Bacchus, see Cyril Mango, *Byzantine Architecture* (Faber & Faber, 1986).

Omitted from this issue, but very prominent during the age of Justinian and Theodora was the Monophysite Controversy. In the early centuries of Christianity, councils met at Nicea and Chalcedon to establish the doctrine of the Trinity [that God is three persons in one nature or essence] and that Jesus had a dual nature—fully God and fully human. Theodora followed the Monophysites who contended that Jesus had a single, divine nature. Justinian held the orthodox dual-nature position most of his life, but converted to Monophysitism, long after Theodora's death and shortly before his own. For more on this controversy, see W. H. C. Frend, *The Rise of the Monophysite Movement: Chapters in the History of the Church in the Fifth and Sixth Centuries* (Cambridge University Press, 1972).

Finally, Judy Chicago chose Theodora as one of the women to occupy a seat at *The Dinner Party*, her massive art installation, in the form of an equilateral triangle, featuring 39 women omitted from history. In storage for decades, *The Dinner Party* has been bought and donated to The Brooklyn Museum, where it will be on display, beginning in early 2007. Theodora's biography and a photo of her magnificent purple, green, and gold mosaic-like porcelain plate can be found in Judy Chicago, *The Dinner Party* (Penguin Books, 1986).

ISSUE 8

Did Environmental Factors Cause the Collapse of Maya Civilization?

YES: David Drew, from *The Lost Chronicles of the Maya Kings* (University of California Press, 1999)

NO: Payson D. Sheets, from "Warfare in Ancient Mesoamerica: A Summary View," in M. Kathryn Brown and Travis W. Stanton, eds., *Ancient Mesoamerican Warfare* (AltaMira Press, 2003)

ISSUE SUMMARY

YES: Writer and documentary presenter David Drew emphasizes environmental factors and their effects on Maya civilization as primarily responsible for its collapse.

NO: Anthropology professor Payson Sheets stresses military expansion as a potential cause of the Maya Collapse.

A notable civilization from long ago wrote in hieroglyphs, developed an accurate calendar, built pyramid-like structures to honor its gods, practiced polytheism with gods represented by animal imagery, and advanced in areas such as mathematics and astronomy. These characteristics could describe the ancient Egyptians. But here they are used to describe the Mayas of Mesoamerica, who established a New World civilization a millennium before the arrival of Europeans. Before their invasion, this Amerindian civilization was in a state of decline. The Spanish conquistadors, following in Christopher Columbus's footsteps, subdued all of Mesoamerica in the sixteenth century and completely destroyed what remained of its civilization. The result of this Spanish action, aided by uncontrolled ecological growth that covered what remained, was the disappearance of this once highly advanced civilization. It would remain obscured until it was rediscovered in the nineteenth century by explorers seeking to find the lost civilization of the ancient Mayas.

Within the last century, work by archaeologists, linguists, and scientists has not only exposed what remains of the Maya grandeur but, by deciphering their language, has uncovered the secrets of their advanced civilization. The continuing discoveries have inspired regular assessments of earlier theories.

It was once thought, for example, that Mayas were peaceful people, with little interest in war as a means to achieving ends. Recent linguistic decipherments now tell us that this was not true. As far as the Mayas are concerned, today's theory is only as good as the latest archaeological discovery or linguistic decipherment, both ongoing processes.

In spite of the wealth of information about the Mayas we now possess, there are still questions that have not been definitively answered. One of the most important questions is what caused the decline of Maya civilization? Maya scholars have developed theories regarding its decline, using the best evidence presently available. However, a consensus has not yet been reached.

This issue seeks to explore the two major theories involving the Mayan decline: (1) It occurred due to internal political, social, and environmental factors that the Mayas could not or would not control; (2) The demise was brought about by factors caused by excessive militarism, which first resulted in territorial expansion and later in weakness and eventual decline. Complicating the search for answers to the cause(s) of the Maya demise are the local/regional differences present in the Maya city-states. Were factors present in the Northern Lowlands states present in their Southern counterparts? And what about their Highland brethren? Could different conditions and circumstances in each area have produced a variety of reasons for their decline? And within a region, can we be sure that the factors that led to one city-states's demise were also responsible for the collapse of others? The possibility exists that each political entity may have had its own unique set of circumstances which contributed to its decline and fall.

In spite of these intrinsic difficulties, Maya scholars continue to explore potential reasons for the civilization's collapse. Both the internal conditions and outside forces theories are considered by David Drew and Payson D. Sheets. In the selections that follow, Drew considers internal stresses—overpopulation, agricultural scarcities, disease, natural disasters—to be the major factors responsible for the collapse of the Maya city-states. Sheets represents those scholars emphasizing the warlike nature of the Mayas and the effects it may have had on the Maya collapse. Future archaeological work in Central America is likely to shed more light on the reasons for the Maya decline.

YES

David Drew

The Lost Chronicals of the Maya Kings

The Maya Collapse

For the early explorers, the enigma of their downfall was perhaps the greatest of the Maya mysteries. The builders of the magnificent cities seemed to have vanished without trace. John Lloyd Stephens saw the 'shattered bark' of Maya civilization left adrift in the jungle, her crew perished and 'none left to tell what caused her destruction'. When had the forests engulfed the temples and pyramids and how had such glory come to pass away? A century later the first question was answered, although it only served to deepen the mystery surrounding the second. As men such as Sylvanus Morley assiduously tracked down dated inscriptions in the forests and excavations proceeded at some of the major sites, it became clear that dynastic role at individual Maya cities had come to an abrupt halt during the course of the ninth century, now known as the 'Terminal Classic' period, No more monuments with dated inscriptions were set up and the construction of palaces and temples ceased. Yet this was mere than the end of kings. For evidence was to accumulate that most of the major cities in the Southern Lowlands were abandoned, their populations never to return, Classic Maya civilization had folded utterly and the signs were that this 'Collapse', as it came to be called, had been a disaster of such a magnitude that it had little precedent in world history. . . .

Half a century ago a range of explanations had already been offered to account for what had happened, including plague, agricultural failure, earthquake, invasion from beyond the boundaries of the Maya world and peasant revolt. Today scholars shy away from presenting the fall of the Classic Maya as a tidy sequence of any single root cause and effect. For if factors can be identified which may ultimately have served to trigger the collapse of particular cities, these only operated because of deep-seated structural problems within the fabric of Maya society. In a pattern of cyclical inevitability that the Maya themselves would have understood, any civilization tends to accumulate imbalances and tensions within the very system that has created its success. The Maya were no exception, for centuries of growth produced intolerable strains which in the end proved socially and politically explosive. Yet if one had to select a fundamental 'cause', it must have lain in the glaring imbalance between the burgeoning Maya population and the productive capacity of their agriculture. . . .

If the evidence suggests that populations were increasing rapidly and that most available land was turned over to agriculture, the other element in the equation, the question of how much food the land could have produced, is of course impossible to answer. We now have an impressionistic picture of the range of Maya adaptations. We know that their agriculture was considerably more intensive than once thought, but any more precise understanding of the nature and effectiveness of cultivation across the Southern Lowlands will elude scholars for many years to come. Much as with population estimates, the evidence to date is limited and comes from scattered studies that have covered in detail only a tiny fraction of the region. And what they do reveal is great variability, that topography, differing soil fertility and localized weather patterns would have rendered conditions for agriculture very different from one area to another. There seems little doubt, however, that the land must have been under tremendous pressure. Over much of the region slash-and-burn agriculture would still have been the mainstay of the farming regime. Farmers who practise the same system today testify that even where a regular period of fallow is maintained, soils will naturally decline over the years in fertility and crop yields. The responsible farmer will see that from time to time fields are rested for longer periods. But with more and more mouths to feed and nowhere to move to, no other lands to till, this may have been impossible at the end of the Late Classic. Indeed many believe that the reverse was increasingly the case, that they would have been forced to shorten the period of fallow on already tired fields. This would have been an extremely risky strategy, courting disaster for short-term ends.

The increasing dearth of forest would have had a profound impact, firstly in encouraging soil erosion. But trees were also vital for so many aspects of life. Originally, of course, there would have been quite enough to go round and large areas of forest would have formed buffer zones between territories. Tracts of jungle must have been safeguarded and harvested as a renewable resource. But by the end of the eighth century one can well imagine strategic decisions being made to fell many of the remaining areas of virgin forest. The Maya were without doubt responsible farmers, with two thousand years' experience of conjuring harvests of maize from sparse tropical soils. They must have been aware of the impact they were having on their environment. But they could no longer afford to be enlightened guardians of forest and field. The picture that emerges is of the environment progressively degraded, of Maya agriculture reaching the very limits of its capacity and being unable to feed populations adequately. The key evidence comes from the bones of Maya people throughout the region. Studies from sites such as Tikal, Altar de Sacrificios and La Milpa tell the same story of an increasingly unhealthy and stressed population. Skeletons had shrunk, the life expectancy of children was beginning to decrease rapidly and disease was commonplace in a manner not observed in the more robust bones of earlier centuries. On the whole, kings and nobility continued to live well and remain healthy, but this would not be the case for long.

Another variable that has to be considered in the overall picture is that of climate change. Over the centuries the climate and patterns of rainfall in the Maya lowlands have been inherently unstable. Modern statistics reveal that rainfall varies considerably in quantity from year to year. Localized droughts are common and when the rains do come they can appear with extraordinary violence in the form of hurricanes that sweep in from the Caribbean. In 1961, for example, Hurricane Hattie wrecked Belize City and then headed inland to bring havoc to much of the Petén. At the time of writing, much of Nicaragua, Honduras and the Caribbean coast of Guatemala is still recovering from the devastating effects of Hurricane Mitch. Spanish accounts of the conquest period speak of an equally unpredictable climate and, in the northern Yucatán in particular, the common occurrence of drought. Diego de Landa was struck by this in talking to local people and records that in 1535, there was a terrible drought when 'such a famine fell upon them that they were reduced to eating the bark of trees . . . nothing green was left'. Such uncertainties undoubtedly preoccupied the Prehispanic Maya and underlined the need, revealed in the codices, for effective divination and the right ritual action to be taken, in the way of suitable offerings for the gods, to avert such calamities.

Given the seemingly precarious situation at the end of the Late Classic, short-term changes in weather patterns or sudden natural disasters could have proved catastrophic in a way that they would not have done in previous centuries. There is now evidence that they may have been confronted by problems of a different order entirely. As we know to our cost today, the removal of large areas of tropical forest does not simply degrade the soil but also adversely affects the climate. Any more localized changes of this kind in the Southern Lowlands may be difficult to detect since, as Don Rice points out in his survey of the eighth century Maya environment, both human impact and climate change leave traces—in the pollen record, for example—which are very difficult to tell apart. But in northern Yucatán, at some distance from the great Classic cities to the south, the analysis of sediments from the remote Lake Chichancanab has suggested that a period of consistent dryness set in throughout the Maya area between 750 and 800 and may have lasted for two centuries. There is some evidence for longer term shifts or cycles of climate change in earlier periods . . . . notably dry episode may have contributed to the downfall of The Late Preclassic city or El Mirador. But that which began in the later eighth century appears to have been the most severe in the Maya region for thousands of years and could have brought prolonged droughts of a kind that the Maya would never have experienced before. Thus to people living on the edge, this may have acted as the final blow which led to social breakdown and disaster.

The exact circumstances and the pattern of events at each of the major cities as they fell apart undoubtedly differed from place to place. The wealth of archaeological and epigraphic evidence from Copán and its region makes it the only example to date where it is possible to reconstruct plausibly and in some detail the end of a Classic Maya city. After its foundation by Yax K'uk Mo in 426, the city and royal dynasty at Copán flourished. To begin with it was a small centre amidst rich farmland overlooking the river. The abundance and increased prosperity amply justified the king's role as leader of his society. The 'semi-divine' authority, the lavish display and the trappings of Copán's kings increased. It was all a great success and the city attracted more and more people to it, even from as far away as central Honduras. But, as the population grew, the urban nucleus expanded over the most fertile bottom-land into a continuous, densely packed residential mass. Gradually there became less and less good land available for cultivation and they began to farm the slopes of the surrounding hills, all the while making sizeable inroads into the local forest cover. Eventually the hills, too, were dotted with groups of houses and trackways, much as they are today, and as the eighth century wore on, Copán's farmers were forced to till the very poorest soils around the hill-tops. Finally, by the end of the century, deforestation, soil erosion and dramatically falling crop yields meant that the valley could no longer feed itself. For a time, perhaps the city was able to depend for food upon tribute in kind from the satellite communities that it dominated. But they, too, would have been feeling the strain, with little surplus to spare, and have been increasingly disinclined to support the demands of the centre. . . .

The end of dynastic rule at Copán is signalled by two most unusual monuments. The first is an unprepossessing, damaged stela of curiously rounded, columnar form known as Stela. It depicts the standing figure of the already dead Yax Pac descending into the jaws of the Underworld. On the back of the stone is a short inscription which has so far proved impossible to decipher in its entirety. But, following an abbreviated date which almost certainly corresponds to 820, the second glyph block features the verb *hom*, which David Stuarr has interpreted as to 'dismantle' or 'destroy'. The next glyph includes the word for 'founder' as it appears in the inscription on top of Altar Q, where it refers to the foundation of the Copán royal line some 400 years earlier by Yax K'uk Mo. On Stela 11 this reference to the founder is coupled with the suffix *nah* meaning 'house'. Put together, what this would mean is 'the founder's house is destroyed', in other words the dynasty which began with Yax K'uk Mo had come to an end. If the interpretation is correct, this inscription is unique in actually announcing the termination of a royal line. It is an extraordinary and quite uncharacteristic admission of failure. . . .

There is no means of knowing what happened to the members of the royal family, although there is evidence that the residential compound of Yax Pac and his line may have been destroyed at about this time. Somewhat later, William Fash suggests, his tomb may have been looted and his funerary temple ransacked. There is no sign, however, of any major upheaval or of what might be termed a popular uprising. Fash believes that the political end-game at Copán amounted to a nobles' revolt. Perhaps it was a takeover by the heads of those non-royal lineages who commanded popular support in the countryside and could distance themselves from the perceived failures of the ruling family. For the houses of these lineages continued to be occupied and indeed were added to over the following century. Thus at Copán rule by a single king seems to have devolved to that of the group. These leading families evidently attempted to stay on and revive the valley's fortunes. But after a century or so, perhaps because of renewed infighting and the continuing decline of agriculture, they appear to have drifted away to smaller, still fertile areas of land in the surrounding hills. At least here, on the less crowded fringes of the Maya world, they had somewhere to go. They reverted, it seems, to a simpler, decentralized way of life, of the kind that had existed before the onset of dynastic rule. Between about 1000 and 1200, the population of Copán fell away rapidly. From the evidence of their rubbish dumps and burials, small groups continued to inhabit parts of the city, but after this time the valley was largely abandoned.

The uniquely detailed picture that emerges from Copán offers a model of how some of the principal elements in the process of Maya 'Collapse' fitted together. Deterioration of the environment and the failure of agriculture imposed intolerable strains on the political system, which finally came apart and led to the toppling of royal scapegoats. In essence this pattern must have been repeated in many other cities, though elsewhere, where kingdoms jostled more densely together, the drift towards failure was more chaotic and more violent. Along the Usumacinta and Pasión rivers, and in the heartland region of the Petén and adjacent areas, the old system of alliances formed around Tikal and Calakmul had broken down by the middle of the eighth century. It is obvious enough today that the only thing which might have enabled the Classic Maya to surmount their problems was political unity and co-operation. This was clearly impossible. Under pressure the political system atomized, reverted to type, with each one of a host of now antagonistic city-states looking to its own interests in what became a struggle for survival. For in many areas, especially those away from the major rivers or lakes, the strain on the environment and the decline of agriculture was in all probability much greater than that visible at Copán. The only option that would keep kings in power and feed their populations was to take land and desperately scarce resources from others. Inscriptions suggest that the incidence of warfare and, most would conclude, its intensity, increased markedly during the latter part of the eighth century. The pattern may have been set with the destruction of Dos Pilas and the conflagration in the Petexbatún area that began in the 760s. This was all-out, brutal war that laid waste the whole region. Along the Usumacinta the last texts that survive from the major cities all speak of warfare, and at some of them there are signs of destruction. Buildings were burnt and monuments defaced at Piedras Negras, and at Yaxchilán archaeologists have recently discovered that a section of the city known as the 'Little Acropolis' was fortified with hastily erected walls, and projectile points covered the ground that Yaxchilán, like Dos Pilas, may finally have fallen in war. . . .

Payson D. Sheets

 **NO**

Warfare in Ancient Mesoamerica: A Summary View

This [article] focuses on warfare in ancient Mesoamerica rather than violence or conflict. The latter two may occur on the interpersonal or interfamilial level and often do not preserve well archaeologically. However, warfare as a socially sanctioned and planned aggressive activity can be preserved reasonably well, especially in a society with considerable architecture as well as writing and art in various media. The objective of this [article] is to briefly consider the history of Mesoamerican warfare . . . and to comment on current status of Mesoamerican warfare in general. It is refreshing for me to summarize and comment on a book on Mesoamerican warfare not written by the traditional "big gun" distinguished scholars but by the next generation of archaeologists exploring the nature and implications of war with new data and ideas.

Overview of Mesoamerican Warfare Studies

The first European contact with a New World civilization was in war, as the Spanish and their Tlaxcalan and other allies conquered the Aztec capital Tenochtitlán. As the Spanish expanded their contacts and attempted to establish control in the sixteenth century, they chronicled warfare and sacrifice throughout Mesoamerica. Despite Spanish documentation of Contact period indigenous warfare, scholars in the early and middle part of the twentieth century often depicted ancient civilizations as peaceful. As scholars have depicted societies as bellicose or peaceful or as they have explored the reasons for warfare, they often have revealed more about their own assumptions and desires than the subject matter under study.

As reflected in this volume, Mesoamerican scholars in recent years have recognized the abundant and wide range of material correlates that warfare has left in the archaeological record. Those material correlates range from the instruments of warfare and fortifications through artistic depictions to textual statements of warfare and its consequences. Certainly, warfare was initiated as a means to capture sacrificial victims for largely religious purposes on occasion, but even then can this be divorced from a function of bolstering political authority? As the evidence for warfare in Mesoamerica accumulates, we must also consider that warfare was an integral component to the emergence of middle range and complex societies throughout the Formative, Classic, and Postclassic.

Warfare in pre-Columbian Oaxaca has been studied for more than half a century, beginning with Caso at Monte Albán. Marcus and Flannery have broadened and deepened our understanding of conflict within and surrounding the Oaxaca Valley, including some evidence of warfare prior to the founding of Monte Albán about 500 B.C. Redmond and Spencer convincingly documented the conquest of the Cuicatlan Canada north of the Oaxaca Valley by Monte Albán. However, as Joyce argues in this volume the claims of militarism from Monte Albán may have been exaggerated. He searched the lower Verde Valley for evidence of Monte Albán conquest in the Late Formative and found little. Ironically, he did find evidence for a strong presence of a different foreign polity a few centuries later that could have had military aspects. Teotihuacan entered the area in a major way in the Early Classic, as evidenced by the lower Verde area having the highest percentage of green Pachuca obsidian of any area outside the Basin of Mexico, along with some settlement shifts to defensible locations and some ceramic changes. Judging from present evidence, if this area had been conquered, it was more likely by Teotihuacan than Monte Albán.

These issues in Oaxaca are exemplary of deeper questions in Mesoamerican archaeology. Often we ask, Was the expansion of society X of an economic nature, or was it theocratic, or was it political? The issues are often simplified to a prime motivator for expansion that can focus on mercantile objectives versus religious conversion or conquest and domination. However, what many of these essays indicate to me is that our Western categories may be useful for initial heuristic purposes but may be misleading if they are allowed to stand unchallenged in the final analysis. Most expansions involved what we would categorize as economic, political, and religious phenomena in deeply intertwined manners.

The recognition of the centrality of warfare to the Classic Maya has been a long time coming. Thompson, the great mid-twentieth-century Mayanist, did acknowledge that warfare existed, but he emphasized warfare in Postclassic and historic times. In his magnum opus *The Rise and Fall of Maya Civilization* (1st ed. 1954, 2nd ed. 1966), he argued that all Mesoamerican warfare originated in the need to obtain captives for the sacrifices needed to nurture the deities. He viewed the Mexicans as more warlike than the Maya, a trend that culminated with the Aztecs.

Thompson did refer to the jaguar and eagle as war gods, which was a step toward the current recognition of the two warrior orders, of eagle and jaguar knights, that were at Teotihuacan and were adopted by the Maya at Tikal and other areas. They become common in the Late Classic (at Bonampak) and Epiclassic (at Cacaxtla) as well as the Early Postclassic (at Tula) . . . and Late Postclassic (at Tenochtitlén). In Aztec mythology, the opposition of jaguar and eagle knights represented the earth and the sky and thus femaleness and maleness. Not only did the warrior orders operate in military campaigns, but they figured prominently in public performances while presenting their captive victims to ensure the proper working of the cosmos.

As early as 1940, Means perceived a fundamental difference between Andean and Middle American warfare. He saw Inka warfare directed toward conquest and acculturation, to bring other peoples into Inka civilization. In contrast, he, like Thompson, viewed Middle American warfare as oriented toward capturing opposing warriors to sacrifice them to provide sustenance for their deities. I believe the fact that it is the only reference to warfare in the Maya area in the index of that entire synthesis volume *The Maya and Their Neighbors* indicates how unimportant warfare was considered by the principal scholars of those decades.

One discovery that made scholars rethink the "peaceful Maya" were the huge ditch-and-parapet fortifications constructed in the Late Formative by Tikal to protect them from Uaxactún. After Tikal apparently conquered Uaxactún, the earthworks no longer served any purpose, and they fell into disrepair. The discovery a decade later of defensive fortifications around Becán indicated the threat of warfare was more widespread among the Maya. More recently, Demarest and Inomata have shown the intensity and social consequences of warfare in the Petexbatun region that led to the end of civilization as the Classic Maya knew it in that area.

Artistic evidence of warfare has also accumulated in the nineteenth and twentieth centuries, as stela scenes and painted evidence from ceramics and murals have become available and are better understood. Hieroglyphic evidence has accumulated more in the "punctuated equilibrium" model rather than a "uniformitarian" accumulation. Throughout most of the past two centuries, epigraphic evidence of warfare grew very slowly, but that changed dramatically with the decipherment of the "shell/star" hieroglyph for warfare and the linking of it with the Venus cycle, captives, and Tlaloc-Venus warfare and numerous hieroglyphic decipherments, particularly in the southern Maya lowlands.

Warfare was woven deeply into the social fabric of most Formative and all Classic and Postclassic Mesoamerican civilizations. It appears that all levels of those societies, from commoners to elites, believed that sacrifice was essential for the proper functioning of the cosmos. Based on the core belief that one does not receive something for nothing, people would offer sacrifices in various forms to receive rain, a good crop harvest, a propitious marriage, recovery from disease, or other anxious need. The sacrifice could take the form of bloodletting, sacrificing food or drink, or the sacrifice of a person. Sacrifice of a person captured in warfare became very common in the Classic and Post-classic. Sacrifice in general and human sacrifice in particular probably had deep roots in the Formative period, with origins possibly in the Archaic or earlier, but it is not until the Late Formative that sacrifice is commonly preserved in the archaeological record.

Evidence of Warfare in Mesoamerica

One of the advantages of studying Mesoamerican warfare is that a wider range of phenomena is available to the scholar than in other pre-Columbian culture area of the New World. I note a dozen of them here with the objective of encouraging future scholars to spread a wide net in their studies.

Fortifications. Site fortification is prima facie evidence of fear of attack, and in many cases one can identify from whom that fear developed. The Tikal ditch-and-embankment built in fear of Uaxactún is a good example. As that feature seems to have no other function than defense, it is unusually unequivocal evidence. In contrast, the apparent fortifications of sites such as Becán, Cacaxtla, Xochicalco, and Monte Albán could also have had residential and/or agricultural functions.

Art and iconography. The prominent display of trophy heads in skull racks or display of them in sculpture or other forms of art are generally the result of opposing warriors being captured in battle and brought into the victorious settlement for sacrifice. The five-point star is now widely recognized as indicating Venus and the need to capture victims for sacrifice in the Classic and Postclassic of Mesoamerica. Headrick provides a good example of the iconography of aggression.

Weapons. The discovery of weapons of war in sites and the depiction of war weapons in art are reasonably reliable indicators of warfare. McCafferty notes a large number of dart points associated with Structure 1 at Cholula that, combined with other evidence, indicates warfare activity. However, the presence of items that *could* be used in war does not mean that they *were* used in war because such implements can be used in hunting or in art as mythology or as symbolic of hunting, war, aggression, or defense. A technology that could have been used in war but evidently was much more important in hunting is illustrated by the bow and arrow coming into ancient El Salvador in the Terminal Classic (ca. A.D. 800). The evidence is the ubiquity of the small projectile points made from snapped prismatic blade sections. They must be arrow points, as they are too small and fragile to be atlatl dart points or spear points. They commonly are found in the most mountainous of terrain, far from any human settlements, and evidently were used for hunting, particularly of deer. The rarity of other indicators for warfare in pre-Columbian El Salvador further substantiates the argument that these artifacts were not used for intraspecies purposes.

The weapons depicted in sculptures, such as the atlatls and darts in the hands of the atlantid figures at Tula, are unequivocal. Equally convincing are the weapons depicted in aggressive murals at Chichén Itzá and other Classic and Postclassic sites. In addition to bows and arrows and atlatls and darts, spears and clubs were used in war. The latter, resembling a baseball bat but with obsidian or occasionally chert prismatic blade segments inserted longitudinally, must have had a horrific impact, as the lithics shattered on impact, macerating tissue and causing massive hemorrhaging. Such a club is illustrated on Stela 5 at Uaxactún. These clubs with lithic inserts would be useful only in warfare and not in hunting or other uses. As LeBlanc notes, the sling is useful to herding peoples and as an implement of war. It is also useful to agriculturalists to discourage herbivory by birds in maize fields.

Epigraphy. It has taken Mayanists a long time to get past their suspicions about the possible reliability of the written record of the Classic period. We all learned at an early age what liars the Aztecs were, deliberately rewriting their history for self-aggrandizement to look eminently civilized in the finest aggressive Mesoamerican sense. Fortunately, it turns out that the Maya texts are generally reliable. Thus, the Maya text describing a battle, a capture, or a decapitation should be taken seriously. The texts are often limited to the victor proclaiming the outcome, with no details about the scale of battle, the reasons for it, and the planning for it.

Osteology. Skeletal analyses can divulge evidence of trauma. An occasional broken bone is not reliable evidence of warfare, but a high frequency of parry fractures in the radius and ulna of young adult males is a good indicator. Skull fracture patterns can also be evidence of warfare, as can simultaneous multiple burials. Decapitations can be indirect indications, after a captive was hauled into the victorious polity and sacrificed.

Artifacts. Warfare, especially toward the severe end of the spectrum, can result in abrupt changes in artifact or architectural styles or frequencies. However, it is risky to argue in the other direction, of artifactual changes indicating warfare in the absence of supporting data, as so many ecologic, economic, religious, demographic, social, adaptive, or political phenomena can also spread or suppress artifact and technologies.

Assimilation or elimination. Warfare can cause a functioning polity to disappear rapidly, but so can other factors. A sudden change in upper-level administration, as apparently occurred in the Early Classic period in Uaxactún, can be evidence of a conquest.

Language and cognition. The terms and concepts used by a society at the time when warfare is being studied or perhaps later among members of the same ethnic-linguistic group can provide extraordinary insight into warfare. This category provides a hearty dose of *their* view, of the emic perspective. Many other indicators here discussed are our interpretive impositions on the archaeological record, with all the dangers inherent in that. Those dangers include the fact that so often we see what we are trained to see and want to see in the archaeological record. Thus, their cognitive categories act as an antidote to exclusively relying on our etic categories. At least knowing their categories helps us be aware of our projecting our own biases onto the archaeological record. . . .

(T)he Classic Maya had four distinct linguistic categories of warfare. *Chu-c'ah,* or "capture," warfare involves the planning of a battle, a successful encounter with the opposition, and the capture of at least one opposing warrior. Both sides could win, each by capturing someone from the other side. The capture of a person can symbolically extend to the defeat of the opposing polity, but this obviously is not a defeat in warfare as conceptualized in the modern Western world. A *ch'ak,* or "axe," event is similar to the capture event, but the person captured is an elite. The capture of 18 Rabbit from Copan by Quirigua and his subsequent decapitation is the best-known example. A *hubi,* or "destruction," is of greater societal consequence and is more similar to warfare as practiced by modern "civilizations." The most severe form of warfare was the "shell-star" battle, where a polity can conquer and assimilate another, resulting in the long-term or even permanent suppression of political and economic independence. Certainly an important endeavor by Maya archaeologists would be to identify the material correlates of each of these emic types of warfare and see how they change through time or vary among contemporary polities.

Ethnohistory and history. The Spanish in the sixteenth century recorded warfare throughout Mesoamerica. Their recording of chronic warfare among pre-Columbian societies should be taken with a grain of salt. For instance, the Aztec claims of their military struggles with Tlaxcala seem exaggerated, and I suspect the Aztecs completely surrounded Tlaxcala with conquered peoples and maintained Tlaxcala as a convenient nearby hunting preserve where their youths could prove themselves in battle and bring captives back to Tenochtitlán. I would not call Tlaxcala an independent polity. And it was to the advantage of the Mexican warrior who brought back a Tlaxcalan captive to believe and act as if he was obtained from an enemy warring state rather than from a hunting preserve. If this interpretation is correct, the Tlaxcalans were subjugated more profoundly by their being maintained as a hunting preserve than were many societies that were militarily conquered by the Aztec war machine and only loosely assimilated into their empire. McCafferty's chapter further underscores the inconsistencies of the ethnohistoric record and illustrates the need for archaeological evidence in conjunction with the written record to provide a more complete picture.

Oral history, mythology, and religion. Sources such as the Chilam Balam, Popol Vuh, Mixtec codices, and the Florentine Codex provide insights on competition, sacrifice, and warfare.

Settlement patterns. The finding of contested zones, of "no-man's-lands" between polities, can be indications of protracted hostilities. They can occur between states, between city states, or between chiefdoms, as illustrated by the uninhabited zones between the Barriles chiefdoms in western Panama.

Desecratory termination rituals. Several chapters in this volume make significant progress in identifying deposits that may often represent the result of warfare in the deliberate termination of buildings and the supernatural powers in them, as different from dedicatory and reverential termination rituals. One key difference is the scale and intensity of architectural destruction, and the term *desecration* is appropriate here. And it is important to note that if these identifications are correct, Brown and Garber . . . have moved the earliest identification of warfare in the Maya area into the Middle Formative period. Their estimated date of about 650 B.C. is slightly earlier than the time that Marcus and Flannery see the earliest warfare in the Oaxaca Valley. The differences between dedication, desecration, and reverential termination rituals are subtle, yet they are of great importance and deserve considerable research attention to improve our understanding of warfare.

Several studies in this volume successfully combine several lines of evidence to better illuminate our understanding of ancient Mesoamerican warfare. In particular, Freidel and colleagues, provide an excellent example of how to closely examine epigraphic, architectural, sculptural, artistic, and artifactual evidence to distinguish conquest of one polity by another versus internal strife and usurpation of power. These authors suggest that the Maya rules of dynastic succession at Tikal were magically manipulated by Nuun Yax Ain (Curl-Snout), who took the Tikal throne from Toh-Chak-Ich'ak (Great-Jaguar-Paw) with the assistance of Siyah K'ak' (Smoking Frog). They suggest that Nuun Yax Ain performed magical rituals that legitimated his place in the Tikal dynastic sequence. What actually happened at Tikal, two-thirds of the way through the fourth century, is far from being well understood. However, I am optimistic that by conjoining multiple lines of evidence and analyzing them carefully, Mayanists might convince even a jury in Los Angeles.

It is instructive to review the history of studies of Mesoamerican warfare to see the changes in assumptions and understandings as twentieth-century archaeologists have explored the topic. One of the most important recent changes is the combination of field archaeology with epigraphy and iconography, which has combined emic with etic approaches. I believe one area that needs further development is for archaeologists to move beyond the assumption that warfare occurred just on the battlefield at a distance from the city. I suggest that at the first stages of preparation for warfare, the action in fact did occur at a distance (such as setting the field of battle with the battle standards). I suspect a participant in the battle might emphasize the more important battle was occurring in the supernatural realm. And the end of the battle is not the end of the story. Perhaps we can learn more about Mesoamerican warfare by studying the next steps, of bringing the captives back, of creation of "stage space" in which to reenact battles, in which the captives shed blood and lose their lives in order that the cosmos may continue functioning. The Western view of war emphasizes the field of battle, body counts, and equipment destroyed, but to understand Mesoamericans we must also emphasize the public performances within the city before and especially after the battle was completed. Mesoamerican city planning not only took into account the cardinal-cosmological directions but also built stage space in overt ways to render visible and audible the enactments of battles and communications with the supernatural realm. Maya stage space in their cities certainly was not a proscenium stage.

Warfare should not be seen as a monolithic repetitive entity among Mesoamerican societies. Rather, warfare varied considerably, depending on factors such as the degree of political centralization, presence or absence of competitive nearby polities, demographic and ecologic processes, ritualization of warfare, resource unpredictability, and economic and technological changes. Hassig deals with some of these factors, and I anticipate that future warfare research will both broaden and deepen them. Are there correlations between the degree of political centralization and the nature of warfare? In a general sense, there is a relationship, as both of the most highly urbanized and centralized civilizations, Teotihuacan and the Aztecs, waged war with standing armies against external polities. Hassig characterizes Teotihuacan and the Aztecs as meritocratic states with some social mobility for individuals based on their military successes. Both states were relatively innovative in military techniques and technology, and both developed large standing armies that expanded over much of Mesoamerica, but neither society lasted for a long time. In contrast, the Maya waged aristocratic wars, were more conservative, avoided having large standing armies of commoners, and as a result were less expansionistic and in the long run more stable. I believe that we can include the Olmec with the Maya in these characteristics. Additionally, I believe that the Zapotecs more closely resemble the Maya than the Basin of Mexico states. Occasional incorporations of the Basin of Mexico style of dispersed leadership occurred in the Maya area in the very Late Classic at Seibal and at about the same time at Chichén Itzá. I believe that Hassig under-estimates the degree to which religion permeated Mesoamerican warfare, particularly in those societies that waged aristocratic wars, but his distinctions are significant and bear further scrutiny. That Teotihuacan and, to a lesser degree, the Aztecs avoided the cult of the king and avoided prominent public depictions of supreme rulers is an important symptom of the significant differences in internal organizational principles among Mesoamerican states.

Conclusions

Many scholars have studied warfare in Mesoamerica. In retrospect, the way research questions have been phrased has often overly focused the domain under consideration. The scholars who argue about what was the "real" nature of war among Mesoamerican societies may have prematurely limited their answers because in the two societies where war is better understood, the Aztec and the Maya, there were quite different kinds of warfare practiced, with markedly different tactics and societal implications. Thus, the scholars who argue that one kind of war is the "true" warfare can be as correct as the schol-ars who argue a different kind of war is the "true" form. Thus, we need not a leveling of the playing field but rather an acknowledged broadening of the playing field.

It is my opinion that the debate over whether warfare in Mesoamerican societies was motivated primarily by political, economic, religious, or demo-graphic-ecologic factors is healthy and eminently worthwhile. And I am confi-dent that the debate will go on indefinitely because thorough and precise knowledge of the cause(s) of warfare is not attainable. Even under the ideal circumstances for warfare scholarship, having unrestricted access to a recent and historically documented war and to participants in that war, it is not pos-sible to accurately know the role of all factors. The factors vary with different participants in the war and even with a particular participant over time. But that is not cause for pallo-despair, as debate and skepticism can stimulate bet-ter scholarship to move us slightly closer to understanding the behaviors and beliefs of warfare, some of the instigating pressures, and occasionally some-thing about the motivations of ancient wars.

I also look forward to Mesoamerican archaeologists incorporating the research of cultural anthropologists. For instance, Ember and Ember "con-ducted a detailed multivariate study of 186 preindustrial societies to explore the reasons why they went to war. The Embers found that the single highest predictor of warfare is a society's fear of resource unpredictability, often due to apparently capricious natural disasters that destroy food resources. Predict-able, chronic natural disasters, such as long-term drought, are less causative of warfare. Unless a society is already greatly stressed, it can accommodate to a long-term drought by such means as intensifying water control. I suspect that the migration of the Anasazi from the Mesa Verde region to the middle Rio Grande was such an accommodation to the long drought of the late thirteenth century in the Southwest. The fear of future sustenance loss or loss of other resources rather than actual deprivation seems to be the strongest motivator for warfare according to the Embers. The second-strongest predictor, about half as strong as resource unpredictability, is a society socializing their members for mistrust of the "other." These two strongest factors certainly are far from being mutually exclusive, and when a society fears an unpredictable nature and foments distrust and hatred for "outside" societies, warfare is a common result. Although many societies in their sample are not state level, these results are intriguing and eminently researchable among Mesoamerican societies from the Formative through the Postclassic. I look forward to explorations to see how fear of an unpredictable nature and fear of others may have underlain Mesoamerican warfare and how a range of coping mechanisms ranging from extending water control through fortifications to developing supernatural access may have been involved.

POSTSCRIPT

Did Environmental Factors Cause the Collapse of Maya Civilization?

In studying the decline of civilizations, it is generally easy to see that, in most instances, a combination of internal and external factors is responsible for their demise. This is certainly true for the Mayas. Both Drew and Sheets would agree that there is no single explanation for the Maya collapse; the question seems to be, which set of factors was more responsible for the demise? Complicating the search for answers to the Maya collapse are the regional and individual differences that existed within the myriad of city-states that provided the civilization with its political base. It should be noted that the reasons for their collapse could also differ due to regional or local conditions. Today's research seems to bear out the legitimacy of this dichotomy.

Studying the reasons for the Maya collapse offers an opportunity to compare/contrast it with another civilization that experienced a similar rise/decline/fall trajectory. In Norman Yoffee and George L. Cowgill, eds., *The Collapse of Ancient States and Civilizations* (University of Arizona Press, 1988), the rise and fall of Mesopotamia, Rome, and Ancient China are compared with those of the Mayas.

There are many highly recommendable books on the Mayas. Some of the recent additions to the field of Mayanology are David Webster, *The Fall of the Ancient Maya: Solving the Mystery of the Maya Collapse* (Thames and Hudson, 2002) and Arthur A. Demarest, *Ancient Maya: The Rise and Fall of a Rainforest Civilization* (Cambridge University Press, 2004). Several anthologies offer new insights on the Maya collapse: Arthur A. Demarest, Prudence M. Rice, and Don S. Rice, eds., *The Terminal Classic in the Maya Lowlands: Collapse, Transition, and Transformation* (University of Oklahoma Press, 2003); and M. Katherine Brown and Travis W. Stanton, eds., *Ancient Mesoamerican Warfare* (AltaMira Press, 2003). Recently the role of drought in the Maya collapse has been emphasized by some. For information, consult Richardson Benedict Gill, *The Great Maya Droughts: Water, Life, and Death* (University Of New Mexico Press, 2001).

ISSUE 9

Could the Crusades Be Considered a Christian Holy War?

YES: Arthur Jones, from "Memories of Crusades Live on in Today's War," *National Catholic Reporter* (October 26, 2001)

NO: Jonathan Phillips, from "Who Were the First Crusaders?" *History Today* (March 1997)

ISSUE SUMMARY

YES: Editor-at-large Arthur Jones presents a case for calling the Crusades a Christian holy war and finds resonances of that long-ago conflict in today's Muslim-Christian conflicts.

NO: Lecturer in medieval history Jonathan Phillips finds motivations for the Crusades in religious fervor, the desire for wealth, and a family history of pilgrimage, not in holy war.

Arthur Jones begins his essay with President Bush's inadvertent use of the word "crusade" on September 16, 2001 ("This crusade, this war on terrorism, is going to take a long time)—a word he claims echoed into Muslim memories of centuries of Christian incursions. Point-of-view is pivotal. Christians might view the Crusades as a noble effort to reclaim the central sites of their faith, or as an unfortunate but long-forgotten chapter in world history. Muslims, by contrast, may have fresh memories of "the holy religious war of the Christians" and their own "war against the cross" that began in the eleventh century and continues today.

Christianity began as a persecuted sect in the Roman Empire that took seriously its founder's injunction to "turn the other cheek" and repay evil with good. Early Christians would have no part of war. But by the fourth century, Constantine, the Holy Roman Emperor, had won battles with the cross on his shield and made Christianity the official faith of the Empire. Even against this background, however, papally sanctioned violence was something new, Jones suggests.

Muhammad's revelation from God ignited a fervor on the Arabian Peninsula that swept across north Africa and into Christian Europe, beginning in the seventh century. By 750 it had spread throughout the Byzantine

Empire. At least in part, Jones argues, the Crusades can be viewed as a Christian counteroffensive, designed to take back their conquered territories and reclaim the Holy Land, the site of Jesus's ministry, death, and burial.

Muslims regard both Jews and Christians as People of the Book, praise their prophets—Abraham, Moses, and Jesus—and permit them to worship freely. The higher head tax Jews and Christians had to pay in Muslim-controlled lands was another disincentive to convert them. So, in the Fertile Crescent, Muslims and Christians had lived together for centuries before the First Crusade—in mutual toleration, if not friendship. One key to the ferocity of the First Crusade is its point of origin. Most Frankish knights would have had no contact with Islam. However, their epic poem *The Song of Roland* changed the "enemy" that defeated Charlemagne's rearguard in the Pyrenees from the Basques, who were the actual victors, into the "treacherous" Muslims of Spain.

Jonathan Phillips situates the Crusades within the social, intellectual, religious, economic, and psychological realities of late eleventh-century Europe, which he calls "one of the most guilt-ridden societies in history." People, he argues, would have had many reasons for joining a crusade—the promise of salvation, the lure of wealth, and family traditions of pilgrimage. And, Pope Urban II's original goal was a very specific one—to assist the Byzantine emperor Alexius in his struggle against the Seljuk Turks of Asia Minor. These motivations, Phillips contends, are sufficient to account for the 60,000 who joined the first Crusade. It is not necessary to posit a holy war as motivation.

Fulcher of Chartres, the priest-chaplain of the First Crusade, described "a new path to heaven" and said confidently that those who undertook this "holy war" would experience "forgiveness of sins." Those who quest for God— in the eleventh century of the twenty-first—believe they will be blessed. During the Seventh Crusade, led by St. Louis, King of France, Yves le Breton reported encountering an old woman who wandered the streets with a dish of fire in her right hand and a bowl of water in her left hand. With the fire, she explained, she would burn up Paradise, until there was nothing left of it, And with the water, she would put out the fires of Hell, until nothing remained of them. "Because," she said, "I want no one to do good in order to receive the reward of Paradise, or from fear of Hell; but solely out of love of God."

YES

Arthur Jones

Memories of Crusades Live on in Today's War

Crusade!

On Sept. 16, the word shot around the Islamic world. And shocked it. President George W. Bush thought he'd used the term innocently enough. On that Sunday, walking from his helicopter to the White House, he said of U.S. retaliation to the Sept. 11 attacks, "this crusade, this war on terrorism, is going to take a long time."

As the Muslim uproar swelled, Bush quickly apologized. But damage had been done. The BBC, for example, in its Persian and Uzbeck broadcast news services, had translated Bush's remark in the way the Islamic world understands it, as "the war of those signed with the cross," and "the holy, religious war of the Christians." (In Islam's many national languages, from Arabic to Farsi to Urdu, the Muslims call their defense against the crusaders, "the war against the cross.")

Only a minority of Muslims actually believe America had declared a "holy war" against them, cautions Paul E. Chevedden of the University of California, Los Angeles. And Georgetown University's Zahid H. Bukhari, speaking of both Muslims and Westerners, said, "Certain lobbies, certain people, do use the word [crusade] to project what is happening because they have their own agendas to present. They like the terminology and can be more effective because of it."

To Muslims, whose memory of historic grievances may be sharper than that of most Christians, the concept of a "holy war" has implications lost in history's mists. To some millions of Muslims within the Islamic world, crusade still means centuries of bloody Western Christian incursions fought over the Holy Land. Those memories are like ghosts dancing to the U.S. drums of war.

NCR talked to historians of religion and those engaged in Muslim-Christian dialogue and, as the globe's sole superpower searches for one man among the rocks and caves of Islamic Afghanistan, learned lessons for today from the history of the medieval crusades. From today's perspective, there are some surprises, some odd similarities and parallels.

Christians did indeed at one time have their "holy wars," accompanied by language that could have come from bin Laden himself.

The historical record tells us that Fulcher of Chartres (1058–1130), priest-chaplain on the First Crusade, wrote in his eyewitness account that this Crusade was a *novum salutis genus*, "a new path to Heaven." Those Christians

From *National Catholic Reporter,* Volume 38, issue 1, October 26, 2001, pp. 1(3). Copyright © 2001 by National Catholic Reporter. Reprinted by permission.

who followed this "holy war" path would, wrote Fulcher, experience "full and complete satisfaction" and "forgiveness of sins."

A World Bursting Apart

To Chevedden, however, who is an associate at UCLA's Gustav E. von Grunebaum Center for Near Eastern Studies, the Crusades have to be understood as part of tremendous geo-political, socio-economic and religious shifts underway at the time. "The Mediterranean world of the 11th century was changing in a remarkable manner; it was witnessing the birth of a new world. The Crusades were the product of the sudden and all-transforming change that produced Western European civilization. An old world burst apart, and a new one took its place."

Bukhari, director and principal co-investigator for Georgetown's Muslims in the American Public Square project, and Fr. James Fredericks of Loyola Marymount theology department, see similar shifts underway today. Bukhari explained that during a period of great transformation "the Crusades were a clash of religions. In the transformations of modern times, we have a clash of civilizations. To some extent there is the same connotation, the whole West as a symbol of Christianity, the entire Muslim world as the symbol of Islam."

But what must be taken into account, he said, is the evolution underway. One aspect of that, he said, is "the evolving debate within Islam about living according to Islamic beliefs, to divine guidance. The notion of how to do that has been evolving since World War II, which triggered the end of colonialism. Among Muslim countries and the Muslim world (which includes those Muslims who live as minorities in non-Muslim countries), there is a debate over issues of democracy, civil rights, human rights, the role of women and living with people of other faiths."

And that debate, he said, "will be violent in some places, look absurd in others, be serious in others, but evolve ultimately, hopefully, in a positive direction."

Bukhari, a Pakistani who has lived in the West for 17 years, said that when "looked at in the time period of 30 to 40 years, things are going very much in a positive direction. Especially with those Muslims living in Western societies. But we are talking only about 30 to 40 years. What evolution will the next 30 to 40 years bring?"

Fredericks, a priest of the San Francisco archdiocese whose field is comparative religion, comments, "We Americans are so concerned with the violent [Islamic] fringe, we miss what's going on at a deeper level."

To Fredericks, the geo-politic transformations Islam is signaling are enormous. This is a huge, huge topic. First, Christianity and Islam—you cannot say it about Judaism—are religions that have been at the foundations of empires. Further, Christianity and Islam are the bases of entire cultural outlooks.

Christian nations today are, by and large, secular societies, in which Protestantism was able to adjust more quickly than Roman Catholicism. "Christianity has made its peace—an uneasy truce—with secular culture. Christianity," he continued, "has grudgingly yielded its place at the center of culture. It isn't that anymore."

The peace isn't total, and opposition to the peace does not just come from Christian reactionaries, traditionalists and conservatives. "We see opposition," he said, "not just from the new religious right, though in the culture wars they get all the publicity, but in the theology of liberation. The theology of liberation also says that religious voices, religious values, need to be very public realities at the center of culture.

"The other thing—and it's such a complicated picture," he said, "there is something in the very character of Christianity that resists privatization. Christianity wants to be a very public religion. So when Christianity becomes a private religion, it is in a rather anomalous situation."

The same statement, he said, can be made about Islam. "Islam wants to be a very public force, a very public reality." Islam wants of its very character to be the basis of society. It always has.

"From the beginnings of Islam," said Fredericks, "submitting to Islam meant renouncing one culture that was sinful and violent and discriminatory and based on petty racial and ethnic rivalries, and recognizing there is this universal humanity, universal morality. A powerful conversion takes place from an immoral society to a moral society." In fact, he said, submission—submission to Allah—is what Islam means.

For Islam to accept a privatized place within secular society "is very, very difficult. We in the West tend to presume that this is an inevitable process. I think that's naive."

Fredericks argues that because Christians "slowly and begrudgingly, and with a great deal of violence" more or less worked out a modus vivendi with the secular nation, Muslims will not necessarily follow suit.

"Why should we presume that that's normative?" he asked.

"Alternative Modernities"

Speaking to Bukhari's point about Islam in the recent post-colonial period, Fredericks talked of "alternative modernities," of Islamic states developing in unique and non-Western ways.

He uses Indonesia, the largest of all Islamic nations, as an example. "If one allows, and it is controversial to do so, that Indonesia's Sukarno [1949–1967] and Suharto [1967–1998] regimes were aftermaths connected to Dutch colonialism, then what we're hearing from Indonesia's Muslims today is, 'We want to be a nation. We don't want to go back to the Middle Ages. And—the West doesn't get this—we want to be a modern nation. We just don't want to be modern the way you're modern. We think that's sick.'"

Think of such a development, says Fredericks, in terms "of 'religious nationalism' as an alternative to Western secularism. Islam saying our religious nationalism is a way of being a modern, national state: Economically competitive, a state able to provide basic social services to its population. We want to be a success. But secularism—with all the immorality that comes with it—isn't going to cut it for us. We're not that kind of people. We want to be an Islamic state."

What the world may be witnessing, contends Fredericks, is not just a violent fringe but manifestations of religious nationalism that from Egypt to

Iran to Indonesia "may have more in common with the theology of liberation than we've recognized. Both are a critique of Western secular, capitalist, consumerist, materialist, globalist secularism. And that's something we ought to pay attention to and be respectful of." Like Islam, liberation theology seeks to put Christian values, such as a preferential option for the poor, at the center of culture.

Scott Bartchy, director of the Center for the Study of Religion at UCLA, said Americans need to understand that at the deepest level they have been moving away from cultural values built around honor–shame–still the dominant framework for values around much of the world. In contrast, the United States "has an achievement-guilt culture focused almost entirely on the individual," he said.

"Certainly we have very little sense of honor," he said. "Most Americans will say honor is nice, but give me the check instead. And if we had any shame, we wouldn't have had the last 20 years of U.S. politics."

Bartchy said that in Germany in the 1970s, Chancellor Willi Brandt resigned as a matter of honor when an East German mole penetrated West Germany's security services. In Japan, "CEOs or government officers caught in whatever, resign." By contrast, he said, "in America if you get caught out, you back and fill. You don't resign, you just tough it out."

The 80 percent of the world living with honor-shame values have strict gender divisions and roles, systems that generate enormous competition among the males, and a sense of bonding within the family. "Islam," he said, "has created a sense of what anthropologists call 'fictive' and I choose to call 'surrogate' kinship: It goes beyond the family to create a sense of brotherhood. It's no accident that the extremist group in Egypt is the 'Brotherhood.'"

In many ways, said Bartchy, "Islam, for all the way it looks, is still kind of a thin overlay of ancient tribal cultures." For example, nothing in the Quran or the Islamic tradition supports honor killing of women, yet in some countries women are killed if they have been raped, he said. "If the father isn't strong enough, the brothers are supposed to go out there and kill that woman. And if they can kill her in public it's even better, because that at least eliminates the shame from the family."

The only groups in the United States that live up to these strong honor-shame codes, Bartchy said, are inner-city gangs and the Mafia. They cannot allow themselves or their family to be "dissed, or shamed." Every time they step over the threshold, they are in competition with the world outside. "From the time you're 3 years old until you die, you do and say those things that will bring honor back to your family."

Which, in part, said Bartchy, explains Osama bin Laden's popularity in Afghanistan. "Whatever else he was doing," he said, "Osama was accumulating an enormous amount of honor. Spending his own wealth initially on the widows and orphans of the mujahideen–an enormous contrast to what the royal elites back home in Saudi Arabia were doing."

In bin Laden's eyes, said Bartchy, these Saudis were not sharing, and Islam requires it. As bin Laden and those sympathetic to him looked at the United States, "they saw the ever-increasing gap between the elite–the enormously rich—and the Americans at the bottom. Then Osama and his allies looked at the Saudi leadership doing the same and reasoned: 'How did Saudis learn that those values are OK? Because they looked to the West.'" (Bartchy left unanswered the next question: "How did the West learn that those values are OK?")

"Basically," he said, "what Muslims in the Near East want is the same things we want. Even the most conservative bring their kids to the United States to be educated. What they can't understand is how we say we're so strong for democracy and participation and yet we continue to prop up regimes in their part of the world they regard as terribly oppressive and corrupt."

At home what bothers Bartchy is the tone of the American popular response, even among his students. They believe, he said, "the only way to look at us is as the victims. We can do anything we damn well please overseas, and that should never have any effect on what comes down."

What the Peeves Really Are

Bush used the word crusade and apologized. He warned against racism and bigotry, and visited with Muslims at Islamic centers. Sound moves?

If Bush wants support, to prove he's not against Islam "the first place you start is at home," said Yvonne Haddad, professor of the history of Islam and Christian-Muslim relations at Georgetown University. "And his rhetoric—in the speech to Congress, listening to it as an American, I was impressed. Listening with the other ear, as Muslims overseas would hear it, it was awful: he talked about 'us' and 'them,' you're either with us or against us. He showed no reflection on what the issues, the peeves, really are."

And some of those peeves can be seen as related to the Crusades. Israel occupies the same geographic area the Crusades were about, she said. "Therefore anybody who supports Israel's policies is perceived as continuing the Crusades."

And a thousand years after the first one, the Crusades remain a source of contention.

Pressures That Led to an Empire-wide Movement

The Nine Crusades, which took place in the 11th, 12th and 13th centuries, were a counteroffensive by Christians against Muslims occupying the Holy Land.

Was the Islamic threat real? "You betcha," said Professor Paul E. Chevedden. "Islamic conquest had taken from Christendom its choicest province—Syria, Egypt, North Africa and Iberia [Spain and Portugal]."

Islam pushed its way north into Italy until it captured Monte Cassino, St. Benedict's monastery, then moved into eastern Switzerland. On the Great St. Bernard Pass, Muslims even captured the abbot of Cluny, France.

The Crusades, in response, were applications of Roman Catholicism's "just war" tradition, said Chevedden of UCLA's Gustav E. von Grunebaum Center for Near Eastern Studies. Islam had the Holy Land, and the pope wanted it back.

A grave pitfall for today, insists Chevedden, would be to view the Crusades in isolation from the world-transforming events in the Mediterranean and in western Asia at the turn of the second millennium. Those events included pressures from expanding populations, rapidly developing urbanism, intellectual and technological inquiries and advances, plus rising commerce pushing into new areas.

The clash between Christendom and Islam was a 1,000-year struggle, the most protracted conflict in human history. What should not be overlooked, Chevedden said, is that, for the most part, Islam, rather than Christianity, was in the ascendancy.

Scott Bartchy, director of UCLA's Center for the Study of Religion, though well aware of what Islam gave to the West during those 1,000 years, looks at the early heritage of both Christianity and Islam from the perspective of violence/non-violence.

During the first 250 to 300 years of Christianity, it was initially persecuted, then scapegoated through four more tense periods, as it became an empire-wide movement. "Never," emphasized Bartchy, "never once during this period is anybody killed in the name of Jesus. The Christians are not a guerrilla band, they are not social bandits. They stay in the urban environment, gain a reputation not only for helping their own widows and orphans, but others' as well. Not only burying their own dead but—a major deal at that time—other people's as well. They never become violent."

Bartchy called it "remarkable" that Jesus' nonviolence had taken "such a hold" across those early centuries. It was Emperor Constantine's adopting Christianity as the Roman Empire's religion in the fourth century that "wrecked things. He never got it," said Bartchy. "He puts the Chi-Rho symbol on Roman shields, and for the first time Christians start killing people in the name of Jesus."

Bartchy contrasts that Jesus with Islam's Muhammad who, in the early seventh century, "goes into Medina and in effect becomes the civil authority. Functionally he's an innovator, a Jesus of Nazareth and a Constantine, all rolled into one."

Bartchy said Muhammad "never ever renounces violence, and for all the fine things in the Islamic tradition, there's never been any serious commitment to nonviolence. In a war, if you follow the prophet, you shouldn't hurt women or children. Or trees. Quite charming that. And the violence should be defensive."

Bartchy said that after the Crusades the Near Eastern Islamic world felt itself transgressed upon, "and there's a certain victim mentality." Culturally, he said, Muslims saved much from the Greek philosophers that the West later appropriated. Technologically Islam held its own, even into the 16th and 17th centuries. "But then the West got the technological edge in military stuff and began pushing," said Bartchy, "and the Muslims again get into the mentality of being victims."

Consequently, Bartchy summarized, today "some of the more extreme people have given themselves permission to do almost anything in the name of defense. And that's what we see."

The Crusades were religious, political and economic. The First Millennium had just ended, the 11th century was the setting of an enormous spiritual revival. For centuries, with the Holy Land under benign Islamic rule, pilgrims traveled together to Jerusalem under arms to protect themselves from robbers. Confessors in that era regularly gave pilgrimages as a penance, so ensuring the safety of pilgrims was one element of the Crusades.

Other elements included merchants in Italian cities wanting Eastern trading outlets and the ambitions of chivalrous knights—high-born youths looking for action and conquest.

There also was a shift within Islam precipitating the Crusades. The more restrictive Turkish Muslims had taken over the Holy Land, and the pope, disenchanted with the warring European nobles' inability to form a coalition to battle Islam, brought his own unifying authority to bear.

The scene was set, and all the elements combined in the urge to free the Holy Land from Islam. Thus nine Crusades, each generally less successful than the one before it.

Crusaders Went from Victory to Disaster

In box scores, there were nine Crusades between 1095 and 1272. The outcome was Crusaders 2, Muslims 5, plus two negotiated ties. And the Muslims remained in control.

The Crusades (1095–1272) got their name from the crosses Pope Urban II distributed in 1095 after he called on the factious European kings and princes to band together and recover the Holy Sepulcher from the Muslim Seljuk Turks.

They agreed. It would be the first of nine crusades.

Even as the potential First Crusaders were looking into strategy and logistics, peasants in France heard the papal call. Less worried than their leaders about tactics and supplies, several thousand started marching. They resupplied themselves by sacking Belgrade. German peasants set out and financed themselves by attacking Jews.

At Constantinople, what was left of these ragtag bands joined forces, sailed to Jerusalem, dispersed the Turks and declared a victory.

The European nobility finally set off, led by Raymond IV of Toulouse and Bishop Ademar. The First Crusade (1096–99) took Nicea, Antioch and consolidated Western control over what they now called the Latin Kingdom of Jerusalem, with Godfrey of Bouillon as ruler.

The Muslims retaliated. The Second Crusade (1147–49) failed to recapture cities taken by the Turks; the Third Crusade (1189–91) failed to retake Jerusalem, which was back in Muslim hands. But Saladin decreed Christians could have access to the Holy Sepulcher.

The Fourth Crusade (1220–04) got bogged down in the more profitable venture of fighting Venice, sacking Constantinople, crushing the Byzantine Empire and establishing the Latin Empire of Constantinople.

Quite disastrous was the 1202 Children's Crusade, led by two young peasants. Stephen in France and Nicolas in Germany led several thousand children out of their homelands and into starvation and disease, and into the arms of adults who sold them into slavery and other fates worse than death.

The second longest crusade, the Fifth Crusade (1218–21) was an unsuccessful war against Egypt, and the Sixth Crusade (1228–29), which eschewed military arms, was led by Holy Roman Emperor Frederick II who negotiated a degree of Christian control over the holy sites.

France's Louis IX led the next two crusades, the Seventh (1248–50) and Eighth (1270), with no noticeable gains. Louis died in North Africa, and the Eighth Crusade was called off. The English launched the Ninth Crusade (1271–72) under Prince Edward. It changed nothing, though the prince later became King Edward I.

Jonathan Phillips

 **NO**

Who Were the First Crusaders?

Who were the people who answered Urban II's call to crusade between 1096 and 1099? Jonathan Phillips investigates their origins and motives.

The canons of the council summarised the offer made by Urban II as he launched the First Crusade:

> Whoever, for devotion alone, not to gain honour or money, goes to Jerusalem to liberate the Church of God can substitute this journey for all penance.

In other words, if people fought God's enemies on earth and completed a pilgrimage to the Holy Land, their actions would receive a spiritual reward of remarkable magnitude. Urban blended the familiar ideas of pilgrimage and penance with the more radical notion of papally-sanctioned violence to produce what a contemporary writer described as "a new means of attaining salvation." He followed the speech at Clermont with an extensive preaching tour through France and by the dispatch of letters and legations elsewhere in Europe.

The response to his appeal was remarkable, and in total almost 60,000 people set out for the Holy Land. The population of Europe at the end of the eleventh century is estimated to have been around 20 million, so clearly the vast majority of people chose to remain in the West. If, however, one adds contact through ties of family and friendship then it is clear that the crusade touched the lives of millions.

Fulcher of Chartres, a participant in the crusade, wrote that people "of any and every occupation" took the cross. He also commented "whoever heard of such a mixture of languages in one army, since there were French, Flemings, Frisians, Gauls, Allobroges [Savoyards], Lotharingians, Allemani [South Germans and Swiss], Bavarians, Normans, English, Scots, Aquitainians, Italians, Danes, Apulians, Iberians, Bretons, Greeks and Armenians." Representatives of the last two groups probably joined the expedition en route, but the remainder had been attracted by Urban's initial call to arms. The crusade therefore appealed to people from almost every level of society right across Christian Europe. The purpose here is to give some insight into who the First Crusaders were, to explain why they took the cross, and to understand the importance of identifying those who took part in the expedition.

From *History Today,* Vol. 47, No. 3, March 1997, pp. 16(7). Copyright © 1997 by History Today, Ltd. Reprinted by permission.

The reasons for such a wide-ranging response are complex. Our distance from events and the nature of the surviving evidence mean that we can never achieve a perfect insight into a crusader's mind. We should not necessarily look for a single motive in determining an individual's desire to take the cross, although certain themes emerge more clearly than others. An understanding of the actions of each crusader must be grounded in the cultural, political and economic context of the time.

Spiritual concerns were a prominent factor governing people's lives in the late eleventh century. It was an intensely religious age; pilgrimage and monastic life flourished, and donations to ecclesiastical institutions were increasingly commonplace. Christian Europe was also one of the most guilt-ridden societies in history. Sin was ubiquitous in everyday life and the images of fire and torture so frequently depicted on churches reinforced the fear of eternal damnation. The need for all people—whether rich or poor, nobles or labourers—to atone for their actions helps to explain the level of enthusiasm for the First Crusade and also the crusaders' determination to fulfil their vows by completing the journey to Jerusalem.

The pope's original conception of the crusade was for a compact contingent of knights to assist Emperor Alexius of Byzantium in his struggle against the Seljuk Turks of Asia Minor before marching on to the Holy Land. His appeal was directed, therefore, towards the knightly classes of his native France, a region of weak central authority and endemic lawlessness which was often initiated by the knights themselves. The crusade may have been one way to channel this violence elsewhere as well as giving the knights an opportunity of salvation. The knights responded in large numbers and formed the backbone of the Christian army.

As we have seen, however, Urban's offer was so attractive that almost all elements of society were represented on the crusade. The most notable exception to this was the absence of any kings. Urban regarded the crusade as a papally-directed enterprise and had not explicitly invited the secular monarchs to become involved. In any case, Philip I of France was excommunicated on account of an adulterous relationship with the Countess of Anjou; Henry IV of Germany was the papacy's principal opponent in a bitter struggle concerning the supremacy of lay versus sacral power (known as the Investiture Contest), and William Rufus was too entangled in the government of England to be particularly interested. It was not until the crusade of Sigurd of Norway (1107–10), that a king participated in a campaign in the Holy Land, although it should be noted that the rulers of Spain had long been involved in the Reconquista, their own struggle against the Muslims.

While the non-participation of kings may be regarded as part of Urban's design, the pope had not anticipated that his call would appeal to monks. He wrote "we do not want those who have abandoned the world and vowed themselves to spiritual warfare either to bear arms or to go on this journey; we go so far as to forbid them to do so." Other churchmen such as priests and clerks, were permitted to join as long as they secured the permission of their bishop, and in any case, some religious officials were needed to administer to the crusaders' spiritual needs during the course of the expedition. Urban's message also struck a deep chord with the wider populace, including women, children, the old, the infirm and the poor. Clearly these groups would hinder the progress of an army because they had to be fed and protected. The pope tried to limit their involvement by requiring people to consult their parish priests before taking their vows, but this measure failed and the crusade set out accompanied by many noncombatants. In the course of the crusade the majority of this anonymous mass perished through starvation or disease, deserted, or were enslaved.

It is among the members of the noble and knightly classes that we can begin to pinpoint the individuals who took the cross. In part this is because, as men of standing, their deeds feature in the narrative accounts of the crusade. Some, such as the southern Italian knight, Hugh the Beserk, are mentioned on only one occasion for an act of particular bravery: in this case because Hugh had single-handedly defended a tower for an entire day against Turkish attacks during the siege of Antioch. For the leaders of the major contingents, however, there is a much fuller picture, particularly when their force happens to have included a chronicler. The anonymous author of the Gesta Francorum, for example, was a member of Bohemond of Taranto's army, and Raymond of Aguilers was the chaplain to Raymond of Saint-Gilles, the Count of Toulouse. The latter writer noted "It seems too tiresome to write of each journey . . . so we have taken care to write of the Count of Saint-Gilles without bothering with the others." In the case of Hugh of Vermandois, younger brother of Philip I of France, there is much less information because, as far as we are aware, no member of his contingent wrote an account of the crusade.

While narrative works provide the majority of our material they are not the only source of information for the crusade. In recent years the use of charters has enhanced our understanding of the motivation, financing and family networks of the crusaders. It is the nature of eleventh-century charters which holds the key to this. Charters from later periods tend to convey only a bare minimum of information, such as names, places, dates, and the exact subject of the transaction. Some charters from the time of the First Crusade, however, provide more of a clue to the hopes and fears of individual crusaders, as well as basic factual information.

Crusading was extremely expensive. To equip oneself with chainmail, horses and supplies would cost a great deal—some estimates suggest over four years' annual income. However, the recent experience of the Norman Conquest, for example, would have given people some idea of the resources needed to fight a large-scale and lengthy military expedition. In order to finance the crusade it was often necessary to mortgage or sell lands and rights to the church. The records of these transactions give further indication as to who took part and how they raised money for the journey. Incidentally, the issue of cost is another reason why the old cliche of crusaders being freebooting younger sons is deeply suspect, simply because such men would have been unable to afford to set out in the first instance.

In fact, largely through the use of charters, all sorts of combinations of family members can be found on the crusade. For example, Hugh of Merysur-Seine mortgaged lands at Rosnay to the abbey of Molesme in order to pay for both his own and his brother's journey. Jonathan Riley-Smith has traced the remarkable involvement of the Montlhery clan. One member, Miles of Bray, was accompanied on the First Crusade by his son, Guy, his brother-in-law, Walter of St. Valery, and two of Walter's sons; his nephew, Baldwin (later Baldwin II of Jerusalem), and two other nephews—Humberge of Le Puiset and Everard III of Le Puiset—were amongst members of the network to take the cross in 1095–96.

Some crusader families had an existing tradition of pilgrimage to the Holy Land which may have formed a further reason for their taking the cross. For example, both the great-grandfather and the grandfather of the First Crusader, Adhemar III of Limoges, had been to Jerusalem in the course of the eleventh century. The influence of pilgrimage is a theme more thoroughly explored in the work of Marcus Bull.

Although the religious motivation of the First Crusaders should be emphasised, it would be naive to argue that other interests were absent. When a noble embarked upon the crusade it was inevitable that he would be accompanied by his household retainers. He would have to provide support for his knights, squires and servants. All were an integral part of a medieval army and, because of this, ties of allegiance and loyalty should be advanced as a further reason for taking the cross, even though such a commitment was, in theory, a strictly voluntary exercise. The desire for land was a further motive, but it did not apply to all the crusaders. Many charters contain clauses detailing financial arrangements that would come into force only if the crusader died during the expedition. Such measures suggest that the participants were well aware of the dangers of the crusade, but hoped to return home once the vow was completed. Two brothers, Bernard and Odo, entered into an agreement with the abbey of Cluny:

> For the remission of our sins, setting out with all the others on the journey to Jerusalem, we have made over for 100 solidi . . . a manor known as Busart. We are making this on the condition that if, on the pilgrimage that we are undertaking, we may die, the manor may remain in perpetuity under the control of . . . the monastery of Cluny. But if we may return . . . we may keep it in our lifetime, but after our death it may not come into the possession of our heirs . . . but will pass to Cluny.

The fact that the Crusader States were seriously undermanned throughout their existence also indicates that relatively few crusaders chose to remain in the Levant and become settlers. Some men, however, were explicit in their intention never to return to the West and clearly planned to carve out new territories for themselves in the East. Raymond of Saint-Gilles was rumoured to be one such person. The French knight Achard of Montmerle might also have been planning to stay in the Holy Land. The charter detailing his agreement with the abbey of Cluny includes the clause "if I die, or if I choose to remain in those lands [the Levant] . . ." shows at least an awareness of the possibility of settling in the East, a course of action which would presumably necessitate the taking of land.

The need to repay debts incurred in paying for the expedition, coupled with poor economic conditions—a series of droughts and bad harvests had marked the early 1090s—suggests that the desire for money may have been a priority for the crusaders. Perhaps the search for salvation and the wish for financial gain seem too mutually exclusive in our eyes. One has only to think of TV evangelism to shudder at the potential for abuse in this connection, yet it is not improbable or contradictory that pious men took the cross also hoping to improve their financial and material prospects. There must also have been crusaders for whom the wish to accumulate wealth predominated. The sources indicate that such people must have been gravely disappointed. There is remarkably little evidence of people returning from the crusade with new-found riches. One rare example is reported by Abbot Suger of Saint Denis. He wrote that Count Guy of Rochefort "returned from the expedition to Jerusalem renowned and rich," an ironic reversal of Urban II's injunction against crusaders seeking honour or money.

People certainly brought back relics from the Holy Land. Lord Riou of Loheac, for example, acquired a fragment of the True Cross and bequeathed it to his local church when he died in 1101. But the experience of the First Crusade does not suggest that it was the route to easy profit. None-the-less, the narrative sources contain frequent reports of the crusaders seeking booty. After the siege of Ma'arrat an Nu'man (December 1098) Muslim graves were dug up and the bodies slit open to check if any treasure had been swallowed. Acts of a similarly brutal nature were repeated elsewhere. The most likely explanation for this behaviour is that substantial sums of money were required to keep the expedition going.

The duration and rigour of the campaign exhausted the resources of the vast majority. Crusaders endured terrible suffering during the march across Asia Minor and at the siege of Antioch (October 1097–June 1098). Food prices became grossly inflated and losses of horses and equipment were enormous. It is an important distinction, therefore, that acts of greed were usually initiated in response to the need to survive, rather than the long-term motivation to accumulate treasure. For those interested solely in money, the cost of warfare and the duration of the expedition meant that the depredation of land closer to home had to be a safer option than going on crusade. If some had set out hoping to acquire untold riches it seems that the hardships of the expedition soon deterred them because throughout the course of the crusade a stream of deserters left the main army unable to endure the experience.

News of the expedition to Jerusalem spread rapidly across Northern and Central Europe and also down through Italy and to Sicily. The pope accepted the reality of the situation and began to dispatch letters of instruction and encouragement to these areas. The only region where he actively discouraged recruitment was the Iberian peninsula because he did not want people distracted from the "reconquista," although we know that some Spanish crusaders ignored him and travelled to Jerusalem. When the forces of the First Crusade began to assemble in 1096 the racial mix of the armies is an impressive testimony to the power of Urban's appeal. Another indication of the range of participants involved is provided by Raymond of Aguilers. He relates that in the Provencal contingent alone no less than seven different currencies were in circulation. He mentioned the use of coins from Lucca, Chartres, Le Mans,

Melgueil, Le Puy, Valence and Poitou. Currency from the first five places have been discovered in a single collection at Antioch and tentatively associated with the siege that took place there.

Because almost every region of Latin Christendom was represented on the First Crusade difficulties emerged in communication and leadership. Problems also arose on account of hostility between regional contingents of the army. An episode related by Ralph of Caen—a visitor to the Levant soon after the First Crusade—serves to illustrate the tensions that sometimes broke out in the course of the campaign. As morale sagged during the siege of Antioch, gangs of northern and southern French grouped up on linguistic lines to forage for supplies. They assaulted or freed their captives according to the language they spoke, while those responding in tongues other than Occitan or a northern French dialect were spared as neutrals.

In the course of the crusade and afterwards, the Franks (as they were known collectively) established a series of states in the Levant. During the early years of settlement the polyglot nature of the crusader army was, to some extent, distilled. In some states the origins of the dominant Latin Christian element reflected the ancestry of the particular leader who had based himself there. Bohemond of Taranto's principality of Antioch had a strong contingent of Normans from Southern Italy. Similarly, because it was Raymond of Saint-Gilles who had set up the county of Tripoli, the area had a Provencal influence. The kingdom of Jerusalem, in consequence of its spiritual importance, attracted sellers from a wider number of regions and represented, therefore, a more diverse grouping.

The creation of the Frankish states, each with its own character and links to the West, as well as the over-arching bond of Latin Christianity, meant that strong ties existed between the settlers and their co-religionists in Europe. As the Muslim jihad gathered momentum in the course of the twelfth century, the Franks in the East needed military and financial help. It is interesting to note that traditions of crusading and ties of kinship between those in the Holy Land and the West were two ideas that the settlers emphasised in their attempts to secure support.

Pope Eugenius III drew attention to the concept of crusading ancestry in Quantum Praedecessores his appeal for the Second Crusade (1145–49). He wrote:

> It will be seen as a great token of nobility and uprightness if those things acquired by the efforts of the fathers are vigorously defended by you, their good sons. But if, God forbid, it comes to pass differently, then the bravery of the fathers will have proved to be diminished in the sons. We impress upon you . . . to defend in this way the Eastern Church, which was freed from their [the Muslims'] tyranny, as we have said before by the spilling of your fathers' blood.

In effect this amounted to an appeal to those families with traditions of crusading. The counts of Flanders were a group particularly receptive to such a message. They also had close family ties with the settlers. When Count Thierry took the cross in 1146 he was perpetuating a well-established line of involvement with the Holy Land. His grandfather, Robert I, had mounted a large-scale pilgrimage to Jerusalem in 1087–90. His uncle, Count Robert II, was one of the leading figures on the First Crusade. His cousin, Count Charles the Good, had visited Jerusalem around 1107, and was probably offered the throne of the kingdom of Jerusalem in 1123–24. In 1134 Thierry gained close links with the house of Jerusalem through his marriage to Sibylla of Anjou, a daughter of King Fulk. Thierry had also journeyed to the Holy Land in 1139 and seems to have planned another trip in 1142 only to turn back at an early stage.

An awareness of the identity of the First Crusaders reveals the impact of Pope Urban's call on the people of Europe in 1095–96. But answering the question "Who were the First Crusaders?" can tell us more. We are able to use the answer to start following traditions of crusading and the creation of family ties between the Levant and the West and from this information we have a better understanding of the nature of Latin settlement in the East and the subsequent history of the crusades.

POSTSCRIPT

Could the Crusades Be Considered a Christian Holy War?

With the emergence of Islamic revivalism in the modern world, the historical relationships between the West and the Muslim world have taken center stage. Are the Crusades at the root of this contemporary conflict? The Islamic world has always viewed the Crusades as an invasion of its territory by a foreign power; the west has not shared this perspective. This issue asks: To what extent can the Crusades be viewed as a Christian Holy War? As the West responds to radical Islamic-inspired terrorism today with shock and outrage, is it not possible that a millennium ago, Middle Eastern Muslims responded in the same manner to the European crusaders?

Both struggles spring, at least in part, from religious motivation present. Christian crusaders believed they were fighting a just war in the service of God; securing indulgences for services rendered; and the ultimate prize, gaining the right to eternal salvation. With a slight change in language, we hear the same promises in Islamic revivalism—fighting the infidels in the name of Allah; participating in a fierce struggle between the forces of good and evil; and ultimately acquiring a special place in heaven as martyrs of the faith. Failure to hear these resonances might prevent us from learning a lesson form history.

For sources on the Crusades from a Muslim viewpoint, see: Amin Maalouf, *The Crusades Through Arab Eyes* (Schocken Books, 1985); Francesco Gabrieli, ed., *Arab Historians of the Crusades* (University of California Press, 1984); and Carol Hillenbrand, *The Crusades: Islamic Perspectives* (Routledge, 2000). Karen Armstrong's *Holy War: The Crusades and their Impact on Today's World* (Anchor Books, 2001) is a Western source that speaks of the Crusades in an objective and critical manner, especially their links with contemporary conflicts among Muslims, Christians, and Jews in the Middle East.

As far as general sources on the Crusades are concerned, start with Steven Runciman's three-volume work *A History of the Crusades*, 4th ed. (Cambridge University Press, 1954). Jonathan Riley-Smith's *The First Crusaders, 1095–1131* (Cambridge University Press, 1997) represents current scholarship. Smith states that the Crusades "drew on the tradition of Pilgrimage to Jerusalem . . . and pious violence" as motivating forces. He also points out that many of the Crusaders from the times he researched came from the same families and clans, and concludes that the sustenance they received from these ties helped make the Crusades possible. A readable, popular account of the Crusades, which features many interesting illustrations and useful maps, is W. B. Bartlett, *God Wills It: An Illustrated History of the Crusades* (Oxford University Press, 1999). Another general source is Thomas F. Madden, *A Concise History of the Crusades* (Roman & Littlefield, 1999).

ISSUE 10

Does the Modern University Have Its Roots in the Islamic World?

YES: Mehdi Nakosteen, from *History of Islamic Origins of Western Education: A.D. 800–1350* (University of Colorado Press, 1964)

NO: Walter Rüegg, from "The University as a European Institution," in Hilde De Ridder-Symoens, ed., *A History of the University in Europe, volume I* (Cambridge University Press, 1992)

ISSUE SUMMARY

YES: Professor of history and philosophy of education Mehdi Nakosteen traces the roots of the modern university to the Golden Age of Islamic culture (750–1150 C.E.). He maintains that Muslim scholars assimilated the best of classical scholarship and developed both the experimental method and the university system, which they passed on to the West before declining.

NO: Emeritus professor of sociology Walter Rüegg calls the university "the European institution *par excellence*," citing its origin as a community of teachers and taught, accorded certain rights that included the granting of degrees, and as a creation of medieval Europe—the Europe of papal Christianity.

As in many other issues, much depends on how we define a university. If one thinks of "higher education"—a serious pursuit of advanced learning, under the tutelage of scholars of acknowledged reputations—we can trace one path of historical research. If, instead, we define the university as a corporation, dedicated to learning rather than commerce, and possessing specialized functions and titles, we might travel a different path. Since the cultural world of medieval Europe is better known, let's begin with the forces and events that created the Muslim world of the same time period.

In the seventh century of this era, the prophet Muhammad united the Arab world under the banner of a new monotheistic religion, Islam, which means "surrender" to Allah or God. Muhammad's 622 "flight" from Mecca to Medina, known as Hijra or the breaking of former ties, marks the beginning of the Muslim lunar calendar. The Christian solar calendar begins with the birth of Jesus, calling everything after that date A.D. for *anno Domini* (in the year of our Lord) and everything before that date B.C. (before Christ). The year 2000 on the Christian calendar was 1420 A.H. [*anno Hegirae*] on the Muslim calendar. Scholars often use C.E. (common era) to replace A.D. and B.C.E. (before the common era) to replace B.C. You will find the A.H. and A.D. designations used in the following selections.

United under Islam, Arab warriors conquered the Persian Empire, took some Byzantine cities, crossed north Africa, and invaded Europe. Stopped at 732 in Tours, France, the Islamic conquest ushered in a "golden age" of learning centered in Cordoba, the capital of Muslim Spain. At that time, Muslims claim that the largest monastery library in Europe contained fewer than 100 books, whereas the library in Cordoba contained over 500,000. At a time when Europe had lost much of its Greco-Roman intellectual heritage and learning was at a low point, Muslim scholars were translating Greek works from the Persian and Byzantine cultures into Arabic and commenting on them. This learning, along with their original contributions in mathematics, medicine, science, and philosophy, was passed on to the West when Islamic culture was conquered first by the Seljuk Turks and later by Genghis Khan and the Mongols of Central Asia.

The Western intellectual debt to Islamic scholars is accepted widely. However, what about the college or university as an institution of higher learning? Were Western scholars able to take the world's heritage of learning and use it to fashion the modern world because they invented the university or because it, too, was borrowed from the Islamic world? It has been said that where you stand determines what you see. In the following selections professors Nakosteen and Rüegg stand within different cultural and academic traditions. Taking the "golden age" of Islamic culture into account permits Nakosteen to build a case for the Islamic origins of the university. If civilization began with the Greeks, however, and the Greeks had no universities, then Europeans logically conclude that the university must have been invented by Europeans. As predecessors and components of universities, colleges have a different history. Here, we find a point of agreement, as professor Rüegg grants they might be traced to Islamic models.

Nakosteen argues that the language barrier and general inaccessibility of historical material to Western scholars, along with religious prejudice and the decline of Islamic culture, have made it easy for Europeans to assume credit for the modern university. In actuality, he maintains, the university is rooted in the Islamic world. Rüegg, however, is concerned primarily with determining which European city—Bologna or Paris—can claim to be the first university. Using his definition of what constitutes a university, Rüegg cannot grant Muslim institutions of higher learning the title or status of a university.

The challenge put forth by Nakosteen is part of the revisionist process that has been going on in history for the last 30 or so years. Part of that process is challenging assumptions that have gone unchallenged for centuries. As other issues in this book have demonstrated, modern scholars are examining the influence of Africa on the Greeks and considering the contributions from Asia and the Arabic world with a new openness. Decide for yourself which definition of the entity called university is more accurate and which path of historical inquiry you find more compelling.

YES

Mehdi Nakosteen

The Nature and Scope of Muslim Education, 750–1350

All dates refer to A.D. unless otherwise specified.

Europe was in its medieval period when the Muslims wrote a colorful chapter in the history of education. Many of their greatest contributions, particularly to Western education, have gone unnoticed because of religious prejudice, language barriers, the decline of Islamic culture, and inaccessibility of historic materials for Western historians of education. The Muslims assimilated through their educational system the best of classical cultures and improved them. Among the assimilated fields were philosophy and Hellenistic medical, mathematical, and technological sciences; Hindu mathematics, medicine, and literature; Persian religions, literature, and sciences; and Syrian commentaries on Hellenistic science and philosophy. By applying the classical sciences to practical pursuits, the Muslims developed the empirical-experimental method, although they failed to take full advantage of it. Later the method was adopted in Europe. They encouraged free inquiry and made available to the public the instruments of research and scholarship. They opened their public and even private libraries to public use, not only regionally but internationally. At a time when books were "published" only through the tedious labor of copyists, they made hundreds, even thousands, of copies of reference materials and made them available to all caring to learn from them. Often they allowed scores of books—sometimes more than a hundred per person—to be borrowed for an almost indefinite time for special studies and prolonged research. They provided food, lodging, and even incidental money for scholars from far away; they made their great teachers internationally accessible by encouraging the concept of the travelling scholar.

In the golden age (750–1150) of their cultural-educational activities they did not permit theology and dogma to limit their scholarship. They searched into every branch of human knowledge, be it philology, history, historiography, law, sociology, literature, ethics, philosophy, theology, medicine, mathematics, logic, jurisprudence, art, architecture, or ceramics. They respected learning; they honored the scholar. They introduced the science and philosophy of the Greeks, Persians, and Hindus to Western Christian schoolmen. But the story of Western education's debt to Islam is still to be written with

From Mehdi Nakosteen, *History of Islamic Origins of Western Education A.D. 800–1350* (University of Colorado Press, 1964), pp. 37–42, 52–53, 61–63. Copyright © 1964 by University of Colorado Press. Reprinted by permission. Some notes omitted.

fullness of knowledge and without prejudice and predetermination of results. What kind of education was responsible for so much in so short a time?

Muslim education went through two distinct periods. First was the period covering the ninth and tenth centuries, when schools developed spontaneously with private endowments interested in public enlightenment; and second the period beginning in the eleventh century and developing through the twelfth and thirteenth centuries, when education became the function of the state, and schools were institutionalized for purposes of sectarian education and political indoctrination.

Madrasahs and Nizamiyyas

A new type of school was conceived as a state institution to promote religious indoctrination of the Sunnite Islamic faith and political indoctrination of a Turkish-Persian style, aside from general learning and particular training. Nizam-al-Mulk (d. 1092; 485 A.H.), the founder and popularizer of these *madrasahs* (schools of public instruction), was a famous vizier (prime minister) in the administration of the Seljuq sultans in the eleventh century. He established the madrasah about the middle of that century, which, though not the first school in Islam, was the first system of special schools geared to that state and Sunnite Islam. The madrasahs had, aside from their zest for learning, both political and religious purposes—the moulding of public opinion in Sunnite orthodox Islam against the Shi'ah branch. Large sums of money were allotted for the establishment and maintenance of these schools with generous scholarships, pensions, and rations granted to all worthy students. In fact, Nizam arranged for regular stipends to all students. The schools were institutionalized under state control and support, and standardized madrasahs were established in all large cities within Islam, with the exception of Spain and Sicily. The greatest of these academies was the one established by Nizam in Baghdad, the famous *Nizamiyyah*, which opened for teaching in 1066–67 (459 A.H.) and continued as a center of learning for several centuries, motivated primarily by religious and literary pursuits. Altogether, Nizam-al-Mulk made the greatest single contribution to education in founding and extending an almost universal system of schools (madrasahs) throughout Eastern Islam.[1] He was one of the most learned men of his time, greatly versed in Muslim hadith, or tradition, and one of the great political theorists of Islam, as shown in his famous *Siyasat-Namah*. His passion for universal education was limited only by the means at his disposal. The schools he founded all over the empire were endowed generously. He supplied them with libraries, the best professors he could find, and a system of scholarships to aid all the students. Let us look into his educational enterprise in some detail.

Nizam-al-Mulk and Muslim Education

The opening of the first school carrying the name of the Persian statesman, Nizam-al-Mulk, took place in 1066 (459 A.H.). It marks the transition from the mosque schools and the beginning of a system of public schools, or madrasahs, throughout the vast area of the Muslim world, which was under strong Persian cultural and administrative influence. This influence continued, first under Arab political supremacy under the Abbassides from the middle of the eighth century to the ninth, and again during the long period of Turkish (Ottoman) politico-religious supremacy, to the early decades of the sixteenth century (1517). It is true that the earlier Turks had a simple culture and were given to warfare and conquest. But settling down to administer their empire, they learned from the superior cultures of the Persians and the Arabs, adopted the Arabic alphabet, and accepted Islam. In time they adapted the foreign cultures to their own needs and tastes, and encouraged the establishment throughout their empire of schools to perpetuate Sunnite Islam and Turkish politics and policies. Tarikh Zaidan, in his *Al-Tamaddun al-Islami (History of Islamic Civilization)*, states that the Turkish princes encouraged learning and increased the number of schools in their empire, guided by three motives: The type of heavenly reward; the fear of losing their fortunes to more greedy superiors or antagonists, so that they utilized their wealth in establishing schools; finally, but most important of all, the desire to indoctrinate religious beliefs of the founder and to combat opposing religious views.

It was the employment of the school for sectarian indoctrination and political influence and propaganda that led the famous Seljuk Sultan Saladin to found madrasahs and also to close the college of Dar al-Ilm (The House of Learning) in Cairo in order to eliminate its Shi'ite influence. In fact it was not uncommon to dismiss professors during this period from the madrasahs because of their religious beliefs, particularly Shi'ite. Muslim scholasticism (*Ilm al-Kalam*) developed in these sectarian colleges of Sunnite or Shi'ite beliefs.

The Sunnite belief received its most sweeping expression under Nizam-al-Mulk. Before his day, there were several institutions of learning in the Islamic world which resembled a college, such as Al-Azhar in Cairo, Egypt, in the last quarter of the tenth century; Dar al-Ilm and Dar al-Hikmah, also in Cairo, in the early decades of the eleventh; Bait-al-Hikmah in Baghdad during the reign of al-Ma'mun; and Baihaqiyyah at Nishapur in Khrasan, Persia. But to Nizam-al-Mulk goes the distinct credit for having founded an institution for instruction and indoctrination under government and religious control, for political and religious ends—a sectarian system of public education with secular emphasis and political motivation.

With these objectives in mind, Nizam-al-Mulk established schools in every city and village of Iraq and Khorassan. Even a small place, such as "Kharn al-Jabal near Tus . . . had its teacher and school." These schools were well distributed from Khorassan in the east to Mesopotamia in the west. These so-called madrasahs soon became standardized, and many of them were built after the example of the one in Baghdad, which was built by Nizam-al-Mulk himself, and named Nizamiyyah (or Nidhamiyyah) in his honor.

> Nizamiyyahs . . . were founded not only in Baghdad, but in Nisabur, Balkh, Herat, Isfahan, Marw, Basrah and Mosul. Not only did Nizam-al-Mulk establish these academies or colleges, but he endowed them. It is estimated that $1,500,000 was spent annually on educational, semi-educational and religious institutions.

Nizamiyyah University, the most famous of the chain of madrasahs, was built in Baghdad in 1065 under the educator's personal supervision. The earliest account of this university is given by ibn Khaldun, the great Arab philosopher-historian, who says:

> Nizam-al-Mulk ordered that Abu Is'haq al-Shirazi should be its professor, but when the people were assembled to hear him he did not appear. He was searched for, but was not to be found; so Abu Nasir ibn-al-Sabbagh was appointed to the post. Later Abu Is'haq met his classes in his mosque, but his students showed their dissatisfaction with his action and threatened to go over to ibn al-Sabbagh unless he accepted the professorship at the Nizamiyyah. Finally he acceded to their wishes, and ibn al-Sabbagh was dismissed after having lectured for only twenty days.

The chief reason for Abu Is'haq's refusal to teach at the Nizamiyyah was, according to ibn Khallikan, that he was "informed that the greater part of the materials employed in the construction of the college have been procured illegally." But the foregoing quotation is of extreme interest for the information it gives us that the mosques were the chief places of learning before the foundation of universities. There were over one hundred such mosques in Baghdad alone.

The principal motive in founding the Nizamiyyah was religious. Its objective was the teaching of "The Shafi'ite (Sunni) school of law," its sole emphasis being upon the teaching of theology and Islamic law, and it stood as a university of Islamic theological learning for several centuries. The great mystic al-Ghazzali taught there twenty-five years after its founding. Al-Abiwardi (d. 1104; 498 A.H.) and ibn Mubarak (d. 1184; 580 A.H.) were associated with it. Ibn Jubair who visited the school about the middle of the fourteenth century, said of it: "And in the midst of Suq al-Thalatha (Tuesday market) is the wonderful madrasah Al-Nizamiyyah, whose beauty has become proverbial."

Aims of Muslim Education

The aims of Muslim education in "medieval" times may be defined as follows:

1. Religious aims, based on (a) *Qur'an* as source of knowledge, (b) spiritual foundation of education, (c) dependence upon God, (d) sectarian morals, (e) subordination of secular subjects to religion, (f) equality of all men before God and man, (g) supremacy of Muhammad over all other prophets, (h) belief in the six articles of Imam or Creed (God, angels, scripture, prophets, judgment, decrees) and (i) belief (and application) in A'amal or religious duties, including confession of faith (There is no God but God), prayers, alms, fasting, and pilgrimage.

2. Secular aims, the importance of which is well suggested by a Muslim tradition, attributed to Muhammad, which says, "The best among you are not those who neglect this world for the other, or the other world for this. He is the one who works for both together." Among these aims were pursuit of all knowledge, as the revelation of the nature of God; education open to all on equal terms, limited only by ability and interest; and guidance and teaching as essential to promote (initiate) knowledge and education.

The *Mutakallimun (Loquentes)*, the Muslim scholastic teachers (speakers of truths), stressed the importance of teachers whose knowledge may be traced back to relevation or may have been made manifest directly by intuition. This was the view of the theologian-philosopher-educator al-Ghazzali, who believed in three degrees of knowledge: (a) Common-sense knowledge, restricted by undisciplined sense-experience and dependent upon external authority; (b) scientific knowledge; (c) intuitive knowledge.

It is of interest to note that al-Ghazzali's concept of scientific knowledge includes seven basic principles or conditions: Stimulation of the search for scientific knowledge; application of scientific arts; advancement of applied sciences and extensive application of them; development of laboratory and experimental pursuits; encouragement of arts and crafts (It was Aristotle in particular, from among the Greeks, who appealed to Islam. This was because of the Greek master's application of philosophy and science to the arts and needs of everyday living and because of the adaptability of his philosophic and scientific concepts to the art of living and the necessities of individual and civic life); encouragement of individual initiative and academic freedom for both teachers and pupils (in the college of Baghdad an inquiring student, who greeted the great teacher with devoted *salams* [bows], often ended the day with an intellectual fist fight with his master in defense of some principles, refutation of others, or hairsplitting argument over insignificant details); attainment of excellence, to produce great men of learning and leaders in public affairs. The pragmatic spirit of their education is indicated by development of textile fabrics, of irrigation systems, of iron and steel products, of earthenwares, and leather products, by architectural innovations, weaving of rugs and carpets, manufacture of paper and gunpowder, maintenance of a merchant marine of a thousand ships, and advancement of commercial activity.

Although Muslim education aimed at practical training, such training was a rule based upon instruction in fundamental sciences. Thus, in the system, practice was sustained by theory; theory verified in practice. Even in commercial training, economics as a science was a foundational training.

It is of interest to note that as Islam began to decline after the end of the eleventh century, the number of its schools of higher learning increased and flourished. These colleges were, however, almost all denominational schools opened and supported by leaders of various Islamic religious factions. Each denominational college was open, with few exceptions, only to followers of a given sect. Religious and literary studies and Arabic language and grammar dominated the subject matter at the expense of philosophy, science, and social studies. The very abundance of these religious schools indicated the gradual decline which was under way. These colleges were intolerant of innovations, suspicious of secular studies, and aloof from creative scholars. Some of these colleges survived destruction by the Mongols in the thirteenth century and remained centers of dogmatic theological instruction to the fourteenth and fifteenth centuries.

There was competition among these denominational schools, particularly between the Shi'ite and Sunnite (Hanafite) religious factions. This competition proved healthy in the increase of these colleges and in their facilities, endowments, and the like, and would have been a tremendous educational power except for their limitations because of their religious nature.

It is of interest also to note that during this same period new universities were beginning to develop in western Europe, particularly in Italy, Germany, France, and England. But unlike the Islamic denominational schools, the Western universities were preserving the best intellectual elements that Islamic research and scholarship had developed during its creative centuries, from the ninth to the twelfth centuries. Islamic works were reaching Europe at about the same period (twelfth and thirteenth centuries) when secular learning was declining in Islam. The works of hundreds of translators not only enriched and created or enlarged many Western universities but brought about the Western Renaissance of the fourteenth and fifteenth centuries. One reason for this, of course, was the revival of secular interest and research in the West, which, though curtailed by religious passion until the seventeenth and eighteenth centuries, was left relatively free from then on to discover new knowledges and usher in the modern world. . . .

The Curriculum of Muslim Schools

The curriculum of Muslim education at that time reminds us in its extensive and intensive nature of curricular programs of modern advanced systems of education, particularly on higher levels of education. It was not unusual to find instruction in mathematics (algebra, trigonometry, and geometry), science (chemistry, physics, and astronomy), medicine (anatomy, surgery, pharmacy, and specialized medical branches), philosophy (logic, ethics, and metaphysics), literature (philology, grammar, poetry, and prosody), social sciences, history, geography, political disciplines, law, sociology, psychology, and jurisprudence, theology (comparative religions, history of religions, study of the *Qur'an*, religious tradition [*hadith*], and other religious topics). They offered advanced studies in the professions, for example, law and medicine.

Their vocational curriculum was varied and founded on the more general studies; in fact, it appears generally to have been as comprehensive as their education was universal. The extent and depth of Muslim curriculum can be detected by references to a number of encyclopedias of general knowledge and specific disciplines, among them the celebrated *Encyclopedia of the Ikhwan al-Safa* (the *Brethren of Purity or Sincerity*), which was known to and respected by European schoolmen.

Another indication of the extent of Muslim curriculum is manifested in the fact that one Arabic dictionary contained sixty volumes, with an illustration for each definition. Again, its richness may be determined by its practical and useful consequences, leading to such ventures as calculating the angle of the ecliptic, measuring the size of the earth, calculating the procession of the equinoxes, inventing the pendulum clock, explaining in the field of optics and physics such phenomena as "refraction of light, gravity, capillary attraction and twilight," using the globe in teaching the geography of a round earth, developing observatories for the empirical study of heavenly bodies, making advances in the uses of drugs, herbs, and foods for medication, establishing hospitals with a system of interns and externs, improving upon the science of navigation, introducing new concepts of irrigation, fertilization, and soil cultivation, discovering causes of certain diseases and developing correct diagnoses of them, proposing new concepts of hygiene, making use of anesthetics in surgery with newly innovated surgical tools, introducing the science of dissection in anatomy, furthering the scientific breeding of horses and cattle, and finding new ways of grafting to produce new types of flowers and fruits. In the area of chemistry, the curriculum led to the discovery of such substances as potash, alcohol, nitrate of silver, nitric acid, sulphuric acid, and corrosive sublimate. It also developed to a high degree of perfection the arts of textiles, ceramics, and metallurgy. . . .

Some Muslim Contributions to Education

Before concluding this brief summary of "medieval" Muslim education, it may be well to point out some of its basic contributions to educational theory and practice, and state also its basic shortcomings.

Throughout the twelfth and part of the thirteenth centuries, Muslim works on science, philosophy, and other fields were translated into Latin, particularly from Spain, and enriched the curriculum of the West, especially in northwestern Europe.

1. The Muslims passed on the experimental method of science, however imperfect, to the West.
2. The system of Arabic notation and decimals was introduced to the West.
3. Their translated works, particularly those of men such as Avicenna in medicine, were used as texts in classes of higher education far into the middle of the seventeenth century.
4. They stimulated European thought, reacquainted it with the Greek and other classical cultures and thus helped bring about the Renaissance.
5. They were the forerunners of European universities, having established hundreds of colleges in advance of Europe.
6. They preserved Greco-Persian thought when Europe was intolerant of pagan cultures.
7. European students in Muslim universities carried back new methods of teaching.
8. They contributed knowledge of hospitals, sanitation, and food to Europe.

The strength of the Muslim educational system lay in the following areas: It produced great scholars in almost every field. It developed literacy on a universal scale when illiteracy was the rule in Europe. It transmitted the best features of classical cultures to the West. It led the way in the development of libraries and universities. Its higher education in its creative centuries was open to rich and poor alike, the only requirements being ability and ambition. It held teachers and books in reverence, particularly on higher levels of instruction. The teacher, the book, the lecture, the debate—these were the nerve centers of its educational system.

The curriculum, which was in the early centuries balanced between sectarian and secular studies, became in the later centuries scholastic, making all or practically all secular studies subject to religious and theological approval. The curriculum became formal, fixed, traditional, religious, dogmatic, backward looking. It encouraged static minds and conformity. It became authoritarian and essentialist.

Whereas in its early centuries Muslim education encouraged debates, experimentation, and individualism, in its later stages it encouraged formal methods, memorization, and recitation. A system which was in its early stages rather spontaneous and free, encouraging individuals to pursue learning and inspire others to enlightenment, lost in the later stages this sense of intellectual adventure and its direction became superimposed from the top (the state and church) rather than inspired by the people. This led in time to an elite and aristocratic concept of education, replacing its early democratic educational spirit. Muslim education did not, and with its scholastic disciplines could not, take advantage of the tools of science and experimentation which it had inherited and improved upon. Rather, it passed on these tools to European men of science, who utilized them effectively after the Renaissance and thus initiated and developed the modern world of science.

Note

1. Among the leading founders of schools in Islam should also be mentioned al Ma'mun (d. 833; 218 A.H.), who supported and endowed the first great Muslim educational center in Baghdad, the famous *Bait-al-Hikmah*, and was instrumental in having Greek, Persian, and Hindu translations made into Arabic by the greatest scholars of the time; Nur-al-Din (d. 1173; 569 A.H.), the Sultan of the kingdom of Syria who, after the dissolution of the Seljuq Empire, founded schools in Damascus and throughout his kingdom, including Egypt; Saladin (d. 1193; 589 A.H.), who extended the school systems in Syria and Egypt.

Walter Rüegg

 **NO**

The University as a European Institution

T he university is a European institution; indeed, it is the European institution *par excellence*. There are various reasons for this assertion.

As a community of teachers and taught, accorded certain rights, such as administrative autonomy and the determination and realization of curricula (courses of study) and of the objectives of research as well as the award of publicly recognized degrees, it is a creation of medieval Europe, which was the Europe of papal Christianity. This is shown in the first volume of our history.

It is, moreover, the only European institution which has preserved its fundamental patterns and its basic social role and functions over the course of history; it has indeed been strengthened and extended in these respects—as the four volumes will show. Of the three acknowledged powers of medieval European society—*regnum, sacerdotium*, and *studium*—the first, political power, has undergone profound changes. The second has, in the Roman Catholic Church, preserved its structure and expanded over the whole planet but it has lost the monopoly which it once possessed of providing the conditions of salvation. The same may be said for the other institutional and cultural creations of the Middle Ages, i.e. the distinctively European forms of organization of a money economy, the plastic arts, architecture, and music.

No other European institution has spread over the entire world in the way in which the traditional form of the European university has done. The degrees awarded by European universities—the bachelor's degree, the licentiate, the master's degree, and the doctorate—have been adopted in the most diverse societies throughout the world. The four medieval faculties of *artes*—variously called philosophy, letters, arts, arts and sciences, and humanities—law, medicine, and theology have survived and have been supplemented by numerous disciplines, particularly the social sciences and technological studies, but they remain none the less at the heart of universities throughout the world. Even the name of the *universitas*, which in the Middle Ages was applied to corporate bodies of the most diverse sorts and was accordingly applied to the corporate organization of teachers and students, has in the course of centuries been given a more particular focus: the university, as a *universitas litterarum*, has since the eighteenth century been the intellectual institution which cultivates and transmits the entire corpus of methodically studied intellectual disciplines.

From A HISTORY OF THE UNIVERSITY IN EUROPE by Hilde DeRidder-Symoens, pp. xix–xx, xxvi–xxvii, 3–8. Copyright © 1992 by Cambridge University Press. Reprinted by permission.

Moreover, the university is a European institution because it has, in its social role, performed certain functions for all European societies. It has developed and transmitted scientific and scholarly knowledge and the methods of cultivating that knowledge which has arisen from and formed part of the common European intellectual tradition. It has at the same time formed an academic elite, the ethos of which rests on common European values and which transcends all national boundaries.

The various efforts which were made after the Second World War to establish 'European' universities were largely unsuccessful because of the resistance of the existing universities, which regarded themselves as European. Indeed, they pointed out that the diversity of national traditions was a precious European heritage and that, by means of their different national components, they contributed to the European community of scholarship and scholars.

It may be asked whether this account does in fact characterize the present situation. Are not the universities of Europe equally, if not more deeply, marked by the differences among the European national states which began to take form in the late Middle Ages and during the Reformation and which, particularly since the nineteenth century, changed the universities of the European continent *de facto*—and often *de jure* as well—into parts of the governmental system? Do they perform genuinely European functions when, in any particular member state of the European community, only about 1 per cent of the student body is made up of those who come from any of the other member states of the community and when, in many European countries, professors from other countries cannot be appointed or can be appointed only in exceptional circumstances? Can the existing European universities be said to be performing their proper social role when the rising generation of European scientists and scholars prefers to continue its studies in universities of another country where the European traditions of scientific and scholarly research and of the academic ethic are pursued with more enthusiasm, seriousness, commitment, and effectiveness than they are in Europe?

The Social Role of the European University

By social function or role is implied the totality of the actions performed in response to the expectations of conduct which others direct toward the incumbent of the particular role. These expectations are based on values towards which conduct is oriented, and the values are translated into norms which guide the socially expected conduct. Expectations, values, and norms are delineated by the explicit and implicit interests of the various social actors and they are often mutually contradictory.

Conflicts are inherent in social roles, and not least in those of universities. Their fundamental values and the norms which are binding on their members are not homogeneous. The values of the universal validity of the criteria, methods, and results of scientific and scholarly research cannot always be adhered to in consequence of the limitations on and diversity of the cognitive powers of individual human beings. The equality of opportunity for admission to and continuance of studies at universities is in conflict with the inequality in the distribution of social and economic resources and of alternative uses for these resources. The precedence given to leisure and contemplation, which are necessary for scientific and scholarly research, represents an ideal of the *bios theoretikos*, which ever since the Greek philosophers has been contrasted and in conflict with the ideal of the *bios praktikos*, which gives precedence to social utility in the application of scientific knowledge and in the professional training provided by universities. The *amor sciendi*, which evaluates highly the search for truth by rigorous scientific and scholarly methods, is associated with indifference to the economic value of the results of research and teaching, and it stands in contradiction to the *ambitio dignitatis* and the *individia pecuniae*, the social and economic utilization of the fruits of academic study. Last but not least, the fundamental value of the academic freedom of the university as a corporate community stands in potential conflict, on two fronts: internally between the freedom of the individual and the collegial solidarity of the members of the university, and externally between the requirements of the university for autonomy and control by those who supply the necessary financial resources.

These and other conflicts are inherent in the social history of the university. To show the various forms which they have taken and the various solutions which have been attempted is the most important aim of our enterprise. Indeed, these conflicts, the tensions which arise from them, and the structures and mechanisms through which they are kept in a state of open equilibrium explain to a considerable extent the dynamics of the European universities. When one value becomes too preponderant and shifts the balance too markedly and too long to one alternative and away from the other, for example, to making the university into a governmental institution or into an ivory tower or into a vocational school or into a wholly self-contained scientific institution, the tensions lose their creative power and lead instead to somnolence or excessive superficial and fruitless agitation.

We certainly no longer share the view, which was put forward by Meiners and which was so characteristic of the Enlightenment, that the history of European universities can 'lead in part to the recognition and avoidance of their misconduct, deficiencies, and faults, and in part to the disclosure and emulation of their merits'. Just as a machine can only be repaired and made operable once more when the significance of its parts and their interdependence is understood and tested, so the university, which is a very complex social institution, must from time to time be subjected to a fundamental analysis. This fundamental analysis of its structures and functions, which have developed in the course of history, is indispensable if the deeper aspects of its social role are to be understood and realistically improved.

Themes

No period in the history of universities has been more intensively studied than the Middle Ages. Nevertheless, numerous gaps remain. Many archival documents, innumerable writings, and many of the lecture scripts of university teachers are still unpublished. Biographical accounts of teachers and students, their social and familial origins, their patterns of association in the course of their studies, and their subsequent careers are markedly lacking. Such prosopographical investigations, which have already been taken in hand for particular universities or for certain regions of provenance, are indispensable for a genuinely social history of universities. Only when such studies have been done will it be 'possible to trace the channels of intellectual currents and influence, to reconstruct the composition and structure of intellectual groups and their connections with each other, and the lines of transmission and diffusion of certain intellectual traditions such as Aristotelianism in the thirteenth, Roman law in the fourteenth, humanism in the fifteenth, and the Reformation in the sixteenth centuries'.

For these reasons, our project can reflect only the present state of research. The aim of this introductory chapter is to show, with reference to a few themes, which perspectives have been opened up through studies of medieval universities, which problems have arisen from those studies, and what knowledge can be drawn from them.

Mythology and Historiography of the Beginnings

In 1988, the University of Bologna celebrated its nine-hundredth anniversary. However, neither our own investigation nor that of others into the history of medieval universities has produced any evidence for such a foundation of the University of Bologna in 1088. Rather, the upshot of these investigations is that no such event took place in 1088. In fact, 1088 was chosen a century ago as the 'conventional date' by a committee under the chairmanship of the famous poet Giosue Carducci; 1888 was to be the occasion for a grand jubilee to be celebrated in the presence of the royal family and rectors of universities from all over the world were to attend. The aim of the celebration was to imprint on the consciousness of the Italian people and of the whole world the knowledge that the recent and still not completely consolidated political unification of Italy could point for its legitimacy to the eight-centuries-long tradition of free research and teaching at the University of Bologna and its national and worldwide importance. The celebration of the eighth centenary of the University of Bologna in 1888 was in fact one of the commemorative celebrations and related symbolic manifestations which were arranged in the course of the nineteenth century in order to remind the nations of their past and its historical continuity and to fortify in them a sense of their national unity.

Commemorative celebrations focus on a particular date. For that reason, a particular date had to be found and it had to be one which was as early as possible so that the politically important, symbolic function of the University of Bologna as the 'mother of European universities' could not be challenged on that occasion. Carducci and his medievalist colleagues based their claim on a document of the thirteenth century. According to this document, the 'famous Irnerius' (1055/60–1125) and an 'unknown' Pepo were the first to have delivered lectures on law in Bologna. Jubilees in most instances stimulate historical research. Such research often corrects the date of foundation or shows the historical account of the alleged foundation to be a myth. Even more than the jubilee celebrations of other universities, the celebration of the eight-hundredth anniversary of the University of Bologna released a flood of publications on the history of universities. We know now that Pepo was by no means 'unknown'; he was referred to in 1190 as *'clarum Bononiensium lumen'*, and presented himself at the court of Emperor Henry IV as an authority on Roman law. In this regard, Carducci would not have chosen the 'conventional date' badly, if in fact Pepo was the founder, or at least a member, of a university. The booklet published on the occasion of the celebration of the nine-hundredth anniversary justified 1088 as the date of foundation of the university by the argument that, in that year, there appeared free arrangements for the teaching of law which were independent of the religious schools of Bologna and that such independence was the mark of a university.

Is this argument defensible? No scholar doubts nowadays that, at various places in the eleventh and twelfth centuries, there existed significant schools and that successful teachers appeared as independent masters who gathered around themselves a circle of pupils. In Bologna, *legum doctores*, who were active as lawyers and judges, joined with their pupils to form free corporations. There is also agreement among various investigators—as subsequent chapters show—that it was the associations of students (in Bologna) or of teachers and students (in Paris), which were granted special liberties and privileges in the thirteenth century, that first laid the basis for that form of higher education which in the Middle Ages was called *studium generate* and which later was designated as a university.

For this reason, Abelard, who taught in the first forty years of the twelfth century at Melun, Corbeil, and Paris, in part in a religious school and in part as probably the most famous independent teacher, has long since ceased to be regarded as the founder of the University of Paris. Similarly, the medical school of Salerno has lost its reputation as the oldest European university; it is, at best, regarded as a 'proto-university'. This does not, of course, detract from its scientific significance as a school for physicians in the tenth century, as a medical centre in the twelfth century, and as a model of medical research and teaching in the thirteenth century.

The origin of the first universities is a very complex process, as will be seen in the next chapter. Bologna or Paris may be called the oldest university depending on the weight which one attributes to one or another of the various elements which make up a university. If one regards the existence of a corporate body as the sole criterion, then Bologna is the oldest, but only by a slight margin. It was in Bologna that, towards the end of the twelfth century, the foreign students of law grouped themselves together as 'nations' and therewith developed a basic organizational form of the medieval European university. If one regards the association of teachers and students of various disciplines into a single corporate body as the decisive criterion, then the oldest university would be Paris, dating from 1208.

The question of which university is the oldest is of practical importance only when it has to be decided which rectors should be granted precedence in academic ceremonies and processions. The date of foundation is more important because of the social and psychological significance of jubilees. Yet, . . . it is very difficult and often arbitrary to assign an exact date to the foundation of a particular university. This is true not only for the oldest universities, which arose only gradually and which are officially acknowledged in various written documents as having 'grown through custom', *e consuetudine*, in a sequence of stages. Even where the foundation of a university has occurred through an explicit decree or enactment, *e privilegio*, the question arises as to which particular event should be regarded as the date of foundation. Should it be the decision of a local authority to found a university or to recognize an existing school as a university, or should it be the recognition or endowment by papal, imperial, or royal authority, or should it be the executive decision by the local municipal authority, or the beginning of the teaching?

It is easier to answer the question as to whether the medieval university had forerunners or models. Very much like contemporary universities, the early universities dated their origins as early as possible. In Bologna, between 1266 and 1234, a founding document was forged, which asserted that the university was established in AD 423 by Emperor Theodosius. The University of Paris thought that it had been founded by Charlemagne, and, through his action, it was able to see itself as a continuator of the tradition of Roman higher education. Some claimed for Oxford an even earlier origin: when, following the destruction of their own city of Troy, the Trojans conquered Albion, it was said that they were accompanied by some philosophers who found a suitable place for themselves in Oxford. A more modest tradition contented itself with Alfred the Great (848–99) as the founder of Oxford. All of these fictions, which were questioned or refuted by the humanists, may be traced back to the medieval practice of legitimating an institution by asserting the antiquity of its origin. The assertion of a line of descent which traced medieval universities back to antiquity does have some justification, inasmuch as essential features of their intellectual substance were of classical origin and then christianized by Saint Augustine and other church fathers. Medieval scholars regarded themselves as dwarfs who stood on the shoulders of their gigantic ancient ancestors and who for that reason could see further. Nevertheless, the organizational form of the university cannot be traced to classical antiquity, nor was it influenced by Byzantium.

It seems more plausible to derive the organizational pattern of the medieval university from the Islamic schools of learning . . . British Islamic scholars give an affirmative answer to the question: 'Did the Arabs invent the university?' They maintain that Islamic institutions of learning were the source of the idea of organizing foreign students into nations and that they were also the source of the ideas of the universal validity of the qualification for teaching conferred by the *venia docendi*, of the academic robe, and of the title of the *baccalarius*. Of course, the invocation of such affinities often confuses the *propter hoc* with the *post hoc*; it does not demonstrate whether and how the later forms emerged from the earlier ones. Furthermore, the discernment of such affinities requires an exact knowledge of both traditions. The term *baccalarius* could not be an Islamic importation of the twelfth century because it was already in use in the ninth century as the Latin designation of a preparatory or auxiliary status in a variety of social careers. The American

Islamicist, Makdisi, who is to be taken more seriously, has discovered eighteen substantial affinities between the Islamic and the occidental patterns of the organization of learning and their transmission through institutional arrangements more or less like universities. He has concluded, however, that 'the university is a twelfth century product of the Christian West of the twelfth century, not only in its organization but also in the privileges and protection it received from Pope and King'. But the situation is different with regard to the colleges, which he does derive from Islamic models.

The borrowings which the university made from other medieval institutions were more important. . . . [The] very idea of the *universitas* is drawn from the term for many kinds of cooperative associations. The term had, however, to be supplemented to refer to the special features of the university, namely *universitas magistrorum et scholarium* or *universitas studii*. The corporate features, privileges, statutes, seals, and oaths and the functions and titles of their officials all have a close affinity to contemporaneous legal and organizational forms. Taken as a whole, the medieval university, as is apparent in the various chapters of this volume, is part of and an expression of its social environment.

POSTSCRIPT

Does the Modern University Have Its Roots in the Islamic World?

It is tempting to think that all modern institutions, especially all those that we find admirable, have come down to us in a direct line from our Western intellectual forbears the Greeks. To take the university as a case in point, however, we cannot trace its origins to Greece—neither the Greeks nor Romans had universities. Higher education in the Greco-Roman world was a much less tightly organized enterprise of student-teacher interaction. There were no diplomas, courses of study, examinations or commencements—at least not as we understand these terms today. Agreeing that we cannot trace the Western university to the Greeks, Rüegg and Nakosteen part company on where its roots actually lie. Rüegg finds universities springing up in Bologna, Paris, Salerno, and Oxford out of an existing corporate model that had the blessing of church and state. Nakosteen finds an unbroken line from the eighth-century Islamic world to the late European Middle Ages. The university system, he argues, was formed in an Islamic context and made its way unchanged into a European one.

If we begin a history of education from within the Islamic world, new patterns will emerge. For an introduction to Islam as providing a way to perceive reality, *Islam and the Cultural Accommodation of Social Change* by Bassam Tibi (Westview Press, 1991) offers a clear introduction to the Sunni/Shi'a split in Islam, which persists today, and a discussion of language (in this case Arabic) as the medium in which cultural symbols are articulated. Students may also be interested in Francis Robinson, ed., *The Cambridge Illustrated History of the Islamic World* (Cambridge University Press, 1996), especially Chapter 7, "Knowledge, its Transmission, and the Making of Muslim Societies." In chapter 9 "The Iranian Diaspora: The Edge Creates a Center" of *Islam: A View from the Edge* (Columbia University Press, 1994), Richard W. Bulliet describes the role of Iranian scholars in the spread of *madrasa* or Islamic colleges.

For additional background on European universities of the Middle Ages, see *The Medieval University* by Helene Wieruszowski (Van Nostrand Reinhold, 1966) and *The Scholastic Culture of the Middle Ages: 1000–1300* by John W. Baldwin (D. C. Heath, 1971). The movie "Stealing Heaven" tells the story of Heloise and Abelard. Set in twelfth-century France, it also offers a very realistic portrayal of the emerging European university system of disputation between professor and students. Finally, Norman F. Cantor's *The Civilization of the Middle Ages* (HarperCollins, 1993) has a chapter titled "Moslem and Jewish Thought: The Aristotelian Challenge," which summarizes the influence of Islamic thought on Europe.

ISSUE 11

Did Women Benefit from the Renaissance?

YES: Margaret L. King, from *Women of the Renaissance* (University of Chicago Press, 1991)

NO: Joan Kelly-Gadol, from "Did Women Have a Renaissance?" in Renate Bridenthal, Claudia Koonz, and Susan Stuard, eds., *Becoming Visible: Women in European History*, 2d ed. (Houghton Mifflin, 1987)

ISSUE SUMMARY

YES: Historian Margaret L. King surveys Renaissance women in domestic, religious, and learned settings and finds reflected in their lives a new consciousness of themselves as women, as intelligent seekers of a new way of being in the world.

NO: Historian Joan Kelly-Gadol discovered in her work as a Renaissance scholar that well-born women seemed to have enjoyed greater advantages during the Middle Ages and experienced a relative loss of position and power during the Renaissance.

In 1974 Joan Kelly-Gadol published a pathbreaking essay that challenged traditional periodization. Before that, virtually every publication on the Renaissance proclaimed it to be a great leap forward for everyone, a time when new ideas were widely discussed and the old strictures of the Middle Ages were thrown off. The difficulty for Kelly-Gadol was that her own work on women during the medieval and Renaissance periods told a different story. She was one of the first to raise this troubling question: Are the turning points in history the same for women as they are for men? Kelly-Gadol found that well-born women lived in a relatively free environment during the Middle Ages. The courtly love tradition allowed powerful, property-owning women to satisfy their own sexual and emotional needs. With the arrival of the Renaissance, however, the courtly love tradition was defined by powerful male princes who found it desirable for women to be passive and chaste in order to serve the needs of the rising bourgeoisie.

The field of women's history has a history of its own. Beginning with the pioneering work of historians such as Mary Ritter Beard, *Woman as Force in History: A Study in Traditions and Realities* (Collier Books, 1946), scholars first engaged in what Gerda Lerner has called "compensatory history"—compensating for past omissions by researching and writing about the great women of history. In a second phase, women's history moved to "contributory history." Looking past the great women, historians took all the traditional categories of standard male history and found women who filled them—women who spent their lives as intellectuals, soldiers, politicians, and scientists. The current phase of women's history parallels more general trends in social history, concentrating on the ordinary people who lived during historical epochs. In this more mature phase, the emphasis is on women's culture—how women saw the world from within their own systems and ways of doing things. If Beard was doing compensatory history, Kelly-Gadol might be said to be engaging in contributory history. The women she writes about led lives similar to those of men in their class during the Middle Ages, but Kelly-Gadol contends that they had a different experience during the Renaissance—a contraction of their sphere of influence and a loss of freedom in the expression of their sexual and emotional needs. For the first time, a sexual double standard appeared—men could engage in extramarital liaisons, whereas women had to remain chaste.

One caution to keep in mind is that people are not aware of the times in which they live in terms of the historical periods that scholars later use for identification. People of the past, like people today, are more concerned with their personal lives and fortunes than with historical trends. Periodization, or the marking of turning points in the past, can be useful. It can help to identify broad trends and forks in the road as we explore the past. What women's history has taught us, however, is that looking at the experiences of men may or may not tell us what the experiences of women were like during the same time periods.

Beard's book and the field of women's history that it inspired made possible the work of later scholars such as Kelly-Gadol. Beard challenged traditional notions about the role of women in history; Kelly-Gadol challenged history itself. Margaret L. King's study, from which the first selection is taken, confronts Kelly-Gadol's question directly and explores it in the light of all we now know about the richly diverse lives of women who lived during the Renaissance.

Margaret L. King

Virgo et Virago: Women and High Culture

Women of Might, Power, and Influence

On the stake that supported the burning corpse of the peasant Joan of Arc, who had donned armor and rallied a king, a placard bore the names that the people of the Renaissance gave to the women they hated: heretic, liar, sorceress. The mystery of that hatred has preoccupied the many tellers of the tale of the life of this patron saint of France. Their answers cannot be recounted here, but without simplifying too much they can be summed up in this way: she was hated because she did what men did, and triumphantly. The men who planted stakes over the face of Europe would not tolerate such a transgression of the order they imagined to be natural. In the age of emblems, Joan of Arc is an emblem of the Renaissance women who attempted to partake in the civilization of the Renaissance: not as bearers of children or worshippers of God, but as forgers of its cultural forms. These women did not share her fate, but a few of them understood it.

Foremost among these women, in the records that that age has left us, are those who had no choice about the role they played. Like Joan, they bore arms, or wielded powers still more formidable. They were the queens and female rulers who ruled as the surrogates of their absent husbands, dead fathers, and immature sons. Extraordinary in their personal strengths and achievements, they have left no residue: their capital passed through the male line of descent and not to female heirs—at least not in the centuries of which we speak. But as women who held command, even if briefly and without issue, they deserve our attention.

In Italy later in the same century that Joan illumined with her strength, Caterina Sforza posed a more traditional but still boldly independent figure. The illegitimate granddaughter of Francesco Sforza, who was in turn the illegitimate usurper of the dynasty of the Visconti in Milan, Caterina was propelled into the political maelstrom of quattro-cento Italy by her marriage to Girolamo Riario, nephew of Pope Sixtus IV. After her husband's assassination in 1488, she fiercely defended her family's interests and the cities of Imola and Forli. Greatly outnumbered by her besiegers, she defended Forli against the enemy who held her six children hostage. Twelve years later, she again commanded the defense of those same walls, was defeated, possibly raped, and was brought captive to Rome by Cesare Borgia.

From WOMEN OF THE RENAISSANCE by Margaret L. King, pp. 157–164, 237–239. Copyright © 1991 by University of Chicago Press. Reprinted by permission.

While Sforza, like Joan of Arc, assumed a military role, she secured no power; few women, even of the most exalted noble and royal families, ever did. Two major exceptions were the Italian-born Catherine de'Medici, who as the widow of France's King Henri II was the regent for his successors, François II and Charles IX, and Elizabeth, daughter of the Tudor king of England. Both molded a Renaissance identity for a female sovereign that expressed the ambiguity of their roles. The former adopted for herself the emblem of Artemisia (the type of armed-and-chaste maiden to be considered at greater length below), who was known for her dutiful remembrance of her predeceased husband, Mausolus. Wielding this device, Catherine de'Medici could both act assertively and demonstrate piety to the male rulers between whom she transmitted power. The more independent and bolder Elizabeth was a master builder of her public image and presented herself to her subjects in a variety of feminine identities: Astraea, Deborah, Diana. At the same time, to win support in moments of crisis for the unprecedented phenomenon of a female monarch, she projected androgynous images of her role (man-woman, queen-king, mother-son), and haughtily referred to herself as "prince," with the body of a woman and heart of a king. She defied the identification of her sex with instability and incompetence. In 1601, the elderly Elizabeth asked Parliament in her Golden Speech: "Shall I ascribe anything to myself and my sexly weakness? I were not worthy to live then"; "my sex," she said a few weeks before her death, "cannot diminish my prestige." Had she married, she might have borne an heir. But had she married, she would have fallen under the influence of a male consort. Instead, a complete dyad in herself, she took no husband and declared herself married to England. Her heroic virginity, more in the pattern of the great saints than of a modern woman, set her apart from the other women of her realm who continued to marry and dwell within the family. Her sexual nature was exceptional, just as her kingly authority was anomalous. In and of herself, she insisted on her right to rule, and was the only woman to hold sovereign power during the Renaissance.

Much of the culture of the late sixteenth-century Tudor court revolved around this manlike virgin whose name still identifies it: Elizabethan. Subtly, the poets, playwrights, and scholars of the age commented on the prodigy among them. Foremost among these commentators was William Shakespeare; in the androgynous heroines of his comedies can be found versions of the monarch, sharp-witted and exalted beyond nature. These female characters, played by boys dressed as women who often dressed as boys to create beings of thoroughly confused sexuality, charmed and entranced like the queen herself. The Shakespearean genius also understood how deeply the phenomenon of a queen-king violated the natural order. In the seemingly lighthearted "Midsummer Night's Dream" he spoke about the abnormality of a political order ruled by a woman when the Amazon Hippolyta was wedded at the last to the lawful male wielder of power. Like Joan of Arc, Elizabeth was perceived (and perceived herself) as an Amazon, and deep in the consciousness of the age she dominated was the discomfiture caused by an armed maiden, a rational female, an emotional force unlimited by natural order.

The phenomenon of enthroned women like Catherine and Elizabeth provoked controversy about the legitimacy of female rule. No one was more outspoken than the Presbyterian John Knox, who charged in his *First Blast of the Trumpet Against the Monstrous Regiment of Women* of 1558 that "it is more than a monster in nature that a woman shall reign and have empire above man." "To promote a woman to bear rule, above any realm, nation, or city, is repugnant to nature, contumely to God, . . . and, finally, it is the subversion of good order, of all equity and justice." When a woman rules, the blind lead the sighted, the sick the robust, "the foolish, mad and frenetic" the discreet and sober. "For their sight in civil regiment is but blindness, their counsel foolishment, and judgment frenzy." Woman's attempt to rule is an act of treason: "For that woman reigneth above man, she hath obteined it by treason and conspiracy committed against God. . . . [Men] must study to repress her inordinate pride and tyranny to the uttermost of their power." God could occasionally choose a woman to rule, John Aylmer wrote a year later, refuting Knox; but most women were "fond, folish, wanton flibbergibbes, tatlers, triflers, wavering witles, without counsell, feable, careless, rashe proude," and so on.

Most defenders of female rule in the sixteenth century could not transcend the problem of gender. While Knox was driven to fury by the accession of Mary Tudor to power, the behavior of her successor Elizabeth the Great enraged the French Catholic political theorist Jean Bodin. In the sixth book of his *Six Books of the Republic*, Bodin explored thoroughly the emotional dimension of female rule. A woman's sexual nature would surely, he claimed, interfere with her effectiveness as ruler. As Giovanni Correr, the Venetian ambassador to France, said of another Queen Mary, the unfortunate monarch of Scotland, "to govern states is not the business of women." Other Venetian ambassadors to the court of Elizabeth's successors were more impressed: that queen by her exceptional wisdom and skill had "advanced the female condition itself," and "overcome the distinction of sexes." Male observers thus viewed the sex of the female monarch as an impediment to rule or considered it obliterated, overlooking it altogether, as though the woman was no woman. Spenser simply made his monarch an exception to the otherwise universal rule of female subordination: "vertuous women" know, he wrote, that they are born "to base humilitie," unless God intervenes to raise them "to lawful soveraintie" (*Faerie Queene* 5.5.25).

Although this problem was agonizing for the few women who ruled, there were only a handful who had to face it: it was rare for a woman to inherit power as did these English queens. It required, in fact, the timely death of all power-eligible males. Most women in the ruling classes did not rule, but only shared some of the prerogatives of sovereignty. In the vibrant artistic and intellectual climate of the Renaissance, particularly in Italy, this meant that they exercised the power of patronage. Women who did not rule or direct with their armies the forces of destruction could wield their authority and wealth to shape thought and culture.

Wherever courts existed as centers of wealth, artistic activity, and discourse, opportunities abounded for intelligent women to perform in the role of patroness of the arts and culture. In France, Anne of Brittany, Queen of Charles VIII, commissioned the translation of Boccaccio's *Concerning Famous Women (De claris mulieribus)*, and filled her court with educated women and discussions of platonic love. The same king's sister-in-law Louise of Savoy tutored the future king François I and his sister, Marguerite, according to the principles of Italian humanism. The latter—Marguerite d'Angoulême, later of Navarre—was the director of cultural matters at her brother's royal court and the protector of a circle of learned men. Influenced by the evangelism of Lefèvre d'Etaples and Guillaume Budé, guided in matters of spirit by the bishop Guillaume Briçonnet, she was at the center of currents of proto-reform. An original thinker herself, her collection of stories, the *Heptaméron*, raised questions about the troubled roles of women in a man's world. From this court circle of active patronesses and educators there derived other women of some power and influence: among them the Calvinist Jeanne d'Albret, Marguerite's daughter and the mother of the future king Henry IV, a valiant fighter for her family and religion; and Renée, the heir of Louis XII who was bypassed in favor of her male cousin François I and made wife instead to the Duke of Ferrara, who chose as a companion for her own daughter the adolescent Italian humanist Olimpia Morata.

In Spain the formidable Isabella guided religious reform and intellectual life, while in England, her learned daughter Catherine of Aragon, King Henry VIII's first queen, was surrounded by the leading humanists of the era. It was for her that Erasmus wrote his *Institution of Christian Matrimony (Christiani matrimonii institutio)* and Juan Luis Vives his *Instruction of a Christian Woman (Institutio foeminae christianae)* and other works. She sought Vives as a tutor for her own daughter, the future queen Mary Tudor. A generation earlier, the proto-figure of the royal patroness and learned woman in England was Margaret Beaufort, Countess of Richmond, already noted as the mother of that country's first Tudor monarch. At the courts of Edward IV and Richard III, she had surrounded herself with minstrels and learned men, supported the art of printing (then in its early stages), endowed professorships of divinity at Oxford and Cambridge (where she founded two colleges), supervised the education of her son and grandchildren, and herself translated from the Latin the devotional *The Mirror of Gold of the Sinful Soul*.

In Italy, where courts and cities and talented men clustered, opportunities abounded for the cultivated woman to help shape the culture of the Renaissance. Notable among such patronesses was Isabella d'Este, daughter of the rulers of Ferrara, sister of Beatrice, who was to play a similar but paler role in Milan, and of Alfonso, Ferrante, Ippolito, and Sigismondo, whom she was to rival in fame. Trained by Battista Guarini, the pedagogue son of the great humanist Guarino Veronese, she had mastered Greek and Latin, the signs of serious scholarship, alongside such skills as lute-playing, dance, and witty conversation. Married to the ruler of Mantua, she presided at that court over festivities and performances, artists, musicians and scholars, libraries filled with elegant volumes; she lived surrounded everywhere by statues, ornate boxes, clocks, marbles, lutes, dishes, gowns, playing cards decorated with paintings, jewels, and gold. Ariosto, Bernardo da Bibbiena, and Gian Giorgio Trissino were among those she favored. She studied maps and astrology and had frequent chats with the ducal librarian, Pellegrino Prisciano. Her *Studiolo* and *Grotta*, brilliantly ornamented rooms in the ducal palace, were her glorious monuments. For these and other projects, she designed the allegorical schemes, consulting with her humanist advisers. Ruling briefly when her husband was taken captive during the wars that shook Italy after the invasion of the forces of France, Spain, and Empire, she was repaid with anger for her bold assumption of authority. Her great capacity was left to express itself in patronage.

Also dislodged from the limited tenure of sovereignty was the wealthy Venetian noblewoman Caterina Cornaro. Born to an ancient Venetian noble family with interests in the eastern Mediterranean—her own mother was from a Greek royal family—Cornaro was married in 1472, at age eighteen, to the King of Cyprus, James II. Her city was concerned with her royal marriage from the start: the island of Cyprus was strategically important, and the Serenissima was jealous of its citizens' involvement in consequential foreign affairs. Venetian concern was justified, for Cornaro became queen of Cyprus a year later, after her husband's sudden death, and held unstable sway, racked by conspiracies, for sixteen years. When Cornaro was tempted by a marriage into the Neapolitan royal house, Venice exerted its authority mightily to force her to abdicate the Cypriot throne. A Neapolitan connection would have meant the alienation of Cyprus from Venetian control. The legate dispatched to the island and charged to persuade her to step down was none other than her brother. He came with offers of an annual salary of 8,000 ducats and a small fiefdom on the Venetian terra firma: she would win fame for herself, he promised, and be known forever as Queen of Cyprus, if she donated her husband's island to her *patria*. Thus compensated by fame and wealth, Cornaro left her rich island kingdom for the miniature one at Asolo. In that court she reigned as queen over a coterie of *letterati*: not the least of them Pietro Bembo, who memorialized the activities over which Cornaro presided in the Arcadian dialogue *Gli Asolani*. Published in 1505 by Aldo Manuzio in Venice, ten years after the conversations that sparked Bembo's imagination had taken place, it circulated in twenty-two editions, Italian as well as Spanish and French. Perhaps more significantly, it influenced the even more famous and complex dialogue of Baldassare Castiglione, commemorating a court presided over by another patroness of letters.

Cornaro's court as described by Bembo prefigures the one in Urbino which Castiglione described. There two women—the Duchess, Elisabetta Gonzaga, and her companion, Emilia Pia—guided and inspired the discussions of proper behavior for both sexes that made up the age's principal handbook of aristocratic values, circulated in some hundred editions and translated into all the major vernaculars: *The Book of the Courtier (Il libro del cortigiano)*. For both sexes, that behavior is sharply defined by the phenomenon of the court: men were not to be too boisterous; women were to be occasions of beauty and delight. No court "however great, can have adornment or splendor or gaiety in it without ladies"; in the same way, no courtier can "be graceful or pleasing or brave, or do any gallant deed of chivalry, unless he is moved by the society and by the love and charm of ladies." "Who learns to dance gracefully for any reason except to please women? Who devotes himself to the sweetness of music for any other reason? Who attempts to compose verses . . . unless to express sentiments inspired by women?"

The virtues that women had to possess to inspire these male achievements were manifold. The courtly lady shares some virtues possessed also by the gentleman—she should be well born, naturally graceful, well mannered, clever, prudent, and capable—but also others which are distinctively hers. If married, she should be a good manager of her husband's "property and house and children," and possess "all qualities that are requisite in a good mother." Beauty is a necessity for her, though not for her male counterpart: "for truly that woman lacks much who lacks beauty." Above all, she must be charming: "she will be able to entertain graciously every kind of man with agreeable and comely conversation suited to the time and place and to the station of the person with whom she speaks, joining to serene and modest manners, and to that comeliness that ought to inform all her actions, a quick vivacity of spirit whereby she will show herself a stranger to all boorishness; but with such a kind manner as to cause her to be thought no less chaste, prudent, and gentle than she is agreeable, witty, and discreet." The qualities the court lady possesses are distinct from those of the courtier she is set to amuse: "above all . . . in her ways, manners, words, gestures, and bearing, a woman ought to be very unlike a man; for just as he must show a certain solid and sturdy manliness, so it is seemly for a woman to have a soft and delicate tenderness, with an air of womanly sweetness in her every movement, which, in her going and staying, and in whatever she says, shall always make her appear the woman without any resemblance to a man." Unlike the queen who bears the power and the glory of the males who otherwise occupy her throne, according to Giuliano de' Medici, Castiglione's spokesman by no means hostile to the female sex, the aristocratic lady must be taught to be something other than a man. The same was true of her humbler counterpart in the bourgeois or artisan classes. . . .

A final question remains—the one implied in the title of a work aiming to describe "Women of the Renaissance." Was there a Renaissance for women? Joan Kelly wrote boldly in 1977 that there was not: "at least, not during the Renaissance." At the time, her insight was powerful. For she was the first historian to point unremittingly to the dismal realities of women's lives in the Renaissance centuries. Within the family, they were subject to fathers and husbands and their surrogates in modes that did not relent before the end of Renaissance centuries. They bore special burdens of economic hardship, which limited their dowries and determined their destinies if they were of the elite, or which condemned them (much as it condemned their brothers) to lives of servitude if they were not. Within the church, they were powerless as well. In Roman Catholic countries, those women who chose or were consigned to the religious life were increasingly enclosed, scrutinized, and constrained. In Protestant countries, they were denied the option of convent or anchorage and placed under the spiritual supervision of the same men who decided their social destiny. In both settings, they could seize, at their peril, the option of nonconformity: they could be heretics, prophets, sectaries, or witches. In the world of learning, women remained suspect throughout the period. They snatched an education, in a few cases, from affectionate fathers, brothers, uncles, and grandfathers. But if they wrote, they were declared to be unwomanly; and if they wrote very well, they were labeled Amazons, fearsome and unnatural beings. This does not look like a Renaissance, a rebirth into a new life, but a continuation and in some ways an intensification of the disabilities and prejudices inherited from the Middle Ages and from antiquity.

Yet an argument can be made to the contrary, and has been, for instance, by the splendid historian of Italian society, David Herlihy. Woman's charismatic role, her astonishing success as intermediary with the divine, rooted in her female role as mother projected on a cosmic scale, gave her special prominence precisely in the Renaissance centuries. As it did, in the case of a few exceptional women. One might wonder if the far greater numbers of those who burned and suffered the torments of the torture chamber might overshadow the figures of spiritual prominence; or if the ordinary suffering of the great mass of women overshadows them, for though these women were subject to the same harsh austerities as men of the age, they were deprived, unlike men, of all autonomy. Nevertheless, Herlihy's suggestion is persuasive. Something changed during the Renaissance in women's sense of themselves, even if very little changed or changed for the better in their social condition. That change did have its roots in the spiritual experience of women, and it culminates in the consciousness put into words by the first feminists of the Renaissance. Not monsters, not defects in nature, but the intelligent seekers of a new way, these women wielded the picks of their understanding to build a better city for ladies.

Joan Kelly-Gadol

 **NO**

Did Women Have a Renaissance?

One of the tasks of women's history is to call into question accepted schemes of periodization. To take the emancipation of women as a vantage point is to discover that events that further the historical development of men, liberating them from natural, social, or ideological constraints, have quite different, even opposite, effects upon women. The Renaissance is a good case in point. Italy was well in advance of the rest of Europe from roughly 1350 to 1530 because of its early consolidation of genuine states, the mercantile and manufacturing economy that supported them, and its working out of postfeudal and even postguild social relations. These developments reorganized Italian society along modern lines and opened the possibilities for the social and cultural expression for which the age is known. Yet precisely these developments affected women adversely, so much so that there was no renaissance for women—at least, not during the Renaissance. The state, early capitalism, and the social relations formed by them impinged on the lives of Renaissance women in different ways according to their different positions in society. But the startling fact is that women as a group, especially among the classes that dominated Italian urban life, experienced a contradiction of social and personal options that men of their classes either did not, as was the case with the bourgeoisie, or did not experience as markedly, as was the case with the nobility.

Before demonstrating this point, which contradicts the widely held notion of the equality of Renaissance women with men, we need to consider how to establish, let alone measure, loss or gain with respect to the liberty of women. I found the following criteria most useful for gauging the relative contraction (or expansion) of the powers of Renaissance women and for determining the quality of their historical experience: 1) the regulation of *female sexuality* as compared with male sexuality; 2) women's *economic* and *political roles*, that is, the kind of work they performed as compared with men, and their access to property, political power, and the education or training necessary for work, property, and power; 3) the *cultural roles* of women in shaping the outlook of their society, and access to the education and/or institutions necessary for this; 4) *ideology* about women, in particular the sex-role system displayed or advocated in the symbolic products of the society, its art, literature, and philosophy. Two points should be made about this ideological index. One is its rich inferential value. The literature, art, and philosophy of a

Bridental, Renate, Claudis Koonz, and Susan Stuard, BECOMING VISIBLE: WOMEN IN EUROPEAN HISTORY, Second Edition. Copyright © 1987 by Houghton Mifflin Company society, which give us direct knowledge of the attitudes of the dominant sector of that society toward women, also yield indirect knowledge about our other criteria: namely, the sexual, economic, political, and cultural activities of women. Insofar as images of women relate to what really goes on, we can infer from them something about that social reality. But, second, the relations between the ideology of sex roles and the reality we want to get at are complex and difficult to establish. Such views may be prescriptive rather than descriptive; they may describe a situation that no longer prevails; or they may use the relation of the sexes symbolically and not refer primarily to women and sex roles at all. Hence, to assess the historical significance of changes in sex-role conception, we must bring such changes into connection with all we know about general developments in the society at large.

This essay examines changes in sex-role conception, particularly with respect to sexuality, for what they tell us about Renaissance society and women's place in it. At first glance, Renaissance thought presents a problem in this regard because it cannot be simply categorized. Ideas about the relation of the sexes range from a relatively complementary sense of sex roles in literature dealing with courtly manners, love, and education, to patriarchal conceptions in writings on marriage and the family, to a fairly equal presentation of sex roles in early Utopian social theory. Such diversity need not baffle the attempt to reconstruct a history of sex-role conceptions, however, and to relate its course to the actual situation of women. Toward this end, one needs to sort out this material in terms of the social groups to which it responds: to courtly society in the first case, the nobility of the petty despotic states of Italy; to the patrician bourgeoisie in the second, particularly of republics such as Florence. In the third case, the relatively equal position accorded women in Utopian thought (and in those lower-class movements of the radical Reformation analogous to it) results from a larger critique of early modern society and all the relations of domination that flow from private ownership and control of property. Once distinguished, each of these groups of sources tells the same story. Each discloses in its own way certain new constraints suffered by Renaissance women as the family and political life were restructured in the great transition from medieval feudal society to the early modern state. The sources that represent the interests of the nobility and the bourgeoisie point to this fact by a telling, double index. Almost all such works—with certain notable exceptions, such as Boccaccio and Ariosto—establish chastity as the female norm and restructure the relation of the sexes to one of female dependency and male domination.

The bourgeois writings on education, domestic life, and society constitute the extreme in this denial of women's independence. Suffice it to say that they sharply distinguish an inferior domestic realm of women from the superior public realm of men, achieving a veritable "renaissance" of the outlook and practices of classical Athens, with its domestic imprisonment of citizen wives. The courtly Renaissance literature we will consider was more gracious. But even here, by analyzing a few of the representative works of this genre, we find a new repression of the noblewoman's affective experience, in contrast to the latitude afforded her by medieval literature, and some of the social and cultural reasons for it. Dante and Castiglione, who continued a literary tradition that began with the courtly love literature of eleventh- and twelfth-century Provence, transformed medieval conceptions of love and nobility. In the love ideal they formed, we can discern the inferior position the Renaissance noblewoman held in the relation of the sexes by comparison with her male counterpart and with her medieval predecessor as well.

Love and the Medieval Lady

Medieval courtly love, closely bound to the dominant values of feudalism and the Church, allowed in a special way for the expression of sexual love by women. Of course, only aristocratic women gained their sexual and affective rights thereby. If a knight wanted a peasant girl, the twelfth-century theorist of *The Art of Courtly Love*, Andreas Capellanus, encouraged him "not [to] hesitate to take what you seek and to embrace her by force." Toward the lady, however, "a true lover considers nothing good except what he thinks will please his beloved"; for if courtly love were to define itself as a noble phenomenon, it had to attribute an essential freedom to the relation between lovers. Hence, it metaphorically extended the social relation of vassalage to the love relationship, a "conceit" that Maurice Valency rightly called "the shaping principle of the whole design" of courtly love.

Of the two dominant sets of dependent social relations formed by feudalism—*les liens de d´ependence*, as Marc Bloch called them—vassalage, the military relation of knight to lord, distinguished itself (in its early days) by being freely entered into. At a time when everyone was somebody's "man," the right to freely enter a relation of service characterized aristocratic bonds, whereas hereditability marked the servile work relation of serf to lord. Thus, in medieval romances, a parley typically followed a declaration of love until love freely proffered was freely returned. A kiss (like the kiss of homage) sealed the pledge, rings were exchanged, and the knight entered the love service of his lady. Representing love along the lines of vassalage had several liberating implications for aristocratic women. Most fundamental, ideas of homage and mutuality entered the notion of heterosexual relations along with the idea of freedom. As symbolized on shields and other illustrations that place the knight in the ritual attitude of commendation, kneeling before his lady with his hands folded between hers, homage signified male service, not domination or subordination of the lady, and it signified fidelity, constancy in that service. "A lady must honor her lover as a friend, not as a master," wrote Marie de Ventadour, a female troubadour or *trobairitz*. At the same time, homage entailed a reciprocity of rights and obligations, a service on the lady's part as well. In one of Marie de France's romances, a knight is about to be judged by the barons of King Arthur's court when his lady rides to the castle to give him "succor" and pleads successfully for him, as any overlord might. Mutuality, or complementarity, marks the relation the lady entered into with her *ami* (the favored name for "lover" and, significantly, a synonym for "vassal").

This relation between knight and lady was very much at variance with the patriarchal family relations obtaining in that same level of society. Aware of its incompatibility with prevailing family and marital relations, the celebrants of courtly love kept love detached from marriage. "We dare not oppose the opinion of the Countess of Champagne who rules that love can exert no power between husband and wife," Andreas Capellanus wrote (p. 175). But in opting for a free and reciprocal heterosexual relation outside marriage, the poets and theorists of courtly love ignored the almost universal demand of patriarchal society for female chastity, in the sense of the woman's strict bondage to the marital bed. The reasons why they did so, and even the fact that they did so, have long been disputed, but the ideas and values that justify this kind of adulterous love are plain. Marriage, as a relation arranged by others, carried the taint of social necessity for the aristocracy. And if the feudality denigrated marriage by disdaining obligatory service, the Church did so by regarding it not as a "religious" state, but an inferior one that responded to natural necessity. Moreover, Christianity positively fostered the ideal of courtly love at a deep level of feeling. The courtly relation between lovers took vassalage as its structural model, but its passion was nourished by Christianity's exaltation of love.

Christianity had accomplished its elevation of love by purging it of sexuality, and in this respect, by recombining the two, courtly love clearly departed from Christian teaching. The toleration of adultery it fostered thereby was in itself not so grievous. The feudality disregarded any number of church rulings that affected their interests, such as prohibitions of tournaments and repudiation of spouses (divorce) and remarriage. Moreover, adultery hardly needed the sanction of courtly love, which, if anything, acted rather as a restraining force by binding sexuality (except in marriage) to love. Lancelot, in Chrétien de Troyes's twelfth-century romance, lies in bed with a lovely woman because of a promise he has made, but "not once does he look at her, nor show her any courtesy. Why not? Because his heart does not go out to her. . . . The knight has only one heart, and this one is no longer really his, but has been entrusted to someone else, so that he cannot bestow it elsewhere." Actually, Lancelot's chastity represented more of a threat to Christian doctrine than the fact that his passion (for Guinevere) was adulterous, because his attitudes justified sexual love. Sexuality could only be "mere sexuality" for the medieval Church, to be consecrated and directed toward procreation by Christian marriage. Love, on the other hand, defined as passion for the good, perfects the individual; hence love, according to Thomas Aquinas, properly directs itself toward God. Like the churchman, Lancelot spurned mere sexuality—but for the sake of sexual love. He defied Christian *teaching* by reattaching love to sex; and experiencing his love as a devout vocation, as a passion, he found himself in utter accord with Christian *feeling*. . . .

The Renaissance Lady: Politics and Culture

In his handbook for the nobility, Baldassare Castiglione's description of the lady of the court makes [the] difference in sex roles quite clear. On the one hand, the Renaissance lady appears as the equivalent of the courtier. She has the same virtues of mind as he, and her education is symmetrical with his. She learns everything—well, almost everything—he does: "knowledge of letters, of music, of painting, and . . . how to dance and how to be festive." Culture is an accomplishment for noblewoman and man alike, used to charm others as much as to develop the self. But for the woman, charm had become the primary occupation and aim. Whereas the courtier's chief task is defined as the profession of arms, "in a Lady who lives at court a certain pleasing affability is becoming above all else, whereby she will be able to entertain graciously every kind of man" (p. 207).

. . . The Renaissance lady is not desired, not loved for herself. Rendered passive and chaste, she merely mediates the courtier's safe transcendence of an otherwise demeaning necessity. On the plane of symbolism, Castiglione thus had the courtier dominate both her and the prince; and on the plane of reality, he indirectly acknowledged the courtier's actual domination of the lady by having him adopt "woman's ways" in his relations to the prince. Castiglione had to defend against effeminacy in the courtier, both the charge of it (p. 92) and the actuality of faces "soft and feminine as many attempt to have who not only curl their hair and pluck their eyebrows, but preen themselves . . . and appear so tender and languid . . . and utter their words so limply" (p. 36). Yet the close-fitting costume of the Renaissance nobleman displayed the courtier exactly as Castiglione would have him, "well built and shapely of limb" (p. 36). His clothes set off his grace, as did his nonchalant ease, the new manner of those "who seem in words, laughter, in posture not to care" (p. 44). To be attractive, accomplished, and seem not to care; to charm and do so coolly—how concerned with impression, how masked the true self. And how manipulative: petitioning his lord, the courtier knows to be "discreet in choosing the occasion, and will ask things that are proper and reasonable; and he will so frame his request, omitting those parts that he knows can cause displeasure, and will skillfully make easy the difficult points so that his lord will always grant it" (p. 111). In short, how like a woman—or a dependent, for that is the root of the simile.

The accommodation of the sixteenth- and seventeenth-century courtier to the ways and dress of women in no way bespeaks a greater parity between them. It reflects, rather, that general restructuring of social relations that entailed for the Renaissance noblewoman a greater dependency upon men as feudal independence and reciprocity yielded to the state. In this new situation, the entire nobility suffered a loss. Hence, the courtier's posture of dependency, his concern with the pleasing impression, his resolve "to perceive what his prince likes, and . . . to bend himself to this" (pp. 110–111). But as the state overrode aristocratic power, the lady suffered a double loss. Deprived of the possibility of independent power that the combined interests of kinship and feudalism guaranteed some women in the Middle Ages, and that the states of early modern Europe would preserve in part, the Italian noblewoman in particular entered a relation of almost universal dependence upon her family and her husband. And she experienced this dependency at the same time as she lost her commanding position with respect to the secular culture of her society.

Hence, the love theory of the Italian courts developed in ways as indifferent to the interests of women as the courtier, in his self-sufficiency, was indifferent as a lover. It accepted, as medieval courtly love did not, the double standard. It bound the lady to chastity, to the merely procreative sex of political marriage, just as her weighty and costly costume came to conceal and constrain her body while it displayed her husband's noble rank. Indeed, the person of the woman became so inconsequential to this love relation that one doubted whether she could love at all. The question that emerges at the end of *The Courtier* as to "whether or not women are as capable of divine love as men" (p. 350) belongs to a love theory structured by mediation rather than mutuality. Woman's beauty inspired love but the lover, the agent, was man. And the question stands unresolved at the end of *The Courtier*—because at heart the spokesmen for Renaissance love were not really concerned about women or love at all.

Where courtly love had used the social relation of vassalage to work out a genuine concern with sexual love, Castiglione's thought moved in exactly the opposite direction. He allegorized love as fully as Dante did, using the relation of the sexes to symbolize the new political order. In this, his love theory reflects the social realities of the Renaissance. The denial of the right and power of women to love, the transformation of women into passive "others" who serve, fits the self-image of the courtier, the one Castiglione sought to remedy. The symbolic relation of the sexes thus mirrors the new social relations of the state, much as courtly love displayed the feudal relations of reciprocal personal dependence. But Renaissance love reflects, as well, the actual condition of dependency suffered by noblewomen as the state arose. If the courtier who charms the prince bears the same relation to him as the lady bears to the courtier, it is because Castiglione understood the relation of the sexes in the same terms that he used to describe the political relation: that is, as a relation between servant and lord. The nobleman suffered this relation in the public domain only. The lady, denied access to a freely chosen, mutually satisfying love relation, suffered it in the personal domain as well. Moreover, Castiglione's theory, unlike the courtly love it superseded, subordinated love itself to the public concerns of the Renaissance nobleman. He set forth the relation of the sexes as one of dependency and domination, but he did so in order to express and deal with the political relation and its problems. The personal values of love, which the entire feudality once prized, were henceforth increasingly left to the lady. The courtier formed his primary bond with the modern prince.

In sum, a new division between personal and public life made itself felt as the state came to organize Renaissance society, and with that division the modern relation of the sexes made its appearance, even among the Renaissance nobility. Noblewomen, too, were increasingly removed from public concerns—economic, political, and cultural—and although they did not disappear into a private realm of family and domestic concerns as fully as their sisters in the patrician bourgeoisie, their loss of public power made itself felt in new constraints placed upon their personal as well as their social lives. Renaissance ideas on love and manners, more classical than medieval, and almost exclusively a male product, expressed this new subordination of women to the interests of husbands and male-dominated kin groups and served to justify the removal of women from an "unladylike" position of power and erotic independence. All the advances of Renaissance Italy, its proto-capitalist economy, its states, and its humanistic culture, worked to mold the noblewoman into an aesthetic object: decorous, chaste, and doubly dependent—on her husband as well as the prince.

POSTSCRIPT

Did Women Benefit from the Renaissance?

Once we begin to consider the experiences of women in history as separate from those of men, we meet a new set of challenges. Women are not a universal category, and their experiences throughout history are as varied as their race, social class, ethnicity, religion, sexual orientation, and a host of other categories make them. In recent years historians have begun to consider both the ways in which women's historical experiences are more or less the same (with regard to childbirth, access or lack of access to birth control, and female sexuality, for example) and the ways in which one woman's experience differs radically from another's (because of race, class, or a host of other differences).

The periodization question remains a fascinating one. Following Kelly-Gadol, other scholars began to look at historical periods with which they were familiar with an eye to using women's experiences as a starting point. In *Becoming Visible* (from which Kelly-Gadol's selection was excerpted), William Monter poses this question: Was there a Reformation for women? For a fuller explanation of the differences among compensatory, contributory, and other approaches, see Gerda Lerner's essay "Placing Women in History," in *Major Problems in Women's History*, 2d ed., edited by Mary Beth Norton and Ruth Alexander (D. C. Heath, 1996). This collection also contains Gisela Bock's "Challenging Dichotomies in Women's History" and "Afro-American Women in History," by Evelyn Brooks Higginbotham, which questions the concept of a universal womanhood by exploring the varying experiences of African American women.

For a Marxist analysis of women in history, see Juliet Mitchell's "Four Structures in a Complex Unity," in *Woman's Estate* (Pantheon Books, 1972). In it, Mitchell argues that production, reproduction, sexuality, and the socialization of children must all be transformed together if the liberation of women is to be achieved; otherwise, progress in one area can be offset by reinforcement in another. For a fuller explanation of the differences among compensatory, contributory and other approaches, *Picturing Women in Renaissance and Baroque Italy*, Geraldine A. Johnson and Sara F. Matthews Grieco, eds, (Cambridge University Press, 1997) offers a collection of essays, exploring women as producers, sponsors, and subjects of art—conflicting images of women suggest a lack of fixed gender roles. Catherine King's *Renaissance Women Patrons: Wives and Widows in Italy, c. 1300–c. 1550* (Manchester University Press, 1998) explores women's artistic patronage during a time when artistic patronage was taken seriously. And, finally, *Birth of the Chess Queen* by Stanford gender scholar Marilyn Yalom (Harper Collins, 2004) contends that the arrival of the queen (to replace a weak vizier who could move only one square diagonally per turn) was linked with the rising status of women in medieval Europe.

ISSUE 12

Was Zen Buddhism the Primary Shaper of the Samurai Warrior Code?

YES: Winston L. King, from *Zen and the Way of the Sword: Arming the Samurai Psyche* (Oxford University Press, 1993)

NO: Catharina Blomberg, from *The Heart of the Warrior: Origins and Religious Background of the Samurai System in Feudal Japan* (Japan Library, 1994)

ISSUE SUMMARY

YES: Religious scholar Winston L. King credits the monk Eisai with introducing Zen to the Hōjō samurai lords of Japan who recognized its affinity with the warrior's profession and character.

NO: Japanologist Catharina Blomberg emphasizes the diversity of influences on the samurai psyche—Confucianism, Shinto, and Zen—stressing the conflict between a warrior's duty and Buddhist ethical principles.

The word *Zen* means meditation. From India Buddhist meditation masters brought their method of practice first to China (where it was known as Ch'an) and in the seventh century to Japan, where the school of Buddhism known as Zen began to flourish during the twelfth and thirteenth centuries. What Western thinkers call truth and salvation lay within the person, according to Zen masters, not in sacred texts, rituals, or doctrines. The realization of satori, or enlightenment, was a visceral rather than an intellectual experience and it could be achieved existentially, through a life of action.

From the time of the Hōjō regent Hōjō Tokiyori (1227–1263), Zen and the samurai class became closely allied. However, Buddhism and its Zen offshoot was not the only religious alternative in Japan. The influences of Confucianism, imported from China, and Shinto, the indigenous faith of Japan, were both significant. Like the Chinese, who found themselves Confucian on state occasions, Taoist on matters of health, and Buddhist at the time of death, Japanese people did not feel these religious traditions were mutually exclusive.

The warrior class that developed in Japan between the ninth and twelfth centuries and supported the shogunates that ruled Japan prior to the nineteenth-century Meiji Restoration was also called bushi, and the code by which they lived and died became known as bushido—the way of the warrior. As skilled fighting men, the samurai were, above all, loyal to the emperor, to his overlord or daimyo, and to other samurai of higher rank. Skilled in swordsmanship, horsemanship, and hand-to-hand combat, many were often also adept at painting, calligraphy, and poetry. They lived spartan lives marked by honor, pride, patriotism, and honesty. Prepared at any moment to lay down their lives for their lord, the samurai preferred ritual suicide (known as seppuku or hara-kiri, meaning disembowelment) to capture in battle or to dishonor. Later scholars have found elements of Buddhism, Confucianism, and Shinto in the bushido code and disagree about which influence predominated.

From Shinto comes reverence for the emperor as a god-like father of the nation. Out of this loyalty to the imperial family flows an intense patriotism as well as the promise that to die for one's country in battle is to become god-like oneself. This absolute fidelity of the samurai may be seen continuing into the modern era. Kamikaze pilots and suicide torpedoists who willingly sacrificed their lives for the success of their nation and to honor the emperor during World War II were following their own version of the bushido code.

Confucianism draws attention to the Five Constant Relationships—between parent and child, husband and wife, older and younger sibling, older and younger friend, and ruler and subject—as models for achieving harmony with the Way of Heaven. To know one's place, to do one's duty, to honor those above and act kindly toward those below, this was the way to live a life of balance, to serve the common good, and to please the ancestors. Samurai loyalty to emperor and overlord may be understood within this context of properly lived human relationships.

Buddhism focuses on how to become enlightened—to see things as they actually are—and, thus, to escape the continual round of birth/death/rebirth known as samsara. Zen Buddhism emphasizes meditation as a path to true seeing into the heart of the cosmos and into the Buddha-nature that is within all things. It makes no hard distinctions between sacred and secular, understanding that the way of enlightenment involves the reconciliation of all apparent opposites. Once these artificial distinctions collapse, a genuine experience of things as they are becomes possible.

Each lifetime arises out of the karma of previous lifetimes. Whatever the person desires, whatever the person does not yet understand, these are the karmic predispositions that travel from birth to birth and govern the agenda of a present lifetime. So, despite the Buddhist prohibition against killing (not only other humans but all living things endowed with Buddha-nature), a samurai might see himself as destined by karma to live a warrior's life. As you read the following selections, decide for yourself which influence—Shinto, Confucianism, Zen—predominated in forming the inner life of the samurai warrior.

Winston L. King

The Japanese Warrior Adopts Zen

Zen Buddhism first became an important factor in the training and life of the Japanese warrior class in the thirteenth century. During the late-twelfth-century struggle of the Genji and Heike clans, Jōdo (Pure Land) Buddhism—in which Amida and his infinite mercy and forgiveness were paramount—was perhaps the soldier's favorite religious loyalty, especially in the hour of death. But with the coming of the Hōjō regency to power, Zen Buddhism increasingly took the leading role.

Eisai: "Founder" of Zen

Eisai (1141–1215) is the first name to reckon with in this Zen ascendancy. Sometimes he is called the founder of Zen Buddhism in Japan. This is not strictly true. The Zen practice of meditation, imported from China (where it was known as Ch'an), had been practiced in Japan since the seventh century, where it was considered one of several types of Buddhist spiritual training and given a home at Enryakuji by Tendai Buddhism.

The situation is rather that Eisai (also called Yōsai), a Tendai monk at Enryakuji, attempted to give Zen a more independent status than Enryakuji leaders were willing to allow it. Eisai, wishing to study with some of the masters of the more venerable Chinese tradition, made two trips to China to "renew" and deepen his understanding of Buddhism, and there he came into contact with the respected masters of the independent Ch'an (Zen) school. At the end of his second visit, from 1187 to 1191, he was given ordination as a Rinzai Zen master, and on his return to Japan he sought to establish a temple in Kyoto in which specific Zen training and meditation—of course, Zen means just that, "meditation"—would be given a central place. To the day of his death, Eisai still considered himself to be a Tendai monk. But Enryakuji would have nothing to do with his "new" Tendai Buddhism and frustrated his efforts. Eisai then journeyed to the shogunal headquarters in Kamakura, where he gained the favor of the widow of the first shogun, Minamoto Yoritomo; Eisai was installed as the head of a newly built temple at her behest. Somewhat later he returned to Kyoto by invitation and spent his last years there as an honored monk-teacher.

Rather curiously, Eisai has been memorialized in a very concrete way: the drinking of tea, bitter green tea (*matcha*) that is "brewed" by stirring the powdered tea leaves into boiling hot water in a tea bowl and whipping it to a froth with a special "feathered bamboo" whisk. He held it to be ideal for keeping the meditator awake and good for the health in general. Later, tea drinking was made into a ritualized fine art with skilled tea masters being much sought after and munificently rewarded by such as Toyotomi Hideyoshi, Tokugawa Ieyasu's predecessor in military and political power. Sometimes the tea drinking was a lavish and ostentatious ceremony—as with Hideyoshi, who used it as a means of political maneuver and dominance. In other versions, the emphasis was on perfect (highly polished) simplicity and "naturalness," as befitting its Zen origins. In modern Japan, there are both the genuinely simple-natural drinking of tea in the Zen monastery and an assiduously cultivated commercialized form carried on by modern tea masters.

To return to Eisai: His accomplishments on behalf of Zen were two. First, though he himself remained a Tendai-Zennist, his special emphasis on Zen practice as a somewhat distinctive and independent religious discipline began the process of establishing Zen as a separate sect. Thus his "new" Zen Buddhism became a part of what is known as the Kamakura period populist Buddhism, which brought Buddhism out of its high-class elitism into the life of the common people. His "companions" in this were Hōnen and Shinran, who taught the sufficiency for salvation of the repetition (in faith) of Amida Buddha's name, and Nichiren, who proclaimed the full efficacy of the Lotus Sutra's name as a mantric chant.

The second accomplishment of Eisai was his bringing of Zen practice in its own independent right to the attention of the new lords of Japan, the Hōjō regency samurai government. It was their interest in Zen, their perception of it as congenial to the warrior's profession and character, that brought Zen and the samurai together. However, even though the Hōjō regents gave Zen a friendly interest and preferential treatment, it was some time before Zen freed itself completely from the Tendai qualifications and Shingon esoteric practices imposed on it by Eisai and came to be defined by its own specific genius and quality. This was accomplished by various of Eisai's disciples and by Dōgen (1200–1253), who also studied Ch'an in China from 1223 to 1228 and returned to Japan to found a competing school of Zen, the Sōtō. There was also a continuing stream of Ch'an masters from the mainland who forwarded the process of developing the distinctive independent character of Zen teaching and practice.

Zen as the Warrior's Religion

The fourth Hōjō regent, Hōjō Tokiyori (1227–1263), nearly fifty years after Eisai's death, was the first to give more than a merely general official friendliness to Zen; he became personally interested in Zen practice and was certified by a Chinese master as having attained to enlightenment. From this time on, Zen and the new warrior-masters of Japan were closely related to each other; this personal interest and discipleship carried on over to the Ashikaga shoguns who governed Japan—or the greater part of it—from 1333 to 1573 and who moved the shogunal headquarters from Kamakura back to Kyoto.

Thus it was that from Tokiyori onward, Zen was the unofficial–official religion of the rulers and ruling class. As a matter of course, Zen prospered as sect and institution. The later Hōjō regents, particularly several of the Ashikaga shoguns, were generous patrons of Zen. By the time of Soseki Musō (1275–1351), the most prominent Zen monk of his time, and nearly a century after Eisai, Zen had grown into a nationwide establishment—courtesy of the Hōjō regents and the shogunate. Zen temples were constructed in all the prefectures. The Five Mountain (*gozan*) system of precedence was established, by which five large temples around Kyoto, with Nanzenji at their head, and another five in Kamakura (one of them Eisai's special temple) were given first-rank status. A second-level class (subordinate to the first class), consisting of some sixty temples, was also established. Finally, there were some two hundred local temples scattered through most of Japan. Again, be it repeated, to this establishment the shogunal authorities gave their full backing and support.

And not only did the Zen sect prosper in terms of the favor of high officials, but also among the rank-and-file samurai themselves. It seems that from the beginning of Zen's "new" presence, its meditation and discipline commended themselves to the samurai, of both high and low rank. One samurai vassal counseled his son, "The duty of a warrior like that of a monk, is to obey orders. . . . He must consider his life not his own but a gift offered to his lord." Indeed, the samurai so "adopted" Zen, for practice in meditation and as a Buddhism suited to them, that it became a proverb in the Kamakura era that "Tendai is for the imperial court, Shingon for the nobility, Zen for the warrior class, and Pure Land for the masses."

But the alliance between the Ashikaga shogunate, now settled in Kyoto, led to far more than the nationwide founding of Zen temples. With Ashikaga Takauji, the first of the Ashikaga shoguns, Zen priests became the official advisers to the shogunate. Because Zen monks were the leading scholars of the day, and numbers of them had been to the Chinese mainland, their advisory role had a great influence on many aspects of official policy and national life. Many of them were traveled men of the world whose ordination as Buddhist monks gave them a high social standing and did not exclude them from the world or from taking part in secular life. (It may be remarked in passing that Zen draws no sharp line between the "sacred" and the "secular"; to the enlightened person, the two are one—it is the inner-personal quality of life that is the domain of virtue and holiness. The Buddha-nature is in everything without essential distinction.) Hence they rendered important diplomatic services, were often negotiators with mainland Chinese officials and other foreigners, and were sent as shogunal emissaries. The Shōkokuji Zen temple in Kyoto was the government's operative foreign-relations center for a considerable period of time.

There was another important aspect of Zen influence, one whose marks still remain in the Japanese cultural and artistic tradition. As Heinrich Dumoulin observes: It was the Zen monk-scholar-artist who opened the world of "*haute* culture" to the warrior clans. The Hōjō regency in Kamakura kept its deliberate distance from the Kyoto court circles—the better to keep its political power intact and to avoid the enervating, effeminizing influence of the imperial and aristocratic circles. The rough, stern warrior clans of the north and east disdained and distrusted the soft and cultured life as corruptive of the more stalwart virtues. But this attitude changed with the passing years, especially under the Ashikaga regime when the shogunate moved its headquarters to Kyoto. The warrior leaders found themselves hungry for the literacy and aesthetic attainments they came in contact with in Kyoto. Zen monks as chosen advisers to the shogunate—disciplined in living, skillful in language and a new style of painting, some of them writers, poets, and men of the world as well as redoubtable warriors—thus became tutors to the warrior-class leaders and influential in setting new cultural styles.

So, too, the influence of Zen, direct and indirect, on the art of the day was substantial. There was painting, for example. Zen set a new style of direct, spontaneous, and spare "painting." Zen artist-monks disdained the colorful and decorative for the most part and opted for *sumie* (India ink drawings), also called *suiboku* ("water and ink" creations). There were self-portraits (almost caricatures, designed to express one's personal essence), persons, animals, birds, vegetation, as well as calligraphy. Much of it was a sheerly black-on-white style of instant art—jet-black indelible ink on porous white paper. Such work required complete poise and decisiveness, for the first stroke was also the last; there could be no patching, no alteration. Its production was fully visceral, a disciplined spontaneity. The starkly simple result admirably expressed the Zen "view" of life.

There was also the Noh play, not originated but strongly influenced by Zen in the days of the Ashikaga Shogun Yoshimitsu (1368–1394), who took a strong personal interest in Noh development. Again, as with sumie, the sparse action and enigmatic, suggestive symbolism suited the Zen genius, even though the themes of the plays were Shintoist and Amidist. Yoshimitsu also built the famous "worldly" Golden Pavilion (Kinkakuji); his successor, two generations later, Shogun Ashikaga Yoshimasa, built the Silver Pavilion (Ginkakuji) in 1473 into which to retire for a Zen meditator's life.

Despite all the personal and official favor shown to Zen by individual regents and shoguns and the semiofficializing of Zen as the government's religion, Zen as a sect avoided the political embroilments that were characteristic of the Nara and Enryakuji temples and the Pure Land Ikkō sect. Zen monks counseled shogunal officials and, as already observed, acted as government representatives in international affairs. But there was never a Zen lobbying group at head shogunal quarters or Zen groups or temples maneuvering to gain power at the expense of competitors.

If we ask why this should be the case, three possible factors may be mentioned. The first and most obvious is: Why *should* Zen enter the always dangerous field of religious–political intrigue? It was already the personal practice of several shoguns; within a hundred years after Eisai, its temples had been established throughout Japan, and Zen had been adopted by the shogunal government as a near-official religion; its monks were advisers to the shoguns, and the samurai looked on it as their special religious faith. Besides this, in Zen's heyday of cultural popularity, Zen scholar-monks set the tone and the pace of new cultural styles. What more was there to ask for? What need to intrigue at court?

Another factor of at least some importance in this connection was what might be called Zen anti-institutionalism. In religious terms, Zen was a rejection of many creedal and ritual elements of the Buddhist tradition embodied in most of the other sects; this allowed considerable freedom of action and practice on its part. On the sectarian-institutional level, Zen favored individual rather than factional or organizational action. Some of the leading Zen monasteries were physically large—the Hōjō regents and Ashikaga shoguns had been generous in their support of the Zen "establishment." Despite this, the relationships between Zen and the government, as well as with other groups, tended to be on the level of the personal—influential individuals rather than organizational muscleflexing. Thus no given Zen temple—paralleling Enryakuji of the Tendai, Kōya-san of the Shingon, or the great fortress-temple of the Pure Land Honganji near Osaka—ever became a powerful and belligerent institution seeking to gain political advantages.

The third factor to be noted is only partially explanatory of this situation. The great sectarian temples that were now and again embroiled in conflict with the civilian government—the Nara sects, Enryakuji, and Kōya-san—had been established centuries before Zen came on to the scene as a sect; and in those centuries they had accumulated their great estates, their vested interests, and their armies of soldier-monks. Thus Zen missed out on this enfeudalizing of the religious establishment and the politicizing of its role. Of course, it must be said that so, too, had the Honganji Jōdo Shinshū (Pure Land) sect, for the Pure Land sects were established at roughly the same time as Zen, in the thirteenth century. Yet Honganji Buddhism gave birth to Ikkō militancy. In any case, Zen's nonpolitical character saved it from the bloody purges that Oda Nobunaga inflicted on Enryakuji and the Ikkō barons in the sixteenth century.

There is another aspect of the religious and political situation that is of importance here: the historical framework of the relation of both Shinto and Buddhism to the state. Shinto, as Japan's first and basic religion, had the emperor as its high priest; as guardian of the Three Sacred Treasures and performer of annual fertility-prosperity rituals, his first concern and main function were the preservation of his people in safety and prosperity. Therefore, in times of crisis, such as the Mongolian invasions in the late thirteenth century, Shinto priests assiduously prayed to the gods and believed that they had responded by sending the gales (*kami kaze*) that had wrecked the Mongol fleets.

But it must also be recollected that Buddhism was first brought into Japan in the sixth century primarily as a more potent means to the same end—preservation of the nation. All the Buddhist sects—with the possible partial exception of the Pure Land—well understood this to be their role in times of crisis. When the Mongols attacked, Buddhist clergy joined their sutra chanting to the ritual efforts of the Shinto priests to bring victory—and were rewarded accordingly. Clans often endowed their local Buddhist monasteries and temples to provide prayers in times of crisis or sickness. And with the transformation of Hachiman, the Shinto god of war, into a bodhisattva [a being whose actions promote unity or harmony; one who vows to postpone one's own enlightenment in order to help all sentient beings realize liberation] of high rank. Buddhist warriors could pray to him for victory as well as Shintoists could. Nor did Zen totally escape this influence. It is significant that Eisai entitled his first major writing *Treatise on the Spread of Zen for the Protection of the Nation*.

As an inevitable and natural result, the nonviolent message of Buddhism was qualified, modified, or overlaid by duty to clan lord, so that Buddhist warriors fought other Buddhist warriors to the death, it is to be presumed with only minor twinges of conscience. Of course, this is not unique to Buddhism. After the officialization of Christianity in Europe by the emperor Constantine in 330 C.E. [Christian Era], the followers of the Prince of Peace not only launched massive crusades against the infidel Muslims, but also fought one another savagely over the truth of their differing doctrines.

It should be said in all fairness that many Buddhist warriors did retire to monasteries, in their later years usually, to pursue their spiritual welfare and in some measure atone for their un-Buddhist conduct in killing their fellow men. But there was an inbuilt factor in Buddhism itself that worked against the teaching that all life, especially human life, is sacred. This was the Buddhist teaching of karmic destiny. For instance, some of the warriors portrayed in the *Heike Monogatari* (Tale of the Heike) lamented the fact, at reflective moments or when they had committed some militarily necessary cruelty, that they had been born into a warrior family and thus must carry on with a warrior's bloody career. And free as Zen may have been in some respects from the bonds of the Buddhist tradition, it was not free from the bonds of the teaching of karma.

To this must be added a peculiarly Japanese factor: the strong sense of family loyalty and tradition, especially in the upper classes. Reflecting the Chinese reverence for ancestors, the family—and its role, occupation, business—is a "sacred" inheritance, entailing the son's—especially the eldest son's—following in his father's footsteps. (One contemporary Shinto priest proudly notes that he is the twenty-eighth in the family who has occupied the headship of a particular shrine.) When this is added to, or is seen as the vehicle of, karmic predetermination, the individual is required, even fated, to accept the role that has been given him—for instance, as a samurai whose destined duty was to be a fighting, life-destroying "Buddhist."

For all its freedom from some of the liabilities of the other sects and despite its emphasis on individual freedom and opposition to institutional bonds, Zen did not escape these doctrinal and historical influences. When it was becoming a distinct and independent sect in the thirteenth century, the institutional format of religion in the service of the state and of warlike sects and monk-warriors had been long set. What could be more natural under the circumstances than for Zen monks, favorites of the Hōjō regents and their successors, the Ashikaga shoguns, and as valued spiritual tutors of the fighting forces, to put themselves completely at the service of the state.

Although he belonged to a subsequent period when Zen no longer occupied its privileged and somewhat exclusive position in government circles, Sūden (Den-chōrō, d. 1633) beautifully illustrates the qualities, accomplishments, and diverse roles characteristic of talented Zen monks. He was head of two Kyoto Zen temples, Konchi-in and, the most prestigious temple of all, Nanzenji, to whose restoration he devoted two years. Then in 1608, Tokugawa Ieyasu called Sūden into the service of the shogunate. (He had previously served as a field secretary in Ieyasu's campaigns.) Sūden handled all documents dealing with foreign relations and was placed in general charge of the Tokugawa religious policy—continuing in that post for another seventeen years after Ieyasu's death—working for the regulation and subordination of Buddhist sects to government control and for the exclusion of Christianity.

In his earlier years, just before he entered a monastery on his father's death, he had fought in his father's forces, taking the heads of three enemies as trophies. Hence Ieyasu allowed the temple built at his own place of retirement in Sumpu for Sūden, to display three black stars on its banner in honor of Sūden's prowess as a warrior. Thus was Sūden the warrior, "executive secretary" in the field to the man who became Japan's de facto ruler in 1600, then his "secretary of state" and the director of religious affairs for the shogunate— all the while presumably retaining his standing as a Zen monk. One is reminded of some of medieval Europe's priest-statesmen such as Armand-Jean Cardinal Richelieu.

In the light of these intimate connections between Zen and the ruling warrior class and also the apparent great popularity of Zen meditation among the rank-and-file samurai, especially during the warring centuries (1200–1600), it is necessary to know something of the samurai class to which Zen would prove of such value in their mode of life. That is, their use of Zen in their martial calling can make sense only if something of their history; their weapons—especially the sword—and their manner of using them; their hopes, fears, and ideals; their social role; and their conceptions of themselves and their "calling" are also known to us.

Warrior Ethics East and West

[A] *bushi* was trained from childhood for his future position in society by being taught to observe his father and his male elders and imitate their behaviour. Formal education consisted of the teaching of the Confucian Classics, but *bushi* of low rank were often illiterate until the time of the Tokugawa *Bakufu*, when literacy became exceptionally widespread in Japanese society. The military arts were the most important part of the training of a *bushi*, and were constantly practised from boyhood. Horsemanship, archery and swordfighting techniques were taught to males, whereas girls of *bushi* stock learned how to use the *naginata*, a halberd with a curved blade, in self-defense. *Bushi* women were also instructed in the use of the dagger which they always carried about their person, in order to be able to commit suicide by severing the jugular vein should the need for such action arise. The education of the *bushi* was referred to from the early Kamakura *Bakufu* by the term *Bun-Bu* (Letters and military arts). The study of letters encompassed the five traditional Chinese Classics and the four Confucian books.

The study of martial arts included a theoretial side as well as a practical one. The nature of the theory of *Bushidō* before it was recorded in the seventeenth century can only be gauged from literary references, and as we have seen the *Gunki Monogatari* provide many instances of the *bushi*'s philosophy of life and death. First of all he was aware of the fact that by fulfilling his duties as a professional warrior he was acting against the central principles of both Buddhism and Shinto. By taking life the *bushi* condemned himself to the existence of an *asura*, infernal spirit, in one of the Buddhist hells, of which there are ten cold and ten hot varieties, instead of being able to gain a favourable rebirth and eventual salvation in the Western Paradise of Amida Buddha. The knowledge of this certain damnation did not deter the samurai from giving loyal service to his lord, however, and it was frequently stressed by the authors of the *Gunki Monogatari* that the carrying out of duty was its own reward. This attitude was considerably elaborated upon and much discussed in later writings on *Bushidō*.

The *kuge* [court nobility] and *buke* [warrior family of the samurai social class] continued to lead separate lives after the establishment of the Kamakura *Bakufu*, although members of the *kuge* and the Imperial family occasionally were impressed or influenced by the warlike spirit of the new rulers. Jien wrote with evident disapproval in his *Gukanshō* of the abdicated Emperor

Go-Toba (1180–1239, regnavit 1183–1198) who displayed an unusual interest in such pastimes as archery and horsemanship. Go-Toba established his own guard force, the *Saimen Bushi* (Westface Warriors) modelling it on the *Hokumen Bushi* (Northface Warriors) of Go-Shirakawa, a private guard which had been disbanded by Minamoto Yoritomo. These imperial guard forces became a disruptive element which tended to disregard the *Bakufu*. There were instances of *Bakufu* officials being arrested in Kyoto, and of court titles being conferred directly, without the customary recommendation and approval of the Kamakura government.

The author of the *Tsurezure Gusa*, a title which can be translated as 'Idle Jottings' or 'Adiafora', Yoshida no Kaneyoshi, also known as Kenk⁻o, (1283–1350?) was a *kuge*, descended from the ancient clan of Court diviners, *Urabe*. Having served at the court of Emperor Go-Uda, he took the tonsure on the death of the Emperor in 1324 and lived as a recluse in a hermitage in the country for many years, although he is said to have returned to Kyoto for a period. His book contains a random collection of anecdotes, miniature essays on various topics, and reflexions on the state of the world. Yoshida clearly deplored the tendency of his contemporaries among the *kuge* to take an interest in warlike pursuits. 'Any man is soldier enough to crush the foe when fortune favours him, but War is a profession where he cannot make his name until, his forces exhausted, his weapons at an end, he seeks death at the hands of the foe rather than surrender. So long as he is living he cannot boast of warlike fame. What then does it profit, unless one is of a military family, to devote oneself to conduct removed from human principles and approaching that of the beasts? Such behavior did not suit the *kuge*'s station in life, and should be left to those born into the ranks of the *bushi*.

He could not, however, refrain from expressing admiration for those who lived and died as befitted warriors, as is evident from an anecdote he recorded. This concerned a party of *komusō*, Zen monks of the Fuke school, who were praying in an Amida temple. Another *komusō* entered, demanding to know whether a man whose name he gave was among them, and explaining that he wanted to avenge the death of his master. The man who had killed his master was present, answered in the affirmative, and arranged to meet his challenger outside the temple, so as not to pollute it or disturb the service in progress. The two men met outside, sword in hand, and fought a duel in which both of them died. 'Wilful and determined, they appear to be devoted to the Way of the Buddha, but they make strife and quarrel their business. Though dissolute and cruel in appearance, they think lightly of Death, and cling not at all to Life. The bravery of such men having impressed me, I set this down as it was related to me.' This, albeit somewhat reluctant, expression of admiration is rather far removed from the unmitigated disdain shown by the Heian literary ladies four centuries previously. It demonstrates how by this time the attitudes of the *bushi* had at least become accepted as a viewpoint which, even if it was not to be emulated, was regarded as worthy of consideration as an alternative to the *kuge* way of life. The *kuge* continued to regard themselves as the only true nobility, while the buke saw them as exponents of the remote and largely inconsequential court system.

The ethics and morals governing the life and thought of the *bushi*, and forming the guidelines for warrior comportment, bore a striking resemblance to contemporary European codes of chivalry. If we examine one of the most famous European works on the subject, *Libre del Orde de Cauayleria* (The Book on the Order of Chivalry), written in Catalan by Raymond Lull around 1280, we find a way of reasoning which is similar to many of the ideas and sentiments expressed in the *Gunki Monogatari* and the legal codes of the Hōjō and Ashikaga rulers. These similarities are entirely fortuitous, but nevertheless interesting and illuminating when we take the widely differing background and development of the two feudal systems into account.

Not unlike different religions, which display affinities of ideas arrived at from diametrically opposed standpoints, the ethical and practical demands of the two types of chivalry demonstrate a certain universality in human thought and endeavour. It must be remembered also that when dealing with European chivalry as well as *Bushidō* we are contemplating an ideal whose attainment might vary quite considerably, according to circumstances, and from one individual to another, and that far from every knight or *bushi* even attempted to attain this ideal although he was certainly aware of its requirements.

Religion was at the back of both kinds of chivalrous behaviour. The European knight was constantly reminded that he was a Christian knight, and that his duty at all times was to uphold the principles of charity, loyalty, truth, justice and virtue, protecting the weak against the strong and defending widows and fatherless children. Lull went to great lengths in his treatise to explain the religious and symbolic significance of the knight's arms, pointing out the resemblance of both his sword and dagger to a cross. The *bushi*, on the other hand, was not expected to uphold justice, truth and virtue *ad majorem Dei gloriam*, but because the quality of *gi* 'duty' or 'righteousness' was demanded of him by the Confucian doctrine to which he adhered.

Whereas the Christian knight could obtain absolution from his sins, e.g. of taking life, through confession, the *bushi* accepted with fortitude that he was condemned according to the tenets of Shinto as well as Buddhism. When we consider the sword of the *bushi* we find that it also had religious connotations, being dedicated to and protected by Buddhas, Bodhisattvas and minor Buddhist deities. The most significant difference between Europe and Japan, however, lay in the fact that not every man born of a knightly family in Europe actually entered an order of knighthood, while in Japan every male of the warrior nobility was a *bushi* by birth. In Europe the new knight was invested in a religious ceremony, usually held on one of the major feast days of the church, and we may compare this ceremony with the *genbuku* (coming of age) ceremony of the young *bushi*. . . .

In Japan the only refuge for a man of *bushi* stock who did not wish to lead the life of an active warrior was to take holy orders and enter the Buddhist priesthood. Buddhist temples and monasteries served as sanctuaries for young survivors of clan feuds, such as Minamoto Yoshitsune, whose life was spared by Taira Kiyomori after the execution of his father on the condition that he enter the Buddhist priesthood where he would be unable to avenge the death of his father. The same course of action was not infrequently taken also in

Europe. Although Christianity and Buddhism are religions devoted to peaceful pursuits and spiritual needs, there existed in Japan as well as in Europe a powerful *ecclesia militans*. In Japan the so-called 'warrior monks', *sōhei*, who first appeared in the Heian period, were a notable feature in the *Gempei* War as well as during the *Sengoku jidai*. Already in 970, Ryōgen, the abbot of the Hieizan monastic complex, laid down rules designed to curtail the activities of armed monks who disrupted the religious services. These regulations seem to have been largely ineffective, if we consider the amount of political power wielded by the armed clerics toward the end of the Heian period, and also the very serious disturbances created during the *Sengoku jidai* by the *Ikkō-ikki*.

The *sōhei* appear to have originated as a result of disputes over the ownership of land rather than over matters of doctrine, and many fights took place between two monasteries belonging to the same school of Buddhism. The warrior monks were not recruited among the high-ranking ecclesiastics, and quite a few laymen were also employed by the temples and monasteries to provide armed protection. Prior to the Kamakura period the *sōhei* wore the ordinary habit of a Buddhist monk, with the addition of a long scarf-like piece of cloth which was wound around the head and neck, covering the face and leaving only a space open for the eyes. They originally carried a staff and a sword, and only during the *Gempei* War did they begin to wear armour and other weapons. The *Heike Monogatari* provides vivid pictures of warrior monks, especially of one who took part with distinction in the Battle on Uji Bridge in 1180, fighting on the Minamoto side. 'Among the warrior-monks was one Tsutsui no Jōmyō Meishū. He wore armour laced with black leather over a deep blue battle robe. The thongs of his helmet with five neck-plates were tied tightly under his chin. He carried a sword in a black lacquered sheath, twenty-four blackfeathered arrows, a bow thickly bound with lacquered rattan, and his favourite wooden-shafted sickle-bladed halberd. He stepped forward onto the bridge and thundered: "You have heard of my fame as a valiant warrior. Take a good look at the pride of Mii-dera, I am Tsutsui no Jōmyō Meishū—among the dōju I am worth a thousand soldiers. Is there any among you who thinks himself a great warrior? Let him come forward!"'

The *Heike Monogatari* then goes on to tell how he performed outstanding feats of marksmanship, killing twelve enemies and wounding eleven more with as many arrows, and swordsmanship, cutting down five men with his halberd and eight more with his sword. After these extraordinary exploits Jōmyō retired to the Byōdōin temple nearby, where he counted the sixty-three dents in his armour and his five wounds, which he cauterised by applying burning grass to them. 'Then', says the *Heike Monogatari*, 'he wrapped a piece of cloth around his head, donned a white robe, and took up a broken bow for a staff. Chanting "Hail Amida Buddha", he went off toward Nara.'

We may compare the important part played by the warrior monks in the Japanese civil wars with the not dissimilar phenomenon in Medieval Europe of the spiritual orders of knights, notably the Templars, Hospitallers, and the Teutonic Order. The Order of the Knights of the Temple was founded in 1118 for the protection of pilgrims on their way to Jerusalem, and the other orders soon followed. They established a network of hospices and churches all over

Europe and the Near East, and became a factor of the utmost importance in the Crusades through their knowledge of the countries around the Mediterranean and their languages and customs. Although their origins and the conditions which brought about their foundation were widely different, the Japanese warrior monks and the military orders of Europe shared one fundamental trait, namely the fact that they had to justify the taking of life. The *sōhei* were either laymen serving in a temple or monastery, or low-ranking monks, and the Knights Templar and Hospitaller were members of religious orders within the Roman Catholic church, and subject to rules of poverty, chastity and obedience like monks and clerics.

The problem was one of morals and ethics, and the main question was whether the ultimate end could be said to justify the use of means which were theoretically forbidden. Buddhism, like Christianity, categorically forbids the taking of all life, going indeed a step further than Christianity by forbidding also the killing of animals, including insects. The person who instigates, or even condones, a killing, is as guilty as the person who carries it out, according to Buddhist doctrine, and in war all soldiers are equally guilty of taking life, whether they actually kill an enemy or not. The negativism of Buddhism, however, which teaches that all is suffering and that nothing really exists, can easily be interpreted as inimical to life itself. The idea of reincarnation may seem to favour the ending of the present existence in order to try again under different and perhaps better circumstances. This is not possible, however, owing to the belief in *karma*, the sum total of the individual's actions, which adheres to its bearer throughout the cycle of reincarnations. There is no getting away from the influence of *karma*, and only by leading a virtuous and pious life and refraining from sinning, can the individual hope to improve his chances of a more favourable rebirth in the next existence.

In Buddhism, as in Christianity, however, there is a considerable divergence between philosophical speculation on doctrine and dogma and popular ideas, and it is not difficult to see that the taking of life could be condoned under special circumstances, even among members of the clergy. The *sōhei* developed parallel to the *bushi* in a society which became increasingly dependent on warlike qualities for maintaining stability, and in the end the *bushi* were forced to eliminate the *sōhei* in order to gain political supremacy and unify the country.

Most of the *sōhei* appear to have been recruited from the popular Amidist schools of Buddhism. Zen Buddhist monks played a more ambivalent part. The Zen schools were introduced in Japan in the early years of the Kamakura *Bakufu*, and Zen monks seem to have taken an active part in the power struggles between the Hōjō *Shikken*, the Imperial court, and the Ashikaga *Shōguns*. As we have seen, the mental discipline taught by Zen came to influence the art and techniques of fighting, especially swordsmanship, to a very large extent. The Zen masters seem to have gone in for theory rather than practice, however, and Zen monasteries did not figure prominently among the religious institutions which were annihilated in Oda Nobunaga's purge of the politicised clergy of the *Sengoku jidai*.

One line of defence adopted by the Buddhist clergy to justify their taking up arms was the simple and apparently irreproachable fact that they were defending their religion against the enemies of the faith. Since they were fighting against their co-religionists of other Buddhist schools, this meant that they considered themselves as defenders of the true religion against false or heretical doctrines. In Europe, the religious orders reasoned in a similar vein, and in the Crusades they felt called upon to rescue one of the most sacred monuments of Christendom, the Holy Sepulchre, from infidel dominance. There is a comprehensive Buddhist tradition of armed divinities protecting the faith against all forms of evil influences, including the *Niō-ō*, the *Shitennō*, and the *Myō-ō*, as well as Bodhisattvas like Monju. The profound influence of the *bushi* on the militant side of Buddhism did not fail to impress the Buddhist clergy, and the prevailing atmosphere was one of warlike exploits rather than peaceful pursuits, however pacifist the Buddhist doctrine may have been originally. . . .

The most important and influential Buddhist monasteries, nunneries or temples, as well as the major Shinto shrines, as a rule chose their abbots and abbesses or chief priests and priestesses among junior members of the Imperial family until modern times. Among the *bushi*, for whom lineage was of the utmost importance, the possibility of entering their ranks from below did however exist until the late sixteenth century. Later, in the latter half of the Tokugawa *Bakufu*, adoption for men and marriage for women became other means of gaining admittance into a *bushi* family. Even such a very powerful man as the autocrat Toyotomi Hideyoshi, who was given a family name and pedigree by Imperial decree, was never able to forget or conceal his plebeian origins. He was greatly feared and in complete command, but nevertheless despised by the old *kuge* and *buke* families. There is no doubt that some families over the centuries managed to get away with spurious and newly fabricated pedigrees, but despite the prevalence of natural disasters such as earthquakes and typhoons, Japan is a country where families have managed to preserve their documents and records from the early Heian period until this day to a remarkable degree.

POSTSCRIPT

Was Zen Buddhism the Primary Shaper of the Samurai Warrior Code?

Because it insists on "no reliance on words or concepts," Zen is difficult to approach by way of printed texts. However, *Zen Flesh, Zen Bones: A Collection of Zen and Pre-Zen Writings*, compiled by Paul Reps (Doubleday, 1989) introduces us to monks who drop sacred texts into the fire, spend years facing walls in silent meditation, and even cut off their own arms to show zeal. This brings us closer to what in Zen might have touched the heart of a samurai.

Two other classics are Miyamoto Musashi, *A Book of Five Rings* (Overlook Press, 1974) and Yamamoto Tsunetomo, *Hagakure: The Book of the Samurai* (Kodansha International, 1983), both easily accessible. Musashi's guide to strategy was based on kendo, or sword fighting, but is consulted by business people who find the challenges faced and the tactics needed today little changed in 350 years. *Hagakure's* central contention is that bushido is a way of dying and that only a samurai prepared and willing to die at any moment can be totally faithful to his lord.

In The *Modern Samurai Society: Duty and Dependence in Contemporary Japan* (Amacom, 1982), Mitsuyuki Masatsugu traces the evolution of the loyal samurai warrior of the past into the devoted samurai executive of today. A similar aim motivates Eiko Ikegami's *The Taming of the Samurai: Honorific Individualism and the Making of Modern Japan* (Harvard University Press, 1995). However, she roots Japan's tradition of competitive individualism in samurai honor consciousness. Haru Matsukata Reischauer's *Samurai and Silk: A Japanese and American Heritage* (Harvard University Press, 1986) honors her two grandfathers—one a provincial samurai who became a founding father of the Meiji government, and the other from a wealthy peasant family who almost singlehandedly developed the silk trade with America.

Finally, Akira Kurosawa's 1954 film *The Seven Samurai* has inspired hundreds of imitators. Seven ronin (freelance samurai, not in service to a feudal lord) are called upon to aid villagers at an isolated outpost who are beleaguered by invading bandits. The honor code of the samurai is a key theme in this classic film as well as in one of its most popular descendants, John Sturges's *The Magnificent Seven*, as well as Ed Zwick's 2003 epic "The Last Smurai." Hired by the Emperor to train Japan's first modern army, Captain Nathan Algren (Tom Cruise) is captured and won over by a pair of Samurai warriors. For classroom and library, Films for the Humanities & Science offers Samurai Japan (ISBN 0-07365-0642-X).

On the Internet . . .

The Great Chinese Mariner Zheng He

This brief site contains an account of Zheng He's travels, a map depicting one of his voyages, and several other useful visuals. What is more important is other links that provide useful information on the great Chinese admiral.

http://www.chinapage.com/zhenghe.html

Columbus and the Age of Discovery

This university-run Web site includes a "computerized informational retrieval system," which contains 1,100 text articles related to Christopher Columbus.

http://muweb.millersville.edu/_columbus

Selected Works of Martin Luther (1483–1546)

From the "Project Wittenberg Website," this site features primary source materials on all of Luther's major works, including the famous 95 Theses.

**http:www.iclnet.org/pub/resources/text/
wittenberg/wittenberg-home.html**

European Witch Hunts (15th–17th Century)

Provides brief information about the witch hunts and their ramifications; also contains a short, but relevant annotated bibliography of important sources.

http://kings.edu/womens_history/witch

The Scientific Revolution: Readings, Resources, Link

A site that explores every facet of the movement; includes essays written by professors, outlines of important material, and many useful resources, print and electronic.

**http://www.clas.ufl.edu/users/rhatch/
pages/03-Sci-Rev/SCI-REV-Home/**

Internet Medieval Sourcebook: Exploration and Expansion

Contains primary source information on a variety of "Age of Discovery" subjects, including: Western Orientalism, Explorers, and Other World Cultures and Exploration.

http://www.fordham.edu/HALSALL/sbook1z.html

PART 3

The Premodern World

*B*oth China and Europe had their Ages of Exploration. Europe's continued and a new continent became populated with Europeans. China abruptly ceased its extensive commercial and maritime adventures during the Ming Dynasty, with very different results. A Reformation within Christianity broke apart a powerful medieval synthesis and facilitated the development of national states. In this more modern world both barbaric witch hunts and the scientific method were born. As the West attempted to spread its dominance, older civilizations responded.

- Did China's Worldview Cause the Abrupt End of Its Voyages of Exploration?

- Did Columbus's Voyages Have a Positive Effect on World History?

- Did Martin Luther's Reforms Improve the Lives of European Christians?

- Were the Witch-Hunts in Premodern Europe Misogynistic?

- Was the Scientific Revolution Revolutionary?

- Did the West Define the Modern World?

ISSUE 13

Did China's Worldview Cause the Abrupt End of Its Voyages of Exploration?

YES: Nicholas D. Kristof, from "1492: The Prequel," *The New York Times Magazine* (June 6, 1999)

NO: Bruce Swanson, from *Eighth Voyage of the Dragon: A History of China's Quest for Seapower* (Naval Institute Press, 1982)

ISSUE SUMMARY

YES: Journalist Nicholas D. Kristof states that China's worldview, shaped by centuries of philosophical and cultural conditioning, was responsible for its decision to cease its maritime ventures during the Ming dynasty.

NO: Naval historian Bruce Swanson acknowledges that China's worldview played a role in its decision to cease its maritime programs, but maintains that there were other, more practical considerations that were responsible for that decision.

$\mathbf{F}$ew historical figures of the last 500 years can match the name recognition of Christopher Columbus, whose voyages and what resulted from them forever altered the course of history. But what about Zheng He? Does his name have the same evocative power as Columbus's? Probably not, and yet in the same century, Zheng He led more and longer naval expeditions, commanded larger ships and more men, and was within the Asian world as popular and as noteworthy as Columbus. An interesting historical lesson, replete with "what might have beens," can be learned from the life and career of the "Chinese Columbus."

Zheng He's life is in itself an interesting story. Born to Muslim parents living in China, he was a young boy when he was captured by the Chinese army and eventually castrated, a common practice for prisoners of war at that time. Eventually, he came into the service of Chinese royal prince Zhu Di, one of twenty-six sons of the Chinese emperor, whom he served with honor and distinction. As a result of an internal power struggle, Prince Zhu Di seized the royal throne from his nephew and became the Ming dynasty's Emperor Yongle, who would rule China from 1402 to 1424. Zheng He played a significant role in this chain of events and would soon be rewarded for his meritorious service.

China's new emperor was an ambitious man who set out to establish his legacy as one of China's greatest rulers. As ameans to achieve this exalted status, he emphasized the importance of China's need to re-establish its role in the commercial and maritime affairs of Asia. When it was time to select someone to command this project, the new emperor selected Zheng He.

For more than two decades Zheng He ran China's maritime operations for his emperor, and his plan included seven major voyages. In the process, "Admiral Zheng visited 37 countries, traveled around the tip of Africa into the Atlantic Ocean and commanded a single fleet whose numbers surpassed the combined fleets of all of Europe. Between 1405 and 1433, at least 317 ships and 37,000 men were under his command" (Admiral Zheng's Fleet: www.oceans online.com/zheng.htm)

China's dominance of Asian waters brought the anticipated fame, wealth, and glory to Emperor Yongle and his eunuch admiral. However, when the former died suddenly in 1424, his successor decided to de-emphasize China's international maritime policies and ordered plans already under way for Zheng He's seventh voyage to be halted. This proved to be only a temporary setback when a new emperor, interested in reviving Yongle's maritime policies, ordered Zheng He's seventh voyage to proceed at once. It would prove to be China's last government-sponsored maritime venture.

Zheng He died in 1433, and soon after China began to lose interest in overseas exploration and eventually scrapped its maritime projects. This would have grave consequences for China when, later in the century, European countries began to send ships into Asian waters. What began as exploration eventually turned into domination, conquest, colonization, and imperialism—with dire consequences for China and the rest of Asia. Much of what follows is historical speculation, but one wonders what would have occurred if those first Western explorers who rounded Africa and headed toward Asia ran into a strong maritime force the size of Admiral Zheng's. And, if China had continued to support its maritime ventures after his death, perhaps history would have had to credit one of his successors with the discovery of the "New World."

There are numerous reasons given for China's retreat from maritime excellence. Some state that a Ming court conflict between eunuchs and Confucian scholars, traditional rivals in court politics, occurred, and the latter eventually won by depicting China's maritime expeditions as costly, eunuch-induced extravagances and not in China's best long-range interests. Others stress a series of other factors, including 1) fear of future Mongol invasions; 2) population shifts away from costal provinces; 3) a desire to promote internal trade efforts; 4) the high cost of supporting the maritime ventures, including the money spent to prevent piracy and the profits lost to it; 5) the corruption which emanated from the costly maritime programs.

In the following selections, Nicholas D. Kristof argues that China gave up on its maritime efforts because these efforts contradicted the worldview that China had cultivated for thousands of years. Navel historian Bruce Swanson counters that this was only one of many factors responsible for China's retreat from naval supremacy.

1492: The Prequel

For most of the last several thousand years, it would have seemed far likelier that Chinese or Indians, not Europeans, would dominate the world by the year 2000, and that America and Australia would be settled by Chinese rather than by the inhabitants of a backward island called Britain. The reversal of fortunes of East and West strikes me as the biggest news story of the millennium, and one of its most unexpected as well.

As a resident of Asia for most of the past 13 years, I've been searching for an explanation. It has always seemed to me that the turning point came in the early 1400's, when Admiral Zheng He sailed from China to conquer the world. Zheng He (pronounced jung huh) was an improbable commander of a great Chinese fleet, in that he was a Muslim from a rebel family and had been seized by the Chinese Army when he was still a boy. Like many other prisoners of the time, he was castrated—his sexual organs completely hacked off, a process that killed many of those who suffered it. But he was a brilliant and tenacious boy who grew up to be physically imposing. A natural leader, he had the good fortune to be assigned, as a houseboy, to the household of a great prince, Zhu Di.

In time, the prince and Zheng He grew close, and they conspired to overthrow the prince's nephew, the Emperor of China. With Zheng He as one of the prince's military commanders, the revolt succeeded and the prince became China's Yongle Emperor. One of the emperor's first acts (after torturing to death those who had opposed him) was to reward Zheng He with the command of a great fleet that was to sail off and assert China's pre-eminence in the world.

Between 1405 and 1433, Zheng He led seven major expeditions, commanding the largest armada the world would see for the next five centuries. Not until World War I did the West mount anything comparable. Zheng He's fleet included 28,000 sailors on 300 ships, the longest of which were 400 feet. By comparison, Columbus in 1492 had 90 sailors on three ships, the biggest of which was 85 feet long. Zheng He's ships also had advanced design elements that would not be introduced in Europe for another 350 years, including balanced rudders and watertight bulwark compartments.

The sophistication of Zheng He's fleet underscores just how far ahead of the West the East once was. Indeed, except for the period of the Roman

Empire, China had been wealthier, more advanced and more cosmopolitan than any place in Europe for several thousand years. Hangzhou, for example, had a population in excess of a million during the time it was China's capital (in the 12th century), and records suggest that as early as the 7th century, the city of Guangzhou had 200,000 foreign residents: Arabs, Persians, Malays, Indians, Africans and Turks. By contrast, the largest city in Europe in 1400 was probably Paris, with a total population of slightly more than 100,000.

A half-century before Columbus, Zheng He had reached East Africa and learned about Europe from Arab traders. The Chinese could easily have continued around the Cape of Good Hope and established direct trade with Europe. But as they saw it, Europe was a backward region, and China had little interest in the wool, beads and wine Europe had to trade. Africa had what China wanted—ivory, medicines, spices, exotic woods, even specimens of native wildlife.

In Zheng He's time, China and India together accounted for more than half of the world's gross national product, as they have for most of human history. Even as recently as 1820, China accounted for 29 percent of the global economy and India another 16 percent, according to the calculations of Angus Maddison, a leading British economic historian.

Asia's retreat into relative isolation after the expeditions of Zheng He amounted to a catastrophic missed opportunity, one that laid the groundwork for the rise of Europe and, eventually, America. Westerners often attribute their economic advantage today to the intelligence, democratic habits or hard work of their forebears, but a more important reason may well have been the folly of 15th-century Chinese rulers. That is why I came to be fascinated with Zheng He and set out earlier this year to retrace his journeys. I wanted to see what legacy, if any, remained of his achievement, and to figure out why his travels did not remake the world in the way that Columbus's did.

Zheng He lived in Nanjing, the old capital, where I arrived one day in February. Nanjing is a grimy metropolis on the Yangtze River in the heart of China. It has been five centuries since Zheng He's death, and his marks on the city have grown faint. The shipyards that built his fleet are still busy, and the courtyard of what had been his splendid 72-room mansion is now the Zheng He Memorial Park, where children roller-skate and old couples totter around for exercise. But though the park has a small Zheng He museum, it was closed—for renovation, a caretaker told me, though he knew of no plans to reopen it. . . .

The absence of impressive monuments to Zheng He in China today should probably come as no surprise, since his achievement was ultimately renounced. Curiously, it is not in China but in Indonesia where his memory has been most actively kept alive. Zheng He's expeditions led directly to the wave of Chinese immigration to Southeast Asia, and in some countries he is regarded today as a deity. In the Indonesia city of Semarang, for example, there is a large temple honoring Zheng He, located near a cave where he once nursed a sick friend. Indonesians still pray to Zheng He for a cure or good luck.

Not so in his native land. Zheng He was viewed with deep suspicion by China's traditional elite, the Confucian scholars, who made sure to destroy the archives of his journey. Even so, it is possible to learn something about his story from Chinese sources—from imperial archives and even the memoirs of crewmen. The historical record makes clear, for example, that it was not some sudden impulse of extroversion that led to Zheng He's achievement. It grew, rather, out of a long sailing tradition. Chinese accounts suggest that in the fifth century, a Chinese monk sailed to a mysterious "far east country" that sounds very much like Mayan Mexico, and Mayan art at that time suddenly began to include Buddhist symbols. By the 13th century, Chinese ships regularly traveled to India and occasionally to East Africa.

Zheng He's armada was far grander, of course, than anything that came before. His grandest vessels were the "treasure ships," 400 feet long and 160 feet wide, with nine masts raising red silk sails to the wind, as well as multiple decks and luxury cabins with balconies. His armada included supply ships to carry horses, troop transports, warships, patrol boats and as many as 20 tankers to carry fresh water. The full contingent of 28,000 crew members included interpreters for Arabic and other languages, astrologers to forecast the weather, astronomers to study the stars, pharmacologists to collect medicinal plants, ship-repair specialists, doctors and even two protocol officers to help organize official receptions.

In the aftermath of such an incredible undertaking, you somehow expect to find a deeper mark on Chinese history, a greater legacy. But perhaps the faintness of Zheng He's trace in contemporary China is itself a lesson. In the end, an explorer makes history but does not necessarily change it, for his impact depends less on the trail he blazes than on the willingness of others to follow. The daring of a great expedition ultimately is hostage to the national will of those who remain behind. . . .

The disappearance of a great Chinese fleet from a great Indian port symbolized one of history's biggest lost opportunities—Asia's failure to dominate the second half of this millennium. So how did this happen? While Zheng He was crossing the Indian Ocean, the Confucian scholar-officials who dominated the upper echelons of the Chinese Government were at political war with the eunuchs, a group they regarded as corrupt and immoral. The eunuchs' role at court involved looking after the concubines, but they also served as palace administrators, often doling out contracts in exchange for kickbacks. Partly as a result of their legendary greed, they promoted commerce. Unlike the scholars—who owed their position to their mastery of 2,000-year-old texts—the eunuchs, lacking any such roots in a classical past, were sometimes outward-looking and progressive. Indeed, one can argue that it was the virtuous, incorruptible scholars who in the mid-15th century set China on its disastrous course.

After the Yongle Emperor died in 1424, China endured a series of brutal power struggles; a successor emperor died under suspicious circumstances and ultimately the scholars emerged triumphant. They ended the voyages of Zheng He's successors, halted construction of new ships and imposed curbs on private shipping. To prevent any backsliding, they destroyed Zheng He's sailing records and, with the backing of the new emperor, set about dismantling China's navy.

By 1500 the Government had made it a capital offense to build a boat with more than two masts, and in 1525 the Government ordered the destruction of all oceangoing ships. The greatest navy in history, which a century earlier had 3,500 ships (by comparison, the United States Navy today has 324), had been extinguished, and China set a course for itself that would lead to poverty, defeat and decline.

Still, it was not the outcome of a single power struggle in the 1440's that cost China its worldly influence. Historians offer a host of reasons for why Asia eventually lost its way economically and was late to industrialize; two and a half reasons seem most convincing.

The first is that Asia was simply not greedy enough. The dominant social ethos in ancient China was Confucianism and in India it was caste, with the result that the elites in both nations looked down their noses at business. Ancient China cared about many things—prestige, honor, culture, arts, education, ancestors, religion, filial piety—but making money came far down the list. Confucius had specifically declared that it was wrong for a man to make a distant voyage while his parents were alive, and he had condemned profit as the concern of "a little man." As it was, Zheng He's ships were built on such a grand scale and carried such lavish gifts to foreign leaders that the voyages were not the huge money spinners they could have been.

In contrast to Asia, Europe was consumed with greed. Portugal led the age of discovery in the 15th century largely because it wanted spices, a precious commodity; it was the hope of profits that drove its ships steadily farther down the African coast and eventually around the Horn to Asia. The profits of this trade could be vast: Magellan's crew once sold a cargo of 26 tons of cloves for 10,000 times the cost.

A second reason for Asia's economic stagnation is more difficult to articulate but has to do with what might be called a culture of complacency. China and India shared a tendency to look inward, a devotion to past ideals and methods, a respect for authority and a suspicion of new ideas. David S. Landes, a Harvard economist, has written of ancient China's "intellectual xenophobia"; the former Indian Prime Minister Jawaharlal Nehru referred to the "petrification of classes" and the "static nature" of Indian society. These are all different ways of describing the same economic and intellectual complacency.

Chinese elites regarded their country as the "Middle Kingdom" and believed they had nothing to learn from barbarians abroad. India exhibited much of the same self-satisfaction. "Indians didn't go to Portugal not because they couldn't but because they didn't want to," mused M. P. Sridharan, a historian, as we sat talking on the porch of his home in Calicut.

The 15th-century Portuguese were the opposite. Because of its coastline and fishing industry, Portugal always looked to the sea, yet rivalries with Spain and other countries shut it out of the Mediterranean trade. So the only way for Portugal to get at the wealth of the East was by conquering the oceans.

The half reason is simply that China was a single nation while Europe was many. When the Confucian scholars reasserted control in Beijing and banned shipping, their policy mistake condemned all of China. In contrast, European countries committed economic suicide selectively. So when Portugal slipped into a quasi-Chinese mind-set in the 16th century, slaughtering Jews and burning heretics and driving astronomers and scientists abroad, Holland and England were free to take up the slack. . . .

If ancient China had been greedier and more outward-looking, if other traders had followed in Zheng He's wake and then continued on, Asia might well have dominated Africa and even Europe. Chinese might have settled in not only Malaysia and Singapore, but also in East Africa, the Pacific Islands, even in America. Perhaps the Famao [a clan of people who live in Pate, an island off the coast of Africa, and who are rumored to be descendents of Chinese shipwreck survivors from countless generations ago] show us what the mestizos [racially mixed people] of such a world might have looked liked, the children of a hybrid culture that was never born. What I'd glimpsed in Pate was the high-water mark of an Asian push that simply stopped—not for want of ships or know-how, but strictly for want of national will.

All this might seem fanciful, and yet in Zheng He's time the prospect of a New World settled by the Spanish or English would have seemed infinitely more remote than a New World made by the Chinese. How different would history have been had Zheng He continued on to America? The mind rebels; the ramifications are almost too overwhelming to contemplate. So consider just one: this [selection] would have been published in Chinese.

Bruce Swanson

 **NO**

Continental and Maritime Ideologies in Conflict: The Ming Dynasty

In 1405, China's progressive attitude toward exploitation of the sea culminated in a series of naval expeditions into the South China Sea and the Indian Ocean. The latter expeditions included visits to Ceylon, India, the Persian Gulf, and Africa. These spectacular voyages, in fact, proved that China was the supreme world seapower whose shipbuilding techniques and navigational abilities were unmatched by any other nation.

But China's prominence as the world's greatest naval and maritime power was short-lived. The last of seven expeditions ended in 1433; never again were naval expeditions attempted by emperors. As a result, it is tempting to dismiss these voyages as a temporary aberration of the Chinese emperor who sponsored them. To do so, however, would be to ignore the ineluctable influence of the maritime spirit on China, particularly the growing awareness of the potential of seapower to expand and control the tribute system. At the same time, the subsequent cessation of the voyages clearly highlights the equally strong force of continentalism among members of the imperial court as they attempted to steer China away from maritime pursuits.

Early Ming Strategic Considerations

Before discussing the voyages and their itineraries, it is important to examine certain factors that reflected China's continuing struggle between supporters of continentalism on the one hand and the maritime ideology on the other.

The First Ming Emperor

The first Ming emperor, Zhu Yuanzhang, was an orphaned peasant from the riverine area near Nanjing. As a child, he had been taken in by Buddhist monks and educated in a monastery. Upon leaving the monastery, he was unable to gain employment and was soon begging for a living. At the age of twenty-five, the vagrant joined a rebel band that fought government soldiers for over a decade in the central China river valleys. Warfare finally wore down the Mongol-backed local forces and the entire Yangzi Valley came under rebel control. In due course, Zhu assumed leadership of the rebels and defeated the

From Bruce Swanson, *Eighth Voyage of the Dragon: A History of China's Quest for Seapower* (Naval Institute Press, 1982). Copyright © 1982 by The United States Naval Institute, Annapolis, Maryland. Reprinted by permission. Notes omitted.

government forces. He then established his capital at Nanjing in 1356. Twelve years later, after taking his rebel army north and capturing Beijing from the Mongols, Zhu founded the Chinese Ming dynasty.

Although Zhu, being from a riverine area, had presumably come into contact with many men who had knowledge of the sea, his initial concerns lay in consolidating Chinese rule and making China's borders and strategic cities safe from Mongol invasion. Accordingly, he took several actions that temporarily stifled maritime activities.

Walls, Canals, and Coastal Defense

With the Mongols only recently defeated, Zhu set about improving city defenses. For example, he directed the construction of a protective wall some 20 miles in length around Nanjing. The barrier was 60 feet high and nearly impenetrable by a force armed with the weapons of the time.

On the coast, Zhu faced the problem of piracy by Japanese and Chinese freebooters, which had increased alarmingly. He ordered that Chinese not be permitted to go overseas—those who violated his edict would be executed as traitors. In 1374 Zhu backed up his decree by abolishing the superintendencies of merchant ships at the ports of Ningbo, Quanzhou, and Guangzhou. Next, he strengthened coastal defenses by constructing forts; in the four-year period from 1383 to 1387, more than one hundred thirty forts were built in the Zhejiang-Fujian coastal zones. In Zhejiang alone, more than fifty-eight thousand troops were conscripted to man the provincial coastal forts.

Zhu also directed the Board of Works to undertake extensive reconstruction of the canal system, which had been damaged by flood and warfare. One of the long-term projects called for enlarging the Grand Canal, which upon completion was to replace the pirate-plagued sea route. The latter route had been reopened earlier when civil strife closed down the canal.

The Tribute System

The first Ming emperor wasted little time before trying to reestablish the tributary system. He ordered missions to proceed to peripheral states such as Japan, Annam, Champa, and Korea, where it was proclaimed that all who wished to enter into relations with China must acknowledge the suzerainty of the new emperor. Very soon some of these states sent reciprocal missions to Peking where Zhu received their kowtows acknowledging him as the Son of Heaven. These missions also served other purposes, such as providing the new Chinese dynasty with information on the current situations in border areas. . . .

The Mongol-Muslim Alliance

The first Ming emperor also had to deal with the continuing threat posed by the retreating Mongols. It took Zhu's armies until 1382 to drive remaining Mongol military units from Yunnan in southwest China. Moreover, during the next twenty years, periodic "mopping-up" operations continued beyond the Great Wall in northeast China and in Korea as well.

For the Ming government, the biggest threat lay westward. A Turkic nomad and Muslim named Timur, or Tamerlane, was conquering the entire central Asian region from Siberia to the Mediterranean and southward to the Indian Ocean. Included in the ranks of his fierce Muslim cavalry were remnants of the retreating Mongol armies.

According to an official Ming history, Zhu was anxious to bring Timur into the tribute system. He sent several small missions on the overland caravan route to seek out the Muslim leader. The Chinese apparently were unaware of just how paltry their offer of suzerainty appeared to the ferocious Timur. The Muslims, in fact, scorned the Chinese. "Because they believe [that] our people [are] wild and boorish, they do not hope for politeness, nor respect, nor honor, nor law from us; and apart from their own realms they do not know of a city [anywhere] in the world."

In 1394, after only a quarter century of Ming rule, an incident occurred that would seriously jeopardize the Chinese dynasty. At that time, Zhu received what he thought was a tribute mission from Timur that delivered a letter acknowledging the Chinese emperor as the ruler of all mankind. The letter, forged by an ambitious merchant or court official, led Zhu to send a return mission to central Asia in appreciation of Timur's vassalage. In 1395, when the Chinese embassy reached Timur and delivered Zhu's note, the Muslim leader became so enraged that he advised his staff to prepare for an invasion of China to bring down the Chinese "infidels." He took the Chinese mission hostage. By 1404 his plans were nearly complete, and he had massed two-hundred thousand Muslim and Mongol cavalrymen in the Pamirs, near modern-day Afghanistan.

Fortunately for the Chinese, Timur died in 1405, following an all-night drinking bout. On his deathbed he reportedly "expressed his regret in having neglected the conquest of such infidel countries as China and drawn his sword against Muslim armies." Two more years passed before the Chinese heard from the freed hostages that Timur had died.

Foreign Policy Under the Second Ming Emperor

While Timur was preparing to invade China, the death of Zhu Yuanzhang in 1398 produced another period of civil war lasting until 1403. Succeeding Zhu was his grandson, a young boy whose court remained in Nanjing. In the north, however, Zhu's fourth son, Chengzu, decided to overthrow his nephew from the southern capital. As the military commander responsible for anti-Mongol operations in the Peking area, he controlled some of the best troops in China. His ultimate success came in 1403, when he defeated the Nanjing forces loyal to his father and assumed the throne with the name Yongle, meaning "perpetual happiness."

Clearly, Yongle's ambition and leadership ability forecast a dynamic reign. As with his father before him, one of Yongle's primary objectives was to establish his sovereignty throughout the tribute system by reinstilling the belief among all foreign states that China was supreme. In order to persuade the tributaries, however, Yongle had to work out a strategy that would both gain respect for Chinese power and enrich the imperial treasuries.

He dealt with Japan first. In 1403 the superintendencies of merchant shipping were reopened and new hostels were built to house Japanese tributary missions coming by sea. A system was devised whereby legitimate Japanese merchants were given trading passports that could be checked by Chinese authorities on each visit. In this way pirates could be identified, while honest Japanese and Chinese businessmen were free to carry on lucrative trade.

In Annam Yongle faced a critical problem. In 1400, while he was fighting to usurp the throne from his nephew, events there were coming to a head. Hanoi had fallen to Champa and the Annamese Tran dynasty was destroyed. The South China Sea was now in the hands of Cham and rebel Annamese pirates, and Chinese merchant shipping, both official and unofficial, was seriously disrupted. In 1406 Yongle decided to attack across the land border in order to pacify the two warring states and then reestablish Annam as a Chinese province. Hanoi was captured in 1406, but the Chinese armies soon bogged down in Annamese cities awaiting reinforcements and supplies. Before long nearly ninety thousand Chinese troops were in Annam attempting to control the countryside through a costly sinicization program.

Problems in inner Asia were developing concurrently with the Annam invasion. Word of the Muslim conquests in central Asia had reached Yongle, but the distance and harsh nature of that western area precluded the dispatch of a large army to confront Timur. Caution got the better of Yongle. He elected to send a small fact-finding mission to Timur in 1402 to inquire why the Muslim leader, since 1395, had failed to pay tribute. In a move that suggested that Yongle would settle for political equality with remote central Asia, he approved the construction of a Muslim mosque in Peking. This may have been done to induce the warring Muslims to keep open the silk route connecting western China with the cities of the Timurid empire (these included Gilgit and Herat, located in modern-day Pakistan and Afghanistan, respectively).

With the silk route used only sporadically, the wealthy classes, the court, and the treasury had become heavily dependent upon southern maritime trade for the import of precious stones, fragrant woods, spices, and rare objects. To ensure the safety of Chinese traders on the sea and the uninterrupted flow of luxury items, it was essential that Yongle build a navy that would convince the ocean states of China's "world supremacy." He devised a forceful plan calling for the aggressive use of seapower to underline Chinese suzerainty over the peripheral southern ocean states. Since the first expedition was to sail all the way to the Muslim states of Aden, Mecca, Djofar, and Hormuz, Yongle likely concluded that the voyages would also be useful in countering Timur's influence in that area.

The Ming Ships and Expeditions

In 1403, a year of momentous decisions, Yongle directed Chinese shipyards in Fujian to undertake an aggressive shipbuilding effort that would result in the construction of more than two thousand large seagoing vessels over the next sixteen years.

The *baochuan*, or treasure ships, were the largest vessels constructed by the Chinese. Their size has been the subject of many arguments among scholars. Ming histories record that the treasure-ships were 440 feet long and 180 feet wide (an unlikely construction ratio of 5:2). At best, this configuration is an exaggeration, for such broad-beamed vessels would be unresponsive even under moderate sea conditions. In fact, acceptance of these figures degrades the reputation of Chinese shipbuilders of the period, who would have recognized that such vessels were impractical to build. Until research proves otherwise, it is this writer's opinion that the largest vessels were shaped much like the three largest junks, of which records are available. These, the Jiangsu trader, the Beizhili trader, and the Fuzhou pole junk, were built on a proportion of about 6.4:1— much closer to the modern naval architecture ratio of 9:1. The former was about 170 feet long and had five masts, while the latter two had lengths of 180 feet with a beam of 28 feet. It may be significant that Fujian shipyards were give the first-order calling for the construction of 137 ships, since these were the yards that probably developed the technique for building the Fuzhou pole junk. . . .

Zheng He

In addition to overseeing the construction of the Ming fleet, Yongle selected the senior officers who were to lead the expeditions. For overall commander the emperor picked a Muslim eunuch named Zheng He, who had been in his service since 1382. As a small boy, Zheng He had been taken prisoner in Yunnan during the final rout of the Mongols.

Following his capture, Zheng He, by custom, was castrated and subsequently made an officer in Yongle's army, where he distinguished himself during the successful usurpation campaign of 1403. For his loyal service, Zheng He, at age thirty-three, was made a grand eunuch and appointed superintendent of the Office of Eunuchs. His military prowess, along with his knowledge of Turku languages and Islam, made Zheng He the ideal choice for senior admiral of the Ming fleet. He was given the name Sanbao Taijian, meaning "three-jewelled eunuch."

During his voyages, Zheng He was accompanied by other Chinese Muslims, including one named Ma Huan, who came from the Hangzhou Bay area. Ma was knowledgeable in matters of the sea and in the Arabic and Persian languages. His chief distinction, however, was the account of three voyages he made with Zheng He.

From Ma Huan we learn that Zheng He's general procedure was to bring the fleet together in late spring near modern-day Shanghai, where a series of briefings and religious ceremonies was conducted. Once prayers had been offered, and the fleet had been organized and briefed, it sailed leisurely on a four- to eight-week "shakedown cruise" to an anchorage at the mouth of the Min River in Fujian Province. There the ships would carry out further intensive training throughout the late summer and early fall. Finally, in December or January, they would set sail during the favorable monsoon.

The Sea Routes

The sea routes followed by Ming naval captains had been known and used for several centuries. Since the Song dynasty, in fact, the routes had been systematized into two major sea lanes: the East Sea Route and the West Sea Route. Each was subdivided into a major and minor route. For example, the major East Sea Route extended to northern Borneo and the Philippines. The minor West Sea

Route encompassed ports in Sumatra and the Malay Peninsula. The major West Sea Route was that route taken to the Indian Ocean via the Malacca Strait.

Following the period of intensive training, the fleet wound its way through the Taiwan Strait and sailed directly into the South China Sea, where land falls were made on Hainan Island and the Xisha Islands (Paracel Islands). From the Xishas the fleet turned westward and made for an anchorage at modern-day Qui Nhon on the Champa (southern Vietnam) coast. The total time of the Fujian-Champa transit was about ten days. Once there, provisions were taken aboard and the crews had "liberty" and "swim call." From Qui Nhon the fleet sailed south-ward toward the west coast of Borneo, making land falls on the various islands in the southern portion of the South China Sea.

After rounding Borneo, the ships entered the Java Sea and sailed to Sarabaja in Java. At this port Chinese crews were again rested for several months, until about July, when the period of favorable winds occurred. They then sailed through the Malacca Strait via Palembang and thence westward to Sri Lanka. From Sri Lanka the ships made their way to Calicut on the Indian coast, where the fleet was divided into smaller "task forces." Some went to Chittagong in modern-day Bangladesh; others went to Hormuz, Aden, and Jidda; and some visited the African coast near the mouth of the Red Sea. Hormuz usually was reached in January of the first year, and the Chinese returned to Malacca by March. They remained in Malacca only briefly, sailing northward to the Yangzi River by July of the second year. . . .

The Decline of Maritime Spirit in the Ming

During the Ming expeditions, a number of political, military, social, and economic factors acted to slow and then finally halt the policies that had promoted maritime experimentation and growth.

The Grand Canal

One of the first indications of China's impending maritime collapse occurred when the Grand Canal was reopened in 1411, making it again possible to ship grain via the inland route. This event marked another closing of the coastal maritime route, and many personnel of the coastal fleets were reassigned to work on the canal. In 1415 the government officially banned grain transport by sea and authorized the construction of three thousand shallow-draft canal barges. This diversion of man-power and shipbuilding expertise was soon felt in the maritime industries. Ocean-going ship construction lagged and was halted altogether by Yongle's successor in 1436. At the same time, regulations were issued that reassigned the men of the Indian Ocean expeditionary force to canal duties as stevedores.

Population Shifts

Significantly, the conclusion of Ming voyages caused a shift of population away from the sea coast that, from 1437 to 1491, resulted in a loss of eight million people in the three principal coastal provinces of Zhejiang, Fujian, and Guangdong. Meanwhile, inland areas such as Yunnan and Hebei gained four million in population. Many coastal inhabitants also emigrated to southeast Asia.

Warfare and Border Pressure

During the fifteenth century China suffered several serious military setbacks along its land borders that deflected interest in maritime expeditions. In 1418 Annam, tiring of the Chinese presence, launched a war of independence. In a way similar to recent United States efforts, the Chinese tried to carry the fight for some nine years, but Annamese guerrilla tactics eventually prevailed. In 1420 the Ming navy lost a battle on the Red River; in 1427 the Chinese emperor finally grew weary of increased war costs and evacuated nearly one hundred thousand Chinese soldiers from Annam. Chinese suzerainty was maintained, however.

In the north, China faced a graver threat in the form of continued Mongol raids along the entire length of the Great Wall. In 1421, in an effort to counter the resurgent Mongols, Yongle moved the capital from Nanjing to Beijing. Troops were shifted from the seacoast to shore up the northern capital's defenses, which lay less than 100 miles from one of the strategic northern passes that intersected the Great Wall. Despite these precautions, the Chinese emperor was captured in 1449, and the Ming court was forced to resurrect its continental defense strategy completely. These policies did little to diminish the northern nomad threat, however; the critical northern frontier remained under nomad pressure for the next three hundred years. Martial law was periodically imposed, and senior military officials spent their careers defending the north rather than performing naval and coastal defense duties.

Corruption in Government

Politics within the Ming court also began to turn attention away from the sea, as eunuchs and Chinese bureaucrats vied for power. The praise and favors lavished on palace eunuchs in the early Ming period eventually led to their complete domination of governmental affairs. By the middle of the fifteenth century, the first in a series of eunuch strongmen ascended to power. Very quickly they set about sealing their hold over the most important government agencies, taking control of the army, the police, and finance ministries. When opposed, the eunuchs often resorted to terrorist tactics, arresting and executing those that dared question their authority. Many became quite corrupt, employing ships and crews to transport ill-gotten goods and transferring soldiers to palace construction work.

By 1480 the political intrigues had increased to such an extent that when a powerful eunuch initiated a request to prepare another series of maritime expeditions in emulation of Zheng He, he was greeted by fierce opposition within the ranks of government bureaucrats. Jealous officials within the Board of War conspired to have records of the Indian Ocean voyages destroyed, so as to frustrate any attempt to imitate the early Ming expeditions.

Piracy

As officials became more absorbed in intrigues at court, they too tended toward corruption, which carried over to coastal trade. Unscrupulous merchants regained control as the government's monopoly on foreign trade was relinquished, and smuggling and piracy flourished. The Ming histories record that "the powerful families of Fujian and Zhejiang traded with the Japanese pirates. Their associates at court protected them and carried out their bidding. . . . Palace attendants outfitted merchant ships and the criminal elements of the coast abetted them in making profit." In fact, while Zheng He and his companions were conducting their voyages, Japanese pirates successfully carried out five major incursions against the Chinese mainland. In 1419 the northern coastguard fleets were helpless in preventing a sizeable force of several thousand pirates from landing on the Liaodong Peninsula. It required a well-trained force of Chinese army troops to subdue the pirates. As an example of the magnitude of this action, the Chinese army commander captured 857 pirates alive and beheaded another 742.

Although Japanese piracy continued to plague the Chinese, it ceased in 1466 when Japan fell into civil war. By 1523, however, Japanese and Chinese raiders were again launching attacks along the coast. Ningbo was burned in that year, and in 1552 a flotilla sailed up the Yangzi, sacking cities without opposition. Natives of the coast fled further inland to escape the ravages of these attacks. In 1555 Nanjing came under seige and the port of Quanzhou in Fujian was plundered. In an attempt to stop these raids, Ming provincial administrators resorted to the Tang dynasty's practice of constructing beacon stations to give advance warnings of pirates. By 1562, 711 beacon stations lined the coast from Jiangsu to Guangdong. By 1563 the army had to be used to combat the sea rovers, who controlled nearly all of the Fujian coast.

Scholarship and Neo-Confucianism

Finally, a version of neo-Confucianism developed that was markedly idealistic and influenced by Buddhism, resulting in a loss of interest in geomancy and maritime expansion. As early as 1426, a minister memorialized the court, stating the following:

> Arms are the instruments of evil which the sage does not use unless he must. The noble rulers and wise ministers of old did not dissipate the strength of the people by deeds of arm. This was a farsighted policy. . . . Your minister hopes that your majesty . . . would not indulge in military pursuits nor glorify the sending of expeditions to distant countries. Abandon the barren lands abroad and give the people of China a respite so that they could devote themselves to husbandry and to the schools. Thus, there would be no wars and suffering on the frontier and no murmuring in the villages, the commanders would not seek fame and the soldiers would not sacrifice their lives abroad, the people from afar would voluntarily submit and distant lands would come into our fold, and our dynasty would last for ten thousand generations.

Such statements helped check Chinese maritime pursuits and force China to restore continentalist policies. Scholars who devoted their lives to the classics were again revered, while the military class was looked upon with great suspicion by the gentry and officials.

By the early fifteenth century, regulations were again in force that made it a capital offense to build a seagoing junk with more than two masts. By

1525 an imperial edict authorized coastal officials to destroy all ships of this kind and place the crews under arrest.

The timing of Chinese maritime decline could not have been worse, for it coincided with European maritime expansion into Asia. The Portuguese arrived in 1516, and although they were expelled in 1521, their exodus was short-lived. They returned and established settlements in Xiamen in 1544 and Macao in 1535. The Spanish occupied the Philippines in 1564 and established trade relations with China shortly thereafter. Then, in the seventeenth century, the Dutch arrived in Asia just as the Ming dynasty was being conquered by the Manchu cavalry that overran Beijing in 1644. Thus was the stage set for the last foreign imperial rulers in China—the Qing.

POSTSCRIPT

Did China's Worldview Cause the Abrupt End of Its Voyages of Exploration?

In this book's last issue, two historians debate the extent to which the West dominated the modern world through an extension of its power and culture. One is left to wonder whether this western intrusion would have been possible if a strong Chinese naval presence had existed. Perhaps the course of world history would have been altered. No colonialism; no imperialism!

The role of court eunuchs throughout Chinese history has been a turbulent one; sometimes they're portrayed as loyal civil servants, other times as despised outcasts. No one however can question their staying power, as during the reign of Pu Yi (1903–1912), who would be China's last emperor, they were still a troublesome court presence. In Bernardo Bertolucci's Academy Award-winning film, *The Last Emperor*, they are shown as having a corrupting influence on the court and are eventually banned from the "Forbidden City." Although historically they were far from angelic, they have sometimes been blamed for conditions and events that were not of their making. Shih-Shan Henry Tsai attempts to correct the myths and stereotypes regarding eunuchs in his *The Eunuchs in the Ming Dynasty* (State University of New York Press, 1996), which provides a badly needed fresh look at the eunuchs in the period covered by this Issue.

For other works on the subject, see Shi-Shah Henry Tsai, *Perpetual Happiness: The Ming Emperor Yongle* (University of Washington Press, 2001) which provides a fresh look at the man responsible for Ming China's maritime activities; Timothy Brook, *The Confusions of Pleasure: Commerce and Culture in Ming China* (University of California Press, 1999) is more useful for general information on Chinese society during the Ming dynasty than specific information of Zheng He and his voyages. An ancillary work, *Chinese Maps: Images Of 'All Under Heaven'* by Richard J. Smith provides background to China's worldview and its development and displays the advanced Chinese map work completed during its history.

Last year, Gavin Menzies's *1421: The Year China Discovered America* (William Morrow, 2003) was published. It extended the breadth of China's maritime efforts by claiming that it was the Chinese who discovered America during the Ming era. However, most who reviewed the book found it long on claims and short on documentation.

Finally, two important reference works on Ming China, both edited by Frederick W. Mote and Denis Twitchett are: *The Cambridge History of China: The Ming Dynasty, 1368–1644, Part I* (Cambridge University Press, 1988); and *The*

Cambridge History of China: The Ming Dynasty, 1368–1644, Part II (Cambridge University Press, 1998).

The recent publication date on many of these books, and the presence of numerous computer web sites containing information about Zheng He, show the timeliness of the subject and give hope that more information on a neglected figure in Chinese and world history will be forthcoming.

ISSUE 14

Did Christopher Columbus's Voyages Have a Positive Effect on World History?

YES: Robert Royal, from "Columbus and the Beginning of the New World," *First Things: A Monthly Journal of Religion and Public Life* (May 1999)

NO: Gabriel Garcia Marquez, from "For a Country Within Reach of the Children," *Americas* (November/December 1997)

ISSUE SUMMARY

YES: Robert Royal states although there were negatives that emanated from Columbus's New World discoveries, they continue to "remind us of the glorious and ultimately providential destiny on the ongoing global journey that began in the fifteenth century."

NO: Nobel laureate Gabriel Garcia Marquez argues that Columbus's voyages had a negative effect on the Americas, much of which is still felt today.

In October 1998, a *New York Times* article covered a dispute between Hispanic-Americans and Italian-Americans with regard to which ethnic group should play the more important role in the organization of New York's Columbus Day Parade. While both groups had legitimate claims to the Columbus legacy (after all, Columbus was a Genoese Italian, but he did his most important work for the Spanish nation), the dispute must have drawn an ironic response from those who witnessed the revisionist bashing that the "Admiral of the Ocean Sea" had received in recent years.

In the five centuries since "Columbus sailed the ocean blue," his historical reputation and the significance of his accomplishments have undergone a series of metamorphoses. In the distant past, an eclectic collection of Columbus critics would number essayist Michel Montaigne, English writer Samuel Johnson, philosopher Jean-Jacques Rousseau, and French historian and philosopher Abbe Guillaume Reynal, some of whom believed that the world would have been better off without the admiral's discoveries.

It has only been in the last two centuries that Columbus's stock has risen in the theater of public opinion and historical significance. There were many reasons for this change including: (1) the United States acting as a model for democratic government in a 19th/20th-century world living under monarchial/autocratic rule; (2) the part played by the U.S. in the Allied victory during World War I, which ended the German, Austrian, Ottoman, and Russian Empires and brought a greater level of democracy to many parts of Europe; (3) the role assumed by the U.S. in saving Europe and the world from the specter of fascist militarism during World War II. All affected the reversal of Columbus's historical fortunes, as many wondered what the world would have become if the U.S. had not been there to provide inspiration and assistance in these times of need. Thus, some of the credit our nation accrued was passed on to Columbus, whose work had made our nation possible. Samuel Eliot Morison's 1940 book, ADMIRAL OF THE OCEAN SEA, marked the climax of this laudatory view of Columbus and his accomplishments.

Historians and publishers love anniversaries and the publicity they generate, and, next to a millennial celebration, none may be more significant than a quincentennial one. Thus, on the 500th anniversary of Columbus's first voyage, the requisite number of tomes on Columbus and his accomplishments were made ready for an eager market. But the world of 1992 was different than the world of Morison's "Admiral of the Ocean Sea," and the historical profession had changed along with it.

The end-of-the millennium generation of historians treated Columbus differently than had their immediate predecessors. Operating from a different world view, Columbus became to many of them a flawed figure responsible for the horrors of the trans-atlantic slave trade, the annihilation of Native American civilizations through cruelty and disease, and the ecological destruction of a continental paradise.

The recently published books about Christopher Columbus opened a national dialogue on the subject. A national Columbus exhibition in Washington, D.C. was received with skepticism by some and quiet reverence by others. While some participated in the national Columbus Day celebration on October 12, 1992, others declared it a day of mourning in honor of those who lost their lives as a result of Columbus's enterprises. A cultural hornet's nest was unleashed, and any who entered into the Columbus fray had to have the thickest of skin.

Fortunately, as is usually the case, time has a soothing effect, and we will have to wait until the year 2092 for the next major Columbus debate. For now, we have the opportunity—with cooler heads and calmer temperaments—to examine the Columbus legacy.

In this Issue, Robert Royal stresses the positive elements that came from Columbus's discoveries. Gabriel Garcia Marquez emphasizes their negative impact on the New World and its peoples.

YES

Robert Royal

Columbus and the Beginning of the New World

. . . The world we know began in the fifteenth century. Not the world of course in the sense of human life or human civilizations, which had already existed for millennia, but the world as a concrete reality in which all parts of the globe had come into contact with one another and begun to recognize themselves as part of a single human race—a process still underway. The spherical globe we had known about since the classical world; in the Middle Ages, readers of Dante took it for granted. Yet it was only because of a small expedition by a few men driven by a mishmash of personal ambition, religious motives, and the desire for profit that an old mathematical calculation was turned into a new human fact. Or as a historian sixty years later accurately characterized the discovery of the New World, it was "the greatest event since the creation of the world (excluding the incarnation and death of Him who created it)."

In our own confused way, we continue to pay homage to that achievement. In 1999, NASA will put a satellite into an orbit a little less than a million miles out into space in what is called L-l, the libration point where the gravity of the earth and the sun exactly balance one another. Equipped with a telescopic lens and video camera, it will provide a twenty-four-hour-a-day image of the surface of the earth. Not surprisingly, one of the enthusiasts behind the project is Al Gore, probably the most environmentally agitated public figure alive. But in spite of the damage that Gore and many others believe we humans have inflicted on the planet since our first large steps in exploring it, and despite the laments of multiculturalists about Europe's rise to world dominance, the new satellite will be called Triana, after Rodrigo de Triana, who first spotted lights on land from the deck of the Pinta during the first voyage of Columbus.

Perhaps the name is only a bow to growing Hispanic influence in the United States; perhaps it hints that we would like to think of ourselves as equally on the verge of another great age of discovery. But whatever our sense of the future, the Columbus discoveries and the European intellectual and religious developments that lay behind them are today at best taken for granted, at worst viewed as the beginning of a sinister Western hegemony over man and nature. The last five centuries, of course, offer the usual human spectacle of great glories mixed with grim atrocities. But we cannot evaluate the voyages of discovery properly—much less the fifteenth-century culture from which they sprang—without gratitude for what they achieved or understanding of their human dimensions. In the fifteenth century, the discoveries were rightly regarded as close to a miracle, especially given the way the century had begun.

The early 1400s were marked by profound religious, political, economic, and even environmental turmoil. At one point in the first decade of the century, there were simultaneously three claimants to the papal throne and three to the crown of the Holy Roman Empire. And the large-scale institutional crises were only a small part of the story. Europe was still suffering from the devastation wrought at the height of the Black Death over half a century earlier and in smaller waves thereafter. Overall, something like 40 percent of the population disappeared in the mid-fourteenth century, in some regions even more. Land lay fallow for lack of workers, villages were deserted, poverty spread. As many modern environmentalists have devoutly wished, nature took its vengeance as human population decreased. Wolves multiplied and returned, even appearing in capital cities. Human predators—in the form of brigands—made travel unsafe over wide areas. The consequences of the retreat of civilization spurred Henry V, fabled victor of Agincourt, to offer rewards for the elimination of both types of pests. Though the beauty of landscapes emerged as never before in contemporary painting and literature, it was not a century that indulged itself in easy sentimentality about the goodness of unimproved nature, human or otherwise. On the contrary, natural hardships spurred the fifteenth century to nearly unparalleled achievements.

But if the internal situation were not enough, Europe was also being squeezed by forces from outside. In 1453, the Ottoman Turks finally succeeded in taking Byzantium. Turkish troops had already been fighting as far into the Balkans as Belgrade a few years earlier. Otranto, in the heel of Italy, fell to them in 1480 for a time. We might have expected the Christian powers to lay aside rivalries momentarily and defend themselves from an alien culture and religion. But the main Atlantic nation-states—England, France, and Spain—were still only beginning to take shape. The rest of Western Europe was broken, despite the theoretical claims of the emperor, into a crazy quilt of competing small powers. So no coordinated effort occurred, though Plus II and other popes called for a crusade. Plus even wrote to Sultan Muhammad II, conqueror of Constantinople, inviting him to convert to Christianity. Whether this letter was intended seriously or as a mere pretext for further action, it failed. Neither "European" nor "Christian" interests were sufficiently united to galvanize the effort. The Pope died in 1464 at the eastern Italian port of Ancona waiting for his people to rally behind him.

A crusade to retake the Holy Land was sometimes a mere pipe dream, sometimes a serious proposal during the course of the century. Ferdinand of Spain listened frequently to such plans, but refrained from doing much. (Machiavelli praises him in The Prince as one of those rulers who shrewdly take pains to appear good without necessarily being so.) Charles VIII of France invaded Italy in 1494 but also had in mind an attempt to retake

Constantinople and restore the Eastern Christian Empire. Earlier, Henry V, on his way to Agincourt, proclaimed his intentions not only to assume the French throne but to "build again the walls of Jerusalem." Western Europe had a persistent if vague sense of responsibility to defend Christianity front Islamic military threats and a deeper need to recover the parts of Christendom lost to Muslim conquest, even if the good intentions were thwarted by intra-European distractions.

Had Islam continued its advance, much of Europe might have then resembled the cultures we now associate with the Middle East. The Americas might have been largely Muslim countries as opposed to largely Christian ones. Islam was more advanced than Europe in 1492, but in the paradoxical ways of culture, its very superiority contributed to its being surpassed. Muslims do not seem to have taken much interest in Western technical developments in navigation, and even well-placed countries like Morocco were never moved to brave the high seas in search of new lands. European technological innovation and military advance may have been born of necessity, given the superiority of outside cultures and the conflicts and rivalries among European nations.

This reminds us of something often overlooked in most contemporary historical surveys. The "Eurocentric" forces, of which we now hear so much criticism, were actually something quite different in the fifteenth century. What we today call "Europeans" thought of themselves as part of Christendom, and a Christendom, as we shall serf, that desperately needed to return to some of its founding truths. Similarly, they did not regard themselves as the bearers of the highest culture. Ancient Greece and Rome, they knew, had lived at a higher level, which is why the Renaissance felt the need to recover and imitate classical models. The fabled wealth of the distant Orient and the clearly superior civilization of nearby Islam did not allow Christendom to think itself culturally advanced or, more significantly, to turn in on itself, as self-satisfied empires of the time such as China did. Contemporary European maps—the ones all the early mariners consulted in the Age of Discovery—bear witness to their central belief: Jerusalem, not Europe, was the center of the world.

But this very sense of threat and inferiority, combined with the unsettled social diversity of Europe at the time, gave Europeans a rich and dynamic restlessness. Not surprisingly, the rise towards a renewed Europe began in the places least affected by the population implosion and, therefore, more prosperous: what we today call the Low Countries and, above all, Northern Italy. Renascences, as Erwin Panofsky demonstrated a few decades ago, had been occurring in Europe since the twelfth century. But the one that took place in Northern Italy in the fifteenth century—the one we call the Renaissance—produced multiple and wide-ranging consequences.

Pius II was in many ways emblematic of the mid-century. A cultivated humanist born in Siena in 1405 with the imposing name Aeneas Sylvius Piccolomini, he initially came under the spell of St. Bernardino, who preached a strictly observant reformed Franciscan life (of which more anon). But he shortly became attracted to the exciting life of the Renaissance Italian humanists, which is to say libertinism and literary pursuits. He shifted parties among papal contenders, pursuing his own ambitions for many years, wrote a popular history (Historia rerum ubique gestarum) that gathered together wide-ranging facts and fictions about foreign lands, and even became imperial poet and secretary to the Holy Roman Emperor Frederick III. But compared with the squabbling popes and anti-popes who preceded him and the colorful escapades of the Borgias, Pius had his virtues. He was learned and hard-working, enjoyed nature, sought reform, and could have made a difference in Europe had his office enjoyed the respect it once had and was to have again later. The religious renaissance, however, like the cultural, scientific, and artistic one with which we are more familiar, had to come from other sources.

Renaissance achievements found multiple and overlapping uses in a Europe in ferment. The geometry developed by the Florentine Paolo Toscanelli allowed Fillippo Brunelleschi, over the objections of a commission of Florentine experts, to dare construction of the unsupported dome that crowns the magnificent Florentine Duomo. Just a few decades later, an intellectually curious Genoese mariner corresponded with Toscanelli in preparation for his attempts to convince another panel of experts in Spain that it was possible to sail west to the Indies (no serious thinker at the time, by the way, believed the earth was flat). His figures were wrong; the distance was greater than he claimed. The experts—and perhaps Columbus himself—knew it. But it was an age when for various reasons people had the faith to attempt things beyond what was previously thought possible. It is worth looking closely at some of those reasons.

Much has recently been written, for example, claiming that the Christian dimension of Columbus' personality was merely a cover for greed and ambition. These alleged traits are then read as a metaphor for a hypocritical European expansion under the cover of religion. Hypocrites certainly existed in the fifteenth century, as they do today. But real history—as opposed to anachronistic morality tales—is always more complex than the simple motives we project back onto figures quite different from ourselves. Like the Italian humanists, who are often wrongly portrayed as modern unbelieving intellectuals, Columbus combined his faith with new knowledge and new interests. But that did not make his faith any less real. He wanted that Renaissance ideal, glory: in this case, that of an unprecedented voyage. He drove hard bargains with Ferdinand and Isabella to secure the financial benefits of his discoveries for himself and his descendants. (The Muslim conquests and consequent monopolies over Eastern trade routes made the European search for alternate routes all the more necessary and profitable.) Yet when all the mundane reasons have been listed, the spiritual dimension of the project remains in ways that are quite unexpected.

In the preface to his Libro de las profecias (Book of Prophecies), an anthology of prophetic texts that he compiled near the end of his life, Columbus relates to Ferdinand and Isabella how, long before he ever approached them, he had become convinced that the westward voyage was not merely possible but his own personal vocation:

> During this time, I searched out and studied all kinds of texts: geographies, histories, chronologies, philosoph[ies], and other subjects. With a hand that could be felt, the Lord opened my mind to the fact that it would be possible to sail from here to the Indies, and He opened my will to desire to

accomplish this project. This was the fire that burned within me when I came to visit your Highnesses.

Of course, the reading alone suggests we are dealing with an unusual kind of sailor, one who, like the humanists of his day, has engaged in sifting and comparing ancient and modern knowledge for new purposes. There is some irony, then, in the fact that he claims that God intended to produce a milagro ebidentisimo ("highly visible miracle") in this enterprise by using an uneducated man: "For the execution of the journey to the Indies, I was not aided by intelligence, by mathematics, or by maps. It was simply the fulfill-ment of what Isaiah had prophesied."

Columbus clearly employed considerable intelligence, mathematical skill, and geographical knowledge in planning his route. He also knew from much experience at sea that winds in the Atlantic nearer the equator would carry him west, those to be found more to the north would take him east, back to Europe. And he was alert to other environmental signs. Late in the first voyage he turned south to follow a flock of birds that he rightly assumed were headed towards land. Without this chance or providential fact, he probably would have come ashore somewhere between Virginia and Florida instead of the Caribbean, with doubtless immensely different effects on subsequent world history.

Despite all the knowledge, abstract and practical, that Columbus brought to bear on his task, the religious intuitions he describes may strike us as border-ing on delusion, on a par with the equally unexpected mystical speculations of the mathematician Pascal, or Newton's commentaries on the prophecies in the Book of Daniel. But anyone familiar with how prophecies have functioned throughout history knows they often work themselves out in ways their authors never envisioned. In Columbus' case, we may wish to avoid judging too quickly the "hand that could be felt" and other evidence that at times he seems to have heard something like divine locutions. They may have been delusions, intui-tions, or something else moving in the depths of human history.

Far from being a later and idealized reinterpretation of his own past, Columbus' remarks are confirmed by a curious source. Recent scholars have discovered notes in Columbus' own hand dated 1481, over a decade before his first voyage, in the back of a copy of Aeneas Sylvius Piccolomini's (the later Pius II) Historia rerum ubique gestarum. There Columbus compiles a shorter list of prophecies from various sources which, it now seems perfectly clear, guided his whole life project. . . .

Much of this real history has been obscured for a long time by persons who found it expedient to use Columbus as a symbolic figure. For most older Americans, he was presented as a heroic proto-American, combating the obscurantism of reactionary Spanish Catholics who thought he would sail off the end of the flat earth. (As we have seen, neither Columbus nor his intellec-tual critics believed in such absurdities.) In that reading, he became a forerun-ner of American Protestantism, modern science, and capitalist enterprise. It is no great loss that we have discarded that historical illusion.

Columbus also did service as an ethnic hero for Catholics, mostly Irish and Italian, during the large waves of immigration at the end of the nineteenth and beginning of the twentieth century. There was less harm here, because he was a true hero. Enthusiasm grew so heated that on the four hundredth anniversary of his voyage in 1892 efforts were made to have him canonized. But Leo XIII, fully aware of Columbus' irregular marital situation (for reasons of inheritance he never married the woman he lived with after his wife died), contented himself with praising his human virtues: "For the exploit is in itself the highest and grandest which any age has ever seen accomplished by man; and he who achieved it, for the greatness of mind and heart, can be compared to but few in the history of humanity."

In recent years, of course, Columbus' standing as hero has come under severe assault. He and the culture he represented have been castigated for initiating the modern cultural dominance of Europe and every subsequent world evil: colonialism, slavery, cultural imperialism, environmental damage, and religious bigotry. There is a kernel of truth in these charges, but obviously to equate a single individual or a complex entity like a culture with what are currently judged to be the negative dimensions of the emergence of an interconnected human world is to do great historical injustice to both individuals and ideas.

Europeans, for example, had an ambivalent stance towards the new peoples they encountered. On the one hand, there arose almost instantaneously the beginnings of the "noble savage" myth, which had a varied career in the hands of writers like Thomas More, Montaigne, and Rousseau. On the other hand, actual experience of the new cultures revealed peoples who displayed much savagery and sometimes little nobility.

Columbus himself adhered to one side or the other in this culture war at different times in his life. In one of his first communications with the Spanish monarchs after the discovery, he described the Tainos of the Caribbean in glowing terms:

> I see and know that these people have no religion whatever, nor are they idolaters, but rather they are very meek and know no evil. They do not kill or capture others and are without weapons. They are so timid that a hundred of them flee from one of us, even if we are teasing. They are very trusting; they believe there is a God in Heaven, and they firmly believe that we come from Heaven. They learn very quickly any prayer we tell them to say, and they make the sign of the cross. Therefore Your Highnesses must resolve to make them Christians.

As the self-contradictions of this passage suggest, Columbus was under the spell of one current in European mythology that believed such "uncivilized" peoples to be somehow closer to the conditions of the Garden of Eden than those enmeshed in the conflicts of "civilization."

In fact, the Tainos themselves were enmeshed in the tribal raiding, slavery, and cannibalism that existed in the Caribbean long before any European arrived (the word "cannibal" is a corruption of the native term for the fierce Caribs who eventually gave their name to the whole region). Columbus was for a while on surprisingly good terms with his Tainos, who in turn used the Spaniards to their advantage against their enemies. But the distance between the cultures was great, and, with the arrival of less-than-ideal explorers in subsequent voyages, the situation took a bad turn. Towards the end of his third voyage, Columbus wrote to complain about criticism of his governorship over both natives and Spaniards:

> At home they judge me as a governor sent to Sicily or to a city or two under settled government and where the laws can be fully maintained, without fear of all being lost. . . . I ought to be judged as a captain who went from Spain to the Indies to conquer a people, warlike and numerous, and with customs and beliefs very different from ours.

Columbus had discovered that the Indians were real flesh-and-blood human beings, with the same mix of good and evil that everywhere constitutes the human condition.

Today, the usual way of characterizing the behavior of the Europeans at this early stage is to fault them for not having the kind of sensitivity to the Other that a modern anthropologist or ethnologist would bring to such situations. Overlooked in this condemnation is the fact that it was precisely out of these tumultuous conflicts that the West began to learn how to understand different cultures as objectively as possible in their own terms. Columbus himself astutely noted differences between the various subgroupings of Tainos as well as their distinctiveness from other tribes. And even when he was driven to harsh action—against both Indians and Spaniards—it was not out of mere desire for power. Bartolome de las Casas, the well-known defender of the Indians, notes the "sweetness and benignity" of the admiral's character and, even while condemning what actually occurred, remarks, "Truly I would not dare blame the admiral's intentions, for I knew him well and I know his intentions were good." Las Casas attributes Columbus' shortcomings not to malign intent but to ignorance concerning how to handle an unprecedented situation.

This raises the question of larger intentions and the world impact of fifteenth-century European culture. The atrocities committed by Spain, England, Holland, and other European powers as they spread out over the globe in ensuing centuries are clear enough. No one today defends them. Less known, however, are the currents within that culture that have led to the very universal principles by which, in retrospect, we criticize that behavior today. For instance, not only Las Casas, but a weighty array of other religious thinkers began trying to specify what European moral obligations were to the new peoples.

Las Casas, who was the bishop of Chiapas, Mexico, where relations between mostly native populations and the central government remain dicey even today, bent over backwards to understand local practices. He once even described human sacrifices as reflecting an authentic piety and said that "even if cruel [they] were meticulous, delicate, and exquisite," a view that some of his critics have remarked exhibits a certain coldness towards the victims. Other missionaries learned native languages and recorded native beliefs. The information coming from the New World stimulated Francisco de la Vitoria, a Dominican theologian at the University of Salamanca in Spain, to develop principles of natural law that, in standard histories, are rightly given credit as the origin of modern international law. To read Vitoria on the Indies is to encounter an atmosphere closer to the UN Universal Declaration of Human Rights than to sinister Eurocentrism.

Las Casas and Vitoria influenced Pope Paul III to make a remarkable statement in his 1536 encyclical Sublimis Deus:

> Indians and all other people who may later be discovered by the Christians are by no means to be deprived of their liberty or the possession of their property, even though they be outside the faith of Jesus Christ. . . . Should the contrary happen it shall be null and of no effect. . . . By virtue of our apostolic authority we declare . . . that the said Indians and other peoples should be converted to the faith of Jesus Christ by preaching the word of God and by the example of good and holy living.

The Spanish crown itself had moral qualms about the conquest. Besides passing various laws trying to eliminate atrocities, it took a step unmatched before or since by any expanding empire: it called a halt to the process while theologians examined the question. In the middle of the sixteenth century, Charles V ordered a theological commission to debate the issue at the monastery of Valladolid. Las Casas defended the Indians. Juan Gines de Sepulveda, the greatest authority on Aristotle at the time, argued that Indians were slaves by nature and thus rightly subject to Spanish conquest. Though the commission never arrived at a clear vote and the Spanish settlers were soon back to their old ways, Las Casas' views were clearly superior and eventually prevailed.

Conquest aside, the question of even peaceful evangelizing remains very much with us. Today, most people, even Christians, believe it somehow improper to evangelize. The injunction to preach the gospel to all nations, so dear to Columbus' heart, seems an embarrassment, not least because of the ways the command has been misused. But some of the earlier missionaries tried a kind of inculturation that recognized what was good in the native practices and tried to build a symbolic bridge between them and the Christian faith. The Franciscans in New Spain and the Jesuits in Canada, for example, tried this approach. Not a few of them found martyrdom.

Many contemporary believers do not think that there was much need to evangelize. This usually arises out of the assumption that native religions are valid in their own way. It will not do, however, given the anthropological evidence, to make facile assumptions that all spiritual practices are on an equal plane. The early explorers who encountered them did not think so, and neither should we. For example, the Mexican novelist Carlos Fuentes, no special friend of Christianity or the Spanish conquest, in the very act of admiring the richness of Aztec culture, characterizes the Aztec gods as "a whole pantheon of fear." Fuentes deplores the way that missionaries often collaborated with unjust appropriation of native land, but on a theological level notes the epochal shift in native cultures thanks to Christian influence: "One can only imagine the astonishment of the hundreds and thousands of Indians who asked for baptism as they came to realize that they were being asked to adore a god who sacrificed himself for men instead of asking men to sacrifice themselves to gods, as the Aztec religion demanded."

This Copernican Revolution in religious thought has changed religious practice around the world since it was first proclaimed in Palestine two millennia ago, yet is all but invisible to modern critics of evangelization. Any of us, transported to the Aztec capital Tenochtitlan or to many other places around the world before the influence of Christianity and Europe, would react the way the conquistadors did—with rage and horror. We might not feel much different about some of the ways that Europeans, imitating Islamic practice, evangelized at times by the sword and perpetrated grave injustices around the world. But it is reductionist in the extreme to regard evangelization simply as imperialism. The usual uncritical way in which we are urged to respect the values of other cultures has only the merest grain of truth buried beneath what is otherwise religious indifferentism.

For all our sense of superiority to this now half-millennium-old story, we still face some of the same questions that emerged in the fifteenth century. We still have not found an adequate way to do justice to the claims of both universal principle and particular communities. We have what Vaclav Havel has called a "thin veneer of global civilization" mostly consisting of CNN, Coca Cola, blue jeans, rock music, and perhaps the beginning glimmer of something approaching a global agreement on how we should treat one another and the planet.

But that minimal unity conceals deeper conflicts involving not only resistance to superficiality but the survival of particular communities of meaning. We say, for example, that we have an equal respect for all cultures—until we come up against religious castes and sexism, clitorectomies and deliberate persecution. Then we believe that universal principles may take precedence. But whose universal principles? A Malaysian prime minister has lately instructed us that, contrary to international assumptions, "Western values are Western values: Asian values are universal values." It may take another five hundred years to decide whether that is so, or whether the opposition it assumes between East and West will persist.

All of this may seem a long way from the fifteenth century. But it is not mere historical fantasy to see in that beginning some of the global issues that are now inescapably on the agenda for the new millennium. Christianity and Islam, the two major proselytizing faiths in the world, are still seeking a modus vivendi. The global culture initiated by Columbus will always be inescapably European in origin and, probably, in basic shape. We chose long ago not to stay quietly at home and build the otherwise quite wonderful contraptions called cuckoo clocks. That decision brought (and brings) many challenges, but the very struggle should remind us of the glorious and ultimately providential destiny of the ongoing global journey that began in the fifteenth century.

Gabriel Garcia Marquez  **NO**

For a Country Within Reach
of the Children

Christopher Columbus, with the authorization of a letter from the Spanish monarchs to the emperor of China, had discovered this paradise through a geographical error that changed the course of history. On the eve of his arrival, even before he heard the wings of the first birds in the darkness at sea, Columbus detected the scent of flowers on the wind coming off the land, and it seemed the sweetest thing in the world to him. He wrote in his shipboard diary that they were met on the beach by natives as naked as the day they were born, handsome, gentle, and so innocent they traded all they had for strings of colored beads and tin trinkets. But his heart almost burst from his chest when he discovered that their noserings were made of gold, and their bracelets, necklaces, earrings, and anklets; that they had gold bells to play with, and some sheathed their private parts in gold. Those splendid ornaments, and not their human values, condemned the natives to their roles as protagonists in the second Genesis which began that day. Many of them died not knowing where the invaders had come from. Many of the invaders died not knowing where they were. Five centuries later the descendants of both still do not know who we are.

It was a more discovered world than anyone believed at the time. The Incas had a well-organized, legendary state with ten million inhabitants and monumental cities built on the Andean peaks to touch the sun god. To the amazement of European mathematicians, they had masterful systems of numeration and computation, archives and records for general use, and an unremitting veneration for public works, whose masterpiece was the garden of the imperial palace with its life-size trees and animals, all of gold and silver. The Aztecs and Mayas molded their historical consciousness into sacred pyramids among active volcanoes, and they had clairvoyant emperors, celebrated astronomers, and skilled artisans who overlooked the industrial uses of the wheel but utilized it in children's toys.

At the juncture of the two great oceans lay a territory of forty thousand square leagues, barely glimpsed by Columbus on his fourth voyage although today it bears his name: Colombia. For some ten thousand years it had been inhabited by scattered communities with different languages, distinct cultures, and their own well-defined identities. They had no notion of the state or of political cohesion but had discovered the political miracle of living as equals despite their differences. They possessed ancient systems of science and

From *Americas Magazine*, Vol. 49, No. 6, November–December 1997, pp. 28(12). Copyright © 1997 by Americas Magazine. Reprinted by permission.

education, and a rich cosmology linked to brilliant metalwork and inspired pottery. In their creative maturity, they had aspired to incorporate art into daily life—perhaps the supreme destiny of the arts—and achieved their goal with remarkable success, in household utensils as well as in the way they lived. For them, gold and precious gems did not have exchange value but cosmological and artistic power, although the Spaniards viewed them with Western eyes: more than enough gold and gems to leave the alchemists idle and pave the streets of heaven with pieces of four. This was the motive and force behind the Conquest and the Colonization, and the real origin of what we are. A century went by before the Spaniards shaped the colonial state with one name, one language, one god, and the same borders and political division into twelve provinces that it has today. Which gave rise, for the first time, to the notion of a centralized, bureaucratic nation, creating out of colonial lethargy the illusion of national unity. Sheer illusion in a society that was an obscurantist model of racial discrimination and larval violence beneath the cloak of the Holy Office. The cruelty of the conquistadors, and the unknown diseases they brought with them, reduced the three or four million Indians encountered by the Spaniards to no more than a million. But the racial mixing known as mestizaje had already become a demographic force that could not be contained. The thousands of African slaves brought here against their will for barbaric labor in mines and on plantations contributed a third notable element to the criollo crucible, with new rituals of imagination and memory and other, distant gods. But the Laws of the Indies imposed millimetric standards of segregation according to the degree of white blood in each race: several categories of mestizos, black slaves, free blacks, varying classifications of mulattoes. It became possible to distinguish as many as eighteen different degrees of mestizos, and the white Spaniards even set their own children apart, calling them criollo whites. Mestizos were not permitted to fill certain high positions in government, to hold other public offices, or to enroll in secondary schools and seminaries. Blacks lacked everything, even a soul; they did not have the right to enter heaven or hell, and their blood was deemed impure until distilled by four generations of whites. Because of how difficult it was to determine the intricate demarcation lines between races, and given the very nature of the social dynamic that created mestizaje, such laws could not be enforced with too much rigor, yet racial tensions and violence increased. Until just a few years ago the children of unmarried couples were still not admitted to secondary schools in Colombia. Blacks have achieved legal equality but still suffer many forms of discrimination in addition to the ones peculiar to poverty.

The generation that won independence lost the first opportunity to eradicate this deplorable legacy. The group of young romantics inspired by the enlightenment of the French Revolution established a well-intentioned modern republic but could not eliminate these vestiges of colonialism. Even they were not free of its evil influence. At the age of thirty-five, Simon Bolivar ordered the execution of eight hundred Spanish prisoners, even those lying wounded in a hospital. Francisco de Paula Santander was twenty-eight when he gave the order to shoot thirty-eight Spaniards, including their commanding officer, who had been captured at the Battle of Boyaca. In an indirect way, some of the virtuous aims of the republic fostered new social tensions between poor and rich, laborers and artisans, and other marginal groups. The savage civil wars of the nineteenth century were an outgrowth of these inequalities, as were the countless political upheavals that have left a trail of blood throughout our history. Two innate abilities have helped U.S. to elude our calamitous fate, to compensate for the gaps in our cultural and social circumstances and carry on a fumbling search for our identity. One is a talent for creativity, the supreme expression of human intelligence. The other is a fierce commitment to self-improvement. Enhanced by an almost supernatural shrewdness, and as likely to be used for good as for evil, they were a providential resource employed by the Indians against the Spaniards from the very day they landed. To get rid of Columbus they sent him from island to island, always on to the next island, to find a king covered in gold who never existed. They deceived the conquistadors, already beguiled by novels of chivalry, with descriptions of fantastic cities built of pure gold, right there, on the other side of the hill. They led them astray with the tale of a mythical El Dorado who covered his body with gold dust once a year and plunged into his sacred lagoon. Three masterpieces of a national epic, used by the Indians as an instrument of survival. Perhaps another of the pre-Columbian talents that we have inherited is an extraordinary flexibility in adapting without delay to any environment and learning with ease the most dissimilar trades: fakirs in India, camel drivers in the Sahara, English teachers in New York.

On the other hand, a trait that may come from the Spanish side is our congenital status as immigrants with a spirit of adventure that seeks out risks rather than avoiding them. Of the five million or so Colombians who live abroad, the immense majority left to seek their fortune with nothing but their temerity, and today they are everywhere, for good reasons or bad, for better or worse, but never unnoticed. The distinguishing Colombian trait in world folklore is that they never let themselves die of hunger. Even more striking is that the farther away they are from Colombia, the more Colombian they become.

This is true. They have assimilated the customs and languages of others and made them their own but have never been able to shake the ashes of nostalgia from their hearts, and they miss no opportunity to express this with every kind of patriotic ceremony, exalting all that they long for in the distant homeland, even its defects.

In the most unexpected countries you can turn the corner and find a living replica of any spot in Colombia: the square, its dusty trees still hung with paper garlands from the last Friday night party; the little restaurant named for an unforgotten town, with the heartbreaking aromas of Mama's kitchen; the July 20 school next to the August 7 tavern that plays music for crying over the sweetheart who never was.

The paradox is that, like their forebears, these nostalgic conquistadors were born in a country of closed doors. The liberators tried to open them to fresh winds out of England and France—the legal and ethical theories of Bentham, the education of Lancaster, the study of languages, the popularization of arts and sciences—in order to eradicate the vices of a Spain more Catholic than the Pope and still wary after the financial harassment of the Jews and eight hundred years of Muslim occupation. The nineteenth century radicals, and then the Generation of the Centenary, proposed the same idea with policies of massive immigration aimed at enriching the culture of mestizaje, but all of them were frustrated by our almost theological fear of foreign devils. Even today we have no idea how much we depend on the vast world we know nothing about. We are conscious of our ills but have exhausted ourselves struggling against the symptoms while the causes go on forever. An indulgent version of our history, meant to hide more than it clarifies, has been written for us and made official; in its original sins are perpetuated, battles are won that never were fought, and glories we never deserved are sanctified. In short, we indulge ourselves with the delusion that although history may not resemble the Colombia we live in, one day Colombia will resemble her written history.

In similar fashion, our conformist, repressive education seems designed to force children to adapt to a country that never took them into account, rather than placing the country within their reach and allowing them to transform and enlarge it. The same kind of thoughtlessness inhibits their innate creativity and intuition, thwarts their imaginations and precocious insights, their wisdom of the heart, until children forget what they doubtless knew at birth: that reality does not end where textbooks say it does; that their conception of the world is more attuned to nature than any adult's; that life would be longer and happier if all people could do the work they like and only the work they like.

These intersecting destinies have forged a dense, indecipherable nation where improbability is the only measure of reality. Our banner is excess. Excess in everything: in good and evil, in love and hate, in the jubilation of victory and the bitterness of defeat. We are as passionate when we destroy idols as when we create them.

We are intuitive people, immediate and spontaneous autodidacts, and pitiless workers, but the mere idea of easy money drives us wild. In our hearts we harbor equal amounts of political rancor and historical amnesia. In sports a spectacular win or defeat can cost as many lives as a disastrous plane crash. For the same reason we are a sentimental society where action takes precedence over reflection, impulsiveness over reason, human warmth over prudence. We have an almost irrational love of life but kill one another in our passion to live. The perpetrator of the most terrible crimes is betrayed by his sentimentality. In other words, the most heartless Colombian is betrayed by his heart.

For we are two countries: one on paper and the other in reality. We are precursors of the sciences in America but still take a medieval view of scientists as hermetic wizards, although few things in daily life are not scientific miracles. Justice and impunity cohabit inside each of us in the most arbitrary way; we are fanatical legalists but carry in our souls a sharp-witted lawyer skilled at sidestepping laws without breaking them, or breaking them without being caught. We adore dogs, carpet the world with roses, are overwhelmed by love of country, but we ignore the disappearance of six animal species each hour of the day and night because of criminal depredations in the rain forest, and have ourselves destroyed beyond recall one of the planet's great rivers. We grow indignant at the nation's negative image abroad but do not dare admit that often the reality is worse. We are capable of the noblest acts and the most despicable ones, of sublime poems and demented murders, of celebratory funerals and deadly debauchery. Not because some of us are good and others evil, but because all of us share in the two extremes. In the worst case—and may God keep us from it— we are all capable of anything.

Perhaps deeper reflection would allow us to determine to what extent our character comes from our still being essentially the same clannish, formalistic, introverted society that we were in colonial times. Perhaps calmer reflection would allow us to discover that our historical violence is the force left over from our eternal war against adversity. Perhaps we are perverted by a system that encourages us to live as if we were rich while forty percent of the population exists in abject poverty, that fosters in us an elusive, instantaneous notion of happiness: we always want a little more of what we already have, more and more of what once seemed impossible, much more of what the law allows, and we obtain it however we can, even if that means breaking the law. Realizing that no government can satisfy these desires, we have become disbelieving, non-participatory, ungovernable, and characterized by a solitary individualism that leads all of us to think we depend only on ourselves. More than enough reason to go on asking ourselves who we are and by which face we wish to be known in the third millennium.

POSTSCRIPT

Did Christopher Columbus's Voyages Have a Positive Effect on World History?

Pouring through the many Columbus-oriented works which were products of the quincentennial anniversary is likely to leave one bewildered and perplexed. One wonders how many writers can take the same information and come to diametrically opposed conclusions concerning Columbus and his place in history. Of course, as is usual in historical matters, one's experiences and the perspective derived from them are important determinants in drawing conclusions form the historical process.

It is worth noting that when the Columbus "iconography" was established in the West, the perspective on civilization was a Eurocentric one, and many of its potentionally-negative voices were muted or silent. As Western history became more "inclusionary" and a multi-cultural view of history made its way into the public consciousness, these voices began to be heard. They produced an alternative interpretation of Columbus's voyages and their impact on history for different from their predecessors. What the future will hold for the subject remains to be seen.

One important question germane to the Columbus debate is: To what extent can he be held personally responsible for the transatlantic slave trade, the annihilation of Native American populations, the ecological destruction of the Western Hemisphere, and other evils that were committed long after his death? Any assessment of Columbus's role in world history needs to explore answers to this question.

The post-quincentennial Columbus years have produced a large volume of works on the subject. Some of those on the negative side of the admiral's contributions to world history include Basil Davidson, *The search for Africa: History, Culture, Politics* (Random House, 1994)—that contains a chapter entitled "The Curse of Columbus"—which blames him for the horrors of the transatlantic slave trade. David Stannard, *American Holocaust: Columbus and the Conquest of the New World* (oxford University press, 1992) goes so far as to hold Columbus responsible for the genocidal acts committed against Native American populations. Kirkpatrick Sale's *The Conquest of Paradise: Christopher Columbus and the Columbian Legacy* (Penguin Books, 1991) takes a more philosophical approach, but still considers Columbus's legacy to be a negative one, especially as far as the environment is concerned.

Columbus has not been without support. The late Italian historian Paolo Emilio Taviani (1913–2001), in *Columbus: The Great Adventure: His Life, His Times, and His Voyages* (Orion Books, 1991) makes a passionate plea for history to view the positive side of the Columbus legacy. Several articles do the same, including: Robert Royal, "Columbus as a Dead White Male: the Ideological Underpinnings of the Controversy over 1492." *The world and I* (December, 1991); Dinesh D'Sousa, "The Crimes of Christopher Columbus," *First Things* (November, 1995); Michael Marshall, "Columbus and the Age of Exploration," *The World And I* (November, 1999).

ISSUE 15

Did Martin Luther's Reforms Improve the Lives of European Christians?

YES: Robert Kolb, from *Martin Luther as Prophet, Teacher, Hero: Images of the Reformer, 1520–1620* (Baker Books, 1999)

NO: Hans Küng, from *Great Christian Thinkers*, trans. John Bowden (Continuum, 1996)

ISSUE SUMMARY

YES: Religion and history professor Robert Kolb contends that Martin Luther was seen as a prophetic teacher and hero whose life brought hope, divine blessing, and needed correctives to the Christian church.

NO: Theologian and professor emeritus of theology Hans Küng views Martin Luther as the inaugurator of a paradigm shift and as the unwitting creator of both bloody religious wars and an unhealthy subservience by ordinary Christians to local rulers in worldly matters.

When Martin Luther was born in 1483, his father, Hans, hoped the boy would become a lawyer. Instead, a mystical experience during a thunderstorm led Martin to enter religious life as an Augustinian monk. Scrupulous in observing his religious duties, Luther became increasingly aware of his own sinfulness and his fear of divine justice. He came to believe that fallen humans, on their own, can never do anything to merit salvation; it is the grace of God alone that "justifies" them.

Sent by his order to teach philosophy at the University of Wittenberg, Luther was appalled at the selling of indulgences (pardons for sins) and denounced the practice, along with other abuses, in 95 theses of protest addressed to the Archbishop of Mainz in 1517. The newly invented printing press spread his ideas throughout the German states and beyond. Summoned to appear before the Imperial Diet at Worms in 1521, Luther clung to his beliefs, displeasing the emperor and earning himself a condemnation. Hidden from danger by his patron, the Elector Frederick of Saxony, Luther translated the Bible into German, unaware that he had launched a radical religious revolution.

Eager for reform rather than revolution, Luther sought to modify what he regarded as abuses within the Christian church. His intention was to strip the modern church of power and corruption and return it to its roots—the pristine days of early Christianity (see Issue 5 for another look at this period). Certainly he had no intention of founding a new religion. This theological conservatism was matched by his opposition to the Peasants' Revolt of 1524–1525. Siding emphatically with the forces of law and order, Luther urged the princes to put down the rebellion and safeguard the God-given social order. In many ways, he was a reluctant revolutionary.

Lutherans (as they called themselves against Luther's wishes) gathered to read the scriptures in their own language, sing, pray, and listen to sermons. Widespread anticlerical feeling inspired many to challenge the wealth and influence of what they saw as an Italian church. Luther's religious alternative was also attractive to those whose feeling of national pride in the semi-autonomous German states made them resent pronouncements from Rome. Violent conflict between Protestant princes and imperial Catholic forces broke out during Luther's lifetime, and people were instructed to follow the religion of their local prince—Lutheran or Catholic.

Luther married a former nun, Katherine von Bora, and fathered a number of children. Living a family life, like those in his congregation, rather than observing the Catholic requirement for celibacy, Luther may have seemed more approachable than the Catholic priests. Insisting on "the priesthood of all believers," he urged his followers to read the scriptures for themselves and find the truth within them. But as the Reformation spread to Switzerland, England, and beyond, thousands died in religious conflicts, and Christianity became increasingly fragmented. At the time of Luther's death in 1546, much of Western Europe was dissolving centuries-old ties that had bound people and nations into a spiritual and temporal unity called Christendom.

If we admit that reform was needed, the next question becomes, Was the reform movement initiated by Luther worth the theological, political, and, especially, human cost? For Robert Kolb, Luther was filled with the dynamism that sprang from his spiritual conviction. Regarded as divinely called to a holy mission, Luther was able to inspire others to an intense, personal relationship with the God of history and the redeemer of human frailty and despair. Luther's writings continued to inspire hope during the troubled century that followed his death.

Hans Küng asserts that Luther has the New Testament on his side in support of the key Reformation concepts of justification, grace, and faith. Also, Luther was a charismatic reformer, without whom there would have been no Reformation in Germany. Having broken with the distant authority of Rome, however, Luther was faced with challenges from both "enthusiasts" on the left and "traditionalists" on the right. Religious wars divided territories into those practicing the "old faith" and those following the reformist "Augsburg Confession." Far from guaranteeing freedom of religion, this division led instead to religion by region. Luther's doctrine of state and church as two realms led, unfortunately, to the subordination of churches to their local princes, who acted as "emergency bishops," and not all of whom were like Frederick "the wise."

YES

Robert Kolb

Martin Luther as Prophet, Teacher, Hero

Introduction

In an attack published in 1529, Johannes Cochlaeus, Martin Luther's fierce foe and first biographer, characterized the Reformer as having seven heads. Throughout the almost five centuries since then, Luther has been depicted by friend and foe alike as having many more than seven faces. The image makers of his own age began immediately to project into public view a picture which reflected their experience of Luther. Their successors have taken the raw material of his life and thought and cast it into forms which would serve their own purposes—with varying degrees of historical accuracy. Few public figures have enjoyed and suffered the process of publicity as has Martin Luther.

Most ages seize historical personalities as clay from which they mold icons of mythical proportions to embody their values and aspirations. Into the apocalyptically charged atmosphere of late medieval Germany stumbled Martin Luther, whose career coincided with the invention of the medium of print. At the outset of his career, historical and religious conditions, medium, and man came together in a unique manner to begin fashioning a public persona which soon loomed larger than life over the German and western European ecclesiastical landscape. Read in the streets of towns and discussed in the taverns of villages, his own publications and the representations of his thought and person by other pamphleteers produced a cultural paragon which his followers in the sixteenth century put to use in several ways.

In the conclusion to his pioneering assessment of the changing views about the Reformer from Wittenberg, Horst Stephan observed that new images of Luther are always "born out of a new encounter with the testimony of the original image, and they are reflections of his form in water of different depths and different hues." To a degree perhaps unique in the history of the church since the apostolic age, the image of this single person, Martin Luther, has directly shaped the institutions and life of a large body of Christendom. He has influenced his followers both as churchman and as teacher of the church. Calvinist churches, of course, look to John Calvin as model and magister for their ecclesiastical life. John Wesley exercises a continuing role in the Methodist churches. To a far greater extent, however, Lutheran churches have found in Luther not only a teacher but

From MARTIN LUTHER AS PROPHET, TEACHER, HERO: IMAGES OF THE REFORMATION, 1520–1620 by Robert Kolb, pp. 9–13, 225–230. Copyright © 1999 by Baker Book House. Reprinted by permission.

also a prophetic hero and authority. Heinrich Bornkamm's observation extends beyond the borders of the German cultural realm which he was sketching: "Every presentation and assessment of Luther and the Reformation means a critical engagement with the foundations of our more recent history. Like no other historical figure, that of Luther always compels anew a comprehensive reflection on the religious, spiritual, and political problems of our lives."

Since Stephan's study others have examined the interpretation of Luther's thought and work both within and outside Lutheranism. None of these, however, has focused in detail on the ways in which Luther's image and thought shaped Lutheran thinking and action during the century following his appearance on the stage of Western history. From the very beginning Luther's students and friends regarded him as a figure of more than normal proportions. Some saw him as an illustrious hero of the faith. Others regarded him as a powerful doctor of the church in line with Moses, Paul, and Augustine. Many also regarded him as a unique servant of God, a prophet and the eschatological angel who is depicted in Revelation 14 as the bearer of the gospel in the last days and whose authority could be put to use in governing and guiding the church, particularly in the adjudication of disputes over the proper and correct understanding of biblical teaching.

Without taking into account the conceptual framework of biblical humanism on the one hand, and that of late medieval apocalyptic on the other, such images seem strange to us moderns. Within the context of Luther's time, however, they provided vehicles by which people could make sense of Luther's impact on their lives and his role on the stage of human history. With such images of Luther in mind his followers set about to reshape the institutions and ideas which held their world together.

This inquiry will review how Luther's message and his career reshaped sixteenth-century German Lutherans' views of God and human history. Three conceptions of the Reformer emerge, reflecting a variety of needs in his society, which was organized around religious ideas and ecclesiastical institutions and practices. Although all three of these conceptions appeared in the first few years of public comment on Luther, they developed in different ways as the years passed. Their influence can best be presented through a chronological tracking of their evolution as exhibited in representative writings from the pens of his disciples. To be sure, historians' analyses always oversimplify: the categories are not so distinct and discrete that they can be neatly separated from each other. Thus our discussion of each motif will reveal aspects of the others.

First, for some of his followers during the subsequent decades, the Reformer functioned as a prophet who replaced popes and councils as the adjudicating or secondary authority (interpreting the primary authority, Scripture) in the life of the church. Like almost every age, the late Middle Ages were a period of crisis, and people were rethinking questions of authority in various aspects of life. Within the church Luther's challenge to the medieval papacy heightened the crisis by confirming doubts about the old religious system. Although Luther and his adherents did not discard the ancient fathers of the church nor disregard their usefulness, they did affirm the primacy of biblical authority; for them Scripture was the sole primary source of truth.

The church, however, always needs a more elaborate system of determining the meaning of the biblical message; and the tradition, in the hands of popes, bishops, and councils, could no longer suffice to adjudicate differences in interpretation of the Scripture. To replace the medieval authorities who had interpreted biblical dicta regarding truth and life, Luther emerged as a prophet of God in whose words a secondary level of doctrinal authority could be found. Those who believed that this Wittenberg professor was God's special agent—a voice of divine judgment upon the corruption of the old system—were able to ascribe such authority to him without difficulty. When the living myth had disappeared into his tomb, and could no longer adjudicate disputes by composing letters or formal faculty opinions, his writings—widely available in print—were used as a secondary authority by some of his disciples.

Second, over the years Luther functioned as a prophetic teacher whose exposition of the biblical message supported and guided the biblical exposition of his followers. Luther based his perception of life and truth upon his conviction that God has spoken reality into existence and shaped human life through his world. Teaching—the content of the Word—thus was paramount in Luther's conception of the way in which God came to people in the sixteenth century and functioned as their God. While the Reformer was still alive and writing, his vast literary output enabled him to influence a broad circle of readers and of nonreaders who heard his ideas from them. When he died, his adherents continued to learn and to teach others through the published corpus of his thought. In elaborating Luther's role as teacher, we must pay attention to the ways in which his writings were reproduced and used in the Lutheran churches of Germany after his death. For his heirs not only reprinted his complete corpus and individual treatises in it; they also repackaged and organized Luther's thought topically for handy reference in the pastor's library. In this manner Luther continued his teaching activity after his death through citations, reprintings, and the organizing of his thought for consumption in a new era.

Third, for his German followers Luther remained above all a prophetic hero whom God had chosen as a special instrument for the liberation of his church—and of the German people—from papal oppression and deceit. As a heroic prophet, Luther symbolized the divine Word which brought God's judgment upon the old papal system, and he embodied the hopes of the people and the comfort of the gospel which brought new heavenly blessings upon the faithful children of God. In their troubled times his followers saw in Martin Luther the assurance that God would judge their enemies and intervene eschatologically on their behalf with the salvation he had promised. . . .

Conclusion

Theander Luther

Five hundred years after his birth Martin Luther continues to engage and fascinate those who encounter him. The testimony of his biography and his writings continues to cast "reflections of his form in water of different depths and hues," as Horst Stephan commented nearly a century ago. Modern scholars have formed their own judgments of Luther and have put his thoughts to their own use on bases different from those that motivated his contemporaries. Apt is Mark Edwards's observation that twentieth-century accounts often give a false representation of sixteenth-century perceptions, "not because the historian knows too little but because the historian knows too much." This is the case because historians have a view "from above"—a more comprehensive view of Luther's context, of his impact, even of the corpus of his writings—a view which none of Luther's contemporaries, nor Luther himself, could have had. For instance, as Edwards observes, "we forget that, except perhaps for a few of Luther's students, no contemporary read Luther's works in light of his pre- Reformation lectures on Psalms, Galatians, and Romans." In fact, the few who had read manuscript notes on these lectures preferred his later works, which more reflected what they had heard from him.

On the other hand, when modern historians come to what Luther wrote and wrought, they do not bring the yearnings and longings shaped by the spirit of medieval apocalyptic nor the humanistic adventure of return to the sources. Instead, we bring our own conceptual framework and our own questions and goals to the texts and story of Martin Luther. Further, it is impossible to return to the pristine sources of the 1510s, 1520s, and 1530s uninfluenced by the interpretations of Luther forged by his students and contemporaries and those who followed them in the succeeding two generations.

From the perspective of the sixteenth century, Luther had seven heads or more. To a remarkable if not unique degree this monk and professor became a fixation for foes and friends alike. Whatever the reasons (as assessed by twentieth-century scholars) may have been, this widespread fixation developed less on the strength of political power or economic resources or social status than on the strength of his ideas and through the public presentation and projection of these ideas. His disciples perceived him to be an authoritative prophet or an insightful teacher or a national and cultural hero, or one who combined two or all of these roles.

As Luther's supporters praised him by recounting his heroic deeds or by repeating his insightful instruction or by putting his image and ideas to use in the life of church and society, they inevitably cast the raw material of his life into forms dictated by the challenges and concerns of their own times. Around 1520 a host of images were marshaled to describe this prophetic figure. In the first decade of his emergence in public he was seen as an authority for determining the proper exposition of biblical truth, the new teacher of the church for the last times, and a hero who would end papal tyranny. All three representations of the Wittenberg professor continued to be in vogue throughout his life and in the years immediately after his death. Gradually, however, his role as adjudicatory authority, which was transferred from his person to his writings, appeared ever less able to serve effectively as a means of deciding and defining public teaching. The national hero he remained, ever more simplified and stylized but not less important because of that, particularly as the shadow of the Counter-Reformation grew heavier over evangelical Germany. His role as teacher continued as well, albeit in limited and adapted form. Changing times meant changing use of the individual who had been thought to personify the message of God and to satisfy the longings of the people.

Not all of Luther's followers put him to use as a substitute for popes and councils, as a secondary authority who could adjudicate disputes over the gospel and the practice of the church. Many did, for the church always needs such a secondary authority. The conviction that the papacy was Antichrist and that councils and the Fathers were fallible produced a crisis of authority in the churches of the Reformation. Among Luther's followers biblical authority prevailed unchallenged as the primary authority for determining truth in the presentation of the gospel. The Fathers and councils had also schooled the thinking of the Wittenberg disciples, although they reckoned with the possibility of errors in patristic and conciliar writings and thus dismissed them as secondary authorities. Accordingly, some certain standard for adjudication of disputes over the interpretation of the biblical message was needed.

Luther's prophet-like appearance on the late medieval scene and his own dynamic concept of the Word of God—as it is repeated in the mouths of living speakers of the biblical message—prompted his contemporaries to attribute adjudicatory authority to him. Medieval apocalyptic hopes and humanist convictions regarding the power of effective oral communication combined with his own understanding of the power of God in the living voice of the gospel to create a belief that he was a special tool of God. As such, it was believed, he spoke God's word of condemnation against the deceiving tyrants of the papal system and announced God's word of grace and mercy in Jesus Christ, and he did so with an authority which he had received along with the gift of clear interpretation of the biblical message. But even while he lived, appeals to his authority were restricted to those circles that accepted him as God's authoritative prophet for the latter day. Furthermore, once he died and could no longer directly apply God's Word to current situations, and the church had to rely on the written works he had left behind, it ceased to be practical—and possible— to regard him as a secondary, adjudicatory authority in the church. The written corpus was too bulky. It contained contradictions. It became politically delicate to emphasize Luther so strongly.

The negative side of Luther's proclamation—in defense of the gospel and in opposition to papal oppression—had made him a hero of Herculean proportions to his contemporaries around 1520; and a hero for nation and people, for freedom and humanity, he remained, particularly as the Roman Catholic prelates and princes became increasingly aggressive and the political tensions within the empire mounted—culminating in the Thirty Years' War. In the following centuries, pressed into a variety of images and forms by the governments of divine-right monarchies and by fans of the Enlightenment, by theologians of diverse perspectives and by politicians of various ideologies, Luther's persona continued to prove itself a useful symbol—a hero of one kind or another—even when his authority and indeed his theology were rejected by his partisans. More often than not, misunderstanding of the hero—occasionally perhaps deliberate, often innocent—separated the historical figure of the Reformer from the Luther myths created ever anew for some purpose or another.

Luther has found enduring use as a teacher of the church as well. To a remarkable extent his thought continued to determine the agenda of theological discussion in many parts of Christendom in succeeding generations. Those who claimed his name could not escape addressing the emphases of his theology— justification, the Word of God as means of grace, the authority of Scripture, the nature and effect of the sacraments, to name but a few of his doctrinal accents. Nonetheless, from the beginning his followers' understanding of his teaching was influenced by the medieval heritage which continued to echo through the minds of his contemporaries, by the agenda of polemic set by his foes as well as his friends, by their individual pastoral or professorial concerns, and by the method and theology of his Wittenberg colleague Philip Melanchthon. Melanchthon's practice of theology schematized the thinking of students into the forms dictated by the loci method, and they could recognize no alternative to placing Luther's thought into these Melanchthonian forms.

The dogmatic tradition which ran from Melanchthon through Martin Chemnitz's commentary on his *Loci communes theologici* to Johann Gerhard and the dogmatic works of Lutheran orthodoxy became the standard expression of what Lutherans believed and taught. Other sources may have shaped preaching, catechetical instruction, and pastoral care, but the conceptual framework into which graduates of Lutheran theological faculties placed materials from Luther's pen and the pens of other theologians came from the Melanchthonian dogmatic tradition. Modern scholars may express chagrin or regret over this fact; indeed, they may find Luther more refreshing or relevant than the works of his followers. But his epigones did fulfil the calling of all theologians: they applied the biblical message and the tradition of their church to the lives of their parishioners in their own generation. And however they may have adapted Luther, they adopted what they understood the heart of his message to be, even if from later perspectives they may have sacrificed too much of its peculiar insights.

. . . [T]hat the hero Luther could be honored and celebrated by being cited in formulaic ways made it unnecessary for young pastors to read his writings and glean the fullness of his unique exposition of the biblical message. The dynamic of his homiletical teaching was placed into forms which limited the ways in which Luther could continue to teach his church. The sermonic ways in which he treated and conveyed the biblical message were set aside. The full scope of his teaching was channeled for the usage of a new day.

Indeed, Luther's teaching for the early sixteenth century needed to be reshaped and readdressed to changing patterns of church life and new issues as well as old. In the course of that inevitable process the vigor and vitality of the prophetic teacher were tamed even as the content of his teaching was preserved within the forms which his followers found useful for conveying his message in their generations. At the outset of the seventeenth century Luther continued to teach, particularly through the most practical of his writings: the postils and the commentaries which could aid preaching, his catechisms, his devotional meditations. His followers regarded him as the greatest of their teachers even if they received his teaching through a grid constructed by others, above all Philip Melanchthon. Luther's prophetic authority as a substitute for popes and councils in adjudicating disputes over the biblical message had waned. Although its memory echoed through certain expressions of praise during the closing decades of the sixteenth century and the opening years of the seventeenth, the Book of Concord had become the secondary authority for a majority of Lutheran churches. The authority of Luther's person, and then the corpus of his writings, had been replaced by the authority of his church's confessional documents. Even those images which had given substance to the claim for his authority—above all, angel of the apocalypse and prophet—were by the end of the sixteenth century no longer used as grounds on which to justify his adjudication of doctrinal differences or to define public teaching, but were used instead to focus attention on his heroic deeds of resistance to papal oppression, deeds out of which the new and final revelation of the gospel had appeared.

Nonetheless, the vibrant interest in Luther's person and career, as well as the availability of much of the corpus of his writings, ensured that his voice continued to inform and form the faith and the life of the people of his church. Even though the extravagant appraisal of his contemporaries had been tamed, for most Lutherans of the early modern period this prophet and teacher loomed over their lives as a unique hero of the faith and of God's Word.

Hans Küng  **NO**

Martin Luther: Return to the Gospel as the Classical Instance of a Paradigm Shift

Why There Was a Lutheran Reformation

Hardly a single one of Luther's reform concerns was new. But the time had not been ripe for them. Now the moment had come, and it needed only religious genius to bring these concerns together, put them into words and embody them personally. Martin Luther was the man of the moment.

What had been the preparation for the new paradigm shift in world history immediately before the Reformation? Briefly:

- the collapse of papal rule of the world, the split in the church between East and West, then the twofold, later threefold, papacy in Avignon, Rome and Pisa along with the rise of the nation states of France, England and Spain;
- the lack of success by the reform councils (Constance, Basal, Florence, Lateran) in 'reforming the church, head and members';
- the replacement of the natural economy by a money economy, the invention of printing and the widespread desire for education and Bibles;
- the absolutist centralism of the Curia, its immorality, its uncontrollable financial policy and its stubborn resistance to reform, and finally the trade in indulgences for rebuilding St Peter's, which was regarded in Germany as the pinnacle of curial exploitation.

However, even north of the Alps, as a result of the Roman system, some of the abuses were quite blatant:

- the retrograde state of church institutions: the ban on levying interest, the church's freedom from taxation and its own jurisdiction, the clerical monopoly of schools, the furthering of beggary, too many church festivals;
- the way in which church and theology were overgrown with canon law;
- the growing self-awareness of university sciences (Paris!) as a critical authority over against the church;

- the tremendous secularization even of the rich prince bishops and monasteries; the abuses caused by the pressure towards celibacy; the proletariat, which comprised far too many uneducated and poor people;
- the radical critics of the church: Wycliffe, Hus, Marsilius, Ockham and the Humanists;
- finally a terrifying superstition among the people, a religious nervousness which often took enthusiastic-apocalyptic forms, an externalized liturgy and legalized popular piety, a hatred of work-shy monks and clerics, a malaise among the educated people in the cities and despair among the exploited peasants in Germany . . . All in all this was an abysmal crisis for mediaeval theology, church and society, coupled with an inability to cope with it.

So everything was ready for an epoch-making paradigm shift, but there was need of someone to present the new candidate for a paradigm credibly. And this was done by a single monk, in the epoch-making prophetic figure of Martin Luther, who was born on 10 November 1483 in Eisleben in Thuringia. Although as a young monk and doctor of theology Luther certainly did not understand himself primarily as a prophet but as a teacher of the church, intuitively and inspirationally he was able to meet the tremendous religious longing of the late Middle Ages. He purged the strong positive forces in mysticism, and also in nominalism and popular piety, confidently centred all the frustrated reform movements in his brilliant personality, which was stamped with a deep faith, and expressed his concerns with unprecedented eloquence. Without Martin Luther there would have been no Reformation in Germany!

The Basic Question: How Is One Justified Before God?

But when did things get this far? As a result of acute fear of death during a violent thunderstorm and constant anxiety about not being able to stand in the final judgment before Christ, at the age of twenty-two, in 1505, Luther had entered a monastery against the will of his father (who was a miner and smelter by trade). But when did the Augustinian monk who loyally obeyed the rules and was concerned for righteousness by works become the ardent Reformer of 'faith alone'? Historians argue over the precise point in time of the 'breakthrough to the Reformation'.

Be this as it may, there is no disputing the fact that Martin Luther, who had a very similar scholastic training in philosophy and theology to Thomas Aquinas, was in deep crisis over his life. Being a monk had not solved any of his problems, but had accentuated many of them. For the works of monastic piety like choral prayer, mass, fasting, penitence, penance to which Luther submitted himself with great earnestness as an Augustine eremite could not settle for him the questions of his personal salvation and damnation. In a sudden intuitive experience of the gracious righteousness of God (if we follow the 'great testimony' of 1545), but presumably in a somewhat longer process (if we look at his earlier works more closely), in his crisis of conscience a new understanding of the justification of the sinner had dawned on Luther.

Whenever precisely the 'breakthrough to the Reformation' took place (more recent scholarship is predominantly for a 'late dating' to the first half of 1518), the 'shift to the Reformation' happens here.

So the starting point of Luther's reforming concern was not any abuses in the church, not even the question of the church, but the question of salvation: how do human beings stand before God? How does God deal with human beings? How can human beings be certain of their salvation by God? How can sinful human beings put right their relationship with the just God? When are they justified by God? Luther found the answer above all in Paul's Letter to the Romans: human beings cannot stand justified by God, be justified by God, through their own efforts—despite all piety. It is God himself, as a gracious God, who pronounces the sinner righteous, without any merits, in his free grace. This is a grace which human beings may confidently grasp only in faith. For Luther, of the three theological virtues faith is the most important: in faith, unrighteous sinful human beings receive God's righteousness.

That was the decisive theological factor. But there was a second one: starting from a new understanding of the event of justification Luther hit upon a new understanding of the church. This was a radical criticism of a secularized and legalized church which had deviated from the teaching and praxis of the gospel, and of its sacraments, ministries and traditions. But in this criticism had not Luther broken completely with the Catholic tradition? With his understanding of justification was he not *a priori* un-Catholic? To answer this question, for all the discontinuity one must also see the great continuity between Luther and the theology which preceded him. . . .

Where Luther Can Be Said to Be Right

Does Luther have the New Testament behind him in his basic approach? I can venture an answer which is based on my previous works in the sphere of the doctrine of justification. In his basic statements on the event of justification, with the 'through grace alone', 'through faith alone', the 'at the same time righteous and a sinner', Luther has the New Testament behind him, and especially Paul, who is decisively involved in the doctrine of justification. I shall demonstrate this simply through the key words:

- 'Justification' according to the New Testament is not in fact a process of supernatural origin which is understood physiologically and which takes place in the human subject, but is the verdict of God in which God does not impute their sin to the godless but declares them righteous in Christ and precisely in so doing makes them really righteous.
- 'Grace' according to the New Testament is not a quality or disposition of the soul, not a series of different quasi-physical supernatural entities which are successively poured into the substance and faculties of the soul, but is God's living favour and homage, his personal conduct as made manifest in Jesus Christ, which precisely in this way determines and changes people.

- 'Faith' according to the New Testament is not an intellectualist holding truths to be true but the trusting surrender of the whole person to God, who does not justify anyone through his or her grace on the basis of moral achievements but on the basis of faith alone, so that this faith can be shown in works of love. Human beings are justified and yet always at the same time (*simul*) sinners who constantly need forgiveness afresh, who are only on the way to perfection. . . .

The Problematical Results of the Lutheran Reformation

The Lutheran movement developed a great dynamic and was able to spread powerfully not only in Germany but beyond, in Lithuania, Sweden, Finland, Denmark and Norway. Parallel to the events in Germany, in Switzerland, which had already begun to detach itself from the empire since the middle of the fifteenth century, an independent, more radical form of Reformation had been established by Ulrich Zwingli and later Jean Calvin which, with its understanding of the church, was to make more of an impact than Lutheranism in both the old world and the new. But it was Luther himself at any rate who in the 1520s and 1530s succeeded in establishing the Reformation movement within Germany.

Indeed, Germany had split into two confessional camps. And in view of the threat to the empire from the Turks, who in 1526 had defeated the Hungarians at Mohács and in 1529 had advanced as far as Vienna, Luther had even asked which was more dangerous for Christianity, the power of the papacy or the power of Islam; he saw both as religions of works and the law. At the end of his life Luther saw the future of the Reformation churches in far less rosy terms than in the year of the great breakthrough. Indeed in the last years of his life, although he was indefatigably active to the end, Luther became increasingly subject, on top of apocalyptic anxieties about the end of the world and illnesses, to depression, melancholy, manic depressions and spiritual temptations. And the reasons for this growing pessimism about the world and human beings were real—not just psychological and medical. He was not spared great disappointments.

First, the original Reformation enthusiasm soon ran out of steam. Congregational life often fell short of it; many who were not ready for the 'freedom of a Christian' also lost all church support with the collapse of the Roman system. And even in the Lutheran camp, many people asked whether men and women had really become so much better as a result of the Reformation. Nor can one overlook an impoverishment in the arts—other than music.

Secondly, the Reformation was coming up against growing political resistance. After the inconsequential Augsburg Reichstag of 1530 (the emperor had 'rejected' the conciliatory 'Augsburg Confession' which Melanchthon had the main part in drafting), in the 1530s the Reformation was able at first not only to consolidate itself in the former territories, but also to extend to further areas, from Württemberg to Brandenburg. But in the 1540s the emperor Charles V, overburdened in foreign politics and at home constantly intent on mediation, had been able to end the wars with Turkey and France. Since the Lutherans had refused to take part in the Council of Trent (because it was under papal leadership: Luther's work *Against the Papacy in Rome, Founded by the Devil*, 1545), the emperor finally felt strong enough to enter into military conflict with the powerful Schmalkald League of Protestants. Moreover the Protestant powers were defeated in these first wars of religion (the Schmalkald wars, 1546/47), and the complete restoration of Roman Catholic conditions (with concessions only over the marriage of priests and the chalice for the laity) seemed only a matter of time. It was only a change of sides by the defeated Moritz of Saxony—he had made a secret alliance with France, forced the emperor to flee through a surprise attack in Innsbruck in 1522, and so also provoked the interruption of the Council of Trent—which saved Protestantism from disaster. The confessional division of Germany between the territories of the old faith and those of the 'Augsburg Confession' was finally sealed by the religious peace of Augsburg in 1555. Since then what prevailed was not religious freedom, but the principle *cuius regio, eius religio*, i.e. religion went with the region. Anyone who did not belong to either of the 'religions' was excluded from the peace.

Moreover, the Protestant camp itself was unable to preserve unity. At a very early stage Protestantism in Germany split into a 'left wing' and a 'right wing' of the Reformation.

The Split in the Reformation

Luther had roused the spirits, but there were some that he would only get rid of by force. These were the spirits of enthusiasm, which while certainly feeding on mediaeval roots, were remarkably encouraged by Luther's emergence. A great many individual interests and individual revolts began to spread under the cloak of Luther's name, and soon Luther found himself confronted with a second, 'left-wing' front. Indeed Luther's opponents on the left (enthusiastic turmoil, riots and an iconoclastic movement as early as 1522 in his own city of Wittenberg!) were soon at least as dangerous for his enterprise of Reformation as his right-wing opponents, the traditionalists orientated on Rome. If the 'papists' appealed to the Roman system, the 'enthusiasts' practised an often fanatical religious subjectivism and enthusiasm which appealed to the direct personal experience of revelation and the spirit ('inner voice', 'inner light'). Their first agitator and Luther's most important rival, the pastor Thomas Münzer, combined Reformation ideas with ideas of social revolution: the implementation of the Reformation by force, if need be with no heed to existing law, and the establishment of the thousand-year kingdom of Christ on earth!

But Luther—who politically was evidently trapped in a view 'from above' and has been vigorously criticized for that from Thomas Münzer through Friedrich Engels to Ernst Bloch—was not prepared to draw such radical social conclusions from his radical demand for the freedom of the Christian and to support with corresponding clarity the legitimate demands of the peasants (whose independence was manifestly threatened and increasingly exploited) against princes and the nobility. Despite all the reprehensible outbursts, were not the demands of the peasants also quite reasonable and justified? Or was it all just a misunderstanding, indeed a misuse, of the gospel? Luther, too, could not deny the economic and legal distress of the peasants.

But a plan for reform would by no means *a priori* have been an illusion. Why not? Because the democratic order of the Swiss confederacy, for the peasants of southern Germany the ideal for a new order, could have been a quite viable model. However, all this was alien to Luther, trapped in his Thuringian perspective and now with his conservative tendencies confirmed. Horrified by news of the atrocities in the peasant revolts, he fatally took the side of the authorities and justified the brutal suppression of the peasants.

The Freedom of the Church?

As well as the left-wing Reformation there was the right wing. And here we must note that the ideal of the free Christian church, which Luther had enthusiastically depicted for his contemporaries in his programmatic writings, was not realized in the German empire. Granted, countless churches were liberated by Luther from the domination of secularized bishops who were hostile to reform, and above all from 'captivity' by the Roman Curia, from its absolutist desire to rule and its financial exploitation. But what was the result?

In principle Luther had advocated the doctrine of state and church as the 'two realms'. But at the same time, in view of all the difficulties with Rome on the one hand and with enthusiasts and rebels on the other, he assigned to the local rulers (and not all of them were like Frederick 'the Wise') the duty of protecting the church and maintaining order in it. As the Catholic bishops in the Lutheran sphere had mostly left, the princes were to take on the role of 'emergency bishops'. But the 'emergency bishops' very soon became 'summepiscopi' who attributed quasi-episcopal authority to themselves. And the people's Reformation now in various respects became a princes' Reformation.

In short, the Lutheran churches which had been freed from the 'Babylonian captivity' quickly found themselves in almost complete and often no less oppressive dependence on their own rulers, with all their lawyers and church administrative organs (consistories). The princes who even before the Reformation had worked against peasants and citizens for the internal unification of their territories (which had often been thrown together haphazardly) and a coherent league of subjects had become excessively powerful as a result of the secularization of church land and the withdrawal of the church. The local ruler finally became something like a pope in his own territory.

No, the Lutheran Reformation did not directly prepare the way (as is so often claimed in Protestant church historiography) for the modern world, freedom of religion and the French revolution (a further epoch-making paradigm shift would be necessary for this), but first of all for princely absolutism and despotism. So in general, in Lutheran Germany—with Calvin, things went otherwise—what was realized was not the free Christian church but the rule of the church by princes, which is questionable for Christians; this was finally to come to a well-deserved end in Germany only with the revolution after the First World War. But even in the time of National Socialism, the resistance of the Lutheran churches to a totalitarian regime of terror like that of Hitler was decisively weakened by the doctrine of two realms, by the subordination of the churches to state authority which had been customary since Luther, and the emphasis on the obedience of the citizen in worldly matters. It can only be mentioned in passing here that in the sermons before his death Martin Luther had spoken in such an ugly and un-Christian way against the Jews that the National Socialists did not find it difficult to cite him as a key witness for their hatred of Jews and their antisemitic agitation. But these were not Luther's last words, nor should they be mine.

I would like to close with three great statements which are utterly characteristic of Luther.

First, the dialectical conclusion of his work 'The Freedom of a Christian': 'We conclude, therefore, that a Christian lives not in himself, but in Christ and in his neighbour. Otherwise he is not a Christian. He lives in Christ through faith, in his neighbour through love. By faith he is caught up beyond himself into God. By love he descends beneath himself into his neighbour. Yet he always remains in God and in his love . . . As you see, it is a spiritual and true freedom and makes our hearts free from all sins, laws and commands. It is more excellent than all other liberty which is external, as heaven is more excellent than earth. May Christ give us liberty both to understand and to preserve.'

Then Luther's summary plea before the emperor and the Reichstag at Worms: 'Unless I am convinced by the testimony of the Scriptures or by clear reason (for I do not trust either in the Pope or in councils alone, since it is well known that they have often erred and contradicted themselves), I am bound by the Scriptures I have quoted and as my conscience is captive to the Word of God, I cannot and I will not retract anything, since it is neither safe nor right to go against the conscience. God help me. Amen.'

And finally, the last thing that Luther wrote: 'Nobody can understand Virgil in his *Eclogues* and *Georgics* unless he has first been a shepherd or a farmer for five years. Nobody understands Cicero in his letters unless he has been engaged in public affairs of some consequence for twenty years. Let nobody suppose that he has tasted the Holy Scriptures sufficiently unless he has ruled over the churches with the prophets for a hundred years. Therefore there is something wonderful, first, about John the Baptist; second, about Christ; third, about the apostle. "Lay not your hand on this divine Aeneid, but bow before it, adore its every trace." We are beggars. That is true.'

POSTSCRIPT

Did Martin Luther's Reforms Improve the Lives of European Christians?

More balanced accounts of Luther's life and work that credit him with bringing about needed reforms while acknowledging his personal and professional failings.

Roland Bainton's acclaimed biography *Here I Stand: A Life of Martin Luther* (Abingdon, 1950) is a good place to begin understanding this complex reformer. Bainton profiles Katherine von Bora and other women in *Women of the Reformation in Germany and Italy* (Augsburg Fortress Publishers, 1971). Jonathan W. Zophy's *A Short History of Renaissance and Reformation Europe: Dances Over Fire and Water*, 2d ed. (Prentice Hall, 1998) covers cultural, economic, religious, political, and social developments and includes gender as a significant subject for historical analysis.

Other biographies include Heiko Oberman's *Luther: Man Between God and the Devil* (Yale University Press, 1989) and Eric Gritsch's *Martin—God's Court Jester: Luther in Retrospect* (Augsburg Fortress Publishers, 1983). Which contains an excellent historiographic chapter entitled "God's Jester Before the Court of History." Perhaps the most respected work is Martin Brechts' three-volume biography *Martin Luther*, translated by James L. Schaaf (Fortress Press, 1985). Richard Marius's *Martin Luther: The Christian Between God and Death* (Belknap Press, 1999) laments the carnage that resulted from Luther's reforms. Martin Marty's *Martin Luther: A Penguin Life* (Viking, 2004) is an excellent new popular biography.

For background about the times that produced Luther and other reformers, Vivian Gren's *The European Reformation* (Sutton Publishing Limited, 1998) offers a helpful time line of dates and suggestions for further reading. Its opening chapter "The Medieval Background" sets the context for Luther, Zwingli, the English Reformation, and Calvin, which are discussed more extensively in later chapters. A massive collection of Luther's writings is available in the 55-volume *Luther's Works*, edited by Helmut Lehman and Jaroslav Pelikan (Concordia and Fortress Presses, 1955–1975).

Films for the Humanities & Sciences has released "Revolution of Conscience: The Life, Convictions, and Legacy of Martin Luther" [ISBN 0-7365-8014-X], which includes accessible narration, period paintings, and choral music. In historical fiction, *Children of Disobedience: The Love Story of Martin Luther and Katarina von Bora* (Crossroad, 2000), by award-winning German novelist Asta Scheib, brings a passionate marriage to life. Unfortunately, it offers little insight into Luther's reforms and, in contrast with the historical record, presents Katarina as increasingly afraid and confused.

ISSUE 16

Were the Witch-Hunts in Premodern Europe Misogynistic?

YES: Anne Llewellyn Barstow, from "On Studying Witchcraft as Women's History: A Historiography of the European Witch Persecutions," *Journal of Feminist Studies in Religion* (Fall 1988)

NO: Robin Briggs, from "Women as Victims? Witches, Judges and the Community," *French History* (1991)

ISSUE SUMMARY

YES: History professor Anne Llewellyn Barstow claims that the European witch-hunt movement made women its primary victims and was used as an attempt to control their lives and behavior.

NO: History professor Robin Briggs states that although women were the witch-hunt's main victims, gender was not the only determining factor in this sociocultural movement.

Virgins and whores, goddesses and devils, mystics and conjurers—historically, women have been perceived as "troublesome creatures." Their very existence has often been seen as a threat to human society, especially with regard to their sexuality. This has resulted in constant attempts on the part of the patriarchal system, which has so dominated the course of history, to control women's lives. Sometimes this system has resulted in second-class status, shattered dreams, and crushed spirits for women; other times the treatment of women was downright misogynistic. The witch hunt craze of early modern Europe was one such example.

Although belief in witches and witchcraft dates back to recorded history's earliest days, the persecution of those accused reached its apex in Europe's early modern period, especially the sixteenth and seventeenth centuries. In the northern, western, and central parts of the continent, witch trials became a frightening reality, as thousands were tried and many were executed for their evil doings and "pacts with the devil." Although exact figures are not known, a moderate estimate of 200,000 tried with half of those executed, has been offered by Anne Llewellyn Barstow. And certainly germane to this issue is the fact that 80 percent of both groups, those brought to trial and those executed, were women.

What factors caused this wave of witch hysteria? First of all, the Protestant Reformation had created a religious uncertainty that gave the witch hunts a *raison d'etre*. Protestants and Catholics battled for the hearts, minds, and souls of Europe's populace, and religious wars became the order of the day. *Malleus Maleficarum (A Hammer of Witches) of Heinrich Kramer and James Sprenger,* two Dominican priests, attests to the volatile religious mood of the day. Published in 1487, it describes in graphic detail, the evil committed by witches, instructions on how to thwart their powers, elicit confessions through torture, and how to punish them, all in gruesome detail. With this mindset, the witch hunts were a predictable outcome.

In the political realm, with the growth of national states in Europe and their creation of divine right monarchies, political orthodoxy became as important as religious orthodoxy. Both had to be enforced to keep the dynastic ship afloat. Those who deviated, had to pay the price.

Social factors also entered into the witchcraze fray. Tensions between and amongst classes permeated the era and led to violent behavior usually geared to keeping the lower classes subjugated. If women had any idea of using these conditions to assert themselves, the trials and resultant executions served as brutal reminders of the power of the status quo and the lengths to which those in power would go to maintain societal control.

Of course, one cannot escape the one constant of the multicentury witch hunt: most of the victims were women. But was gender the only factor in determining the outcome of the witch hunts? Were women singled out for prosecution solely on the basis of their sex? Or were there other factors—political, economic, social, legal, or local—that influenced the witch hunts. These questions had been raised in the historical debates of previous generations, but interest was renewed in the 1960s, presumably due to the increased attention given to women's studies. This included the study of violence against women, which has reached epic proportions in the contemporary world. Were there signs of such actions against women in the past? Was the witchcraze just one extreme example of violence against women?

A seminal article by Hugh Trevor-Roper entitled "The European Witchcraze of the Sixteenth and Seventeenth Centuries," *Encounter* (May and June, 1967), later republished in *The European Witchcraze in the Sixteenth and Seventeenth Centuries, and Other Essays* (Harper Torchbooks, 1969) got the historical process started. Still, it was not until recent times that the idea of the witch hunts as exemplary of misogyny or hatred of women reached center stage. Since that time, it has been impossible to remove the gender factor from any witchcraft studies.

The two readings in the issue represent the best in recent witchcraft scholarship. Anne Llewellyn Barstow makes a persuasive case for gender as the key factor in determining witch hunt outcomes. She sees this as part of a long struggle to "keep women down." Robin Briggs admits that the large preponderance of the witch hunt's victims were women, and gender certainly was a factor in the genesis of the craze. But he favors the presence of socio-economic, political, religious, and legal factors as better means to understanding the witchcraze; After all, misogyny had been present since the beginnings of patriarchy.

YES

Anne Llewellyn Barstow

On Studying Witchcraft as Women's History

On average, witchcraft, the ultimate in human evil, was sex-related to women in much the same proportion as sanctity, the ultimate in human good, was sex-related to men.

— Christina Larner, *Witchcraft and Religion*

After years of being relegated to folkloric and esoteric studies, European witchcraft is beginning to emerge as an important chapter in early modern history. In particular, the persecutions of the sixteenth and seventeenth centuries have become the subject of scholarly attention. One might assume that the persecutions have been seen as an integral part of women's history, but that is not the case. The witch craze has been interpreted by most historians as *not* a matter of gender.

Given that over 80 percent of the victims were women, this is a surprising and, I believe, a disturbing conclusion. I will therefore examine what difference it makes when one subjects this material to the insights of women's history.

Historians have in fact interpreted the witch-craze as the result of religious upheaval, of the growth of the nation-state, of the isolation of mountain folk—of anything, in short, rather than of what women were doing or were perceived as being. When one focuses on the roles women played in early modern society, and how those roles changed in the sixteenth century, a different picture emerges. This approach enables one to see that women had served as healers, midwives, and counsellors, using an age-old combination of experience "common sense") and magical techniques to cure and advise. Long respected for these skills, they began to be attacked for them at the end of the Middle Ages. Further, one must ask the economic question: How were women coping with the increasing gap between poor and rich that emerged in the sixteenth century? When one sees how women's basic options narrowed, then one is ready to ask about other changes in sixteenth-century society that affected them, such as legal shifts.

One must remember that European women *as a group* were first subject to criminal persecutions on witchcraft charges. Having been kept out of the courts because they were seen by law as minors, women suddenly were held

From Anne Llewellyn Barstow, "On Studying Witchcraft as Women's History: A Historiography of the European Witch Persecutions," *Journal of Feminist Studies in Religion*, vol. 4, no. 2 (Fall 1988). Copyright © 1988 by Anne Llewellyn Barstow. Reprinted by permission of the author. Notes omitted.

legally responsible for their actions, once witch allegations were made. Seen as a group of independent adults, women thus entered European legal history by being accused of witchcraft. And those accusations were heavily negative about female sexuality: women were blamed for preventing conception, causing miscarriage, abortion, and stillbirth, making men impotent, seducing men, having sex with the devil, giving birth to demons. Underlying these charges lay the fact that women healers were the authorities on sexuality, which led to a deadly professional rivalry between folk healers and priests and university-trained doctors. Added to this rivalry was the conviction that women were more strongly sexed than men, which led to deep-seated fears in some males.

I believe that the sudden rise in prosecutions for witchcraft that began in Europe c. 1560 was related in part to attempts to take away women's control of their sexual and reproductive lives. This fitted into the strongly patriarchal concept of family for which the sixteenth century is known, and into the attack by doctors on midwives and folk healers, and by Reformers, both Catholic and Protestant, on traditional sexual mores.

Although men could be arraigned on the charge of witchcraft, and were prosecuted in small numbers, the craze was aimed mostly at women: 80 percent of the accused and 85 percent of those executed were female. Men were associated with witchcraft chiefly because they were related to women who were already suspect or because they had committed other crimes. And yet, although men "qualified," women were overwhelmingly singled out. The extent of the attack on women becomes clear when we recall that 92 percent of the accused in the English county of Essex were women, and that all but two of the female inhabitants of Langendorf in the Rhineland were arrested. In twelfth-century Kiev when periodic fears of witchcraft arose, all of the old women of the area were seized and subjected to the ordeal by cold water (thrown, bound hand and foot, into the Dnieper River). Christina Larner, the analyst of Scottish witchcraft, observed that there were periods "when no mature woman in Fife or East Lothian can have felt free from the fear of accusation." Given these cases, we see that the notorious examples of the two German villages left with only one female inhabitant apiece and of Rheinback, where one person, most often female, out of every two families was put to death, are not unbelievable. Christina Larner put the question precisely when she asked, "Was witch-hunting also woman-hunting?"

Despite such evidence, historians have for the most part not dealt with the persecutions as an attack on women. And yet the first major research published on witchcraft, the documents book and analysis brought out by Joseph Hansen at the turn of the century, had offered a promising beginning. Hansen recognized that women had been singled out as victims, and he gathered some of the more misogynist materials to illustrate this discrimination. Hansen's insights were not entirely lost on Wallace Notestein, who in 1911 devoted one paragraph of his study of English witchcraft to the subject.

Observing that about six times as many women were indicted as men, he concluded that "this was to be expected." Implying that by nature women would be suspected of witchcraft, Notestein left it at that.

Hansen's insights had no further influence on research for the next half century. While the issue of gender virtually dropped out of the discussions, what remained was a disturbing glimpse of how historians saw women in history. L'Estrange Ewen's first analysis of the English Home Counties trials, for example, provided plenty of information about misogyny in the courts, but he did not mention women as a category at all. Four years later, however, while publishing further trial documentation, he briefly stated his thoughts about the victims:

> That many of the condemned women, although innocent of witchcraft, were really undesirable neighbours cannot be doubted. Mental institutes not being features of the social life, numbers of melancholics were at large, others again, mentally sound, ranked as thieves, cozeners, whores, blasphemers, blackmailers, abortionists, perhaps even poisoners. Mentally degraded, they allowed vermin and domestic animals to suck or lick their blood, although many of such recorded practices can have been nothing more than misunderstanding or hallucination.

Not only condescending to the victims, Ewen went on to libel them:

> At heart they were murderers, and morally as guilty as cutthroat or poisoner. But their confessions are not greatly to be relied upon, obtained as they were by deceit and duress, and, it may be supported, sometimes coloured by vanity.

Although he conceded that "occasionally the witches did possess abnormal power," he had little awareness of the positive role they had filled in premodern society as healers and diviners; instead, he perpetuated the worst of the "hag" stereotype about these women.

In disparaging the very nature of women, writers such as Ewen had of course a long tradition to draw on. In the 1480s when Kramer and Sprenger, authors of the witch-hunters manual, *Malleus Maleficarum*, described women as liars, unfaithful, immoderate, sexually insatiable, and downright evil, they quoted at length from biblical, classical, and medieval sources. As Barbara Walker observes, "From Terrible Crone to castrating witch was not a large step. . . . She had many guises: she-demon, witch, sorceress, succubus, Hag." The witch-hunters of the sixteenth century had models of castrating, death-dealing female types with which to demonize their own women, and many twentieth-century historiographers of the witch-craze have not demythologized their own attitudes toward the women they write about.

In the same category is Julio Caro Baroja's brief mention, at the end of his 1965 book on Basque witchcraft, of the sick, "slightly mad, weird" old women who are his typical witches. Seeing them as pathetic outsiders "with an overdeveloped sense of their own importance," he concluded that "a woman usually becomes a witch after the initial failure of her life as a woman, after frustrated or illegitimate love affairs have left her with a sense of impotence or disgrace," and he regretted that "those unfortunate sick people" were put to death because their type of neurosis was not understood. I conclude from this that it is just as well that most historians did not attempt a gender analysis before we had the insights of women's history to guide us.

The 1967 essay which launched the recent revival of witchcraft studies, H. R. Trevor-Roper's "European Witch-Craze of the Sixteenth and Seventeenth Centuries," while utterly deficient in gender analysis, sheds some light on how historians were missing the point. While making an important analysis of how social tension was generated "by unassimilable social groups," he had a logical opening to discuss women and why some of them were seen as unassimilable. But he could not seem to think of "women" as a group, as a societal category. Sixty pages later, at the end of the essay, he finally identified the victims, calling them "hysterical women in a harsh rural world or in artificial communities—in ill-regulated nunneries . . . or in special regions like the Pays de Labourd, where . . . the fishermen's wives were left deserted for months." Again, we find the theory of the sexually deprived female. But for most of his essay, the victims have no identity. Trevor-Roper understood the dynamics of the medieval persecution of heretics, Jews, and Moors, and realized that the witch-craze was also a persecution of "unassimilable" groups—but thinking of women as either hysterical or as sex-starved individuals, he could not draw any conclusions about them as a group.

Trevor-Roper's controversial essay inspired a series of archival studies of witch trials, written in order to refute him but all showing their debt to him nonetheless. Alan Macfarlane's careful analysis of the Essex trials confirmed that 92 percent of the victims there were women, an extraordinarily high percentage, but he concluded that "there is no evidence that hostility between the sexes lay behind their prosecutions." Keith Thomas in his influential study of English folk religion concurred with Macfarlane. While denying that either misogyny or psychological factors mattered, he made the useful point that economic and social considerations are valid, because women "were the most dependent members of the community, and thus the most vulnerable to accusation." He also pointed out that charges of female sexual irregularities— illegitimacy, promiscuity, sexual voracity—figured in the trials, but he seemed not to realize that these are the stuff of which misogyny is made.

Both Macfarlane and Thomas said that the question of why women are singled out must be looked into—but neither of them did so. Succeeding works documented a vast amount of woman-hatred, making it all the more surprising that scholars still did not see gender as the central issue. Erik Midelfort's research on southwestern Germany is a case in point. While analyzing massive witch panics such as Wiesensteig where sixty-three women were burned to death, and Quedlinburg, where 133 witches, mostly female, were executed in one day, Midelfort suggested that "women seemed . . . to provoke somehow an intense misogyny at times" and asked that we study "why that group *attracted to itself* the scapegoating mechanism." Not content with blaming the victims, Midelfort went on to deny that there had been a particular tradition of misogyny in the sixteenth century. Complaining that this alleged tradition had been documented "only in literary sources," he overlooked the fact that his own material was primary proof for it.

By this time in the development of witchcraft studies, a pattern of denial is clear. Historians were denying that misogyny and patriarchy are valid historical categories and were refusing to treat women as a recognizable historical group. Reading these works is like reading accounts of the Nazi holocaust in which everyone agrees that the majority of victims were Jewish, but no one mentions anti-Semitism or the history of violent persecution against Jews, implying that it was "natural" for Jews to be victims. Without mention of a tradition of oppression of women, the implication for the sixteenth century is that of course women would be attacked—and that it must somehow have been their fault. This is what historians conclude when they have no awareness of traditional misogyny or traditional oppression of women.

In 1948 in the work of the researcher of northern French witchcraft, Emile Brouette, misogyny was finally related again to the persecutions. Even if one believes that it is possible to be antifeminist without burning witches, he maintained, still it is theologically only one step from scorning a woman to believing that she is a servant of the devil. This perception was rejected by Brouette's successor there in witchcraft studies, Fr. Pierre Villette, who insisted that it was "psychologie féminine" and that alone which explained the large numbers of female victims; in other words, women do threaten men and drive them to attack. Villette even excused the virulent misogyny of the authors of the *Malleus Maleficarum,* in light of this frightening "female psychology."

Working twenty years later in the same northern French area as Villette had covered in the 1950s, Robert Muchembled drew quite different conclusions. Ascribing the preponderance of female victims (82 percent) partly to traditional misogyny, literary as well as theological, lay as well as clerical, Muchembled moved the argument along by tying female oppression to the general sexual repression of the two Reformations. His proofs were the increased punishment for prenuptial pregnancy, bastardy, and adultery, with heavier penalties against women than men. He also documented the intrusion of the state into village life, which brought elite fantasies about witches and an impersonal bureaucratic form of justice that seriously disturbed traditional village relationships. As society became more repressive, the charges against alleged witches became wilder: while some of the accused had had reputations for lasciviousness, even women with good names were now accused of having sex with the devil or keeping a demon lover. Muchembled was right to broaden the scope and to see that the witch-hunt involved persecuting women for their sexuality.

The years after 1972, when Midelfort's work was published, show a change in scholars' interpretations of this evidence, a change which must be credited to the nascent movement for women's history. Midelfort himself took a different position nine years later, claiming that "one cannot begin to understand the European witch-hunt without recognizing that it displayed a burst of misogyny without parallel in Western history," and he even suggested that future research should investigate the fantasies of the bishops and university professors who presided over the German trials. This indicates a more sympathetic approach, one perhaps influenced by the work in women's history accomplished in the intervening decade.

In a general interpretation of early witchcraft up to 1500, Jeffrey Burton Russell made a major attempt to place women at the center of the problem. Russell understood one role of medieval women, namely their leadership in heretical groups; he appreciated the extent to which medieval heretical groups appealed to women by offering women roles from which they were excluded by the church. But he failed to see that folk religion (folk magic, witchcraft) was another valid alternative for women. Throughout, he accepted the demonologists' definitions of witchcraft, calling it a "violent form" of "feminine discontent" involving "criminal" activity. Because he insisted on associating witchcraft primarily with heresy, rather than with folk religion, and saw it as ultimately subversive, he was forced to conclude that the alleged witch engaged in violent, even criminal, activity, leaving the issue not far from the "woman as hag" position. In a more recent work, Russell connects suspected women with hags even more strongly: ". . . in Christian Europe, the hag image was projected upon human beings. The European witch, then, must be understood not just as a sorceress, but as the incarnation of the hag. She is a totally evil and depraved person under the domination and command of Satan."

Two new comprehensive studies that cover the entire witch-hunting period, go further in searching for gender factors. In Joseph Klaits's 1985 book, misogyny is dissected as part of theology, medical attitudes, law, art, ageism, and poverty. Woman-hatred is identified in familial attitudes and in sexual exploitation. That Klaits devotes half a chapter to "sexual politics," a discussion he placed early in the book, shows that he understands the institutional nature of the problem—that the social order felt threatened by nonconformist women, felt that church and family, and even the state, were threatened. And he is one of the few (Muchembled is another) who has analyzed the sadistic impulse in the witch-hunt.

But Klaits sees not women but the Reformation (meaning both Protestant and Catholic) as the main factor in the persecutions, blaming both the religious upheaval and, chiefly, the antisexual reformism of the Reformation period for the extremes of the witch-craze, and in doing so he shifts the focus away from women. Women, after all, were not the main actors in the Reformation drama, so Klaits brings us back to looking at what men did. It matters little to witchcraft studies whether one explains witchcraft by what lawyers, judges, doctors, theologians, bishops or Reformers did—all of these explanations miss the central point, because all pull the focus away from the victims, from the women themselves. And Klaits states categorically that women are not the central issue. Even his emphasis on them as sexual objects, true though it is to the trial material, has the effect of showing us the victims from the outside.

Brian Levack's study, intended like Klaits's to be used as a textbook, affirms at one point that witchcraft was sex related, and discusses the many ways in which women were more vulnerable than men to these charges. But Levack seldom mentions gender in the rest of his book.

A model of gender analysis finally appeared in 1976, E. William Monter's study of the witch-craze in the Swiss-French borderlands. Affirming the widespread use of black and white magic in preindustrial Europe, he is sympathetic to women's use of magic as a compensation for their legal and economic disadvantages. He lays their persecution to their gender and maintains unequivocally that sex was the crucial factor, more important than poverty, age, or any other. Defining misogyny as more than the usual woman-hatred in family and in theology. Monter adds the important observation that witch prosecutions rose and fell with legal action against two other sex-linked crimes: infanticide and sodomy. Infanticide was resorted to almost entirely by single women, and both infanticide and sodomy were seen by sixteenth-century society as "unnatural." Since witchcraft was seen as "unnatural," sinful, and a single woman's crime, it is not surprising that the sixteenth century became "interested in executing women as witches." Concluding that "women were the specially designated victims," that "witchcraft, as the demonologists had repeatedly insisted, was sex-linked," Monter set the stage for the type of gender analysis which must be done on the witchcraft materials, but he did not follow through on these insights.

The late Scottish sociologist Christina Larner produced the most thorough gender investigation to date. Using her triple skills in sociology, history, and religion, Larner accepted the positive use of witchcraft by poor village females ("women embracing witchcraft"), saw the persecutions as motivated by a desire to control independent-minded (and -mouthed) women, and made male hatred of the female body into a real, believable factor in the craze. One expects her to conclude that gender is the central issue, and she does affirm that "all women were potential witches," that "the witch hunt was part of the sex war," and that "witch-hunting *is* woman-hunting." And yet she wasn't satisfied with these formulations, and repeatedly modified them: "the reasons why witches were hunted are not directly related to their being women, but to their being thought evil"; "the crime of witchcraft, while sex-related, was not sex specific"; the hunt was "no more a persecution of women than the prosecution of killers was a persecution of men." Finally concluding, that "witch-hunting is *not* woman-hunting." Larner maintained that at any rate the questions raised by the issue of woman-hunting were too narrow. Recommending instead that we ask broader, presumably more important questions of the craze, questions about Christianity as a political ideology, about crises in law and order—that is, the more political questions—she turned away from the theory of persecution by gender, which she more than anyone had validated.

Once again women as a gender group are seen not to matter and the questions of women's history are considered too narrow. Larner's conclusions are the most disappointing of all, for she had a keen awareness of how the oppression of women works in history. She doesn't make clear why one must forego questions about woman-hunting in order to work on the political issues, nor does she see that the woman-hunting questions *are* political. Material that shows women as "threatening to patriarchal order," or religion as "relentlessly patriarchal" is neither narrow nor apolitical.

To sum up: the problems one faces in studying witchcraft as a persecution by gender are many. First one must acknowledge that folk healers and diviners were useful, sought-after members of society, pre-1500. Although they were reperceived after that as suspect, even as evil, by elite groups, and eventually by villagers as well, the historian has no grounds to caricature them as hags. Second the distinction between folk religious practices and witchcraft accusations must be observed. The latter were the grotesque distortions made by the European elite of the actual, useful functions of folk healers and counsellors, made in order to discredit them. Finally, one must distinguish between sex and gender. Despite the emphasis on female sexuality in the trial records and procedures, the historian is ill advised to interpret the victims, no matter how sympathetically, as sex objects. Women were more than sex objects in sixteenth-century society, they served as midwives, healers, counsellors, farmers, alewives, spinners, domestic servants, assistants to their husbands in craft work, etc., and their productive, as well as reproductive, roles shaped how they were seen. Only when the historian distinguishes between gender roles and sexuality can we properly evaluate why women were perceived as a threat.

A lack of understanding of patriarchy as a historical category and of how it functions in society is another weak point in most of the works cited here. Without this understanding one doesn't see that women were accused primarily by men, tried by male juries, searched by male prickers, sentenced by male judges, tortured by male jailers, burned to death by male executioners—while being prayed over by male pastors. The patriarchal system also explains why many women accused other females: if a woman displeased or threatened the men of her community, she would also be seen as dangerous by the women who depended on or identified with those men. The internalization of "who is not acceptable" goes even deeper than that: women—and other oppressed groups—sometimes try to outdo their oppressors in scorning persons perceived as outsiders, in hope of being accepted, or tolerated, themselves. In the witchcraft trials, the poor attacked those even poorer; and poor women attacked those women even further out of power than they.

How misogyny, the hatred of women, in addition to patriarchy, the rule over women, caused females to be singled out, needs to be made clear. It was antiwoman theology that turned the attention of the inquisitional courts to women *as women,* a process that was quickly taken up by secular courts as early as c. 1400. This was not caused by something innately evil about women, nor any change in their nature; the cause was the specific connection that Dominican inquisitors and theologians (de Savigliano, Nider, Jacquier, Kramer, Sprenger) made between witchcraft and women, based on ancient Christian beliefs about the defective, evil nature of women. When historians deal with this tradition of misogyny, rather than blaming the victim for somehow "attracting" hatred, then the persecutions can be understood. Both patriarchy and misogyny are valid, and in this case essential, historical factors.

Furthermore, this is not a one-issue topic. A number of false leads have been followed, and the concept of persecution by gender has been repeatedly denied, in order to narrow down the analysis to some one key factor: the Reformation(s), community tensions, proto-capitalist agriculture, more abstract forms of justice, demographic change (more single women), plague, etc. While all of the above are factors, none of them is *the* factor. I suggest that we stop looking for a central, unifying explanation for this very complex, messy, rich phenomenon. Witchcraft, far from being odd, esoteric, or disgusting, turns out to be a capital topic for studying the transition from medieval to early modern society. By forcing the historian to focus on women's lives and how they were changed and limited by the greater power of the seventeenth-century churches and states, the witchcraft phenomenon illuminates the racism and imperialism that Europeans were beginning to export around the world. What European men and women did to the people whom they colonized, European men first did to European women. Traditional patriarchal structures and misogynistic attitudes were heightened by new legal, religious, and political arrangements. Women's lives *were* changed; some of their old roles were challenged, and as they resisted, they were made the new scapegoats for an expanding but insecure society.

This dynamic history cannot be reduced to a central cause. It must be dealt with as multifaceted, as filled with internal change and contradiction. The thread that runs through it, the only constant, is the gender of the victims. It is from the beginning, and becomes even more emphatically, a persecution of women, which sheds light on the history of persecution, criminality, poverty, religious teaching, the family, and how men and women relate to each other.

Women as Victims?
Witches, Judges and the Community

. . . The identification of witches with women was already standard form, it would appear, in the decades when trials were at their height. The demonologists would have been shocked to find their confident assertions turned against them by modern writers who use the persecution as prime evidence for man's inhumanity to women, often seeming to assume that the sex ratio was not de Lancre's 90 per cent, or even Bodin's 98 per cent, but a stark 100 per cent. This is sometimes coupled with assertions that the numbers executed were of holocaust proportions: a vastly inflated figure of 9 million women supposedly executed as witches in early modern Europe seems to have gained a certain currency. Although no one will ever know the exact number of trials or executions, because of poor record-keeping, the result of every detailed local investigation to date has been to reduce them dramatically. It would seem that 50,000 would be a plausible figure for total executions in Europe, and that some 20 per cent of these would be of men.

So far as the general public is concerned, attacking prevalent myths about witchcraft is likely to have no better results than Don Quixote's assault on the windmills. Among historians one hopes that it may be a different matter, yet the topic still seems to have an alarming capacity to generate heroic oversimplifications or absurdities, which then spill over from one book into another. A classic example is the association of witchcraft with midwives, apparently based on one of the more hysterical passages in the *Malleus malefi-carum*. This hoary old myth is repeated by the great majority of writers on witchcraft, even when they admit that it fails to hold good for their own area; it is cited as evidence for male hostility to a female paramedical specialism, and related to the emergence of men midwifes in the seventeenth century. If appears to be totally unfounded, for a painstaking check of all known British cases reveals precisely two rather dubious instances in England, and 14 out of some 3,000 accused to in Scotland. In both countries midwives are seriously under-represented among the suspects, while in France and Lorraine they are equally elusive; so far just one case has been found in Lorraine, and even after confessing to numerous acts of witchcraft the accused rather touchingly insisted that she had always done her duty as a midwife. All later demonologists seem to have referred back to the *Malleus* and to a brief reference by Nider, these early authors were appropriating a standard charge against the Jews, then turning it into a typical inversion, motif, with the midwife killing the babies instead of protecting them. When an argument sounds plausible, appeals to widely held preconceptions and can be backed up by a few genuine cases, it risks becoming virtually indestructible. Facile general explanations of this kind are frequently applied to aspects of witchcraft, and a recent example has been provided by Stanislas Andreski. He claims that all existing explanations are fundamentally unsound, whereas the obvious answer is that women were being persecuted as the agency for the spread of virulent syphilis. The case is supported on the grounds of general chronological patterns (which are far from convincing even if one accepts this dubious line of reasoning), alongside some passages selected from the demonologists, which refer to disease in general rather than syphilis in particular. The crucial test for any such theory must come through examination of the trial records, which Andreski never attempts. Another book which advances a general theory on a very thin evidential basis is that by Brian Easlea; here again we find a dubious attempt to argue from chronology, as with the assertion that in the 1630s 'more witches were being burned throughout Europe than at any time previously'. The only area where this is remotely arguable is Germany, and even here the group of local epidemics took place between 1627 and 1632. The author goes on to claim that 'in a time of disaster and hideous death scapegoats will in general be sought. The chosen scapegoat in the two centuries after the publication of the *Malleus Maleficarum* was the female sex, particularly those women living beyond the immediate control of men.' He offers no serious explanation for the formation of this supposed misogynistic consensus, admitting that Christian views hostile to women had been, around rather longer. It may nevertheless be the case that Easlea's statement comes alarmingly close to the received wisdom among most early modern historians.

If we discard the more sweeping and untenable generalizations, three eminently plausible suggestions do emerge from the literature of the subject, although no historian has really addressed the central issue of gender directly and extensively in relation to the European material. Firstly, that women were supposed to employ supernatural means to avenge themselves precisely because they had little direct power against their enemies. Secondly, that men felt deeply insecure about the sexual and social domination they were supposed to exercise over their womenfolk, and projected their own aggression into the female sex as a whole, so that they readily saw women as vengeful and hostile. Thirdly, that social and economic changes produced a much larger group of dependent poor, among whom older women were disproportionately numerous. Of these only the last is really a dynamic factor, in the sense that it refers to changes taking place in approximately the right time-scale, yet it is hardly a sufficient explanation on its own. There has been considerable support for a fourth interpretation, which attaches the persecution to the process of slate-building. According to this view, the development of the absolutist state was linked to the assertion of patriarchal authority at all levels, together with the identification and punishment of deviants, and the repression of popular cultural forms. The difficulty with this thesis, which surely does contain some element of truth, is that it is so hard to identify the detailed mechanisms necessary to give it real substance, and even more those which might extend it to women. Medieval states had persecuted minority groups, notably heretics, Jews and lepers; early modern ones similarly engaged in serious and organized campaigns against religious dissidents. By comparison the persecution of witches appears a rather casual and sporadic affair, in which only a handful of rulers or their immediate servants took any known interest. It does seem to tie in with the criminalization of women, in so far as there was a contemporaneous wave of prosecutions for infanticide and a range of sexual offences, all perhaps being linked to the emergence of a category of crimes against society as opposed to the individual. One other serious interpretation has been, offered recently, by Carol Karlsen in the context of New England witchcraft, essentially that women who inherited substantial property were perceived as threatening the natural order of male dominance. There does seem to be some empirical justification for this in her small sample (although she does not use a control group); it is plainly irrelevant to the European context, however, where most of the accused seem to have been wretchedly poor.

What becomes of these more promising general notions when they are compared with the detailed evidence for France and her borderlands? We have to start with the stunning fact that over a large area of France witchcraft seems to have had no obvious link at all with gender. Bodin, de Lancre and most modern historians are simply wrong to assume that witches were always overwhelmingly women. Of nearly 1,300 witches whose cases went to the *Parlement* of Paris on appeal, just over half were men. The appeal system may have been invoked more often by men, yet there are many reasons to doubt that this has more than a modest effect on the figures. In around 500 cases which did not reach the *Parlement,* although there is a small majority of women, men still make up 42 per cent of the accused. Some local studies also show a predominance of men, as do the *arrêts* which de Lancre himself collected and printed in his 1622 volume. It does appear that as one moves to the east of the *Parlement's ressort* the proportion of women rises towards 70 per cent, which fits very well with the picture just across the border, and suggests that the data, are trustworthy, with, the central and western parts of the *ressort* showing a clear majority of male witches. One should add that the *Parlement* was notably lenient, with only 104 of the accused being executed; women came off slightly worse here, 58 to 46. Still more unexpectedly, the torture was totally ineffective, since only one of 185 persons sent to the *question* confessed. Alfred Soman, who has produced these remarkable findings, offers no explanation for the divergence between northern France and most other regions of Europe. Unfortunately the records are relatively laconic, so that it is difficult to test any hypothesis one might form; the great majority of the men accused were poor peasants and artisans, a fairly representative sample of the *menu peuple.* A tentative suggestion is that popular beliefs about the nature and use of magical powers may, in the relevant areas, have given unusual prominence to masculine activity. The tendency to leniency increased steadily after 1600, until in the period 1626–39 we find just three executions, all of men who admitted making written pacts with the Devil. Over the same period the *Parlement* was dealing with a roughly comparable level of infanticide cases, which it treated very harshly by comparison, well over half the accused being executed. It is tempting to add that in the most spectacular trials of the period, those connected with the great possession cases, we find male priests being denounced by women.

Relatively high proportions of male witches are not uncommon. In his study of south-west Germany Midelfort finds figures rising towards 25 per cent by the 1620s, while Monter's sample of well over a thousand cases from the Jura and the Alps has 22.5 per cent of men. For the department of the Nord, then mostly in the Spanish Netherlands, men made up 18 per cent of a much smaller group of 268. A recent collection of essays on peripheral regions of Europe shows some striking discrepancies, with men accounting for 90 per cent of the accused in Iceland and 60 per cent in Estonia, nearly 50 per cent in Finland, but only 10 per cent in Hungary. A random sample of 100 accused witches from Lorraine contains 28 men, and in these cases the survival of full trial records makes deeper probing possible. When the information about individuals reaches a certain density one can actually draw negative conclusions, since their personal and social positions become clear, so that for instance one can decide whether or not they were regular beggars. The first point is that the age distribution is virtually identical for the two sexes, with just over 90 per cent of the accused giving their age as 40 or over; nearly 70 per cent were over 50, with a remarkable 37 per cent claiming to be over 60. Of the 72 women, 36 were married, 34 widows, 2 unmarried. Ten were healers of some kind, although several appear marginal examples, another 10 were regularly dependent on begging. Among the 28 men we find the usual preponderance of artisans and peasants, with 5 who were closely linked to the care of animals as herdsmen and blacksmiths, and one regular beggar. There were just two married couples, while 6 other individuals of each sex had close relatives already accused. As for the outcome, women did fractionally better than men, with 15 being released and 2 banished, as against 5 and 1, although one man did escape after confessing under torture The vast majority of the accused were poor villagers, no more than a handful enjoying even modest prosperity. These data point to considerable diversity among the suspects; although women over 50 compose 51 per cent of the sample, it would be hard to compile a profile of a typical witch without excluding significant groups. One possible conclusion would be that the preponderance of women can be substantially (although not wholly) explained by the large number of widows, the classic dependent and vulnerable group of early modern society.

A rather clearer pattern emerges when we look at the witnesses, for here there is a marked difference between the trials of men and women. In the former men gave testimony three times more often than women, 427 to 144. When women were on trial men still gave testimony more often, but only by 683 to 519, so that 43 per cent of witnesses were women, and in 30 per cent of cases they were in the majority. In due course it should be possible to refine these figures considerably, to discriminate between witnesses in terms of their attitude to the accused, the significance of their deposition, and so forth. It will also be interesting to determine how many bewitchments were alleged to have been committed against men, women and children respectively. What can be said already is that in a society whose formal structures at least were completely dominated by men, the numbers of women testifying are really rather large, while a subjective impression is that they were just as likely to produce damaging evidence as were the men. The readiness of women to accuse other women does not of course disprove the claim that witch-hunting was women-hunting, since women in a patriarchal society are under severe pressure to conform, which may make them very hostile to feminine deviants who indirectly threaten their own security. This argument obviously has force, yet it can easily be abused, for there is no logical reason why it should not be applied to every conceivable situation, and it is therefore very hard to test. Although some witnesses were obviously reluctant, or made it plain their suspicions had only been aroused by communal opinion, this does not appear to relate to gender. Seen at ground level the hunt is quite clearly one for witches, not some complicated mechanism for persecuting women as such. What leaps off the page in virtually every case is the passionate conviction with which witnesses of both sexes asserted they had suffered grievous harm through the ill will of a neighbour; there is no doubt that they believed in witchcraft quite enough to die of it, for all its lack of objective reality.

The notion that the persecution was stage-managed by the elites, to which even so able a historian as Christina Larner could recently subscribe, seems wildly mistaken. Admittedly there are some isolated examples of elite witch-hunters, such as those of the *bailli* Jean Clere and the inquisitor Father Symard in the Franche-Comté, or Pierre de Lancre in the Labourd. Nicolas Remy, *procureur général* of the duchy of Lorraine, might be thought another instance, but this would be to misunderstand his actual role in the trials, and the meaning of his claim to have helped burn over 800 witches He was in effect the chief ducal prosecutor, who participated in the formal process whereby the papers were reviewed in Nancy, making recommendations and requests to the court there for appropriate action. Remy rarely dealt with suspects in person, nor did he initiate any extensive search for them; denunciations emerged from the local community with no specific prompting from above. As is clear from his own text, he took most of the details he reported from the trial records sent up from the local jurisdictions. Until the edict of 1682 which reduced it to the level of fraud, there was never any specific legislation against witchcraft in either France or Lorraine, since judges had no difficulty construing the offence in terms of existing authorities and legal traditions. The *Parlements* could hardly have initiated persecution, unless they issued special commissions, since they normally functioned only as appeal courts for criminal cases. As Dewald suggests for Rouen, there are probably links between the growth in the number of cases coming up from rural jurisdictions and the treatment of witchcraft. Soman has shown how the *Parlement* of Paris was active in repressing abuses from the 1580s onwards; in 1603 it condemned Jean Minard, the hangman of Rocroi, to the galleys for life. Minard, almost certainly the most lethal of all French witch-hunters, had identified several hundred witches by pricking for the mark, most of them from across the border in the Spanish Netherlands.

Even if we take the more general view of the 'social' offences of witch-craft, infanticide and prostitution, it remains doubtful whether there was any real intention to criminalize women as such. There was a natural tendency to expand central justice, as a means both to emphasize royal supremacy and to enhance the prestige of the expanding corps of loyal officials; the ambitions of this latter group were crucial to the whole process. In Lorraine the relatively weak dukes could not imitate the French monarchy directly; nevertheless, they did succeed from around 1560 in establishing a modest element of judicial review by the court of the *echevins* of Nancy. At the most elementary level the persecution of deviants must always have been attractive to the men in power, since it confirmed their authority and gave it added moral force. In any case they sincerely believed in the conceptions of the moral order enshrined in early modern religious and social thought, even if they sometimes hesitated before trying to apply them in all circumstances. Too much concentration on the justice of the *Parlements* and similar courts, however, risks being seriously misleading. The most striking innovation of the sixteenth century in France was the summary justice of the *maréchaussée*, a development of martial law intended to deal with such offenders as deserters, coiners, highway robbers and sturdy beggars. The *prévôis des maréchaux* were widely feared for their arbitrary use of wide powers, subject to no appeal, which led to same spectacular miscarriages of justice. In the absence of decent written records we can only conjecture at their overall performance, but they may well have put more people to death than all the other courts combined, most of them men from among those *gem sans aven* whose lives everyone held cheap. Between 1596 and 1602 the *Parlement* of Paris had to issue six stern *arrêts* to prevent witches being tried *prévôtalement* in Poitou and Basse Marche, where it seems that local judges were trying to go along with popular feeling—the witches involved, incidentally, were predominantly men.

A first general conclusion, therefore, is that there was no grand witch-hunt inspired by higher authority. The general acceptance that witchcraft was a real offence certainly gave some leeway for lesser local judges to encourage prosecutions, but this would seem to have been true from at least the fourteenth century. In France would-be persecutors were severely constrained by the sceptical attitude of most *Parlements,* always anxious to check local abuses. Lorraine is a different story, for the central authorities showed much greater enthusiasm to confirm the sentences of lesser courts. The various officials in the localities had every chance to act as orchestrators of persecutions, yet in practice there is very little sign that they did so on more than the most sporadic basis. If women were being hunted, it was by neighbours who knew little or nothing of the various misogynist doctrines which have often been advanced to explain the whole phenomenon, this does not mean that they were free of gender prejudice, of course, merely that it was of a much more popular and inchoate nature. Such feelings obviously existed, but do not show up often in the records themselves. We may well suppose that there are two basic factors which have always operated to encourage such prejudice. Firstly, the dominance claimed by men in both society and family most have engendered severe tensions, while requiring some kind of justification.

Secondly, almost every individual's fundamental experience of love and hate is with a woman, in the mother-child relationship. This is particularly relevant when one considers the dominant role played by rationalized unconscious processes in witchcraft beliefs and trials.

There can be no doubt that witchcraft persecutions belonged to a general category of scapegoating practices, which invite a mixture of social and psychological explanations. Much of this complex causation fails to show on the surface, even when one can reconstruct cases in great detail; it is of the very essence of the projection mechanism, whereby internal conflicts and guilt are redirected towards another person or group, that the process should be largely opaque to its perpetrators. Statements made during trials also display a certain amount of deliberate coding, for both witnesses and accused tried to represent past events in edited or evasive ways, not least because they knew the judges might not approve of some routine village practices. . . .

In prevailing familial systems of north-western Europe such old women seem often to have found themselves dangerously isolated; once past the stage of bearing and caring for children, their main claim to consideration lay in experience. Knowledge of remedies was a widespread form of this, which did not have to imply any pretensions to special gifts as a healer, so that the request to advise a neighbour must have been common enough. Although the reactions of these suspects probably indicate that they had detected the suspicions which underlay these particular invitations, the mechanism they suggest is still an intriguing one.

An exceptionally full attempt to interpret such materials is to be found in Muchembled's *Les dermiers bûchers*, based on a group of trials in a Flanders village in 1679. He suggests the existence of a large pool of rumours and suspicions, largely sustained by feminine gossip, which could always provide ready-made victims to satisfy demands which usually originated outside the system, arising from economic crisis or elite anxieties. Men were frequently suspected, but even if directly accused were likely to escape formal prosecution. Examined in detail, nearly all the key points in his account of the trials prove to be purely hypothetical, while his methods of linking internal and external forces go against much that has been argued here. In its more descriptive sections, however, his picture of a distinctively feminine sphere is thought-provoking and helpful. Village women do seem to have passed much of their lives in the company of other women, often competing for apparently miniscule satisfactions in turns of social esteem and personal standing. Older women quite often appear as regular if unwelcome visitors to the houses of their younger neighbours. . . .

. . . A subjective impression, which has yet to be tested statistically, is that women dominated unofficial medical practice in Lorraine, at least where remedies for ordinary illnesses were concerned, When one particularly active healer, Claudatte Clauchepled, teamed up with a male vagrant, Jean-don Bassat, his role was merely to find custom for her service If women predominated heavily in prescribing herbal remedies, charms and pilgrimages, men held the same position when it came to the *devins* who effectively operated as witch-doctors. This sexual dimorphism is bard to account for, and perhaps too much

should not be made of it, since female neighbours who were not regular healers were quite likely to identify a sickness as *mal donné*, while *devins* appear
in a substantial minority of all cases, not a majority. They cannot plausibly be
seen as men persecuting women in any case, since their technique; normally
placed the onus for identifying the witch on the client. The mulation of suspicions and rumour into action is indeed the key step which one seeks to
explain, yet which is too often elusive even in well-accorded cases. The example of Jacquotte Gardeux and Marie Canot is unique among the Lorraine trials,
in that it includes specific claims by the accused that the legal process was
being manipulated by rich and powerful families. Even here there is no reason
to suppose that the motivation was political, for the charges against both
women were typical enough; it merely looks as if Marie was accused on the
basis of a single incident. In fact the head of the Cabled family, whom Marie
alleged to be master-minding the affair, gave testimony that he did not share
the suspicions of his wife and sons over the death of one of their horses, while
as a conspiracy it was a distinct failure, since the court treated both women
with unusual leniency, subjecting Jacquotte alone to a mild session of torture
before releasing them. What this case also demonstrated was the danger of
giving a sharp-tongued woman the chance to denounce her neighbours, for
Jacquotte made a remarkable series of charges against the witnesses. Her specific accusations about bastardy, adultery and theft must have left some of
them wishing they had kept their own mouths shut. . . .

    . . . Temporary refuge in the village church provided an exceptional
chance to agree on communal action against a suspect. In more normal circumstances such action probably followed the crystallization of the rumours
which were in regular circulation, a process which followed no standard pattern, and often depended heavily on an individual who was willing to expose
himself to certain risks. He might suffer financial loss if the suspect were
acquitted and the trial costs fell on him, although this would only occur if he
had made himself *apartie formelle*, who undertook to bring forward witnesses
himself. More commonly he must have feared further *maléfices* by the witch,
and the future hatred of her friends and kin. At this crucial point there is no
doubt that men had to take the lead, yet of course one can often detect their
womenfolk close behind. . . .

    . . . Historians naturally assume that kinship is one of the strongest
social bonds, so that family links provide a vital key to the allegiances and
behaviour of individuals. This becomes such second nature that they are liable
to forget a matter of common experience, the fact that the bitterest disputes
are probably those within families. As they emerge from the trials, such tensions might arise over property, stepchildren, unsuitable behaviour by a
spouse, and numerous similar matters. It is apparent that they could also centre on witchcraft itself, with strains developing within the family group over a
wife who was suspect to the community at large Stepmothers were particularly at risk: Colas Jean George said of Claudette Dabo that his late father had
married her as his second wife. He had many disputes with her, partly because
his father . . . left him in charge of the horses and carts. He believed that for
this reason she had caused the deaths of four or five horses; this had hardly

affected her, since she had brought nothing to the household, and by the marriage settlement had merely her keep and a sum of money. Women were surely in a vulnerable position when such quarrels occurred, for marriage separated them to a greater or lesser extent from their own kin by blood, frequently leaving them dependent for protection on their husband's relatives. There are enough cases of this kind to suggest that it was one of several factors which made gender a very relevant, yet not a determining, element in the complex dynamics of persecution. In certain special cases men might actually form a majority of the accused, while in most of Europe they were a significant minority. The predominance of women corresponded to the social dynamics of the supposed crime, which made it the typical revenge of the weak against the strong. The particular position of widows, and of wives within the household, interrelated with the specificities of feminine culture and popular medical practice. A pre-existing cultural stereotype which identified witchcraft with women was reinforced by the experience of trials in which most of the accused were indeed women. As usual with witchcraft, close examination of the facts undermines grand theories, and requires us to devise much subtler explanations for a many-faceted reality.

POSTSCRIPT

Were the Witch-Hunts in Premodern Europe Misogynistic?

Violence against women, which is considered by many to be epidemic in this generation, has caused a re-assessment of misogyny. Domestic violence, spousal abuse, sexual assault, rape, and sexual harassment, have occupied recent headlines and created an acute awareness of woman-as-victim issues. In seeking the roots of such violent behavior, a search for historical antecedents is a logical starting point. Renewed interest in the witch hunt phenomenon has enlivened interest in the subject of violence against women, a unique synthesis of two subjects with such far-reaching results.

Despite a plethora of available information and data, we are no closer today to definitive answers to some of the major questions involving early modern Europe's witch hunt experiences. For example, were the witch hunts a centralized movement initiated from society's "power elite"; or did local variables play a more important role in their development and outcomes? If women's sexuality was a major force in the witchcraze phenomenon, who introduced it into the public record, and why? If socio-economic factors were important to the movement, why did it last for more than three centuries? And if women were viewed as "creatures of God," how could the executions of witches be accompanied by such sadistic tortures? Was there another lesson being taught here?

On the generation-long historiography of the European witchcraze, Hugh Trevor-Roper's essay mentioned in the Introduction is a good place to start. William Monter's *Witchcraft in France and Switzerland: The Borderlands* (Cornell University Press, 1969); and *Ritual, Myth, and Magic in Early Modern Europe* (Ohio University Press, 1984), along with his many articles, are important contributions to the study of the witch hunts. Brian P. Levack's *The Witch-Hunt in Early Modern Europe* (Addison-Wesley, 1995) provides a thorough, textbook-like coverage of the subject. Anne Llewellyn Barstow's *Witchcraze: A New History of the European Witch Hunts* (HarperCollins, 1994) is a recent assessment of the relationship between the witch hunts and gender. An alternative companion piece would be Robin Briggs, *Witches and Neighbors: The Social and Cultural Context of European Witchcraft* (Penguin Books, 1996). A recent addition to the field is Robert W. Thurston, *Witch, Wicce, Mother Goose: The Rise and Fall of the Witch Hunts in Europe and North America* (Longman, 2001).

An excellent primary source book which can be used to shed light on the subject is Alan C. Kors and Edward Peters, eds., *Witchcraft in Europe, 1100–1700: A Documentary Issue* (University of Pennsylvania Press, 1995), which provides among its many primary source pieces, opinions by several popes, Martin Luther, John Calvin, Cotton Mather, Michel de Montaigne, Baruch Spinoza, and countless others. See also Jonathan Barry, Marianne Hester, and Gareth Roberts, eds., *Witchcraft in Early Modern Europe: Studies in Culture and Belief* (Cambridge University Press, 1998), which contains many articles on the subject, written by leading European scholars. Finally, a recent article which brings the historiographical study of the witch hunts and gender up to date is Elspeth Whitney, "The Witch 'She'/the Historian 'He': Gender and the Historiography of the European Witch Hunts," *Women and Language* (Spring, 2000).

ISSUE 17

Was the Scientific Revolution Revolutionary?

YES: **Edward Grant**, from "When Did Modern Science Begin?" *American Scholar* (Winter 1997)

NO: **Steven Shapin**, from *The Scientific Revolution* (University of Chicago Press, 1996)

ISSUE SUMMARY

YES: Distinguished professor emeritus of history and philosophy of science Edward Grant argues that there was a revolution in science that took place in the seventeenth century; however, it might have been delayed by centuries if several key developments between 1175 and 1500 had not paved the way for it.

NO: Professor of sociology and historian of science Steven Shapin questions the idea of a Scientific Revolution, suggesting greater continuity with the past and rejecting a single time/space event we might call a Scientific Revolution.

When you open a history textbook, you will find it conveniently divided into chapters and units with titles that mark the major turning points of history. One of those titles in a text on World History or Western Civilization is likely to be The Scientific Revolution. Known as periodization, this tendency of historians to provide interpretive groupings of events has recently been subjected to reappraisal. If "where you stand determines what you see," then the very act of labeling periods of history makes judgments about what is important and valuable.

The assumption behind periodization is that there are moments when the path of history is re-routed, when a sharp break with the past leads to a new kind of experience or a new way of understanding the world. One of the questions historians must ask, therefore, is whether a particular event or series of events represents primarily continuity with the past or discontinuity from it. Traditional periodization has seen the Scientific Revolution as a classic example of discontinuity—as a sharp break with the medieval past and the ushering in of the modern world. Recently, however, historians have taken a fresh look at the late sixteenth and early seventeenth centuries and wondered how scientific and how revolutionary this period actually was.

A danger historians must also remain alert to is called presentism, the tendency to judge and interpret the past by the standards and concerns of the present. From the perspective of the early twenty-first century, for example, we might be tempted to emphasize progress, as the Industrial Revolution replaced backbreaking labor with the power of machines. People who actually lived through these changes, by contrast, might have focused on the breakup of the productive family unit in the home, as individuals left the home to do wage work. Two questions we must ask ourselves are: Did Europeans living in the seventeenth century experience revolutionary changes? and How much of a break with the past did the scientific discoveries of that century represent?

For Edward Grant, there was undoubtedly a Scientific Revolution. He sees the fields of astronomy, cosmology, and physics undergoing "momentous changes" over the sixteenth and seventeenth centuries. However, he also documents a series of events—the translation of Greek and Arabic scientific/philosophical works into Latin, the formation of the medieval university, and the emergence of a class of theologian/natural philosophers—without which the scientific revolution would not have occurred when it did.

Steven Shapin begins with a boldly revisionist declaration: "There was no such thing as the Scientific Revolution." Reflecting a postmodern view of the world, Shapin questions whether or not it is even possible to speak about an "essence" of something called "science." Instead of a single, discrete entity, he sees a wide variety of ways of understanding, explaining, and controlling the natural world. If we list the characteristics of the so-called revolution, Shapin believes we will find that experimental method, mathematical approaches, and even mechanical conceptions of nature were both advocated and rejected by people who thought of themselves as scientists.

Both Grant and Shapin acknowledge continuity with the medieval past rather than a radical break from it. And, both would agree that the past did not become the "modern world" at a single historical moment. Where they differ, is that Grant does see a seventeenth-century turning point—although rooted in a steady forward progression—whereas, Shapin insists that every development we might label revolutionary had "significantly variant contemporary forms" or was criticized by contemporaries whom we also regard as revolutionary "moderns."

YES

Edward Grant

When Did Modern Science Begin?

Although science has a long history with roots in ancient Egypt and Mesopotamia, it is indisputable that modern science emerged in Western Europe and nowhere else. The reasons for this momentous occurrence must, therefore, be sought in some unique set of circumstances that differentiate Western society from other contemporary and earlier civilizations. The establishment of science as a basic enterprise within a society depends on more than expertise in technical scientific subjects, experiments, and disciplined observations. After all, science can be found in many early societies. In Islam, until approximately 1500, mathematics, astronomy, geometric optics, and medicine were more highly developed than in the West. But science was not institutionalized in Islamic society. Nor was it institutionalized in ancient and medieval China, despite significant achievements. Similar arguments apply to all other societies and civilizations. Science can be found in many of them but was institutionalized and perpetuated in none.

Why did science as we know it today materialize only in Western society? What made it possible for science to acquire prestige and influence and to become a powerful force in Western Europe by the seventeenth century? The answer, I believe, lies in certain fundamental events that occurred in Western Europe during the period from approximately 1175 to 1500. Those events, taken together, should be viewed as forming the foundations of modern science, a judgment that runs counter to prevailing scholarly opinion, which holds that modern science emerged in the seventeenth century by repudiating and abandoning medieval science and natural philosophy, the latter based on the works of Aristotle.

The scientific revolution appeared first in astronomy, cosmology, and physics in the course of the sixteenth and seventeenth centuries. Whether or not the achievements of medieval science exercised any influence on these developments is irrelevant. What must be emphasized, however, is that the momentous changes in the exact sciences of physics and astronomy that epitomized the scientific revolution did not develop from a vacuum. They could not have occurred without certain foundational events that were unique products of the late Middle Ages. To realize this, we must inquire whether a scientific revolution could have occurred in the seventeenth century if the level of science in Western Europe had remained much as it was in the first half of the twelfth century, before the transformation that occurred as a consequence of a great wave of translations from the Greek and Arabic languages into Latin that began around 1150 and continued on to the end of the thirteenth century. Could a scientific revolution have occurred in the seventeenth century if the immense translations of Greco-Arabic (or Greco-Islamic) science and natural philosophy into Latin had never taken place? Obviously not. Without those translations many centuries would have been required before Western Europe could have reached the level of Greco-Arabic science. Instead of the scientific revolution of the seventeenth century, our descendants might look back upon a "Scientific Revolution of the Twenty-first Century." But the translations did occur in the twelfth and thirteenth centuries, and so did a scientific revolution in the seventeenth century. It follows that something happened between, say, 1175 and 1500 that paved the way for that scientific revolution. What that "something" was is my subject here.

To describe how the late Middle Ages in Western Europe played a role in producing the scientific revolution in the physical sciences during the seventeenth century; two aspects of science need to be distinguished, the contextual and the substantive. The first—the contextual-involves changes that created an atmosphere conducive to the establishment of science, made it feasible to pursue science and natural philosophy on a permanent basis, and made those pursuits laudable activities within Western society. The second aspect—the substantive—pertains to certain features of medieval science and natural philosophy that were instrumental in bringing about the scientific revolution.

The creation of an environment in the Middle Ages that eventually made a scientific revolution possible involved at least three crucial preconditions. The first of these was the translation of Greco-Arabic science and natural philosophy into Latin during the twelfth and thirteenth centuries. Without this initial, indispensable precondition, the other two might not have occurred. With the transfer of this large body of learning to the Western world, the old science of the early Middle Ages was overwhelmed and superseded. Although modern science might eventually have developed in the West without the introduction of Greco-Arabic science, its advent would have been delayed by centuries.

The second precondition was the formation of the medieval university, with its corporate structure and control over its varied activities. The universities that emerged by the thirteenth century in Paris, Oxford, and Bologna were different from anything the world had ever seen. From these beginnings, the medieval university took root and has endured as an institution for some eight hundred years, being transformed in time into a worldwide phenomenon. Nothing in Islam or China, or India, or in the ancient civilizations of South America is comparable to the medieval university. It is in this remarkable institution, and its unusual activities, that the foundations of modern science must be sought.

The university was possible in the Middle Ages because the evolution of medieval Latin society allowed for the separate existence of church and state, each of which, in turn, recognized the independence of corporate entities, the university among them. The first universities, of Paris, Oxford, and Bologna, were in existence by approximately 1200, shortly after most of the translations had been completed. The translations furnished a ready-made curriculum to the emerging universities, a curriculum that was overwhelmingly composed of the exact sciences, logic, and natural philosophy.

The curriculum of science, logic, and natural philosophy established in the medieval universities of Western Europe was a permanent fixture for approximately 450 to 500 years. It was the curriculum of the arts faculty, which was the largest of the traditional four faculties of a typical major university, the others being medicine, theology, and law. Courses in logic, natural philosophy, geometry, and astronomy formed the core curriculum for the baccalaureate and master of arts degrees and were taught on a regular basis for centuries. These two arts degrees were virtual prerequisites for entry into the higher disciplines of law, medicine, and theology.

For the first time in the history of the world, an institution had been created for teaching science, natural philosophy, and logic. An extensive four-to-six-year course in higher education was based on those subjects, with natural philosophy as the most important component. As universities multiplied during the thirteenth to fifteenth centuries, the same science-natural philosophy-logic curriculum was disseminated throughout Europe, extending as far east as Poland.

The science curriculum could not have been implemented without the explicit approval of church and state. To a remarkable extent, both granted to the universities corporate powers to regulate themselves: universities had the legal right to determine their own curricula, to establish criteria for the degrees of their students, and to determine the teaching fitness of their faculty members.

Despite some difficulties and tensions between natural philosophy and theology—between, essentially, reason and revelation—arts masters and theologians at the universities welcomed the arrival of Aristotle's natural philosophy as evidenced by the central role they gave it in higher education. Why did they do this? Why did a Christian society at the height of the Catholic Church's power readily adopt a pagan natural philosophy as the basis of a four-to-six-year education? Why didn't Christians fear and resist such pagan fare rather than embrace it?

Because Christians had long ago come to terms with pagan thought and were agreed, for the most part, that they had little or nothing to fear from it. The rapprochement between Christianity and pagan literature, especially philosophy, may have been made feasible by the slowness with which Christianity was disseminated. The spread of Christianity beyond the Holy Land and its surrounding region began in earnest after Saint Paul proselytized the Gentile world, especially Greece, during the middle of the first century. In retrospect—and by comparison with the spread of Islam—the pace of the dissemination of Christianity appears quite slow. Not until 300 A.D. was Christianity effectively represented throughout the Roman Empire. And not until 313, in the reign of Constantine, was the Edict of Milan (or Edict of Toleration) issued, which conferred on Christianity full legal equality with all other religions in the Empire. In 392, Christianity was made the state religion of the Roman Empire. In that year, the Emperor Theodosius ordered all pagan temples closed, and also prohibited pagan worship, thereafter classified as treason. Thus it was not until 392 that Christianity became the exclusive religion supported by the state. After almost four centuries of existence, Christianity was triumphant.

By contrast, Islam, following the death of Mohammad in 632, was carried over an enormous geographical area in a remarkably short time. In less than one hundred years, it was the dominant religion from the Arabian peninsula westward to the Straits of Gibraltar, northward to Spain and eastward to Persia, and beyond. But where Islam was largely spread by conquest during its first hundred years, Christianity spread slowly and, with the exception of certain periods of persecution, relatively peacefully. It was this slow percolation of Christianity that enabled it to come to terms with the pagan world and thus prepare itself for a role that could not have been envisioned by its early members.

The time it took before Christianity became the state religion enabled Christianity to adjust to the pagan society around it. In the second half of the third century, Christian apologists concluded that Christianity could profitably utilize pagan Greek philosophy and learning. In a momentous move, Clement of Alexandria (ca. 150–ca. 215) and his disciple Origen of Alexandria (ca. 185–ca. 254) laid down the basic approach that others would follow. Greek philosophy, they argued, was not inherently good or bad, but one or the other depending on how it was used by Christians. Although the Greek poets and philosophers had not received direct revelation from God, they did receive natural reason and were therefore pointed toward truth. Philosophy—and secular learning in general—could thus be used to interpret Christian wisdom, which was the fruit of revelation. They were agreed that philosophy and science could be used as "handmaidens to theology"—that is, as aids to understanding Holy Scripture—an attitude that had already been advocated by Philo Judaeus, a resident of the Jewish community of Alexandria, early in the first century A.D.

The "handmaiden" concept of Greek learning became the standard Christian attitude toward secular learning by the middle of the fourth century. That Christians chose to accept pagan learning within limits was a momentous decision. They might have heeded the words of Tertullian (ca. 150–ca. 225), who asked pointedly: "What indeed has Athens to do with Jerusalem? What concord is there between the Academy and the Church?" With the total triumph of Christianity at the end of the fourth century, the Church might have reacted adversely toward Greek pagan learning in general, and Greek philosophy in particular, since there was much in the latter that was offensive to the Church. They might even have launched a major effort to suppress pagan thought as a danger to the Church and its doctrines. But they did not.

The handmaiden theory was obviously a compromise between the rejection of traditional pagan learning and its full acceptance. By approaching secular learning with caution, Christians could utilize Greek philosophy—especially metaphysics and logic—to better understand and explicate Holy

Scripture and to cope with the difficulties generated by the assumption of the doctrine of the Trinity and other esoteric dogmas. Ordinary daily life also required use of the mundane sciences such as astronomy and mathematics. Christians came to realize that they could not turn away from Greek learning.

When Christians in Western Europe became aware of Greco-Arabic scientific literature and were finally prepared to receive it in the twelfth century, they did so eagerly. They did not view it as a body of subversive knowledge. Despite a degree of resistance that was more intense at some times than at others, Aristotle's works were made the basis of the university curriculum by 1255 in Paris, and long before that at Oxford.

The emergence of a class of theologian-natural philosophers was the third essential precondition for the scientific revolution. Their major contribution was to sanction the introduction and use of Aristotelian natural philosophy in the curriculum of the new universities. Without that approval, natural philosophy and science could not have become the curriculum of the medieval universities. The development of a class of theologian-natural philosophers must be regarded as extraordinary. Not only did most theologians approve of an essentially secular arts curriculum, but they were convinced that natural philosophy was essential for the elucidation of theology. Students entering schools of theology were expected to have achieved a high level of competence in natural philosophy. Since a master of arts degree, or the equivalent thereof, signified a thorough background in Aristotelian natural philosophy, and since a master's degree in the arts was usually a prerequisite for admittance to the higher faculty of theology, almost all theologians can be said to have acquired extensive knowledge of natural philosophy. Many undoubtedly regarded it as worthy of study in itself and not merely because of its traditional role as the handmaiden of theology. . . .

Medieval natural philosophers investigated the "common course of nature," not its uncommon, or miraculous, path. They characterized this approach, admirably, by the phrase "speaking naturally" (loquendo naturaliter)—that is, speaking by means of natural science, and not by means of faith or theology. That such an expression should have emerged, and come into common usage in medieval natural philosophy, is a tribute to the scholars who took as their primary mission the explanation of the structure and operation of the world in purely rational and secular terms.

The widespread assumption of "natural impossibilities" or counterfactuals— or, as they are sometimes called, "thought-experiments"—was a significant aspect of medieval methodology. An occurrence would have been considered naturally impossible" if it was thought inconceivable for it to occur within the accepted framework of Aristotelian physics and cosmology. The frequent use of natural impossibilities derived largely from the powerful medieval concept of God's absolute power, in which it was conceded that God could do anything whatever short of a logical contradiction. In the Middle Ages, such thinking resulted in conclusions that challenged certain aspects of Aristotle's physics. Where Aristotle had shown that other worlds were impossible, medieval scholastics showed not only that the existence of other worlds was possible, but that they would be compatible with our world.

The novel replies that emerged from the physics and cosmology of counterfactuals did not cause the overthrow of the Aristotelian world-view, but they did challenge some of its fundamental principles. They made many aware that things could be quite different from what was dreamt of in Aristotle's philosophy. But they accomplished more than that. Not only did some of the problems and solutions continue to influence scholastic authors in the sixteenth and seventeenth centuries, but this characteristically medieval approach also influenced significant non-scholastics, who reveal an awareness of the topics debated by scholastics.

One of the most fruitful ideas that passed from the Middle Ages to the seventeenth century is the concept of God annihilating matter and leaving behind a vacuum—a concept used effectively by John Locke, Pierre Gassendi, and Thomas Hobbes in their discussions of space.

A famous natural impossibility derived from a proposition condemned in 1277. As a consequence, it was mandatory after 1277 to concede that God could move our spherical world rectilinearly, despite the vacuum that might be left behind. More than an echo of this imaginary manifestation of God's absolute power reverberated through the seventeenth century, when Pierre Gassendi and Samuel Clarke (in his famous dispute with Leibniz) found it useful to appeal to God's movement of the world. In medieval intellectual culture, where observation and experiment played negligible roles, counterfactuals were a powerful tool because they emphasized metaphysics, logic, theology, and the imagination—the very areas in which medieval natural philosophers excelled.

The scientific methodologies described here produced new conceptualizations and assumptions about the world. Ideas about nature's simplicity, its common course, as well as the use of counterfactuals, emphasized new and important ways to think about nature. Galileo and his fellow scientific revolutionaries inherited these attitudes, and most would have subscribed to them.

Another legacy from the Middle Ages to early modern science was an extensive and sophisticated body of terms that formed the basis of later scientific discourse such terms as potential, actual, substance, property, accident, cause, analogy, matter, form, essence, genus, species, relation, quantity, quality, place, vacuum, infinite, and many others. These Aristotelian terms formed a significant component of scholastic natural philosophy. The language of medieval natural philosophy, however, did not consist solely of translated Aristotelian terms. New concepts, terms, and definitions were added in the fourteenth century, most notably in the domains of change and motion. Definitions of uniform motion, uniformly accelerated motion, and instantaneous motion were added to the lexicon of natural philosophy. By the seventeenth century, these terms, concepts, and definitions were embedded in the language and thought of European natural philosophers.

Medieval natural philosophy played another momentous role in the transition to early modern science. It furnished some—if, it is true, not many—of the basic problems that exercised the minds of non-scholastic natural philosophers in the sixteenth and seventeenth centuries. Medieval natural philosophers produced hundreds of specific questions about nature, the answers to which included a vast amount of scientific information. Most of the questions had multiple answers, with no genuine way of choosing between them. In the sixteenth and seventeenth centuries, new solutions were proposed by scholars who found Aristotelian answers unacceptable, or, at best, inadequate. The changes they made, however, were mostly in the answers, not in the questions. The scientific revolution was not the result of new questions put to nature in place of medieval questions. It was, at least initially, more a matter of finding new answers to old questions, answers that came, more and more, to include experiments, which were exceptional occurrences in the Middle Ages. Although the solutions differed, many fundamental problems were common to both groups. Beginning around 1200, medieval natural philosophers, largely located at European universities, exhibited an unprecedented concern for the nature and structure of the physical world. The contributors to the scientific revolution continued the same tradition, because by then these matters had become an integral part of intellectual life in Western society.

The Middle Ages did not just transmit a great deal of significantly modified, traditional, natural philosophy, much of it in the form of questions; it also conveyed a remarkable tradition of relatively free, rational inquiry. The medieval philosophical tradition was fashioned in the faculties of arts of medieval universities. Natural philosophy was their domain, and almost from the outset masters of arts struggled to establish as much academic freedom as possible. They sought to preserve and expand the study of philosophy. Arts masters regarded themselves as the guardians of natural philosophy and fought for the right to apply reason to all problems about the physical world. By virtue of their independent status as a faculty, with numerous rights and privileges, they achieved a surprisingly large degree of freedom during the Middle Ages.

Theology was always a potential obstacle, true, but in practice theologians offered little opposition, largely because they, too, were heavily imbued with natural philosophy. By the end of the thirteenth century, the arts faculty had attained virtual independence from the theological faculty. By then, philosophy and its major subdivision, natural philosophy, had emerged as an independent discipline based in the arts faculties of European universities. True, arts masters were always subject to restraints with regard to religious dogma, but the subject areas where such issues arose were limited. During the thirteenth century, arts masters had learned how to cope with the problematic aspects of Aristotle's thought. They treated those problems hypothetically, or announced that they were merely repeating Aristotle's opinions, even as they offered elaborations of his arguments. During the Middle Ages, natural philosophy remained what Aristotle had made it: an essentially secular and rational discipline. It remained so only because the arts faculty struggled to preserve it. In doing so, they transformed natural philosophy into an independent discipline that embraced as well as glorified the rational investigation of all problems relevant to the physical world. In the 1330s, William of Ockham expressed the sentiments of most arts masters and many theologians when he declared:

> Assertions . . . concerning natural philosophy, which do not pertain to theology, should not be solemnly condemned or forbidden to anyone, since in such matters everyone should be free to say freely whatever he pleases.

Everyone who did natural philosophy in the sixteenth and seventeenth centuries was the beneficiary of these remarkable developments. The spirit of free inquiry nourished by medieval natural philosophers formed part of the intellectual heritage of all who engaged in scientific investigation. Most, of course, were unaware of their legacy and would probably have denied its existence, preferring to heap ridicule and scorn on Aristotelian scholastics and scholasticism. That ridicule was not without justification. It was time to alter the course of medieval natural philosophy.

Some Aristotelian natural philosophers tried to accommodate the new heliocentric astronomy that had emerged from the brilliant efforts of Copernicus, Tycho Brahe, and Galileo. By then, accommodation was no longer sufficient. Medieval natural philosophy was destined to vanish by the end of the seventeenth century. The medieval scholastic legacy, however, remained—namely, the spirit of free inquiry, the emphasis on reason, a variety of approaches to nature, and the core of legitimate problems that would occupy the attention of the new science. Inherited from the Middle Ages, too, was the profound sense that all of these activities were legitimate and important, that discovering the way the world operated was a laudable undertaking. These enormous achievements were accomplished in the late Middle Ages, between 1175 and 1500.

To illustrate how medieval contributions to the new science ought to be viewed, let me draw upon an analogy from the Middle Ages. In the late thirteenth century in Italy, the course of the history of medicine was altered significantly when human dissection was allowed for postmortems and was shortly afterward introduced into medical schools, where it soon became institutionalized as part of the anatomical training of medical students. Except in ancient Egypt, human dissection had been forbidden in the ancient world. By the second century A.D., it was also banned in Egypt. It was never permitted in the Islamic world. Its introduction into the Latin West marked a new beginning, made without serious objection from the Church. It was a momentous event. Dissection of cadavers was used primarily in teaching, albeit irregularly until the end of the fifteenth century. Rarely, if at all, was it employed to enhance scientific knowledge of the human body. The revival of human dissection and its incorporation into medical training throughout the Middle Ages laid a foundation for what was to come.

Without it, we cannot imagine the significant anatomical progress that was made by such keen anatomists as Leonardo da Vinci (1452–1519), Bartolommeo Eustachio (1520–74), Andreas Vesalius (1514–64), and many others.

What human dissection did for medicine, the translations, the universities, the theologian-natural philosophers, and the medieval version of Aristotelian natural philosophy did collectively for the scientific revolution of the seventeenth century. These vital features of medieval science formed a foundation that made possible a continuous, uninterrupted eight hundred years of scientific development, a development that began in Western Europe and spread around the world.

Steven Shapin  **NO**

The Scientific Revolution

The Scientific Revolution: The History of a Term

There was no such thing as the Scientific Revolution, and this [selection is from] a book about it. Some time ago, when the academic world offered more certainty and more comforts, historians announced the real existence of a coherent, cataclysmic, and climactic event that fundamentally and irrevocably changed what people knew about the natural world and how they secured proper knowledge of that world. It was the moment at which the world was made modern, it was a Good Thing, and it happened sometime during the period from the late sixteenth to the early eighteenth century. In 1943 the French historian Alexandre Koyré celebrated the conceptual changes at the heart of the Scientific Revolution as "the most profound revolution achieved or suffered by the human mind" since Greek antiquity. It was a revolution so profound that human culture "for centuries did not grasp its bearing or meaning; which, even now, is often misvalued and misunderstood." A few years later the English historian Herbert Butterfield famously judged that the Scientific Revolution "outshines everything since the rise of Christianity and reduces the Renaissance and Reformation to the rank of mere episodes. . . . [It is] the real origin both of the modern world and of the modern mentality." It was, moreover, construed as a conceptual revolution, a fundamental reordering of our ways of *thinking* about the natural. In this respect, a story about the Scientific Revolution might be adequately told through an account of radical changes in the fundamental categories of thought. To Butterfield, the mental changes making up the Scientific Revolution were equivalent to "putting on a new pair of spectacles." And to A. Rupert Hall it was nothing less than "an *a priori* redefinition of the objects of philosophical and scientific inquiry."

This conception of the Scientific Revolution is now encrusted with tradition. Few historical episodes present themselves as more substantial or more self-evidently worthy of study. There is an established place for accounts of the Scientific Revolution in the Western liberal curriculum, and this [selection] is an attempt to fill that space economically and to invite further curiosity about the making of early modern science. Nevertheless, like many twentieth-century "traditions," that contained in the notion of the Scientific Revolution is not nearly as old as we might think. The phrase "the Scientific Revolution" was probably coined by Alexandre Koyré in 1939, and it first became a book title in

A. Rupert Hall's *The Scientific Revolution* of 1954. Before that time there was no event to be studied in the liberal curriculum, nor any discrete object of historical inquiry, called the Scientific Revolution. Although many seventeenth-century practitioners expressed their intention of bringing about radical intellectual change, the people who are said to have made the revolution used no such term to refer to what they were doing.

From antiquity through the early modern period, a "revolution" invoked the idea of a periodically recurring cycle. In Copernicus's new astronomy of the mid-sixteenth century, for example, the planets completed their revolutions round the sun, while references to political revolutions gestured at the notion of ebbs and flows or cycles—fortune's wheel—in human affairs. The idea of revolution as a radical and irreversible reordering developed together with linear, unidirectional conceptions of time. In this newer conception revolution was not recurrence but its reverse, the bringing about of a new state of affairs that the world had never witnessed before and might never witness again. Not only this notion of revolution but also the beginnings of an idea of revolution in science date from the eighteenth-century writings of French Enlightenment philosophes who liked to portray themselves, and their disciplines, as radical subverters of ancient régime culture. (Some . . . seventeenth-century writers . . . saw themselves not as bringing about totally new states of affairs but as restoring or purifying old ones.) The notion of a revolution as epochal and irreversible change, it is possible, was first applied in a systematic way to events in science and only later to political events. In just this sense, the first revolutions may have been scientific, and the "American," "French," and "Russian Revolutions" are its progeny.

As our understanding of science in the seventeenth century has changed in recent years, so historians have become increasingly uneasy with the very idea of "the Scientific Revolution." Even the legitimacy of each word making up that phrase has been individually contested. Many historians are now no longer satisfied that there was any singular and discrete event, localized in time and space, that can be pointed to as "the" Scientific Revolution. Such historians now reject even the notion that there was any single coherent cultural entity called "science" in the seventeenth century to undergo revolutionary change. There was, rather, a diverse array of cultural practices aimed at understanding, explaining, and controlling the natural world, each with different characteristics and each experiencing different modes of change. We are now much more dubious of claims that there is anything like "a scientific method"—a coherent, universal, and efficacious set of procedures for making scientific knowledge—and still more skeptical of stories that locate its origin in the seventeenth century, from which time it has been unproblematically passed on to us. And many historians do not now accept that the changes wrought on scientific beliefs and practices during the seventeenth century were as "revolutionary" as has been widely portrayed. The continuity of seventeenth-century natural philosophy with its medieval past is now routinely asserted, while talk of "delayed" eighteenth- and nineteenth-century revolutions in chemistry and biology followed hard upon historians' identification of "the" original Scientific Revolution.

Why Write About the Scientific Revolution?

There are still other reasons for historians' present uneasiness with the category of the Scientific Revolution as it has been customarily construed. First, historians have in recent years become dissatisfied with the traditional manner of treating ideas as if they floated freely in conceptual space. Although previous accounts framed the Scientific Revolution in terms of autonomous ideas or disembodied mentalities, more recent versions have insisted on the importance of situating ideas in their wider cultural and social context. We now hear more than we used to about the relations between the scientific changes of the seventeenth century and changes in religious, political, and economic patterns. More fundamentally, some historians now wish to understand the concrete human *practices* by which ideas or concepts are made. What did people *do* when they made or confirmed an observation, proved a theorem, performed an experiment? An account of the Scientific Revolution as a history of free-floating concepts is a very different animal from a history of concept-making practices. Finally, historians have become much more interested in the "who" of the Scientific Revolution. What kinds of people wrought such changes? Did everyone believe as they did, or only a very few? And if only a very few took part in these changes, in what sense, if at all, can we speak of the Scientific Revolution as effecting massive changes in how "we" view the world, as the moment when modernity was made, for "us"? The cogency of such questions makes for problems in writing as unreflectively as we used to about the Scientific Revolution. Responding to them means that we need an account of changes in early modern science appropriate for our less confident, but perhaps more intellectually curious, times.

Yet despite these legitimate doubts and uncertainties there remains a sense in which it is possible to write about the Scientific Revolution unapologetically and in good faith. There are two major considerations to bear in mind here. The first is that many key figures in the late sixteenth and seventeenth centuries vigorously expressed *their* view that they were proposing some very new and very important changes in knowledge of natural reality and in the practices by which legitimate knowledge was to be secured, assessed, and communicated. They identified *themselves* as "moderns" set against "ancient" modes of thought and practice. Our sense of radical change afoot comes substantially from them (and those who were the object of their attacks), and is not simply the creation of mid-twentieth-century historians. So we can say that the seventeenth century witnessed some self-conscious and large-scale attempts to change belief, and ways of securing belief, about the natural world. And a book about the Scientific Revolution can legitimately tell a story about those attempts, whether or not they succeeded, whether or not they were contested in the local culture, whether or not they were wholly coherent.

But why do we tell *these* stories instead of others? If different sorts of seventeenth-century people believed different things about the world, how do we assemble our cast of characters and associated beliefs? Some "natural philosophers," for example, advocated rational theorizing, while others pushed a program of relatively atheoretical fact collecting and experimentation.

Mathematical physics was, for example, a very different sort of practice from botany. There were importantly different versions of what it was to do astronomy and believe as an astronomer believed; the relations between the "proper sciences" of astronomy and chemistry and the "pseudosciences" of astrology and alchemy were intensely problematic; and even the category of "nature" as the object of inquiry was understood in radically different ways by different sorts of practitioners. This point cannot be stressed too strongly. The cultural practices subsumed in the category of the Scientific Revolution—however it has been construed—are not coextensive with early modern, or seventeenth-century, science. Historians differ about which practices were "central" to the Scientific Revolution, and participants themselves argued about which practices produced genuine knowledge and which had been fundamentally reformed.

More fundamentally for criteria of selection, it ought to be understood that "most people"—even most educated people—in the seventeenth century did not believe what expert scientific practitioners believed, and the sense in which "people's" thought about the world was revolutionized at that time is very limited. There should be no doubt whatever that one could write a convincing history of seventeenth-century thought about nature without even *mentioning* the Scientific Revolution as traditionally construed.

The very idea of the Scientific Revolution, therefore, is at least partly an expression of "our" interest in our ancestors, where "we" are late twentieth century scientists and those for whom what they believe counts as truth about the natural world. And this interest provides the second legitimate justification for writing about the Scientific Revolution. Historians of science have now grown used to condemning "present-oriented" history, rightly saying that it often distorts our understanding of what the past was like in its own terms. Yet there is absolutely no reason we should not want to know how we got from there to here, who the ancestors were, and what the lineage is that connects us to the past. In this sense a story about the seventeenth-century Scientific Revolution can be an account of those changes that we think led on—never directly or simply, to be sure—to certain features of the present in which, for certain purposes, we happen to be interested. To do this would be an expression of just the same sort of legitimate historical interest displayed by Darwinian evolutionists telling stories about those branches of the tree of life that led to human beings—without assuming in any way that such stories are adequate accounts of what life was like hundreds of thousands of years ago. There is nothing at all wrong about telling such stories, though one must always be careful not to claim too much scope for them. Stories about the ancestors as ancestors are not likely to be sensitive accounts of how it was in the past: the lives and thoughts of Galileo, Descartes, or Boyle were hardly typical of seventeenth-century Italians, Frenchmen, or Englishmen, and telling stories about them geared solely to their ancestral role in formulating the currently accepted law of free fall, the optics of the rainbow, or the ideal gas law is not likely to capture very much about the meaning and significance of their own careers and projects in the seventeenth century.

The past is not transformed into the "modern world" at any single moment: we should never be surprised to find that seventeenth-century scientific practitioners often had about them as much of the ancient as the modern; their notions had to be successively transformed and redefined by generations of thinkers to become "ours." And finally, the people, the thoughts, and the practices we tell stories about as "ancestors," or as the beginnings of our lineage, always reflect some present-day interest. That we tell stories about Galileo, Boyle, Descartes, and Newton reflects something about our late twentieth-century scientific beliefs and what we value about those beliefs. For different purposes we could trace aspects of the modern world back to philosophers "vanquished" by Galileo, Boyle, Descartes, and Newton, and to views of nature and knowledge very different from those elaborated by our officially sanctioned scientific ancestors. For still other purposes we could make much of the fact that most seventeenth-century people had never heard of our scientific ancestors and probably entertained beliefs about the natural world very different from those of our chosen forebears. Indeed, the overwhelming majority of seventeenth century people did not live in Europe, did not know that they lived in "the seventeenth century," and were not aware that a Scientific Revolution was happening. The half of the European population that was female was in a position to participate in scientific culture scarcely at all, as was that overwhelming majority—of men and women—who were illiterate or otherwise disqualified from entering the venues of formal learning.

Some Historiographical Issues

I mean this [selection] to be historiographically up to date—drawing on some of the most recent historical, sociological, and philosophical engagements with the Scientific Revolution. On the other hand, I do not mean to trouble readers with repeated references to methodological and conceptual debates among academics. This [selection] is not written for professional specialized scholars. . . . There is no reason to deny that this story about the Scientific Revolution represents a particular point of view, and that, although I help myself freely to the work of many distinguished scholars, its point of view is my own. Other specialists will doubtless disagree with my approach—some vehemently—and a large number of existing accounts do offer a quite different perspective on what is worth telling about the Scientific Revolution. The positions represented here on some recent historiographic issues can be briefly summarized:

1. I *take for granted* that science is a historically situated and social activity and that it is to be understood in relation to the *contexts* in which it occurs. Historians have long argued whether science relates to its historical and social contexts or whether it should be treated in isolation. I shall simply write about seventeenth-century science as if it were a collectively practiced, historically embedded phenomenon, inviting readers to see whether the account is plausible, coherent, and interesting.

2. For a long time, historians' debates over the propriety of a sociological and a historically "contextual" approach to science seemed to divide practitioners between those who drew attention to what were called "intellectual factors"—ideas, concepts, methods, evidence—and those who stressed "social

factors"—forms of organization, political and economic influences on science, and social uses or consequences of science. That now seems to many historians, as it does to me, a rather silly demarcation, and I shall not waste readers' time here in reviewing why those disputes figured so largely in past approaches to the history of early modern science. If science is to be understood as historically situated and in its collective aspect (i.e., sociologically), then that understanding should encompass all aspects of science, its ideas and practices no less than its institutional forms and social uses. Anyone who wants to represent science sociologically cannot simply set aside the body of what the relevant practitioners *knew* and how they went about obtaining that knowledge. Rather, the task for the sociologically minded historian is to display the structure of knowledge making and knowledge holding *as social processes*.

3. A traditional construal of "social factors" (or what is sociological about science) has focused on considerations taken to be "external" to science proper—for example, the use of metaphors from the economy in the development of scientific knowledge or the ideological uses of science in justifying certain sorts of political arrangements. Much fine historical work has been done based on such a construal. However, the identification of what is sociological about science with what is external to science appears to me a curious and a limited way of going on. There is as much "society" inside the scientist's laboratory, and internal to the development of scientific knowledge, as there is "outside." And in fact the very distinction between the social and the political, on the one hand, and "scientific truth," on the other, is partly a cultural product of the period [I discuss]. What is common sensically thought of as science in the late twentieth century is in some measure a product of the historical episodes we want to understand here. Far from matter-of-factly treating the distinction between the social and the scientific as a resource in telling a historical story, I mean to make it into a topic of inquiry. How and why did we come to think that such a distinction is a matter *of course?*

4. I do not consider that there is anything like an "essence" of seventeenth-century science or indeed of seventeenth-century reforms in science. Consequently there is no single coherent story that could possibly capture all the aspects of science or its changes in which we late twentieth-century moderns might happen to be interested. I can think of no feature of early modern science that has been traditionally identified as its revolutionary essence that did not have significantly variant contemporary forms or that was not subjected to contemporary criticism by practitioners who have also been accounted revolutionary "moderns." . . .

❦

The confrontation over Newton's optical work can stand as an emblem of the fragmented knowledge-making legacies of the seventeenth century. A theoretically cautious and experience-based conception of science was here juxtaposed to one that deployed mathematical as well as experimental tools to claim theoretical certainty. Diffidence was opposed to ambition, respect for the concrete particularities of nature to the quest for universally applicable idealizations, the modesty of the fact gatherer to the pride of the abstracted philosopher. Do you want to capture the essence of nature and command assent to representations of its regularities? Do you want to subject yourself to the discipline of describing, and perhaps generalizing about, the behavior of medium-sized objects actually existing in the world?

Both conceptions of science persist in the late twentieth century, and both can trace elements of their formation back to the seventeenth century. The one is not necessarily to be regarded as a failed version of the other, however much partisans may defend the virtues of their preferred practice and condemn the vices of another. These are, so to speak, different games that natural philosophers might wish to play, and decisions about which game is best are different in kind from decisions about what is a sensible move within a given game: an accurate pass from midfield to the winger in soccer is not a bad jump shot in basketball. In the seventeenth century natural philosophers were confronted with differing repertoires of practical and conceptual skills for achieving various philosophical goals and with choices about which ends they might work to achieve. The goal was always some conception of proper philosophical knowledge about the natural world, though descriptions of what that knowledge looked like and how it was to be secured varied greatly.

POSTSCRIPT

Was the Scientific
Revolution Revolutionary?

This question is a philosophical as well as a historical one. At issue are how we understand key terms such as "science" and "revolution" as well as how we interpret what philosophers call epistemology or knowledge theory. Both historians agree that key people in the past understood what they were doing as a break with the past. And, both agree that there are continuities as well as discontinuities. Taking apart texts to reveal their hidden meanings has led many to question whether it is ever possible to have a single, universal meaning for a term like "science." What the word may have meant to people practicing it in the seventeenth century may be worlds away from what it means to people practicing it today. And those of us outside the scientific community in either period generally have even less idea what may be at stake.

Thomas Kuhn, whose widely-read 1962 book *The Structure of Scientific Revolutions* (University of Chicago, 1962, 1970) has shed some light on this controversy, combines continuity with discontinuity. Revolutions, Kuhn writes, are occasional, dramatic breaks from periods of what he calls "normal science" when everyone in the scientific community operates from within an accepted paradigm. Revolutions occur when experiments repeatedly do not yield the expected results or when data do not conform to predicted outcomes. Scientists struggle to make the new material fit the old paradigm; those who challenge the paradigm are marginalized or forced to conform. When it becomes clear that the paradigm has broken down, a new paradigm is accepted. Then everything is explained in terms of the new paradigm. Students are educated in the new paradigm; textbooks are written to reflect it; research takes it as its starting point. Has the world changed or only our way of explaining it to ourselves?

Rethinking the Scientific Revolution, Margaret J. Osler, ed. (Cambridge University Press, 2000) is a collection of fifteen essays; the first defends the traditional image of the Scientific Revolution and the other fourteen challenge it in various ways. In *Ingenious Pursuits: Building the Scientific Revolution* (Doubleday, 1999), Lisa Jardine, a Renaissance scholar, provides thumbnail biographies of major and minor natural scientists. As a general introduction to this subject, students might try *Encyclopedia of the Scientific Revolution: From Copernicus to Newton,* Wilbur Applebaum, ed. (Garland, 2000). In 700 pages, this volume chronicles the extraordinary changes in natural philosophy from the beginning of the sixteenth century to the end of the seventeenth century. It includes the political, religious, social, and technological factors that affected developments in science, biographical selections and some short bibliographies.

ISSUE 18

Did the West Define the Modern World?

YES: **William H. McNeill**, from *The Rise of the West: A History of the Human Community* (University of Chicago Press, 1991)

NO: **Philip D. Curtin**, from *The World and the West: The European Challenge and the Overseas Response in the Age of Empire* (Cambridge University Press, 2000)

ISSUE SUMMARY

YES: Professor of history William H. McNeill states that in 1500, Western Europe began to extend influence to other parts of the world, resulting in a revolution in world relationships, in which the West was the principal beneficiary.

NO: History professor Philip D. Curtin states that the amount of control the West had over the rest of the world was mitigated by the European colonial process and the reaction it engendered throughout the world.

It seems to be widely accepted that beginning in 1500, Western Europe embarked on a course of world domination, the effects of which are still with us today. Due to factors such as superior military technology, immunity to diseases which ravaged others, and a strong will to succeed, Europeans were able to extend their influence over people in other parts of the world. An immediate result of this was the trans-Atlantic slave trade where Europeans traded products, including firearms, for human cargo. Finding African leaders willing to participate in this horrific practice, the Europeans did not even have to penetrate into the heart of Africa to make their profits. The slaves-to-be were brought to coastal fortresses called "factories" to wait for the western ships and the inhumane exchange to take place. It would not be until the 19th century that Europeans would begin to directly assert themselves into African affairs in what has been called the "Age of Imperialism."

In Asia, the system was different, but with similar economic results. Trading posts were set up throughout Asia, especially in India—and later—China, where the Portuguese, Dutch, French, and British established commercial rivalries. These led to greater control over larger areas where the Europeans exploited the existence of local rivalries and corrupt, incompetent leaders to further their economic interests. These too would lead to a more direct control over some of the nations of Asia during the 19th century, and a more indirect control over others.

Many have assumed that the capitalism and democracy that are so prominent among the world's nations today are part of the legacy that non-Western nations inherited from their contact with the West. In this view, the Western way was the wave of the future. Also, the West's technological and military superiority over the past 500 years has naturally led generations of Western historians to view the last half-millennium through the eyes of their own worldview. When the civilizations of the non-Western world were considered at all, they were simply included in a marginal and ancillary way.

All of this changed with the end of colonialism, an important result of World War II. The former colonies, mandated territories, and Western-controlled areas were now free and independent nations, ready to determine their own destinies—and interpret their own histories. In this process they were joined by a generation of new Western historians who did not see the world through Eurocentric-colored glasses. Together, they forced the historical profession to reevaluate the Eurocentric view of the world's last five hundred years.

William McNeill's book *The Rise of the West*, first published in 1962, has achieved classic status among world history books. In the following selection from that book, McNeill operates from the thesis that from earliest historical times, world civilizations have had contact with one another. He refers to this process as **ecumene** (from the Greek, meaning one world). From these contacts, came exchanges of all types which altered those civilizations in particular, and the world in general. He states that this process has affected the scope of history, although it is the West—as the title of his book implies—that has benefitted the most from the process. McNeill concludes that this superiority began during the Age of Exploration of the sixteenth century and continues to influence the current world.

Philip D. Curtin covers the same time span, and sees similar results—a Western domination which extended throughout the world. However, he discovers as a result of this process, the limited control the West was able to exert over the world. This was due to (1) the nature of the various types of institutional control established by the West; (2) the responses of the world's nations to this European intrusion which lessened their control. It is interesting to note that in place of the more common "The West and the World" titles given to books and chapters in textbooks when describing this period, Curtin uses as his title, *The World and the West*.

YES

William H. McNeill

The Far West's Challenge to the World, 1500–1700 A.D.

The year 1500 A.D. aptly symbolizes the advent of the modern era, in world as well as in European history. Shortly before that date, technical improvements in navigation pioneered by the Portuguese under Prince Henry the Navigator (d. 1460) reduced to tolerable proportions the perils of the stormy and tide-beset North Atlantic. Once they had mastered these dangerous waters, European sailors found no seas impenetrable, nor any ice-free coast too formidable for their daring. In rapid succession, bold captains sailed into distant and hitherto unknown seas: Columbus (1492), Vasco da Gama (1498), and Magellan (1519–22) were only the most famous.

The result was to link the Atlantic face of Europe with the shores of most of the earth. What had always before been the extreme fringe of Eurasia became, within little more than a generation, a focus of the world's sea lanes, influencing and being influenced by every human society within easy reach of the sea. Thereby the millennial land-centered balance among the Eurasian civilizations was abruptly challenged and, within three centuries, reversed. The sheltering ocean barrier between the Americas and the rest of the world was suddenly shattered, and the slave trade brought most of Africa into the penumbra of civilization. Only Australia and the smaller islands of the Pacific remained for a while immune; yet by the close of the eighteenth century, they too began to feel the force of European seamanship and civilization.

Western Europe, of course, was the principal gainer from this extraordinary revolution in world relationships, both materially and in a larger sense, for it now became the pre-eminent meeting place for novelties of every kind. This allowed Europeans to adopt whatever pleased them in the tool kits of other peoples and stimulated them to reconsider, recombine, and invent anew within their own enlarged cultural heritage. The Amerindian civilizations of Mexico and Peru were the most conspicuous victims of the new world balance, being suddenly reduced to a comparatively simple village level after the directing classes had been destroyed or demoralized by the Spaniards. Within the Old World, the Moslem peoples lost their central position in the ecumene as ocean routes supplanted overland portage. Only in the Far East were the effects of the new constellation of world relationships at first unimportant.

From THE RISE OF THE WEST by William McNeill, pp. 565–7, 576–8, 569–74. Copyright © 1991 by University of Chicago Press. Reprinted by permission.

From a Chinese viewpoint it made little difference whether foreign trade, regulated within traditional forms, passed to Moslem or European merchants' hands. As soon as European expansive energy seemed to threaten their political integrity, first Japan and then China evicted the disturbers and closed their borders against further encroachment. Yet by the middle of the nineteenth century, even this deliberate isolation could no longer be maintained; and the civilizations of the Far East—simultaneously with the primitive cultures of central Africa—began to stagger under the impact of the newly industrialized European (and extra-European) West.

The key to world history from 1500 is the growing political dominance first of western Europe, then of an enlarged European-type society planted astride the north Atlantic and extending eastward into Siberia. Yet until about 1700, the ancient landward frontiers of the Asian civilizations retained much of their old significance. Both India (from 1526) and China (by 1644) suffered yet another conquest from across these frontiers; and the Ottoman empire did not exhaust its expansive power until near the close of the seventeenth century. Only in Central America and western South America did Europeans succeed in establishing extensive land empires overseas during this period. Hence the years 1500–1700 may be regarded as transitional between the old land-centered and the new ocean-centered pattern of ecumenical relationships—a time when European enterprise had modified, but not yet upset the fourfold balance of the Old World.

The next major period, 1700–1850, saw a decisive alteration of the balance in favor of Europe, except in the Far East. Two great outliers were added to the Western world by the Petrine conversion of Russia and by the colonization of North America. Less massive offshoots of European society were simultaneously established in southernmost Africa, in the South American pampas, and in Australia. India was subjected to European rule; the Moslem Middle East escaped a similar fate only because of intra-European rivalries; and the barbarian reservoir of the Eurasian steppes lost its last shreds of military and cultural significance with the progress of Russian and Chinese conquest and colonization.

After 1850, the rapid development of mechanically powered industry enormously enhanced the political and cultural primacy of the West. At the beginning of this period, the Far Eastern citadel fell before Western gunboats; and a few of the European nations extended and consolidated colonial empires in Asia and Africa. Although European empires have decayed since 1945, and the separate nation-states of Europe have been eclipsed as centers of political power by the melding of peoples and nations occurring under the aegis of both the American and Russian governments, it remains true that, since the end of World War II, the scramble to imitate and appropriate science, technology, and other aspects of Western culture has accelerated enormously all round the world. Thus the dethronement of western Europe from its brief mastery of the globe coincided with (and was caused by) an unprecedented, rapid Westernization of all the peoples of the earth. The rise of the West seems today still far from its apogee; nor is it obvious, even in the narrower political sense, that the era of Western dominance is past. The American and Russian outliers of European civilization remain militarily far stronger than the other states of the world, while the power of a federally reorganized western Europe is potentially superior to both and remains inferior only because of difficulties in articulating common policies among nations still clinging to the trappings of their decaying sovereignties.

∢◎∢

From the perspective of the mid-twentieth century, the career of Western civilization since 1500 appears as a vast explosion, far greater than any comparable phenomenon of the past both in geographic range and in social depth. Incessant and accelerating self-transformation, compounded from a welter of conflicting ideas, institutions, aspirations, and inventions, has characterized modern European history; and with the recent institutionalization of deliberate innovation in the form of industrial research laboratories, universities, military general staffs, and planning commissions of every sort, an accelerating pace of technical and social change bids fair to remain a persistent feature of Western civilization.

This changeability gives the European and Western history of recent centuries both a fascinating and a confusing character. The fact that we are heirs but also prisoners of the Western past, caught in the very midst of an unpredictable and incredibly fast-moving flux, does not make it easier to discern critical landmarks, as we can, with equanimity if not without error, for ages long past and civilizations alien to our own.

. . . Fortunately, a noble array of historians has traversed the ground already, so that it is not difficult to divide Western history into periods, nor to characterize such periods with some degree of plausibility. A greater embarrassment arises from the fact that suitable periods of Western history do not coincide with the benchmarks of modern world history. This is not surprising, for Europe had first to reorganize itself at a new level before the effects of its increased power could show themselves significantly abroad. One should therefore expect to find a lag between the successive self-transformations of European society and their manifestations in the larger theater of world history. . . .

The Great European Explorations and Their World-Wide Consequences

Europeans of the Atlantic seaboard possessed three talismans of power by 1500 which conferred upon them the command of all the oceans of the world within half a century and permitted the subjugation of the most highly developed regions of the Americas within a single generation. These were: (1) a deep-rooted pugnacity and recklessness operating by means of (2) a complex military technology, most notably in naval matters; and (3) a population inured to a variety of diseases which had long been endemic throughout the Old World ecumene.

The Bronze Age barbarian roots of European pugnacity and the medieval survival of military habits among the merchant classes of western Europe, as well as among aristocrats and territorial lords of less exalted degree, [are worth emphasizing.] Yet only when one remembers the all but incredible courage, daring, and brutality of Cortez and Pizarro in the Americas, reflects upon the ruthless aggression of Almeida and Albuquerque in the Indian Ocean, and discovers the disdain of even so cultivated a European as Father Matteo Ricci for the civility of the Chinese, does the full force of European warlikeness, when compared with the attitudes and aptitudes of other major civilizations of the earth, become apparent. The Moslems and the Japanese could alone compare in the honor they paid to the military virtues. But Moslem merchants usually cringed before the violence held in high repute by their rulers and seldom dared or perhaps cared to emulate it. Hence Moslem commercial enterprise lacked the cutting edge of naked, well-organized, large-scale force which constituted the chief stock-in-trade of European overseas merchants in the sixteenth century. The Japanese could, indeed, match broadswords with any European; but the chivalric stylization of their warfare, together with their narrowly restricted supply of iron, meant that neither *samurai* nor a sea pirate could reply in kind to a European broadside.

Supremacy at sea gave a vastly enlarged scope to European warlikeness after 1500. But Europe's maritime superiority was itself the product of a deliberate combination of science and practice, beginning in the commercial cities of Italy and coming to fruition in Portugal through the efforts of Prince Henry the Navigator and his successors. With the introduction of the compass (thirteenth century), navigation beyond sight of land had become a regular practice in the Mediterranean; and the navigators' charts, or *portolans*, needed for such voyaging showed coasts, harbors, landmarks, and compass bearings between major ports. Although they were drawn freehand, without any definite mathematical projection, *portolans* nevertheless maintained fairly accurate scales of distances. But similar mapping could be applied to the larger distances of Atlantic navigation only if means could be found to locate key points along the coast accurately. To solve this problem, Prince Henry brought to Portugal some of the best mathematicians and astronomers of Europe, who constructed simple astronomical instruments and trigonometrical tables by which ship captains could measure the latitude of newly discovered places along the African coast. The calculation of longitude was more difficult; and, until a satisfactory marine chronometer was invented in the eighteenth century, longitude could be approximated only be dead reckoning. Nevertheless, the new methods worked out at Prince Henry's court allowed the Portuguese to make usable charts of the Atlantic coasts. Such charts gave Portuguese sea captains courage to sail beyond sight of land for weeks and presently for months, confident of being able to steer their ships to within a few miles of the desired landfall.

The Portuguese court also accumulated systematic information about oceanic winds and currents; but this data was kept secret as a matter of high policy, so that modern scholars are uncertain how much the early Portuguese navigators knew. At the same time, Portuguese naval experts attacked the problem of improving ship construction. They proceeded by rule of thumb; but deliberate experiment, systematically pursued, rapidly increased the seaworthiness, maneuverability, and speed of Portuguese and presently (since improvements in naval architecture could not be kept secret) of other European ships. The most important changes were: a reduction of hull width in proportion to length; the introduction of multiple masts (usually three or four); and the substitution of several smaller, more manageable sails for the single sail per mast from which the evolution started. These innovations allowed a crew to trim the sails to suit varying conditions of wind and sea, thus greatly facilitating steering and protecting the vessel from disaster in sudden gales.

With these improvements, larger ships could be built; and increasing size and sturdiness of construction made it possible to transform seagoing vessels into gun platforms for heavy cannon. Thus by 1509, when the Portuguese fought the decisive battle for control of the Arabian Sea off the Indian port of Diu, their ships could deliver a heavy broadside at a range their Moslem enemies could not begin to match. Under such circumstances, the superior numbers of the opposing fleet simply provided the Portuguese with additional targets for their gunnery. The old tactics of sea fighting—ramming, grappling, and boarding—were almost useless against cannon fire effective at as much as 200 yards distance.

The third weapon in the European armory—disease—was quite as important as stark pugnacity and weight of metal. Endemic European diseases like smallpox and measles became lethal epidemics among Amerindian populations, who had no inherited or acquired immunities to such infections. Literally millions died of these and other European diseases; and the smallpox epidemic raging in Tenochtitlan when Cortez and his men were expelled from the citadel in 1520 had far more to do with the collapse of Aztec power than merely military operations. The Inca empire, too, may have been ravaged and weakened by a similar epidemic before Pizarro ever reached Peru.

On the other hand, diseases like yellow fever and malaria took a heavy toll of Europeans in Africa and India. But climatic conditions generally prevented new tropical diseases from penetrating Europe itself in any very serious fashion. Those which could flourish in temperate climates, like typhus, cholera, and bubonic plague, had long been known throughout the ecumene; and European populations had presumably acquired some degree of resistance to them. Certainly the new frequency of sea contact with distant regions had important medical consequences for Europeans, as the plagues for which Lisbon and London became famous prove. But gradually the infections which in earlier centuries had appeared sporadically as epidemics became merely endemic, as the exposed populations developed a satisfactory level of resistance. Before 1700, European populations had therefore successfully absorbed the shocks that came with the intensified circulation of diseases initiated by their own sea voyaging. Epidemics consequently ceased to be demographically significant. The result was that from about 1650 (or before), population growth in Europe assumed a new velocity. Moreover, so far as imperfect data allow one to judge, between 1550 and 1650 population also began to spurt upward in China, India, and the Middle East. Such an acceleration of population growth within each of the great civilizations of the Old World can scarcely be a mere coincidence. Presumably the same ecological processes worked themselves out in all parts of the ecumene, as age-old epidemic checks upon population faded into merely endemic attrition.

The formidable combination of European warlikeness, naval technique, and comparatively high levels of resistance to disease transformed the cultural balance of the world within an amazingly brief period of time. Columbus linked the Americas with Europe in 1492; and the Spaniards proceeded to explore, conquer, and colonize the New World with extraordinary energy, utter ruthlessness, and an intense missionary idealism. Cortez destroyed the Aztec state in 1519–21; Pizarro became master of the Inca empire between 1531 and 1535. Within the following generation, less famous but no less hardy conquistadores founded Spanish settlements along the coasts of Chile and Argentina, penetrated the highlands of Ecuador, Colombia, Venezuela, and Central America, and explored the Amazon basin and the southern United States. As early as 1571, Spanish power leaped across the Pacific to the Philippines, where it collided with the sea empire which their Iberian neighbors, the Portuguese, had meanwhile flung around Africa and across the southern seas of the Eastern Hemisphere.

Portuguese expansion into the Indian Ocean proceeded with even greater rapidity. Exactly a decade elapsed between the completion of Vasco da Gama's first voyage to India (1497–99) and the decisive Portuguese naval victory off Diu (1509). The Portuguese quickly exploited this success by capturing Goa (1510) and Malacca (1511), which together with Ormuz on the Persian Gulf (occupied permanently from 1515) gave them the necessary bases from which to dominate the trade of the entire Indian Ocean. Nor did they rest content with these successes. Portuguese ships followed the precious spices to their farthest source in the Moluccas without delay (1511–12); and a Portuguese merchant explorer traveling on a Malay vessel visited Canton as early as 1513–14. By 1557, a permanent Portuguese settlement was founded at Macao on the south China coast; and trade and missionary activity in Japan started in the 1540's. On the other side of the world, the Portuguese discovered Brazil in 1500 and began to settle the country after 1530. Coastal stations in both west and east Africa, established between 1471 and 1507, completed the chain of ports of call which held the Portuguese empire together.

No other European nations approached the early success of Spain and Portugal overseas. Nevertheless, the two Iberian nations did not long enjoy undisturbed the new wealth their enterprise had won. From the beginning, the Spaniards found it difficult to protect their shipping against French and Portuguese sea raiders. English pirates offered an additional and formidable threat after 1568, when the first open clash between English interlopers and the Spanish authorities in the Caribbean took place. Between 1516 and 1568 the other great maritime people of the age, the Dutch, were subjects of the same Hapsburg monarchs who ruled in Spain and, consequently, enjoyed a favored status as middlemen between Spanish and north European ports. Initially, therefore, Dutch shipping had no incentive to harass Iberian sea power.

This naval balance shifted sharply in the second half of the sixteenth century, when the Dutch revolt against Spain (1568), followed by the English victory over the Spanish armada (1588), signalized the waning of Iberian sea power before that of the northern European nations. Harassment of Dutch ships in Spanish ports simply accelerated the shift; for the Dutch responded by despatching their vessels directly to the Orient (1594), and the English soon followed suit. Thereafter, Dutch naval and commercial power rapidly supplanted that of Portugal in the southern seas. The establishment of a base in Java (1618), the capture of Malacca from the Portuguese (1641), and the seizure of the most important trading posts of Ceylon (by 1644) secured Dutch hegemony in the Indian Ocean; and during the same decades, English traders gained a foothold in western India. Simultaneously, English (1607), French (1608), and Dutch (1613) colonization of mainland North America, and the seizure of most of the smaller Caribbean islands by the same three nations, infringed upon Spanish claims to monopoly in the New World, but failed to dislodge Spanish power from any important area where it was already established.

⚜

The truly extraordinary *élan* of the first Iberian conquests and the no less remarkable missionary enterprise that followed closely in its wake surely mark a new era in the history of the human community. Yet older landmarks of that history did not crumble all at once. Movement from the Eurasian steppes continued to make political history—for example, the Uzbek conquest of Transoxiana (1507–12) with its sequel, the Mogul conquest of India (1526–1688); and the Manchu conquest of China (1621–83).

Chinese civilization was indeed only slightly affected by the new regime of the seas; and Moslem expansion, which had been a dominating feature of world history during the centuries before 1500, did not cease or even slacken very noticeably until the late seventeenth century. Through their conquest of the high seas, western Europeans did indeed outflank the Moslem world in India and southeast Asia, while Russian penetration of Siberian forests soon outflanked the Moslem lands on the north also. Yet these probing extensions of European (or para-European) power remained tenuous and comparatively weak in the seventeenth century. Far from being crushed in the jaws of a vast European pincer, the Moslems continued to win important victories and to penetrate new territories in southeast Europe, India, Africa, and southeast Asia. Only in the western and central steppe did Islam suffer significant territorial setbacks before 1700.

Thus only two large areas of the world were fundamentally transformed during the first two centuries of European overseas expansion: the regions of Amerindian high culture and western Europe itself. European naval enterprise certainly widened the range and increased the intimacy of contacts among the various peoples of the ecumene and brought new peoples into touch with the disruptive social influences of high civilization. Yet the Chinese, Moslem, and Hindu worlds were not yet really deflected from their earlier paths of development; and substantial portions of the land surface of the globe—Australia and Oceania, the rain forests of South America, and most of North America and northeastern Asia—remained almost unaffected by Europe's achievement.

Nevertheless, a new dimension had been added to world history. An ocean frontier, where European seamen and soldiers, merchants, missionaries, and settlers came into contact with the various peoples of the world, civilized and uncivilized, began to challenge the ancient pre-eminence of the Eurasian land frontier, where steppe nomads had for centuries probed, tested, and disturbed civilized agricultural populations. Very ancient social gradients began to shift when the coasts of Europe, Asia, and America became the scene of more and more important social interactions and innovation. Diseases, gold and silver, and certain valuable crops were the first items to flow freely through the new transoceanic channels of communication. Each of these had important and far-reaching consequences for Asians as well as for Europeans and Amerindians. But prior to 1700, only a few isolated borrowings of more recondite techniques or ideas passed through the sea lanes that now connected the four great civilization of the Old World. In such exchanges, Europe was more often the receiver than the giver, for its people were inspired by a lively curiosity, insatiable greed, and a reckless spirit of adventure that contrasted sharply with the smug conservatism of Chinese, Moslem, and Hindu cultural leaders.

Partly by reason of the stimuli that flowed into Europe from overseas, but primarily because of internal tensions arising from its own heterogeneous cultural inheritance, Europe entered upon a veritable social explosion in the period 1500–1650—an experience painful in itself but which nonetheless raised European power to a new level of effectiveness and for the first time gave Europeans a clear margin of superiority over the other great civilizations of the world. . . .

Conclusion

Between 1500 and 1700, the Eurasian ecumene expanded to include parts of the Americas, much of sub-Saharan Africa, and all of northern Asia. Moreover, within the Old World itself, western Europe began to forge ahead of all rivals as the most active center of geographical expansion and of cultural innovation. Indeed, Europe's self-revolution transformed the medieval frame of Western civilization into a new and vastly more powerful organization of society. Yet the Moslem, Hindu, and Chinese lands were not yet seriously affected by the new energies emanating from Europe. Until after 1700, the history of these regions continued to turn around old traditions and familiar problems.

Most of the rest of the world, lacking the massive self-sufficiency of Moslem, Hindu, and Chinese civilization, was more acutely affected by contact with Europeans. In the New World, these contacts first decapitated and then decimated the Amerindian societies; but in other regions, where local powers of resistance were greater, a strikingly consistent pattern of reaction manifested itself. In such diverse areas as Japan, Burma, Siam, Russia, and parts of Africa, an initial interest in and occasional eagerness to accept European techniques, ideas, religion, or fashions of dress was supplanted in the course of the seventeenth century by a policy of withdrawal and deliberate insulation from European pressures. The Hindu revival in India and the reform of Lamaism in Tibet and Mongolia manifested a similar spirit; for both served to protect local cultural values against alien pressures, though in these cases the pressures were primarily Moslem and Chinese rather than European.

A few fringe areas of the earth still remained unaffected by the disturbing forces of civilization. But by 1700 the only large habitable regions remaining outside the ecumene were Australia, the Amazon rain forest, and northwestern North America; and even these latter two had largely felt tremors of social disturbance generated by the approaching onset of civilization.

At no previous time in world history had the pace of social transformation been so rapid. The new density and intimacy of contacts across the oceans of the earth assured a continuance of cross-stimulation among the major cultures of mankind. The efforts to restrict foreign contacts and to withdraw from disturbing relationships with outsiders—especially with the restless and ruthless Westerners—were doomed to ultimate failure by the fact that successive self-transformations of western European civilization, and especially of Western technology, rapidly increased the pressures Westerners were able to bring against the other peoples of the earth. Indeed, world history since 1500 may be thought of as a race between the West's growing power to molest the rest of the world and the increasingly desperate efforts of other peoples to stave Westerners off, either by clinging more strenuously than before to their peculiar cultural inheritance or, when that failed, by appropriating aspects of Western civilization—especially technology—in the hope of thereby finding means to preserve their local autonomy.

Philip D. Curtin  **NO**

The World and the West:
The European Challenge and the
Overseas Response in the Age of Empire

Conquest

The word *colonialism* is often a misnomer, used for any form of domination of one society over another. The original Greek meaning of a colony implied an outward migration from a mother city or metropolis to settle in a new place. True colonization in this original sense is represented today by examples such as the United States and Canada, where culture change took place but was mainly carried by a blanket immigration of Europeans who brought their culture with them. The Native Americans were pushed aside to become a small minority, sometimes culturally assimilated, sometimes not.

Another variety of so-called colonialism is demographically the reverse of true colonization. It is more accurately labeled territorial empire, where Europeans conquered a territory overseas but sent a negligible number of settlers beyond the administrative and military personnel required to control it. Examples of this type would be British rule in India and Nigeria.

A third, mixed case, midway between territorial empire and true colonization, also sometimes occurred. In these instances, European settlers were a substantial minority, living alongside other cultural communities of native inhabitants. The result is often called a plural society. A rough line between plural societies and true empires can be drawn when the settler community reaches more than about 5 percent of the total population. The important instances of plural societies in the past century or so are South Africa, Algeria, Israel, some Latin American countries, such as Peru or Guatemala, and many parts of the former Soviet Union.

The Pattern of Empire

The conventional history of European empire building not only lumps dissimilar experiences under the rubric of colonialism, but it often, and too readily, accepts convenient fictions, concocted by long-dead publicists, historians, and government officials, in place of reality. Historians in recent decades have made great progress in correcting this European bias, but much remains to be done.

From THE WORLD AND THE WEST by Philip D. Curtain, pp. 117–17, 275–277. Copyright © 2000 by Cambridge University Press. Reprinted by permission.

One tendency of past historiography, not yet altogether corrected, is the tendency to read backward from the clear pattern of European dominance in the recent past, assuming that it was the case in earlier periods as well. Territorial empire and large-scale true colonization have origins that can be traced to these earlier times, but they flourished only in the period since about 1800, or even later.

In earlier centuries, the most important modes of culture contact were commercial, mediated by trade diasporas or the settlement of merchants along a trade route to facilitate commerce. These commercial settlers came only in small numbers but were often extremely important in the process of culture change. They were, in a sense, professional cross-cultural brokers, facilitating trade between the home region and its commercial outposts. Examples can be found in the earliest urban societies of Mesopotamia and in the pre-Columbian Americas.

Many early trade diasporas were comparatively peaceful, living on sufferance with the permission, often the good will as well, of the rulers of the territory where they settled. Dating back to the medieval Mediterranean, European trade diasporas often took a more violent form, where Genoese and Venetian not only settled in alien trading towns but seized the towns themselves and used them as bases for intercity competition in warfare as well as commerce. They rarely aspired to territorial control beyond those strong points, which is why militarized trade diasporas of this type are often called trading-post empires.

Between about 1425 and 1525, when the remnants of Magellan's fleet returned to Spain, European mariners revolutionized human ability to travel by sea and return. The achievement depended on a combination of improved vessels and navigational techniques with increased geographic knowledge, including the outlines of the world wind system. Before this time in world history, regular and routine navigation had been limited to coastal voyages and to some travel on inland seas such as the Mediterranean, though offshore voyages were common in the monsoon belt that stretched east and west from Indonesia to Africa and north through the South China Sea to Japan. After the 1520s, however, European mariners could sail to any coast in the world, though at considerable cost and danger at first.

This maritime revolution gave Europeans their first significant military advantage. They had, as yet, no technical advantage in the Mediterranean, where during the 1500s the Ottoman Turks were at least their equal. Overseas it was different. Maritime technology often made Europeans locally supreme in distant seas, where opposing ships mounting effective artillery were virtually unknown. Seapower also had the strategic advantage of mobility to concentrate the available force on a single objective.

It was the mobility of seapower that made it possible for Europeans to build trading-post empires at a time when they were still inferior militarily on land. In the early 1500s, when the Portuguese first began to send naval expeditions east of the Gape of Good Hope, they often chose as their bases islands such as Goa in western India, with secondary centers at Mozambique in East Africa, Melaka in Malaya, and Macau in south China. In the early 1600s, the

Dutch established a similar network based on Batavia (now Jakarta) on Java, with connections westward to Ceylon and the east coast of India and north to an island in Nagasaki harbor in Japan. The English shortly entered the picture at Bombay, Madras, and Calcutta in India. France and other European maritime states followed with their own sets of competing trading posts. These trade enclaves were no threat to major Asian powers, but they were the entering wedge from which territorial empires were to spread in later centuries.

Overland trading-post empires soon began to appear as well. In the 1600s, French fur traders fanned out to the west of the lower St. Lawrence River valley by way of the Great Lakes. English fur traders reached south from Hudson Bay. Neither had any interest in controlling territory or ruling over the Native American populations; they only wanted a secure base for trade and protection from rival European traders. In Asia at the same period, fur traders from Muscovy were extending their trading-post empire eastward across Siberia to the Pacific. In time, these overland trading-post empires were to form the background for territorial empire and true colonization in both North America and Siberia.

Empire in the Americas

In the Americas, and in the Americas alone, European territorial empires date from the 1500s. Here, the European maritime advantage intersected with a particular American vulnerability. The ancestors of the American Indians had crossed the land bridge from Asia during the last Ice Age, up to about 10,000 years ago. Their passage occurred before the agricultural revolution, hence before the development of diseases like smallpox, which grew out of the interaction of humans and their domestic animals. Other serious diseases, such as falciparum malaria, evolved in tropical Africa only after agriculture had made dense human communities possible. Those postagricultural human pathogens came too late to be carried to the Americas by the original immigrants, and the Americas, in isolation, developed no diseases of equivalent seriousness. Meanwhile, the intensity of intercommunication across the Afro-Eurasian land mass made it possible for diseases originating at any point to spread much more widely. Elements of a common disease pool, though with local variations, existed over most of these continents.

Any disease environment tends to build up a pattern of countervailing immunities in the children who grow up there. Victims of most diseases, if they survive, emerge with a degree of protection against further attack. Measles and other so-called childhood diseases mainly affect the young because most people are infected in childhood and are relatively immune later in life. Some diseases are also benign in childhood but more serious for adults. Yellow fever, for example, is often so mild in children that it has no clinical symptoms, yet victims still acquire a lifelong immunity, whereas among adults, yellow fever is often fatal to more than half of its victims.

In the early 1500s, diseases from Afro-Eurasia were devastating for non-immune American populations. Smallpox alone often swept away more than a quarter of the population, leaving the survivors incapable of an adequate military defense. As a result, major American empires such as those of the Aztecs and Incas were unable to withstand Spanish attack. The Portuguese also easily established bases here and there along the Brazilian coast. Even after the initial crisis, the disease impact lasted for decades as one unfamiliar disease followed another. Some of the new diseases, such as smallpox, were common to Africa and Europe alike, but the most commonly fatal of tropical diseases, yellow fever and falciparum malaria, were virtually unknown in Europe, though Europeans accidentally introduced them to the Americas through the slave trade. Amerindian populations declined steeply for about a century and a half after contact, before they stabilized and began slowly to grow again. . . .

Migration and Demographic Transitions

The mass emigration of Europeans is characteristic of the industrial age, beginning in the 1800s, although in any decade before the 1840s more Africans than Europeans crossed the Atlantic. Even though earlier European governments tended to think their best prospects overseas were trading-post empires, small true colonies were an occasional by-product. The Azores, in the mid-Atlantic at the same latitude as Portugal itself, were an uninhabited chain of islands discovered by chance. In the next century, after 1470, they were gradually settled by mainland Portuguese. By the mid-1500s they had become part of Portugal, producing the same wine, wheat, and cattle as peninsular Portugal. The Canaries and Madeira, closer to the African coast, went though phases of trading-post and plantation developments, but they too ultimately became true colonies of Spain or Portugal.

Brazil began as an adjunct to the Portuguese trading-post empire in the Indian Ocean. Ships bound for India had to pass close by. Though they did not often stop off, Brazil in unfriendly hands would have been a potential threat to the safe passage to India. When, by the 1540s, the French and some others became active as dye-wood traders on the Brazilian coast, the Portuguese crown decided to plant a colony there, mainly as the self-supporting nucleus for a garrison to protect a crucial strategic position.

The original expedition of 1549 shows the Portuguese intentions. It included 320 people in the pay of the crown, 400 convicts to supply labor, and about 300 assorted priests and free men as colonists and missionaries. Up to about 1570, European colonists were a majority, but, as the influx of African and Amerindian slaves shifted the balance, northeast Brazil became a plantation colony with European managers and an African and Amerindian working class. It was only in the 1800s that a significant amount of true colonization was again attempted, this time mainly in central and southern Brazil.

In the 1600s, the French and the Dutch pursued a similar strategy of commercial settlements. Some of their Caribbean posts followed the Brazilian precedent and in time became plantation colonies with a majority population from Africa, but others took another direction and became true colonies, more by population growth than by continuous immigration from Europe. The Dutch settlement at the Gape of Good Hope and the French settlement around the mouth of the Saint Lawrence can serve as examples. Both of these settlements were founded in the mid-1600s to protect commerce, but with enough European farmers to produce a local supply of food and to provide local manpower for defense.

New France along the Saint Lawrence was established to serve the fur trade, which required only a few thousand settlers, and that was all that France sent out. During the whole period from its foundation to the conquest by England in 1763, no more than 10,000 immigrants came from France, and some authorities think the number may have been closer to 4,000. Yet the net natural increase of less than 10,000 French settlers led, with only small later additions from Europe, to a French Canadian population of more than five million in North America today.

The purpose of the Dutch settlements at the Cape was similar—to serve as a way station for the Dutch East India Company's trade to Indonesia and India and to provide a garrison to protect the harbor at Table Bay. For several decades after its founding in 1652, Cape Town was a military post and little more. But then, in 1679, the Company decided to increase the number of settlers in order to make the post more nearly self-supporting. The settlers were not on the Company payroll, but they might be called out for militia duty. Meanwhile, they were encouraged to produce food for the garrison and for sale to passing ships. For a time, the Company subsidized, the immigration of German, Dutch, and French Protestants. In all, it sent out some 1,630 people, but in 1707, it ended assisted immigration, and immigration died to a trickle. This European immigration of two thousand or so before 1710 nevertheless grew by natural increase into a white Afrikaans-speaking South African population, which, numbered about three and a half million by the early 1900s.

At the Cape of Good Hope, however, the result was not a true colony on the order of Quebec. The local Khoisan population survived and mixed with European settlers and with slaves from many shores of the Indian Ocean. The result, is the present Cape Colored community, recently numbering more than three million people. The Cape Province thus became a plural Society, but a plural society that absorbed many different cultures. Not only did the small nucleus of European settlers expand through population growth, but their culture became an important ingredient in the culture of the Cape Colored majority. The vast majority of Cape Colored people, for example, speak Afrikaans as their home language.

The European settlements at the Cape and in Quebec illustrate two important differences from other trading-post empires. In both, the settlers were not an all-male military force but included women. They soon developed a normal sex ratio, which led to a natural increase among the European community. European populations in the humid tropics rarely attained a net natural increase, even after many decades, partly for lack of women and partly for lack of immunity to tropical disease. The disease environments of Canada and the Cape of Good Hope, however, were as favorable to European population growth as that of Europe itself, perhaps more so, and settler communities in North America and South Africa soon attained a higher rate of net natural increase than the European populations at home.

The demographic transitions in Spanish America were similar but more complex. By the 1570s, Mexico and Peru had overcome the anarchy of the conquest period to become the first territorial empires in the European world; yet two centuries later, they had become a complex network of plural societies, with little net demographic input from Europe. The Spanish empire in the Americas had begun, not on the initiative of the Spanish government but on that of the conquerors themselves, and they numbered in the low thousands. Their successors were few as well—soldiers, administrators, missionaries, and later on, mine and ranch managers. Spanish America, at any date in the 1500s, was a territorial empire controlled by a tiny European minority.

After that time, the flow of net Spanish immigration to the Americas is difficult to estimate. Some authorities give the figure of 150,000 legal emigrants crossing from Spain to the Americas over the whole period from 1509 to 1740. Others suggest a half million up to 1650 only. These estimates are uncertain because they seldom take account of a large but unspecified number of officials, merchants, and soldiers who returned to Spain after a tour of duty in the Americas. In addition, the migratory flow in the 1500s was largely male—less than 15 percent female before 1550, less than 35 percent female by the end of the century. This suggests that the second generation of Spanish-derived population would be *mestizos*, Spanish only on the father's side.

These patterns of disease, immigration, and reproduction formed the historical demography of Spanish America through the colonial period. No matter what the net migration from Europe, once the sex ratio of overseas Europeans reached parity among American-born Spaniards, the overseas European population rose by natural increase, just as it did at the Gape of Good Hope or in Quebec. So too did the mestizo populations. With time, the Native American decline slowed and stopped, and recovery began, but the timing was not uniform everywhere. Those Amerindian populations that first encountered the alien diseases had begun a strong recovery before the disease crisis reached more isolated regions. . . .

. . . British North America passed through another kind of demographic transition during the 1600s and 1700s. The overseas-European population increased dramatically, as it did elsewhere outside tropical lowlands. The Indians that survived the disease crisis, however, were too few to form a working class, as they had in Spanish America. For the most part, the working class in the northern colonies was made up of indentured European servants and their descendants, a few African slaves, some convicts, and some free settlers.

The English, unlike the other colonial powers, sometimes founded true colonies in North America by intent. In the 1600s, it was a common opinion that England was overpopulated, and this opinion lay behind the colonization of Ireland as well. Some settlements were designed to reproduce the society of the mother country, but not all. New York was partly designed to anchor the fur trade through Albany to the west, just as Quebec was to anchor the fur trade of the Saint Lawrence. The South Carolina low country of the early 1700s was more a plantation colony on the West Indian model than it was a colony of settlement.

Nevertheless, more European migrants went to North America in the colonial period than to all other destinations, and their population growth after arrival was even more important. Recent guesses based on spotty immigration figures put the number of arrivals in the mainland British colonies at 360,000 to 720,000, depending on the mode of estimation. Whatever the actual number within that range, the rate of population growth was so high that this small input produced an overseas European population of more than three million by 1790.

Even so, the volume of the European immigration was insignificant compared to the flow that would follow in the late 1800s. Imprecise estimates of all European movement overseas by 1790 indicate around a million and a half—far fewer than the total of around eight million Africans landed in the Americas before 1800, and insignificant compared to the European emigration overseas in an equivalent time period from 1800 to 1990, sometimes set at sixty million.

Emergence of Territorial Empire

Territorial empire, like the massive European migrations overseas, belongs to the industrial age. Before about 1750, significant European control over territorial empires was still confined to the Americas, but even then the area governed was a shadow of what text-book maps show as Spanish and Portuguese America. The maps show European claims to sovereignty, whereas real government administration as of 1800 covered only the highlands from central Mexico to central Chile, most Caribbean islands, and much of coastal Brazil. Otherwise, the Europeans actually controlled only enclaves within territory they claimed but did not try to govern. Such enclaves to the north of central Mexico included scattered mining centers, trading towns such as Santa Fe, and bits of California surrounding mission stations. Elsewhere in North America, the pattern was similar. Real control extended over the coastal settlement areas from Quebec to Georgia, but beyond the Appalachians the dominant pattern was that of an overland trading-post empire. By 1800, not a quarter of the territory of the Americas was actually governed by Europeans.

North of the Black Sea and south of Muscovy, Europe had another frontier of expanding control to the east. At the beginning of the 1600s, this region had been mainly controlled by Tatar nomads left over from Mongol expansion of the 1200s and later, now contested by sedentary states on the borders—Muscovy to the north, Poland and Lithuania to the west, the Hapsburg domains to the southwest, and the Ottoman Empire to the south. The political and military contest between these sedentary states was more fluid than similar frontier struggles in western Europe. Ultimate political control of bureaucratic structures was less secure than in western Europe; populations were both sparser and more mobile. Over the period from 1600 to about 1800, however, the drift of power was away from the Tatars and Ottomans and in favor of the Russian Empire, and the military and political advance was accompanied by a massive settlement of what was to be Ukraine and southern Russia. It was the beginning of Russian colonization that would ultimately extend beyond the Urals as well.

Before 1800, however, the Russian presence in Siberia took the form of a trading-post empire that stretched eastward to Alaska. The bare beginning of true colonization centered in a narrow strip of land along the line of the later trans-Siberian railroad. In fact, the Russians had begun moving into that corridor a little before 1800, but the main Russian occupation came afterward, along with the Russian acquisition of territorial empire in the Caucasus and Central Asia. In this part of Eurasia, the pattern was that of incipient territorial empires in the south and overland trading-post empires in the north, with enclaves of true colonization scattered in both regions. The whole strategy of European expansion here was under the strong influence of older traditions of conflict between nomadic and sedentary peoples.

Along the southern and eastern coasts of Asia, the pattern of European empire was still that of the trading enclaves, though some territorial control was beginning here and there. In the Philippines, Spain had extended the patterns of control originating in Spanish America. Its bureaucratic administrative structure theoretically covered all the islands, but underneath, strong elements of control remained in local hands, Spanish and Filipino alike. The government in Manila did not even try to administer much, perhaps most, of the Philippine territory it claimed.

The most important European territorial empires in Asia were those ruled by the British and the Dutch East India Companies. They were chartered trading companies, originally intended to supervise trading-post empires. By 1800, the Dutch Company had considerable power over parts of the Indonesian archipelago, but it was mainly exercised for commercial advantage rather than tax revenue, much less day-to-day government administration. The Company's rule over territory, weak as it was, was confined to the western three-quarters of the island of Java. Otherwise it had genuine control over a number of trading-post towns and some islands of particular importance for the spice trade, like the Malukus.

In India as of 1800, the British East India Company was the dominant authority over the provinces of Bengal and Bihar, but the nature of that authority indicates the transitional stage between trading-post empire and real territorial control. Since the 1740s, European powers, especially Britain and France, had begun to be more than simple traders, even armed traders, arid they transferred their European rivalry into Indian politics. The Mughal Empire, which had ruled north India through most of the 1500s and 1600s, was no longer a strong central authority except in name. Provincial rulers held the real power, though they might rule in the Mughal name. This fluid situation opened the possibility for the European companies to recruit Indian soldiers to oppose one another and to use their military power to participate actively in an Indian state system.

At first, the Europeans sought only to influence Indian rulers, but that influence gradually increased to the point that they were de facto rulers. In 1772, the British East India Company became, in theory, a corporate official of the Mughal empire for the provinces of Bengal and Bihar, in the hinterland of Calcutta. It assumed the post of revenue collector, or *diwan*, for those provinces but kept the revenue for itself instead of passing it on to the Mughal capital in Delhi. The actual tax collectors were Indian, as they had always been, but they now worked under supervision of British Company officials. Tax collection led the Company on to take over other administrative and judicial powers, at least over the top level of government. Still later, it began the indirect supervision of Indian "native states," which would agree to accept the authority of a

British "resident," in effect a kind of ambassador whose advice the ruler was bound to accept in crucial matters.

Beginning with these convenient fictions, the authority of the British company increased until by 1805, it was the most powerful single territorial power in India. By the 1840s, the British East India Company was so powerful that its word could often be law even within most Indian states still not formally annexed to British India. Even so, the authority of the Company and of Crown officials above it was imbedded in a congeries of Mughal institutions, which were only gradually Westernized in the course of the 1800s.

The Changing Reality of Imperial Power

The powers of governments have varied over time, although the early industrial age made available a new technology of government, which, with local modification, has become worldwide. In the agricultural age government administration differed greatly from one culture to another. Feudal Europe was very different from Song China. Many historical atlases show a map of "Charlemagne's Empire," in a solid color and stretching over much of northwest Europe from a capital at Aachen. Charlemagne's overrule may have been recognized in some sense over this vast territory, but the levels of literacy and governmental efficiency in Europe at that time were so low that orders could not have been reliably transmitted everywhere, much less obeyed. It is doubtful whether a substantial minority of the population were conscious that they were part of an empire by any name.

Maps of later periods show such events as the transfer of Alsace and Lorraine from France to Germany in 1871. The meaning in that case was far more real. Taxes went to a new destination. Orders given were normally carried out; police and judicial authorities exercised control within a central framework of authority. Public education by that time was nearly universal, and changing the language of education from French to German meant something important, even though the people of Alsace continued to speak their own home language, which was neither. Hardly anyone, however ill-educated, could fail to be aware of the change. European governments in the early industrial age controlled a largely literate population through an increasingly efficient public administration, which controlled wide areas of public service. No preindustrial government had such extensive power to influence its subjects in so many aspects of their lives.

European empires overseas had increasing administrative power as well, but an enormous gap could sometimes exist between their claims to authority and the reality of power they were capable of exercising. The European use of grandiose titles to empire goes back at least to the early 1500s, when Manoel I of Portugal claimed the title "Lord of the Conquest, Navigation, and Commerce of Ethiopia, Arabia, Persia, and India." At the time, very few people in these territories had even heard of Portugal, but the claim is not as foolish as it sounds. In the European context of that time, it was merely the assertion of a Portuguese monopoly over Asian trade, to the exclusion of other Europeans, and a warning that other Europeans who attempted to conquer Asian or African territory could count on Portuguese opposition.

At other times, Europeans underplayed rather than overplayed the reality of their power. In 1882, a British army occupied Egypt, but the European diplomatic setting of the time made it inconvenient for Britain either to annex Egypt or to withdraw. As a way out, the British Foreign Office established its control over major operations of the Egyptian government and ruled Egypt in fact for decades. British overrule began in 1882, and a measure of control over Egyptian foreign policy lasted until 1952, but Egypt was a legal part of the British Empire only from 1914 to 1922. Everybody important knew what was going on, but it was a convenient fiction to call the British governor "consul general" rather than governor, and to rule the protectorate through the Foreign Office rather than the Colonial Office.

Openly disguised control of this kind was common in the age of empire. The map was dotted with *Schutzgebieten*, protectorates, overseas provinces, Socialist Soviet Republics, African Homelands, and other disguised forms of territorial empire. In most cases, the disguise was merely a legal fiction for the sake of public relations, not a serious effort to fool either the conquered people or the world at large.

The true degree of outside control, nevertheless, is sometimes hard to ascertain. It was theoretically possible at the height of European empire to set up a fully bureaucratic imperial administration, with the apparatus of the modern state at its command and with little or no participation on the part of the local population. But this kind of imperial government was rare outside of plural societies such as Algeria or South Africa, where a local population of overseas Europeans was available as administrators. Elsewhere, the vast majority of police, clerical workers, and low-level administrators were recruited locally. Sometimes high-level administrators were local as well, such as the rajas at the head of Native States in India.

The proportion of European administrators to population could vary greatly, but even in the most heavily administered colonies they were comparatively few. The Belgian Congo was tightly ruled, but it had only about one European administrator for 1,500 subjects. In other African territories, where the Europeans made a conscious decision to administer through existing authorities, the ratio might run as high as one to 50,000 or even more.

It was one question to decide how much authority to delegate to local subordinates, a second to decide how much authority to exercise at all. At one end of the spectrum, a European power might claim sovereignty over a territory in order to warn off European rivals but not attempt to rule over it. Actual influence might be limited to threats or an occasional punitive expedition. The Spanish and Portuguese claim to share sovereignty over the Americas in the colonial period was largely of this sort, and well into the twentieth century, Latin American republics left much of the Amazon basin and some of the Pacific coastal plain unadministered. Neither the Australians nor the Dutch attempted to administer all the interior of New Guinea until well after the Second World War. Unless the potential subjects had valuable resources such as minerals or oil, it was sometimes cheaper and easier to let them go their own way.

Another possibility was to divide authority into a European sphere and a local sphere. Europeans often preferred to take over foreign affairs, the military,

revenue collection, or posts and telegraphs, which seemed to affect their interests, leaving other matters to the local authorities, as the British did in Egypt.
In other places, like parts of China in the late 1800s or the Persian Gulf sheik-
doms in the early twentieth century, it is unclear whether Europeans were ruling at all or simply giving advice with a certain weight of power behind it.

A similar problem existed even with territories that were formally under
European rule. Precolonial authorities could be left to rule their territory with
the advice of European officials. Sometimes the advice was perfunctory, but at
other times it was so detailed and precise that the advisers became the real rulers. The reality of imperial rule was therefore highly variable from time to
time and place to place even within a single colonial empire. Published maps
colored appropriately to show French, British, or Portuguese territory merely
showed claims to legal sovereignty, not the reality of power exercised on the
ground.

Afterword

The rise of the West to a position of dominance is one of the most important
developments in world history in recent centuries. Many have dealt with it in
some central framework, whether that of European history, alone, that of economic history, or that of a world system. Everyone writing about the world
beyond Europe has had to take the rise of the West into account, consciously
or unconsciously.

For the world outside the West, the central fact in this period is the challenge of the West and the responses to it, and many historians have dealt with
this subject in different ways. These essays represent a particular approach,
with an emphasis on the non-Western responses seen through case studies of
particular problems, rather than through broad themes and overall generalizations. The choice of cases may appear idiosyncratic, but it was not random.
They were chosen in an effort to look at a wide variety of responses within a
brief scope. The sharp shift in subject matter from a discussion of administrative decisions and their outcomes in Southeast Asia to the affairs of Maya
peasants in Yucatan was intentional. Both views represent only a part of the
whole reality, but together they represent part of the variety of what actually
took place. The essays seek to incorporate the perspective of world history,
not by telling all the important things that happened anywhere—a clear
impossibility—but by telling about a selection of different things that happened in different places within the framework of different human societies.

The essays also incorporate a strand of comparative history, with a particular attitude about which comparisons are valuable. Some compare situations that are similar; others look for common threads, in dissimilar
circumstance. Both approaches have their uses. The comparison of modern-
ization in Japan and Turkey is familiar and has been dealt with by others from
different points of view. The comparison of the Yaqui and the Maya has a
common factor in Spanish and Mexican overrule. Other comparisons are
intentionally distant—like the responses of the modernizing oligarchies in
Japan and Buganda. Such comparisons of events in distant parts of the world

can help to rise above the immediate cultural setting. The chapter about culture change in plural societies as distant as South Africa and Soviet Central Asia had that objective, and so did the pair of chapters about nation building in Ghana and Indonesia.

Some common themes emerge in retrospect. One is a reflection on historical change in general; it is the gap between the intentions of the major actors and the actual outcomes. A second is the degree to which the European empires; were actually, run by non-Europeans. This is not merely a reflection of the fact, that Europe conquered the world mainly with non-European soldiers, though this, too, was the case, but also of the fact that the actual rule over the conquered societies was far more in local hands than in those of European administrators. This theme merges with a third. Cultural borrowing from the West was rarely a matter of wholesale imitation. The borrowed cultural items were fitted into an existing cultural matrix. Nor was the globalization of world cultures a one-way street; Western borrowing from the non-West is less obvious to Westerners because it, too, was fitted into a familiar Western cultural matrix.

One final theme has been more explicit, though not emphasized because it is so obvious. Human cultures have been converging since the invention of agriculture, and the convergence has been more rapid than ever since the beginning of the industrial era. The controversial question is: What, if anything, should or could be done about it? The homogenization of human cultures is only one part of a broader pattern of change making the world a less varied place than it used to be. Biological species are disappearing at a faster rate than ever before, and the technology that has come with the industrial age is largely to blame. Biologists are alarmed and would like to preserve as many species as possible. It is hard to advocate a similar course of action for human cultures, especially regarding cultures other than one's own. Globalization has some benefits, but it also has costs. Perhaps the place to begin is to be conscious that they exist.

POSTSCRIPT

Did the West Define the Modern World?

Changes in the historical profession in the last quarter-century can be seen clearly in the 25th anniversary edition of McNeill's *Rise of the West*. In an essay entitled "The Rise of the West After Twenty-five Years," McNeill states that the first edition of his book was influenced by the post-World War II imperial mood of the United States, which was then at its apex of power and ability to influence world affairs. He now urges historians to "construct a clear and elegant discourse with which to present the different facets and interacting flows of human history as we now understand them." The rise in the number of world history courses in college curricula (replacing the traditional Western history ones) and the number of advanced degrees awarded each year in non-western humanities-related subjects, are the fruits of the new historical labors of which McNeill speaks.

This issue provides interesting tie-in opportunities with Issue 13 and 14 in this volume. It examines the reasons why the Chinese gave up on their maritime campaigns, and the effects of such action are scrutinized and assessed. This Chinese decision is directly related to this issue, especially the McNeill reading, which describes why the West was able to gain the upper hand over the rest of the world during the "Age of Exploration" and after.

But the term dominance should not be taken to imply that the modern world's development has been fueled solely by the centuries of western influence. The work of a new generation of historians, described briefly in this issue's introduction, attests that the countries of Africa, Asia, and Latin America today, owe a great deal to their own home-grown cultures, institutions, and mores.

Some sources helpful to understanding this issue would be: Eric Wolf, *Europe and People Without History* (University of California Press, 1982), a ground-breaking work on the need to provide an all-inclusive view of the world's history; and, Fernand Braudel, *The Perspective of the World* (University of California Press, 1992), the third volume of a multi-volume study of the 15th- through-18th century capitalist world, gives "the people without history" a voice. Finally, for a multi-disciplinary application of these principles, which concentrates on Africa, see Robert H. Bates, V.Y. Mudimbe, and Jean O'Barr, eds., *Africa and the Disciplines: The Contributions of Research in Africa to the Social Sciences* (University of Chicago Press, 1993). Steven Feierman's essay, "African Histories and the Dissolution of World History" is especially useful.

Contributors to This Volume

EDITORS

JOSEPH R. MITCHELL is a history instructor at Howard Community College in Columbia, Maryland, and a popular regional speaker. He received a M.A. in history from Loyola College in Maryland and a M.A. in African American history from Morgan State University, also in Maryland. He is the principal coeditor of *The Holocaust: Readings and Interpretations* (McGraw-Hill/Dushkin, 2001).

HELEN BUSS MITCHELL is a professor of philosophy and director of the women's studies program at Howard Community College in Columbia, Maryland. She is the author of *Roots of Wisdom* and *Readings from the Roots of Wisdom*. Both books were published by Wadsworth Publishing Company and are now in their fifth and third editions, respectively. She has also created, written, and hosted a philosophy telecourse, *For the Love of Wisdom,* which is distributed throughout the country by Dallas TeleLearning. She has earned numerous degrees, including a Ph.D. in women's history from the University of Maryland.

STAFF

Larry Loeppke	Managing Editor
Jill Peter	Senior Developmental Editor
Susan Brusch	Senior Developmental Editor
Beth Kundert	Production Manager
Jane Mohr	Project Manager
Tara McDermott	Design Coordinator
Nancy Meissner	Editorial Assistant
Julie Keck	Senior Marketing Manager
Mary Klein	Marketing Communications Specialist
Alice Link	Marketing Coordinator
Tracie Kammerude	Senior Marketing Assistant
Lori Church	Pemissions Coordinator

AUTHORS

WARREN BARBOUR teaches anthropology at the state University at Buffalo, New York.

ANNE LLEWELLYN BARSTOW is professor of history, retired, at the State University of New York at Old Westbury. She is the author of *Witchcraze: A New History of the European Witch Hunts* (HarperCollins, 1994).

CATHARINA BLOMBERG is a professor at Stockholm University, Sweden. She edited a 14-volume work entitled *The West's Encounter With Japanese Civilization.*

LISA BELLEN-BOYER combines theological and biblical studies with interests in art history and psychology in her interdisciplinary and intercultural work. She is a researcher on the staff of the Newark, New Jersey Museum.

ROBIN BRIGGS, a senior research fellow at All Souls College and a university lecturer in modern history at Oxford University, England, is the author of *Witches and Neighbors: The Social and Cultural Context of European Witchcraft* (Penguin Books, 1996).

RACHEL CASPARI is a teacher and researcher at the University of Michigan.

PAOLO CESARETTI is professor of Byzantine studies at the University of Chieti, Italy, and the author of many books on Byzantine art and architecture.

PHILIP D. CURTIN, emeritus professor of history at The Johns Hopkins University, is the author of *Disease and Empire: The Health of European Troops in the Conquest of Africa* (Cambridge University Press, 1998).

DAVID DREW, an award-winning archaelogy writer and presenter of television documentaries, is also a Fellow of the Royal Geographical Society and the Royal Anthropological Society.

EDWARD GRANT is distinguished professor of history and philosophy of science at Indiana University, Bloomington.

N.G.L. HAMMOND is professor emeritus of Greek at Bristol University, England. He is the author of *Alexander the Great: King, Commander, and Statesman* (Bristol, 1994).

PETER HEATHER teaches history at Worcester College, University of Oxford. He is the author of *On the Fall of the Roman Empire: A New History of Rome and the Barbarians* (Oxford, 2005).

ARTHUR JONES is editor-at-large for *The National Catholic Reporter.*

JOAN KELLY-GADOL (1928–1982) was a Renaissance scholar and theorist in women's history. Her works include *Leon Battista Alberti: Universal Man of the Early Renaissance* (University of Chicago Press, 1969).

KAREN L. KING is professor of New Testament Studies at the Harvard Divinity School. She is the editor of *Images of the Feminine in Gnosticism* (Trinity Press, 2000) and *Women and Goddess Traditions in Antiquity And Today* (Fortress Press, 1997).

MARGARET L. KING is a history professor at the Graduate Center of the City University of New York. She has written extensively on the subjects of Women, Humanism, and the Renaissance.

WINSTON L. KING is professor emeritus at Vanderbilt University. A long-time writer on religion, he is the author of a number of books on Buddhism in Asia.

ROBERT KOLB is assistant professor of religion and history at Concordia College. He has written extensively on religious subjects, including Lutheran Church history and popular christianity.

SAMUEL NOAH KRAMER (1897–1990) was a curator at the Museum of the University of Pennsylvania. He wrote and published widely on Sumerian texts and mythology.

NICHOLAS KRISTOF is a journalist, specializing in Asian affairs. He is coauthor, with his wife Sheryl Wudunn, of *China Wakes* (Vintage Books, 1995).

HANS KÜNG, a Swiss Roman Catholic theologian, is professor emeritus at Tubingen University in Germany and the author of dozens of influential books.

GABRIEL GARCIA MARQUEZ, a Nobel Laureate in literature is the author of many novels among them *One Hundred Years of Solitude and Love in the Time of Cholera*, and a Columbian.

WILLIAM H. MCNEILL taught history at the University of Chicago from 1947 to 1987. He served as President of the American Historical Association in 1981 and received the Erasmus Prize from the Dutch government in 1996.

MEHDI NAKOSTEEN is a former professor of history and the philosophy of education at the University of Colorado. He is the author of *The History and Philosophy of Education* (Ronald Press, 1965).

STEPHEN OPPENHEIMER is a member of Green College, Oxford University, and the author of *The Real Eve: Modern Man's Journey Out of Africa* (Carroll & Graf, 2003).

BERNARD ORTIZ de MONTELLANO teaches at Wayne State University, Pennsylvania.

JONATHAN PHILLIPS is lecturer in medieval history at Royal Holloway University of London and the author of *Defenders of the Holy Land: Relations between the Latin East and the West, 1119–1187.*

PROCOPIUS was a historian during the reign of Justinian and Theodora.

ROBERT ROYAL is vice president of the Ethics and Public Policy in Washington, D.C., and the author of *The Virgin and The Dynamo: Use and Abuse of Religion in the Environmental Debate* (Eerdmans, 1999).

WALTER RUEGG is emeritus professor of history at the University of Berne, Switzerland. He is the general editor of the multi-volume *History of the University in Europe* (Cambridge University Press, 1992).

ANTONIO SANTOSUOSSO is professor of history at the University of Western Ontario and the author of *Barbarians, Marauders, and Infidels: the Ways of Medieval Warfare* (Westview Press, 2004).

STEVEN SHAPIN is professor of sociology at the University of California at San Diego. He is the author of *Leviathan and The Air Pump: Hobbes, Boyle, and The Experimental Life* (Princeton University Press, 1985).

PAYSON D. SHEETS, professor of history at the University of Colorado, has worked at several Mesoamerican archaeological sites.

CHESTER G. STARR (1914–1999) was professor of history of history at the University of Michigan, Ann Arbor. He was the author of many books on the ancient world, including some focusing on Greek and Roman civilization.

BRUCE SWANSON was a well-known authority of Chinese maritime affairs. He has written articles on the subject and was a regular participant in conferences related to the maritime environment in China.

IVAN VAN SERTIMA teaches at Rutgers University, New Jersey, and is the author of *They Came before Columbus: The African Presence in Ancient America* (1976).

GABRIEL HASLIP VIERA is professor of sociology and director of the program in Latin American and Latino studies at the City College of New York.

MILFORD WOLPOFF is professor of anthropology at the University of Michigan at Ann Arbor. He is the author of *Paleoanthropology* (McGraw-Hill Higher Education, 1998).

IAN WORTHINGTON is professor of Greek history at the University of Missouri, Columbus. He is the author of *Alexander The Great: Man and God* (Pearson and Longman, 2003).

Index

Wolpoff, Milford, on Homo sapiens
origins, 9–15
Women's roles: impact of
Renaissance, 191–97, 198–203;
inferences about Sumerian
civilization, 20–26, 27–33;
influence of Christianity, 76–82,
83–90; witch-hunts and, 279–87,
288–96
Worthington, Ian, on Alexander,
64–71
Wu Xinzhi, 9, 12

Y
Y chromosome studies, 4–5
Yellow fever, 330, 331
Yongle Empire, 226, 233–38
Yoshida no Kaneyoshi, 215
Yoshitsune, Minamoto, 216

Z
Zen Buddhism, 207–13, 214–19
Zeno, 131
Zheng He, 226–28, 229, 230, 235
Zhu Yuanzhang, 231–32